BETWEEN HEAVEN AND EARTH

A pied kingfisher (*Ceryle rudis*) among the papyrus marshes. Wall painting from the northern palace of Akhenaten, Amarna (Davies 1936, vol. 2, pl. 76)

BETWEEN HEAVEN AND EARTH
BIRDS IN ANCIENT EGYPT

edited by

ROZENN BAILLEUL-LeSUER

with new photography by

ANNA R. RESSMAN

ORIENTAL INSTITUTE MUSEUM PUBLICATIONS 35
THE ORIENTAL INSTITUTE OF THE UNIVERSITY OF CHICAGO

Library of Congress Control Number: 2012946464
ISBN-10: 1-885923-92-9
ISBN-13: 978-1-885923-92-9

© 2012 by The University of Chicago. All rights reserved.
Published 2012. Printed in the United States of America.

The Oriental Institute, Chicago

This volume has been published in conjunction with the exhibition
Between Heaven and Earth: Birds in Ancient Egypt
October 15, 2012–July 28, 2013.

Oriental Institute Museum Publications 35

Series Editors

Leslie Schramer

and

Thomas G. Urban

with the assistance of

Rebecca Cain

Lauren Lutz and Tate Paulette assisted with the production of this volume.

Published by The Oriental Institute of the University of Chicago
1155 East 58th Street
Chicago, Illinois, 60637 USA
oi.uchicago.edu

Illustration Credits

Front cover: "Birds in an Acacia Tree." Tempera on paper by Nina de Garis Davies, 1932. Catalog No. 11.
Back cover: Head of an owl. Limestone and pigment. Late Period to early Ptolemaic period, 664–150 BC Catalog No. 22

Catalog Nos. 1–2, 5–15, 17–18, 20–27, 29–40: Photos by Anna R. Ressman; Catalog Nos. 3, 16, 19: Copyright the Art Institute of Chicago; Catalog No. 4: A114917d_12A, photo by John Weinstein. Reproduced with the permission of The Field Museum of Natural History, Chicago, all rights reserved; Catalog No. 28: Copyright the Brooklyn Museum, New York

Printed by Four Colour Print Group, Loves Park, Illinois

The paper used in this publication meets the minimum requirements of American National Standard for Information Service — Permanence of Paper for Printed Library Materials, ANSI Z39.48-1984.

∞

TABLE OF CONTENTS

Foreword. *Gil J. Stein* 7
Preface. *Jack Green* 9
List of Contributors 11
Introduction. *Rozenn Bailleul-LeSuer* 15
Time Line of Egyptian History 19
Map of Principal Areas and Sites Mentioned in the Text 20

I. THE REVERED AND THE HUNTED: THE ROLE OF BIRDS IN ANCIENT EGYPTIAN SOCIETY
   1. From Kitchen to Temple: The Practical Role of Birds in Ancient Egypt. *Rozenn Bailleul-LeSuer* 23
   2. The Role of Birds within the Religious Landscape of Ancient Egypt. *Foy Scalf* 33
   3. An Eternal Aviary: Bird Mummies from Ancient Egypt. *Salima Ikram* 41
   4. Sheltering Wings: Birds as Symbols of Protection in Ancient Egypt. *Randy Shonkwiler* 49
   5. Pharaoh Was a Good Egg, but Whose Egg Was He? *Arielle P. Kozloff* 59
   6. Birds in the Ancient Egyptian and Coptic Alphabets. *François Gaudard* 65
   7. Birds and Bird Imagery in the Book of Thoth. *Richard Jasnow* 71
   8. Birds in Late Antique Egypt. *Susan H. Auth* 77

II. ANCIENT EGYPTIAN BIRDS AND MODERN SCIENCE
   9. Bird Identification from Art, Artifacts, and Hieroglyphs: An Ornithologist's Viewpoint. *John Wyatt* 83
   10. Bird Behavior in Ancient Egyptian Art. *Linda Evans* 91
   11. Studying Avian Mummies at the KNH Centre for Biomedical Egyptology: Past, Present, and Future Work. *Lidija M. McKnight* 99
   12. Medical CT Scanning of Ancient Bird Mummies. *Bin Jiang, MD, and Michael Vannier, MD* ... 107
   13. Challenges in CT Scanning of Avian Mummies. *Charles A. Pelizzari, Chad R. Haney, Rozenn Bailleul-LeSuer, J. P. Brown, and Christian Wietholt* 109
   14. Terahertz Pulse Imaging of an Egyptian Bird Mummy. *J. Bianca Jackson, Gérard Mourou, Julien Labaune, and Michel Menu* 119

III. EPILOGUE
   15. The Avifauna of the Egyptian Nile Valley: Changing Times. *Sherif Baha el Din* 125

IV. CATALOG
   Birds in Creation Myths 131
   Pharaoh the Living Horus and His Avian Subjects 135
   Birds as Protection in Life 143
   Fowling in the Marshes and Aviculture 147
      Nina de Garis Davies's Facsimiles from the Painted Tomb-Chapel of Nebamun 152
   Bird Motifs in Ancient Egyptian Arts and Crafts 157
   Birds in the Writing System 167
   Birds in the Religious Life of Ancient Egyptians 177
      Falcon Cults 178
      Ibis Cults 189
   Birds in Death and the Afterlife 201

Appendix: Bird Anatomy 214
Concordance of Museum Registration Numbers 215
Checklist of the Exhibit 216
List of Birds 217
Bibliography 218

FOREWORD

GIL J. STEIN
DIRECTOR, ORIENTAL INSTITUTE

Archaeologists, textual specialists, anthropologists, and art historians know that sometimes a single object, idea, or theme can provide tremendous insights into the character of an entire civilization. The great pioneer of anthropology in the nineteenth century, Frank Hamilton Cushing, wrote an ethnographic masterpiece called "Zuni Breadstuff," in which he showed that a single item — maize or corn — permeated every aspect of the economy, society, and religion in this fascinating Pueblo Indian culture.

The Oriental Institute's new special exhibit Between Heaven and Earth: Birds in Ancient Egypt is a beautiful example of the way that birds can provide an equally fascinating and completely surprising perspective on an entire civilization. Birds held enormous importance in the natural, economic, and spiritual life of ancient Egypt. The exhibit explores the role of birds at the interface between nature and culture, and in doing so gives us a new understanding of the ways that the ancient Egyptians experienced and gave meaning to the world around them.

Working with Chief Curator Jack Green and Special Exhibits Coordinator Emily Teeter, Rozenn Bailleul-LeSuer — the exhibit curator and editor of this catalog — has done a wonderful job in presenting us with a very different picture of ancient Egypt through the topic of birds. Birds were a fundamental link between heaven and earth — between the natural/physical and spiritual realms. Creation itself was understood as the hatching of an egg, just as the beginning of human life was traced to the same metaphor. The migrations of birds, like the inundation of the Nile, provided a seasonal marker that defined the most basic rhythm of life in the annual cycle of ancient Egypt. As beautiful tomb paintings show us, the astounding abundance of wild birds in the marshes along the Nile provided food and feathers to the inhabitants of Upper and Lower Egypt. Domesticated birds such as ducks and geese were prized as an extremely important subsistence resource as well. But beyond their economic role, birds played a fundamental role in the Egyptian cultural understanding of their origins, of kingship, and of the gods themselves. Thus, for example, the beautiful objects and tomb paintings in this special exhibit highlight the importance of Horus, the falcon, as a metaphor for kingship, the unification of Egypt, and as a link to the gods. Thoth, the god of writing, magic, and wisdom, was represented as having the head of an ibis. The pervasive practice of bird mummification further attests to the importance of birds in the religious life of many Egyptians.

Rozenn Bailleul-LeSuer and the entire staff of the Oriental Institute's Museum deserve our thanks for their efforts and creativity in conceptualizing and creating this exhibit. Between Heaven and Earth presents Egypt through a unique and innovative prism — and in doing so greatly enriches our understanding of this ancient civilization.

PREFACE

JACK GREEN
CHIEF CURATOR, ORIENTAL INSTITUTE MUSEUM

I will be the first to admit that I am not a "bird person," a label which has circulated numerous times during discussions and planning for this special exhibit and catalog. Yet during the course of working with guest curator Rozenn Bailleul-LeSuer, I have come to greatly appreciate and understand birds more than I could have imagined, especially given their significance and rich symbolism within ancient Egypt. One of the most important parts played in the preparation of this exhibit has been the innovative and thorough research conducted by Rozenn and a range of contributors. This has resulted in the publication of many objects from this exhibit for the very first time, providing important new insights on objects that may be more familiar to us. An exciting and important aspect of this research has been the contribution of specialist knowledge about birds themselves. Most Egyptologists are not ornithologists, and vice versa, so researchers possessed with knowledge of bird behavior, physical characteristics, habitats, and migration patterns can help to decode and better understand the myriad ways in which birds were perceived and represented by ancient Egyptians. What is particularly striking is the great attention to detail that artists and scribes applied in some of their representations — indicating perhaps much closer relationships with the natural world in the past (however idealized), than we might appreciate in today's industrialized and environmentally compromised world.

Many people helped to bring this exhibit and catalog to fruition. In addition to new research and editing conducted by Rozenn, over twenty authors contributed to the essays and catalog entries in this volume, several of whom are based at the University of Chicago within the Oriental Institute and the Department of Near Eastern Languages and Civilizations (NELC). Colleagues at several museums assisted us with loans, which have helped enhance this exhibit with some quite exceptional objects: We thank Douglas Druick, Karen Manchester, Mary Greuel, and Angie Morrow at the Art Institute of Chicago; John McCarter Jr., James Phillips, Alan Francisco, and John Weinstein from the Field Museum, Chicago; and Arnold Lehmann, Edward Bleiberg, Yekaterina Barbash, and Elisa Flynn from the Brooklyn Museum, New York.

The staff of the Oriental Institute has been, as ever, extremely diligent, supportive, and flexible in the course of the exhibit preparations. I would like to thank Registrars Helen McDonald and Susan Allison, especially for their work on loans, access to the collections, and preparation of object lists; our conservation team, Laura D'Alessandro and Alison Whyte, who ensured that delicate objects such as our bird mummies were well cared for; Museum Archivist John Larson assisted in the sourcing of images and documentary material; Photographer Anna Ressman, assisted by Bryce Lowry and John Whitcomb, for her beautiful new photography of the catalog objects; Curatorial Assistant Mónica Vélez especially for help with image and audio-video procurement and social media promotion; Joshua Day, who helped create the educational touchscreen and digital media for the exhibit; Erik Lindahl and Brian Zimerle of our Preparation Department, assisted by Matt Federico, exerted considerable creative and physical energies to design and build the show. Colleagues in the Public Education and Outreach Department: Carole Krucoff, Wendy Ennes, and Moriah Grooms-Garcia for collaborative help in developing educational activities and programs related to the exhibit. Emily Teeter played her vital role as Special Exhibits Coordinator, keeping the exhibit, catalog, and publicity on schedule, providing expert knowledge and advice to fellow Egyptologist Rozenn, in addition to writing several catalog entries. In our Publications Department, Thomas Urban and Leslie Schramer provided us with a wonderful catalog, and as ever, it has been a pleasure to work with them. We thank the anonymous reviewer of the catalog for their valuable input and feedback. We also thank Oriental Institute Director Gil Stein and Executive Director Steve Camp for their continued and generous support of the exhibit program, and for their close interest and engagement with this show.

Rozenn's acknowledgments can be found in her Introduction on the following pages. They attest to academic rigor, the scope of her research interests, and emergent experience as a curator. A few individuals and institutions already mentioned by her deserve special mention. We are indebted to the University of Chicago Hospitals and their staff for allowing our bird mummies to be studied using their clinical CT scanner (when not in use for human subjects), especially to Dr. Michael Vannier (MD) and his staff for giving us access to this equipment, and to Drs. Charles Pelizzari, Chad Haney, and Christian Wietholt for their access to the microCT scanner and for their participation on the Bird Mummy project. This has allowed fresh data and images to be presented in this catalog and exhibit for the very first time.

PREFACE

Our community focus group assisted with a review of the exhibit in its formative stages. Many thanks to Jacqueline Dace, Nathan Mason, Matt Matcuk, Ray Johnson, Oscar Sanchez, Dianne Hanau-Strain, and Molly Woulfe, who provided many useful comments and ideas that we are integrating in to the exhibit. We are also grateful for support from the Audubon Society, who assisted as co-sponsors with collaborative educational events, including a public symposium coinciding with our exhibition.

Funding and support for this exhibit has come from a number of individuals, most especially from Kitty Picken, whose visionary support played a vital role in development of Between Heaven and Earth. We are grateful to Daniel and Lucia Woods Lindley for their generous support of the exhibition and catalog. We also thank Lewis and Misty Gruber, who reflected their lifelong love of ancient Egypt and birds in their gift to support this endeavor. Thanks also go to Joan Fortune, Doris Holleb, David and Carlotta Maher, and Anna White for their generous gifts. Finally, we thank the Members of the Oriental Institute and our public visitors who regularly contribute donations which help us to present all of our special exhibitions. We hope that our visitors will enjoy our show as much as we have in putting it together.

CONTRIBUTORS

About the Contributors*

Susan H. Auth taught ancient art in the Department of Art History at Rutgers University. She then held the position of curator of ancient art at the Newark Museum for thirty-two years. Her research interests are in ancient glass and Late Antique Egypt. See "An Intarsia Glass Panel of Thomas and the Cross" in *Interactions: Artistic Interchange between the Eastern and Western Worlds in the Medieval Period*, edited by Colum Hourihane (Princeton: Index of Christian Art, Princeton University, 2007, pp. 133–46).

Sherif Baha el Din is a leading ecologist and naturalist in Egypt and the Middle East. For the past thirty years he has been actively promoting nature conservation in the region, establishing the framework for the Egyptian Protected Area network and helped declare and manage many of the protected areas within. He has a long interest and established knowledge of the Egyptian avifauna and herpetofauna, contributing many scientific publications in the field, including important faunal reviews such as the *Birds of Egypt* (1989) and *A Guide to the Reptiles and Amphibians of Egypt* (2006).

RBL **Rozenn Bailleul-LeSuer** is a PhD candidate in Egyptology in the Department of Near Eastern Languages and Civilizations at the University of Chicago and curator of the exhibit Between Heaven and Earth: Birds in Ancient Egypt. After studying chemical engineering in France, as well as Greek and Latin in Vermont, she is now able to combine her passion for birds and her academic interest in ancient Egypt. Her dissertation is entitled "The Exploitation of Avian Resources in Ancient Egypt: A Socio-Economic Study."

J. P. Brown is a conservator and computer scientist working at the Field Museum of Natural History in Chicago. In 2006 he got a chance to use CT scanning on museum artifacts and has been scanning specimens with medical and micro-CT ever since.

Linda Evans is a postdoctoral fellow in the Department of Ancient History, Macquarie University, Sydney, Australia. Her research concerns the role of animals in ancient societies, especially Egypt, with a special focus on ancient knowledge of animal behavior as reflected in art and religion. She has published widely on this topic, including *Animal Behaviour in Egyptian Art: Representations of the Natural World in Memphite Tomb Scenes* (Aris & Phillips, 2010).

François Gaudard is an Egyptologist and research associate for the Chicago Demotic Dictionary at the Oriental Institute of the University of Chicago as well as a co-editor of the Mummy Label Database, a joint project of the Instituto de Lenguas y Culturas del Mediterráneo y Oriente Próximo, Centro de Ciencias Humanas y Sociales - CSIC, Madrid, and of the Oriental Institute. He has been an epigrapher for the Epigraphic Survey, based at Chicago House, the field headquarters of the Oriental Institute in Egypt.

KG **Kenneth Griffin** is a PhD student of Egyptology at Swansea University, United Kingdom, researching the role of the *rekhyt*-people within the Egyptian temple. He has worked at Abydos and Thebes and is currently part of the South Asasif Conservation Project.

Chad R. Haney is a biomedical engineer and has been working on multi-modality imaging to characterize response to cancer therapy for the past nine years. In collaboration with Drs. Pelizzari, Karczmar, and Halpern, he has been attempting to identify a signature for successful treatment of a novel anti-vascular treatment using Magnetic Resonance Imaging (MRI) and Electron Paramagnetic Resonance Imaging (EPRI). He is currently interim technical director of the preclinical nuclear medicine imaging lab, where the micro-computed tomography images seen in this volume were acquired.

Salima Ikram is a professor of Egyptology at the American University in Cairo and has worked in Egypt since 1986. She has directed the Animal Mummy Project, co-directed the Predynastic Gallery Project, and is co-director of the North Kharga Oasis Survey. She has participated in many excavations throughout the Nile Valley and the

---

* Initials identify contributors in the Catalog.

CONTRIBUTORS

Western Desert, many of which focus on animal burials. She has also carried out experimental mummification on a variety of creatures. Dr. Ikram has published extensively, both for children and adults. Her published works include: *Divine Creatures: Animal Mummies in Ancient Egypt*; *An Introduction to Ancient Egypt*; *Death and Burial in Ancient Egypt*; and with A. Dodson, *The Mummy in Ancient Egypt* and *The Tomb in Ancient Egypt*.

J. Bianca Jackson received a PhD in applied physics from the University of Michigan at Ann Arbor in 2008. She is a postdoctoral research scientist with a joint project in France between the Centre de Recherche et de Restauration des Musées de France (Paris) and the Institut de la Lumière Extrême (Palaiseau). She specializes in terahertz applications for cultural heritage science.

Richard Jasnow is a professor of Egyptology in the Department of Near Eastern Studies at Johns Hopkins University. He received his PhD from the Department of Near Eastern Languages and Civilizations at the University of Chicago in 1988 and was a senior epigrapher for the Epigraphic Survey for five years. He is a specialist in the Late Period of Egypt, with a particular interest in Demotic Egyptian. His publications include *The Oriental Institute Hawara Papyri: An Egyptian Family Archive from the Time of Alexander the Great and the Early Ptolemies* (with George R. Hughes, 1997), and *The Ancient Egyptian Book of Thoth* (with Karl-Theodor Zauzich, 2005).

Bin Jiang, MD, PhD, is a visiting scholar at the University of Chicago and radiologist at Tongren Hospital in Beijing, China. She is an associate professor of radiology at the Capital Medical University in Beijing. Her principal interest is head and neck radiology. She holds MD and PhD degrees from Tianjin Medical University in China and has more than twelve peer-reviewed publications.

Arielle Kozloff is an independent scholar and advisor to museums and antiquities collectors worldwide. She was curator of ancient art at the Cleveland Museum of Art from 1975 to 1997, during which time she produced a number of exhibitions including Egypt's Dazzling Sun: The World of Amenhotep III. She has contributed to dozens of publications, and her biography, *Amenhotep III: Egypt's Radiant Pharaoh*, appeared in 2012 from Cambridge University Press.

Julien Labaune received his MS in physics from École Polytechnique, where he recently completed his PhD. He has authored several academic papers, including two invited. His research interests are terahertz in art and archaeology.

Lidija M. McKnight, after studying archaeology (BSc Honours) at the University of York, completed an MSc and PhD in biomedical Egyptology at the KNH Centre for Biomedical Egyptology, University of Manchester. Following her graduation in 2009, she took up the position of research associate working on the Ancient Egyptian Animal Bio Bank Project. Her research interests focus on improving knowledge of the role of animals in ancient Egypt, in particular their postmortem treatment.

Michel Menu received his Doctorate d'Ingénieur in physics and optics from l'Université Pierre et Marie Curie-Paris VI in 1978 and has received a Diplôme d'Habilitation à diriger des recherches en sciences. He has worked at the Research Laboratories of French Museums (now the L-C2RMF) in Paris, France, since 1980 and is currently the chief of research. He has authored over 200 scientific publications, is a member of the editorial board of Applied Physics A, and is the chief editor of *TECHNE*.

Gérard Mourou received his PhD in physics from the University of Paris VI. He is currently the director of the Institut de la Lumière Extrême, professor of physics at École Polytechnique, and professor emeritus at the University of Michigan, where he was the A. D. Moore Distinguished University Professor of electrical engineering and computer science. Dr. Mourou has been a pioneer in the field of ultrafast photonics for nearly twenty years. He has published more than 100 papers and holds over a dozen patents.

Charles A. Pelizzari is an associate professor and director of medical physics in the Department of Radiation and Cellular Oncology at the University of Chicago. His career has focused on the use of medical imaging modalities (CT, MRI, PET, ultrasound) as the source of anatomic and functional information used in planning and guidance of radiation treatments for cancer. He has particular interests in multimodality imaging, image analysis, and 3-D visualization of clinical, preclinical, and specimen image data.

Robert K. Ritner is a professor of Egyptology in the Oriental Institute, Department of Near Eastern Languages and Civilizations, Program on the Ancient Mediterranean World, and the College, University of Chicago. His research interests include Egyptian religion and magic, language, and social history. His monographs include *The*

CONTRIBUTORS

Mechanics of Ancient Egyptian Magical Practice, The Libyan Anarchy, and *The Joseph Smith Egyptian Papyri: A Complete Edition.*

FS **Foy Scalf** is a PhD candidate in Egyptology in the Department of Near Eastern Languages and Civilizations at the University of Chicago. He specializes in the funerary literature of the later periods of Egyptian history and is currently finishing a dissertation on Demotic funerary literature from the Roman period.

RS **Randy Shonkwiler** is a PhD candidate in the Department of Near Eastern Languages and Civilizations at the University of Chicago. He worked for the Epigraphic Survey from 2001 to 2004 and was a member of the Oriental Institute's 2007 Nubian Expedition. Since 2008 Randy has been the breeding bird monitor for the Bird Conservation Network at the Bergman Slough and John Duffy Forest Preserves of Cook County, Illinois.

ET **Emily Teeter** is a research associate and coordinator of special exhibits at the Oriental Institute. She is the editor of the exhibit catalogs *The Life of Meresamun: A Temple Singer in Ancient Egypt, Before the Pyramids: The Origins of Egyptian Civilization,* and *Picturing the Past: Imaging and Imagining the Ancient Middle East.* Her most recent books are *Religion and Ritual in Ancient Egypt* and *Baked Clay Figurines and Votive Beds from Medinet Habu.*

Michael Vannier, MD, is a professor of radiology at the University of Chicago Hospitals and a pioneer in biomedical computer graphics. He serves as editor-in-chief of the *International Journal of Computer Aided Radiology and Surgery.*

Alison Whyte holds a Master of Art Conservation degree from Queen's University and is a conservator at the Oriental Institute Museum. She specializes in the preservation of archaeological material from the Near East.

Christian Wietholt, PhD, is an application engineer working for Visage Imaging, Inc., developer of the Amira visualization software. Using his background in functional imaging he used to conduct small animal imaging research at Marquette University, the National Health Research Institutes of Taiwan, Chang Gung University, and the University of Chicago. With his main focus on traditional radiology and nuclear medicine imaging modalities, he is now developing image analysis and visualization methods for various imaging needs.

John Wyatt read anthropology and ethnography at the University College of Rhodesia and Nyasaland and has been a professional ornithologist, specializing in African birds, for the last forty-four years. He has spent the last six of these researching and writing a book, *Birds in Ancient Egypt: A Guide to Identification,* which is scheduled for publication in 2013/14. He was co-author of the Griffith Institute's 2011 online publication "An Album of Howard Carter's Watercolours of Birds and Animals."

BZ **Brian Zimerle** is the exhibit designer and assistant preparator at the Oriental Institute Museum as well as an artist. He teaches ceramics at the College of DuPage and exhibits nationally. His interests include the recreation of ancient Near Eastern and Asian ceramics and contemporary art practices.

Flock of common teal (*Anas crecca*) at Lake Dahshur, against the backdrop of the Red Pyramid of Snefru (photo by Sherif Baha el Din)

INTRODUCTION

ROZENN BAILLEUL-LeSUER
EXHIBIT CURATOR

> "Egypt is a land of water-birds. In the migration season, the lagoons of the Delta, the reed-banks of the Fayum, the canals, ponds and flooded fields are crowded with thousands of water-birds, ibises, pelicans, cranes, cormorants, herons of all kinds, flamingoes, ducks and geese."
>
> — Hermann Kees,
> *Ancient Egypt: A Cultural Topography*, p. 93

Birds are my passion. They all fascinate me, with no exception, from the house sparrows surrounding me in the city and the starlings exchanging long discussions by my window,[1] to the colorful cardinals and the impressive peregrine falcons that have chosen the University of Chicago campus as their hunting ground. In a world where the human population is constantly growing, and wild habitats are either disappearing or changing, birds' complex behaviors and abilities to adjust to new environments never cease to amaze me; I am constantly finding new reasons to observe them. My scholarly interest in ancient Egypt has given me the opportunity to explore how the inhabitants of the Nile Valley used to view these denizens of the sky, how they interacted with them and incorporated them in their daily life. As Hermann Kees wrote in the above quotation, the wetlands of Egypt are ideally located for the gathering of myriads of migratory birds in need of freshwater, food, and rest after crossing the surrounding barren lands. My research quickly revealed that ancient Egyptians highly valued the birds surrounding them, both symbolically and pragmatically. Early in Egyptian history, these avian visitors became included in all aspects of the local culture: religion, art, writing system, and diet (fig. 1).

Since perusing the companion book Bettina Schmitz and Dina Faltings published in 1987 in conjunction with their exhibit on birds in ancient Egypt at the Pelizaeus-Museum in Hildesheim, Germany,[2] I have aspired to curate a similar exhibit at the Oriental Institute Museum, entirely dedicated to the ancient Egyptian avifauna. While writing a potential narrative for this exhibit, I further realized that similarities between Chicago and the Nile Valley made the Oriental Institute the ideal location for such a special exhibit. Indeed, both Egypt and Chicago are located on migration flyways, making them paradises not only for birds flying back and forth between their winter quarters and breeding grounds, but also for bird-watchers. Furthermore, many inhabitants of the great metropolis of Chicago may have forgotten that this

FIGURE 1. Section of "Geese of Meidum," a fragmentary wall painting from the mastaba of Nefermaat and Itet, now in the Egyptian Museum, Cairo, JE 34571/CG 1742. On the left, a bean goose (*Anser fabalis*) followed by two white-fronted geese (*Anser albifrons*) (photo by George B. Johnson)

INTRODUCTION

city was built on wetlands which used to border Lake Michigan. Efforts have been undertaken to restore some of these marshes on the southeast side of Chicago, which was home to manufacturing and steel industries.

For the first time in the United States, artifacts from the Oriental Institute Museum's collection combined with a few key objects from the Brooklyn Museum, the Art Institute of Chicago, and the Field Museum of Natural History, illustrate the omnipresence of birds in this ancient society, from cradle to coffin. Ancient Egyptians are often described in texts as "having hatched from an egg," that is, their mother's womb, only to return to a variation of it in the form of a coffin, after death.[3]

Since the beginning of time humans have been fascinated by these feathered creatures that are as comfortable in the air as they are in the water and on land, affinities which only emphasize our own limitations. Their ability to fly high in the sky led the ancients to believe that they could join the gods and thus act as divine messengers, if not as receptacles of the divine themselves. Many gods indeed are depicted in the shape of birds, or with a combination of human and avian features (see Chapter 2). Ancient Egyptians especially applied the birds' ability to travel between worlds to their conception of death and men's fate after being deposited in their tombs. While the deceased's body, mummified and tightly wrapped with linen bandages within the coffin and sarcophagus, epitomizes the inability to move, one aspect of his/her personality, the *ba*, depicted with a human head and a bird's body, was released after death and granted total freedom of movement. It could stretch its wings and leave the immobile corpse to re-join the world of the living. Just as the coffin could be described as an "egg" (*swḥ.t*) in Egyptian, the *ba*-bird hatched at death from the coffin to be free and give the deceased a chance for a new life.

Migratory birds also occupied an important place in ancient Egyptian symbolism. Avid observers of nature, the inhabitants of the Nile Valley were aware of the biannual journey of numerous species of birds, and differentiated them from the local birds by giving them specific names (in Egyptian *gš* or *ḫtyw-tꜣ*). Their regular arrival and departure twice a year came to be seen as the symbol for the hope of a new life after death, which was also seen as a journey to another world (Hornung and Staehelin 1976, pp. 135–37). The watery expanses of the Egyptian marshes, filled with thousands of migratory waterfowl briefly joining the local birds, appeared as a reenactment of the moment of creation, when the primeval mound emerged from the watery Nun and birds were crucial actors in the creation of the universe (see "Birds in Creation Myths," in the Catalog). Religious texts even equated birds with the souls of the blessed dead, which were transformed into feathered creatures by the rays of the sun, able to fly and travel between worlds. At night, they reunited with the deceased in the tomb. "Birds, and migratory birds in particular, became symbols of the conquest of death" (Hornung and Staehelin 1976, p. 136).[4]

In addition to giving ancient Egyptians hope for rebirth in the afterlife, birds were also significant during their lifetime. Frequently depicted as lapwings equipped with arms raised in praise before their king, all Egyptians were under the rule of the living Horus, the falcon god, embodied by pharaoh (see Chapter 5). All human beings were thus symbolically imparted with avian characteristics. As mentioned above, gods themselves could be represented as feathered creatures, in many instances protecting the living and the dead with their wide wings, as depicted on every temple's doorways and ceilings (fig. 2; see Chapter 4).

FIGURE 2. Ceiling decoration in the temple of Medinet Habu. Large vultures deploy their wings over the passers by (photo by Rozenn Bailleul-LeSuer)

INTRODUCTION

Children growing up on the banks of the Nile would have been surrounded by a multitude of bird species, whose numbers increased exponentially during migration. The spectacular arrival of millions of waterfowl in the fall coincided with the Nile flood (fig. 3). As the water receded, the rich sediments from the Ethiopian highlands brought a renewed potential for life in the land and would have welcomed large flocks of ducks, geese, and wading birds, finding food aplenty in the low water and mudflats. Fowlers organized expeditions to catch large numbers of these waterfowl using clap-nets. Some of the birds trapped under the net were intended to fill the poultry-yards of households and temples. Others were killed and processed for immediate consumption, or preserved in salt or fat for later use. Either as tasty additions to their diet or as offerings to the gods and dead relatives, birds were first and foremost exploited for their meat, as described in Chapter 1.

These vibrant and colorful flocks of birds did not fail to inspire Egyptian craftsmen and artisans. As early as the predynastic period (ca. 3500 BC), they incorporated the waterfowl motif into their work. Birds fluttering in the marshes were common motifs on palace walls, but also on more mundane objects such as vases, bowls, and cosmetic boxes, thus ensuring fertility and bounty provided by the rich land of the Nile Valley (see Catalog No. 13). Birds were not only included in the artistic representations, they were also involved in the writing system (see Chapter 7). Scribal students had to familiarize themselves with more than sixty bird signs. A Ptolemaic papyrus from Saqqara gives us a glimpse at the mnemonic system which had been devised at the time, if not earlier, to memorize the alphabet (see Chapter 6).

To gain a greater understanding of the ways with which the ancient Egyptians experienced and exploited the birds of the Nile Valley and the surrounding deserts, I benefited from the expertise of many scientists: archaeologist Renée Friedman, who shared with me the exciting discovery of ostrich remains at her site of Hierakonpolis; zooarchaeologist Veerle Linseele, who reminded me of the challenges of studying avian remains at archaeological sites; as well as the biologists and ornithologists of the University of Minnesota Raptor Center, in particular Michelle Willette, who gave me advice on species identification. Collaboration was established with the Zoology (John Bates, Sherif Baha el Din, Steve Goodman, Mary Henein, Holly Lutz, David Willard) and Anthropology (Robert Martin, James Phillips, J. P. Brown, Jamie Kelly) departments of the Field Museum of Natural History and the Division of Biological Sciences at the University of Chicago. Our joint knowledge of birds and ancient Egypt was put to the test when examining a series of bird mummies that entered the Oriental Institute Museum in the late nineteenth and early twentieth century. These mummified bundles were CT scanned using state-of-the-art scanners and data processing to discover their contents. Dr. Michael Vannier gave us access to the clinical CT scanner at the University of Chicago Medical Center and shared his expertise in this domain. Medical physicists Charles Pelizzari, Chad Haney, and Christian Wietholt spent many hours teaching me how to analyze CT scan data sets, and J. P. Brown of the Field Museum gave us the opportunity to use their powerful post-processing software. Finally, veterinarian Kenneth Welle helped me identify the anatomic structures of the birds hidden behind the linen wrappings. I will never be able to thank all of them enough for supporting this project, for their availability and their patience with all my questions.

FIGURE 3. View of the Giza pyramids during the inundation. Photographed by the Zangaki Brothers, 1870s–1890s (P. 9254)

INTRODUCTION

This catalog far from exhausts the topic of birds in ancient Egypt. Rather, it gives an overview of the main themes in which birds play a major role, as well as the most recent scientific research conducted on avian remains, in particular bird mummies. The catalog ends with Sherif Baha el Din's examination of the status of the avian population in modern Egypt and its coping mechanism in response to recent environmental changes.

I would like to conclude by expressing my gratitude to the many people who made this exhibition possible, starting with Gil Stein, director of the Oriental Institute, Jack Green, chief curator of the Oriental Institute Museum, and W. Raymond Johnson, field director of Chicago House and my faculty advisor for the exhibit, who supported my wish to share my interest in the birds of ancient Egypt and who gave me the tools to bring this project to fruition. During the three years of research and teamwork leading to this exhibit and catalog, I had the invaluable opportunity to work alongside the talented staff of the Oriental Institute Museum, in particular Geoff Emberling and Thomas James, who helped me at the inception of the project; Emily Teeter, who was always available to assist me in the complex and fascinating position of guest curator; assistant registrar Susan Allison, and conservator Alison Whyte, with whom I worked all along and who tracked and prepared the many objects on display in the exhibit; Brian Zimerle, who shared with me his knowledge of pottery and gave me a new appreciation for the work of the ancient Egyptian potters; Angela Altenhofen, who kindly agreed to add an artistic touch to the catalog with her work; Carole Krucoff and Wendy Ennes, whose enthusiasm for the show gave me the energy to persevere; Thomas Urban and Leslie Schramer, whose patience and kindness cannot be praised enough during the laborious editing process of the catalog. I also thank faculty members Janet H. Johnson, Nadine Moeller, Brian Muhs, Robert K. Ritner, Donald Whitcomb, and Christopher Woods, for their advice, suggestions on, and contributions to the catalog; Oriental Institute research associate Tasha Vorderstrasse for sharing her knowledge of birds in Byzantine and Islamic art and for her advice on pottery manufacture.

My sincere gratitude goes to the many authors in this catalog, who agreed to participate in this project and temporarily focus their research solely on the fascinating topics in which birds figure prominently. I thank them for kindly sharing their time and expertise on these themes.

I also want to acknowledge the many individuals and institutions contacted during the research for this exhibit who contributed with information and illustrations to this catalog: Sherif Baha el Din, Jackie Garner, George B. Johnson, Jonathan Rossouw, Stefano Vicini, and John Wyatt for their magnificent photographs and watercolors; American University in Cairo (Salima Ikram and Cynthia Sheikholeslami); Brooklyn Museum (Yekaterina Barbash); Egyptian Exploration Society (Joanna Kyffin and Chris Nauton); Hebrew University, Jerusalem (Orly Goldwasser); Institut für Ägyptologie; Instituto de Lenguas y Culturas del Mediterráneo y Oriente Próximo (José Galán); LMU München (Patrick Brose and Dieter Kessler); Macquarie University (Linda Evans and Naguib Kanawati); Metropolitan Museum of Art (Marsha Hill, Heather Masciandaro, Deborah Schorsh, Morena Stefanova); Musée des Confluences de Lyon (Deirdre Emmons and Virgile Marengo); National Museum in Cracow (Dorota Gorzelany); Newark Museum (Andrea Hagy); Russel-Cotes Art Gallery and Museum, Bornemouth (Duncan Walker); Smithsonian Museum (James Krakker and Christopher Milenski); University of Chicago (Special Collections Research Center); University of Illinois at Urbana-Champaign (Douglas Brewer and Kenneth Welle); University of Manchester (Stephanie Atherton and Lidija McKnight); University of Memphis (Nigel Strudwick); University of Michigan (Terry Wilfong); Waseda Institute of Egyptology (Nozumo Kawai).

I am grateful to my assistants Anna Hopkins and Jimmy Mroz, who gathered research material and helped me with editing, and Lauren Lutz, who assiduously read and edited my work, and whom I cannot thank enough for helping me meet the catalog submission deadline.

My deepest gratitude goes to my friends and colleagues with whom I discussed my project ideas for hours and whose suggestions, support, and advice have greatly improved the exhibit and catalog: Bethany Anderson, Natasha Ayers, Kathryn Bandy, Solange Bumbaugh, Lori Calabria, Aleksandra Hallmann, Katharyn Hanson, Megaera Lorentz, Elise MacArthur, Foy Scalf, Tanya Treptow.

Finally, I would like to dedicate this catalog to my French and American families, in particular my husband BoB, for continuously supporting me in my endeavors.

NOTES

[1] See Marcus 2006.
[2] Schmitz and Faltings 1987.
[3] M. Williams 2011, pp. 128–54.
[4] The author's translation of the original German.

TIME LINE OF EGYPTIAN HISTORY

After Hornung et al. 2006 and Eder and Renger 2007

CULTURAL PERIOD	DYNASTIES	DATES
Late Palaeolithic period		ca. 24,000–10,000 BC
PREDYNASTIC PERIOD		**CA. 4000–3100 BC**
Naqada IC period		ca. 3700 BC
Naqada II period		ca. 3500–3200 BC
Naqada III period		ca. 3150–2900 BC
DYNASTIC PERIOD		**CA. 2900–332 BC**
Early Dynastic period	Dynasties 1–3	ca. 2900–2545 BC
Old Kingdom	Dynasties 4–8	ca. 2543–2120 BC
First Intermediate Period	Dynasties 9–10	ca. 2118–1980 BC
Middle Kingdom	Dynasties 11–12	ca. 1980–1760 BC
Second Intermediate Period	Dynasties 13–17	ca. 1759–1539 BC
New Kingdom	Dynasties 18–20	ca. 1539–1077 BC
Third Intermediate Period	Dynasties 21–24	ca. 1076–723 BC
Late Period	Dynasties 25–30	ca. 722–332 BC
GRECO-ROMAN PERIOD		**332 BC–AD 395**
Macedonian dynasty		332–305 BC
Ptolemaic period		305–30 BC
Roman period		30 BC–AD 395
LATE ANTIQUE PERIOD		**ca. AD 300–641 and beyond**
Coptic period		3rd–9th centuries AD

Map of principal areas and sites mentioned in the text

I

THE REVERED AND THE HUNTED

*The Role of Birds
in Ancient Egyptian Society*

1. FROM KITCHEN TO TEMPLE: THE PRACTICAL ROLE OF BIRDS IN ANCIENT EGYPT

ROZENN BAILLEUL-LeSUER

Because of the location of Egypt on a major flyway, millions of fall Eurasian migratory birds, exhausted from their long flight over the arid landscape of the Levant and the Sinai, or from their journey over the Mediterranean Sea, yearly join indigenous species in the wetlands of the Nile Delta.[1] Such a spectacle could not fail to leave a lasting impression on the ancient Egyptians, whose survival depended on their observation skills and their understanding of the environment. A wealth of evidence, in the form of iconography, written material, and faunal remains uncovered near the sites of ancient hunting camps in the Eastern Sahara and in settlements in the Nile Valley and Western Desert oases, indicates that ancient Egyptians capitalized on the providential and cyclical passage of large flocks of birds. They endeavored to capture them; they reared them in captivity and incorporated them in varied facets of daily life. Whether as food for the living or as offerings to the deceased and to the many gods of the Egyptian pantheon, birds remained an intrinsic part of the lives of all ancient Egyptians.

THE CAPTURE OF BIRDS

As early as the late Palaeolithic period, the inhabitants of the Nile Valley were taking full advantage of the resources provided by the fauna surrounding them. In particular, the predictable arrival of millions of birds twice a year during fall and spring migrations appeared as a reliable source of protein, which was complemented by the large number of catfish traveling with the Nile flood, as well as the wild cattle and hartebeests grazing alongside the river (Gautier 1987, p. 431). Already 15,000 years ago, hunters manifested their interest in the avifauna by carving depictions of waterfowl in the company of herds of wild cattle on the cliffs overlooking the Nile River near Qurta

FIGURE 1.1. Clap-netting scene from the tomb of Nakht (TT 52; ca. 1400–1390 BC). A team of four fowlers are shown having caught in their net a wide variety of colorful waterfowl, for the most part ducks and a coot (*Fulica atra*), with black plumage and red eyes (from Nina Davies 1936, vol. 1, pl. 48)

(Huyge 2009; Huyge and Ikram 2009). Archaeofaunal research conducted in Wadi Kubbaniya, Kom Ombo, and the Fayum has confirmed that the diet of the early inhabitants of these regions included migrating waterfowl that spent the winter in Egypt or used the wetlands of the country as a stopover before continuing their long voyage south.[2]

The depictions of daily life activities surviving on the walls of elite tomb-chapels testify to the continued interest of ancient Egyptians in these feathered visitors. A common scene, attested from the Old Kingdom to the Late Period, is the representation of the deceased in the company of family members on board a papyrus skiff, attempting and for the most part being successful at hitting with a throwstick the birds flying away from a papyrus thicket (see Catalog No. 13). This activity might have been a leisurely pursuit of the elite, as they enjoyed spending time in the cooler environment of the marshes;[3] the Egyptians living near wetlands might also have occasionally included wild fowl in their diet by catching a few birds with this simple yet deadly weapon (Catalog No. 12). However, the most effective technique employed to catch large numbers of waterfowl in the marshlands of the country required a clap-net[4] and a well-coordinated team of fowlers under the supervision of an overseer determined to ensure the success of the expedition (fig. 1.1). In some instances, a decoy bird, usually a grey heron (*Ardea cinerea*) (fig. 1.2; see also fig. 10.6), had been placed near the pond with its leg tied to a post before the hunt began: the presence of this traditionally wary bird seemingly reassured other waterfowl flying by, which then landed on the water only to be ensnared in the meshes of the net (Mahmoud 1991, pp. 121–213) (see Chapter 10 in this volume).

Based on textual evidence, the large fowling expeditions took place for the most part in the marshes of the Delta and the Fayum.[5] The Middle Kingdom narrative entitled "The Pleasures of Fishing and Fowling" is indeed set in the wetlands of Lower Egypt (Caminos 1956, p. 4). Moreover, a letter from the Twenty-first Dynasty, probably from El-Hiba in Middle Egypt, specifically mentions the dispatch of a fowler "downstream ... following the fowlers of migratory birds" (Wente 1990, p. 208). Marshes, however, were not limited to these two areas of Lower Egypt. After the departure of the floodwaters, seasonal wetlands were also created near desert margins, in areas called "backswamps" (Butzer 1976, p. 18). The presence of these temporary bodies of water all along the Nile Valley was most attractive not only to resident and wintering waterfowl, but also to the species of birds inhabiting the surrounding arid environments that relied on sources of freshwater. Thus Egyptians from villages located along the Nile River too had the potential to enjoy catching birds and filling their clap-nets with various species of ducks and geese.

FIGURE 1.2. Grey heron (*Ardea cinerea*), Aswan (photo by Jonathan Rossouw)

Undoubtedly, ancient Egyptian artists possessed a developed sense of observation when it came to representing the avian world (see Chapters 9 and 10). Many species of migrant and indigenous birds were thus included in the representations of activities in the marshes (Catalog Nos. 11 and 13). Artists also paid great attention to representing the species of birds destined to enter the menu of the deceased in the afterlife. The elite tombs of the Old Kingdom in particular provide a wealth of information on the species of fowl that were favored for their culinary qualities. The carefully labeled rows of birds presented to the deceased for inspection include not only several species of geese (greylag, *Anser anser*; and white-fronted geese, *A. albifrons*) and ducks (for example, pintail, *Anas acuta*; Eurasian teal, *A. crecca*; and mallard, *A. platyrhynchos*), but, in a few rare instances, also coots (*Fulica atra*) and swans (*Cygnus* sp.) (Mahmoud 1991, pp. 38–93).

The taste for poultry, however, was not limited to waterfowl. Cranes are also a prominent bird in offering scenes (Stupko 2010). A clap-net, with a specific mechanism to trap these long-legged birds, was employed to catch both common and demoiselle cranes (*Grus grus* and *Anthropoides virgo*) (Altenmüller 1974; Henein 2002; Henein 2010, pp. 278–79, 320–23).

1. THE PRACTICAL ROLE OF BIRDS IN ANCIENT EGYPT

FIGURE 1.3. Eurasian hoopoe (*Upupa epops*), Luxor (photo by Jonathan Rossouw)

FIGURE 1.4. In the mastaba tomb of his father, the courtier Mereruka (ca. 2305 BC), Mery-Teti is watching the seining of fish, holding his pet hoopoe by its wings (from Sakkara Expedition 1938, part I, pl. 48C)

Furthermore, representations of activities in orchards and gardens reveal that birds could at times be targeted and captured in trees. Songbirds, in particular doves (*Streptopelia* sp.), pigeons (*Columba* sp.), and golden orioles (*Oriolus oriolus*), could indeed be caught using a large net as they roosted in trees, or a spring trap as they fed on the ground. Capturing these birds had the advantage of "killing two birds with one stone." While it was a promise of a tasty meal, it also rid the orchards and vineyards of flocks of birds, which had the tendency to invade fruit-bearing trees and pilfer the fruits, thus damaging the crops. In several representations, servants are depicted scaring songbirds away by making loud noises or by shaking a cloth in the air. A few hoopoes (*Upupa epops*) (fig. 1.3) were also caught in these large tree nets. While it is unclear whether they were consumed, they are often represented being held by children and it has been suggested that they served as pets (fig. 1.4) (Houlihan 1986, p. 120). Finally, the capture of common quails (*Coturnix coturnix*), which landed in large feathery clouds all along the coast during fall migration and stopped to feed in wheat fields during their spring journey northward, required yet a different method involving a ground net, as clearly represented in the Old Kingdom tomb of Mereruka (fig. 1.5) and on a fragment from the New Kingdom tomb of Nebamun (Parkinson 2008, p. 118, fig. 123).

The Nile Valley and the Delta were by far the areas of choice for both birds and people to settle and flourish. However, the deserts, which lie on both sides of the Nile Valley and represent 95 percent of the territory of Egypt, are not devoid of fauna and are even the favored habitat for a variety of animals that

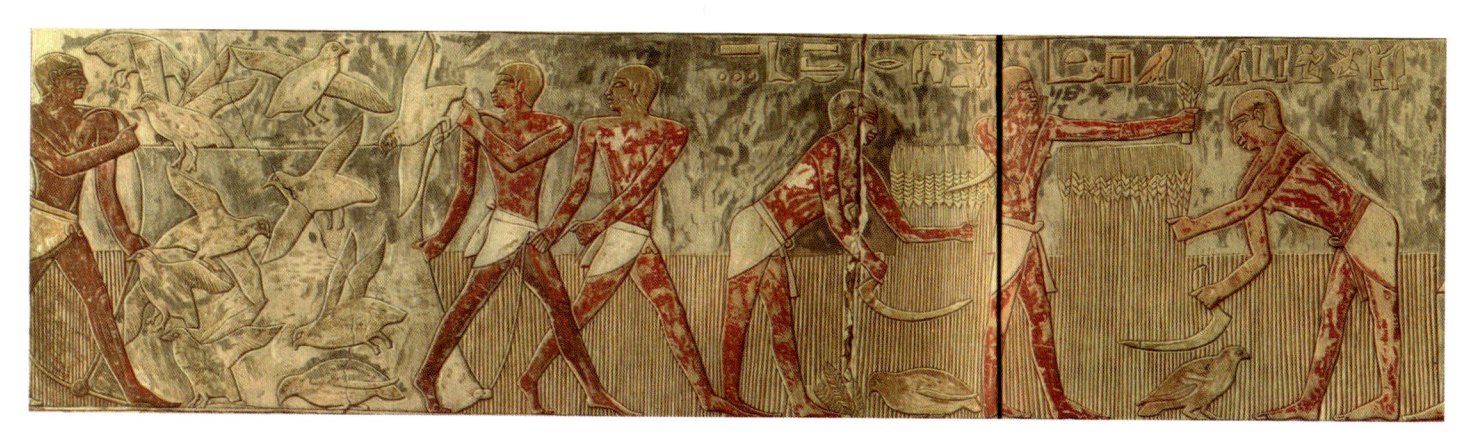

FIGURE 1.5. Quail netting during the harvest, as depicted in the mastaba tomb of Mereruka (ca. 2305 BC) (from Sakkara Expedition 1938, part II, pl. 168)

FIGURE 1.6. Ostriches (*Struthio camelus*) (photo by Jonathan Rossouw)

FIGURE 1.7. Petroglyph in the Wadi Barramiya depicting a flock of ostriches (courtesy of Douglas Brewer)

have adapted to such harsh conditions. The exploitation of the Eastern Sahara started when climatic conditions had yet to be as hyper-arid as they are today. During the crucial period leading to the formation of the Egyptian state at the end of the fourth millennium BC, the region had witnessed a more clement and humid phase during which the Western Desert of Egypt was subject to more frequent rainfall. The desert edges and dry riverbeds, called wadis, supported a vegetation rich enough to attract not only wild mammals, such as gazelles and wild cattle, but also ostriches (*Struthio camelus*) (fig. 1.6) and helmeted guineafowl (*Numida meleagris*). These animals could also graze on the alluvial plain, which had not been fully claimed for agricultural purposes. The early settlers of the Nile Valley thus lived in close contact with this desert fauna (Hendrickx 2010, p. 107). They organized hunting expeditions, whose real or hopeful successes were recorded haphazardly on the cliffs and rocky outcrops of the wadis they used as their hunting grounds. Large mammals fell prey to their arrows. Ostriches are also a common motif in rock art, either as single birds or as flocks (fig. 1.7). In some instances, these large birds were depicted running, flapping their wings and being chased by dogs, indicating that they may have been the object of the hunt (Morrow et al. 2010). A few more explicit scenes involve a hunter pointing his bow and arrows toward a fleeing bird (Winkler 1938, pl. 23). No clear evidence shows that ostriches were exploited for their meat.[6] Their eggs[7] and feathers, however, were already prized objects and continued to be so in pharaonic Egypt (see below).

POULTRY-YARDS AND AVIARIES

While tomb representations clearly show that some birds captured during fowling expeditions were dispatched immediately and further processed — plucked, eviscerated, and in some cases preserved in jars for later consumption (fig. 1.8), a large proportion of the birds was placed into crates and sent by boat to poultry-yards. Several types of aviaries can

FIGURE 1.8. Scene of poultry processing from the tomb of Nakht (TT 52; ca. 1400–1390 BC). A man is shown plucking the feathers of a duck, while another is cutting a bird open on a sloping board. Five birds have already been processed and have been hung to dry. The large jars in the upper right corner most likely contain the fat in which the birds would be preserved (from Davies 1936, vol. 1, pl. 48)

1. THE PRACTICAL ROLE OF BIRDS IN ANCIENT EGYPT

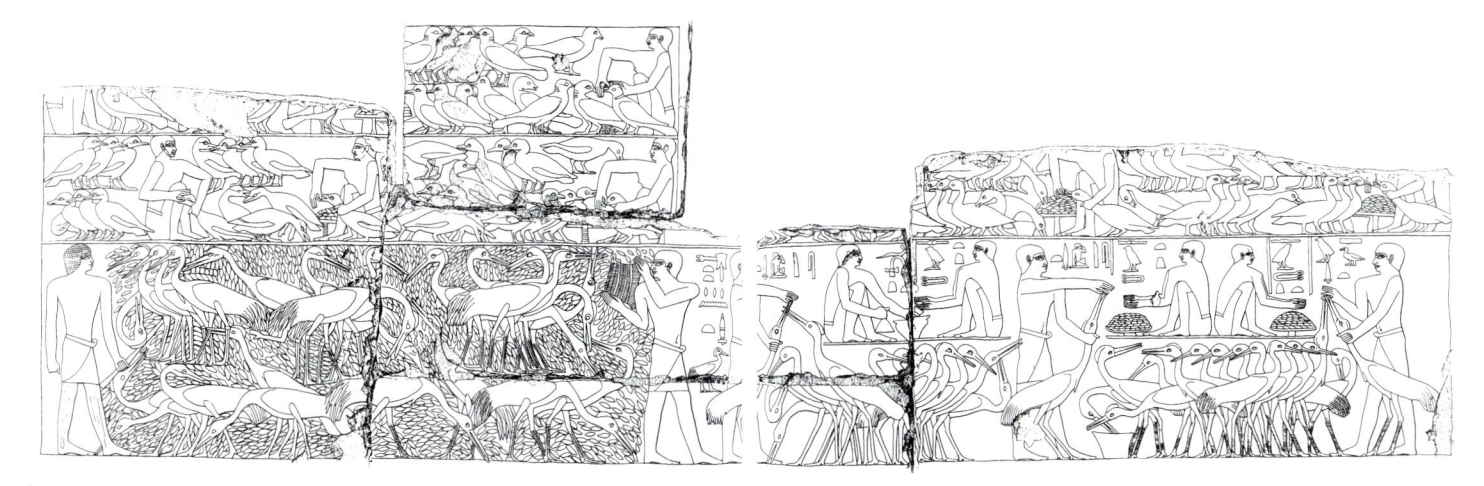

FIGURE 1.9. Force-feeding of a variety of birds: songbirds, perhaps doves and pigeons, in the top left corner; ducks and geese in the central register; cranes, both demoiselle (*Anthropoides virgo*) and common (*Grus grus*), in the bottom right corner. Another flock of cranes is shown feeding on grain poured by an attendant. A herdsman, standing in the bottom left corner, is keeping watch over them (from Sakkara Expedition 1938, part I, pl. 52)

be identified based on the iconographic repertoire of the Old Kingdom.[8] Birds were thus gathered by types: ducks and geese were kept in an enclosure surrounding a water basin; cranes did not require this additional source of water and were kept separately. Grain would be regularly poured over the fence by estate workers. Furthermore, some birds were selected to live in smaller enclosures and be force-fed, so as to improve the quality of their flesh (fig. 1.9). While cages of pigeons and/or orioles are depicted in the midst of offerings during this period, it is not until the Ptolemaic period that dovecotes are attested in the archaeological record (Husselman 1953).

expeditions during the winter. However, the presence of goslings in farmyard representations of the New Kingdom (Catalog No. 14) (fig. 1.10) has led scholars to conclude that some species of geese had been successfully domesticated by that time (ca. 1400 BC). According to J. Boessneck, they include greylag and white-fronted geese, ancestors to domestic geese encountered in modern farmyards (1960; 1988, pp. 88–91). In a similar fashion, doves and pigeons were successfully bred in captivity in most villages of Ptolemaic and Roman Egypt.

DOMESTICATION

Domestication is a slow and selective process. It leads to an animal "whose genetic make-up (and thus whose gene pool) has been altered to satisfy the vital needs of humans, such that if it were released into its natural environment, it would be at a selective disadvantage when competing against its wild counterparts" (Brewer 2001, p. 89). By about 5000 BC, the predynastic inhabitants of the Nile Valley and the Fayum were exploiting domesticated cattle, sheep, and goats. On the other hand, the abundance of waterfowl, their reliable twice-yearly migratory visits to Egypt, and the high potential for fruitful hunting expeditions did not motivate ancient Egyptian aviculturalists to breed these birds in captivity at such an early date. The supply of birds kept in poultry-yards could simply be replenished by new fowling

FIGURE 1.10. Small gaggle of goslings following their parents (D. 17884; photo by Anna Ressman. For full scene, see Catalog No. 14)

BIRDS IN ANCIENT EGYPTIAN CITIES AND VILLAGES

In a letter to his dead mother, written on a bowl that might have contained offerings for her funerary cult, an ancient Egyptian named Shepsi reminds her of all the good deeds he performed during her lifetime. In particular,

> [...] you said to me, your son, "You shall bring me some quails that I may eat them" and I, your son, then brought you seven quails and you ate them [...][9]

This passage unmistakably informs us of the ancient Egyptians' taste for poultry. Members of the elite are also depicted dining on ducklings and other roasted fowl (fig. 1.11). While all levels of society may not have regularly included meat in their diet,[10] it is consistently represented in the iconography of pharaonic Egypt. Geese, ducks, pigeons, and quails were most favored, and could be prepared in various ways. These birds could be roasted, grilled, and salted (Verhöven 1984, pp. 34–39, 59–63, 148–54).

With the increased foreign presence in Egypt during the first millennium BC, a new bird appears on tomb walls among the presentation of offerings, the red jungle fowl, or domestic chicken (*Gallus gallus*). It may have been introduced to Egypt from India by way of Mesopotamia during the Persian period (525–404 BC) (Houlihan 1986, pp. 79–81). Archaeological excavations document that, by the Roman period, chicken had become a bird of choice for the table.[11] Pigeons and doves were also popular. As noted previously, starting during the Ptolemaic period, dovecotes become a standard feature of Egyptian villages.

FIGURE 1.11. In the mastaba tomb of his brother Mereruka, Ihi is shown enjoying some fowl and wine during a boating party in the marshes (from Sakkara Expedition 1938, part I, pl. 44)

FIGURE 1.12. Baskets of eggs beside a small flock of captured Dalmatian pelicans (*Pelecanus crispus*). Tomb of Horemheb (TT 78). Thebes, Eighteenth Dynasty (Davies 1936, vol. 1, pl. 41)

1. THE PRACTICAL ROLE OF BIRDS IN ANCIENT EGYPT

BIRD BY-PRODUCTS

Birds in ancient Egypt were first and foremost valued for their flesh, which constituted a tasty complement to the traditional diet of bread, beer, vegetables, and fish. Eggs have not been documented as being part of a regular diet.[12] They were, at times, represented in piles of offerings, alongside nests of hatchlings (fig. 1.12);[13] however, the symbolism attached to these items, that is, rebirth and fertility, might prevail over their value as food. Furthermore, until the arrival of the chicken in their farmyards, ancient Egyptians' access to eggs was limited to the spring mating season of their fowl. On the other hand, eggs were among the ingredients of medicinal recipes, as was goose and ostrich fat (Darby et al. 1977, p. 330).

Ostriches, those giant birds of the savannah, were a favorite desert game of the king and his elite during dynastic times. During the Eighteenth Dynasty (ca. 1539–1292 BC), ostriches were represented in several Theban tombs being chased and pierced with arrows. While possibly not prized for their meat,[14] their wings and tails provided long feathers for fans.[15] Tribute bearers from Syria, Libya, Nubia, and Punt included this luxury item alongside ostrich eggs among the many goods presented to the king (fig. 1.13) (Catalog No. 1). Containers and beads made of ostrich eggshell have also been recovered from archaeological contexts.

Finally, a less luxurious, but nonetheless highly valued by-product of bird keeping is bird feces, also known as guano. It is recorded that it was gathered from the dovecotes of the Greco-Roman period and used as fertilizer in fields (Houlihan 1986, p. 103). Roman administrators recognized its value and imposed taxes on pigeon-houses (Lichtheim 1957, p. 110).

THE ECONOMIC VALUE OF BIRDS IN VILLAGE LIFE

In the Middle Kingdom Tale of the Eloquent Peasant, a farmer from Sekhet-Hemat, that is, the Wadi Natrun, loads his donkey with "an abundance of all the finest products" of his region, including pigeons, *nʿrw-*, and *wgs*-birds, in order to use them to barter and acquire provisions for his family (Tobin 2003a, p. 26).[16] Ostraca from Deir el-Medina also record transactions in which goods are acquired by exchanging birds:

> [...] as for the goat that I acquired for 20 (pigeons), please give your personal attention and buy 25 pigeons with it." (Wente 1990, p. 158)

These texts demonstrate that fowl were an integral part of the barter system, and therefore the life of the village. Presumably, each household possessed its own fowl-pen, replenished with birds received as rations, or acquired by hunting the local avifauna.

BIRDS IN FUNERARY AND TEMPLE CONTEXTS

THE FUNERARY REALM

To a large extent, our knowledge of ancient Egyptian avifauna comes from the funerary realm. The processions of offering bearers, both on tomb-chapel walls and as models (Catalog No. 39), indicate which birds were most tasty and desired in the afterlife. Food cases containing prepared dishes were also deposited in tombs and victual bird mummies became part of the funerary assemblage of the Theban elite during the Eighteenth Dynasty (Catalog No. 40) (Ikram 1995, pp. 203–04). The deeply rooted belief that death was simply a passage from life on this earth to the afterlife and that deceased relatives continued to partake

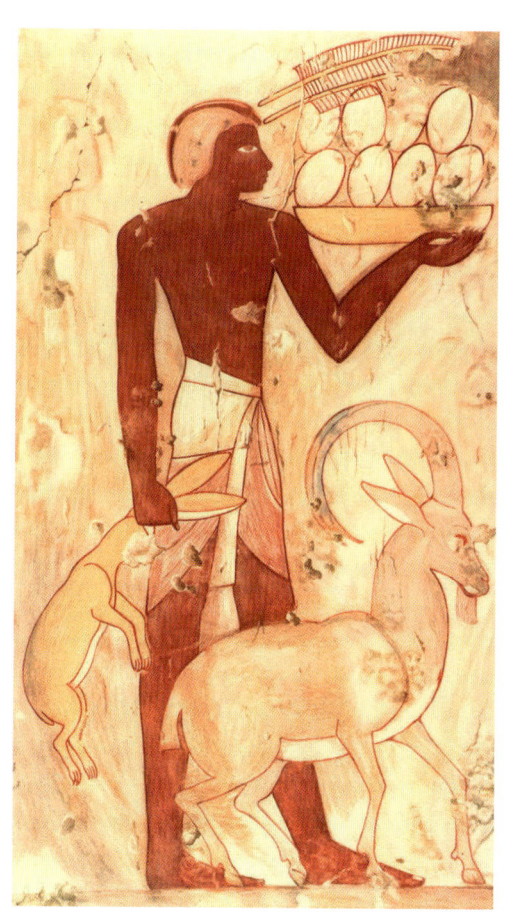

FIGURE 1.13. In the tomb of Horemheb, ostrich eggs and feathers figure among tributes from the desert (from Davies 1936, vol. 1, pl. 38)

in the community's life motivated ancient Egyptians to prepare meticulously for this passage and to devote a portion of their resources to it. Starting in the Middle Kingdom, to multiply their chances of a prosperous afterlife, ancient Egyptians set up stelae and statues in courtyards of temples and pilgrimage sites, before which offerings could also be piled up in their honor. The recitation of the offering formula, known as the *ḥtp di ny-sw.t* formula, inscribed in tomb-chapels, on these stelae, and on statues, magically ensured that the deceased would receive proper nourishment in the afterlife. The provisions traditionally consisted of "1,000 loaves of bread, 1,000 jugs of beer, 1,000 oxen, **1,000 birds**, 1,000 bolts of cloth, 1,000 vessels of alabaster, and 1,000 of every good and pure thing on which gods live ..."

THE TEMPLE

In theory, "land, animals, and labor belonged to the state" (Menu 2001, p. 430). In return, the king maintained cosmic balance, or *maat*, in the country and promised victory and prosperity to his subjects. The king also acted as the high-priest for all the temples in Egypt. To propitiate the gods in his favor, he made ample donations of land and other commodities to all temples and sanctuaries and thus ensured their proper functioning. The voluminous Papyrus Harris I, listing donations made by Ramesses III (ca. 1187–1157 BC) to the temples of Thebes, Heliopolis, and Memphis during his reign, attests to the extent of the king's generosity. During the thirty-one years of his reign, 680,714 birds were donated to these major temples so as to provide offerings for the numerous ceremonies mentioned in the text (Grandet 1994–99). As Jac J. Janssen rightfully asks (1979, p. 170), "what happened with the temple-offerings?" As a matter of fact, the gods enjoyed the appetite-inducing smells that emanated from these foodstuffs only for a short while. All evidence points to the priestly community consuming this food, which, in some cases, did not even reach the altars; rather, it was redistributed immediately to the temple staff, both priests and lay-workers, as well as members of the community.

Starting in the Twenty-sixth Dynasty (664–525 BC), the status of birds in cultic activities reached unparalleled heights in the eyes of pilgrims and temple administrators. Indeed, the cults of sacred animals, such as those of the sacred ibis and the falcon, experienced an exponential growth during the Ptolemaic period and remained popular during the Roman period (see Chapters 2 and 3). Archival documents, especially from the second century BC, as well as collections of ostraca, include detailed information on the cult of the ibis, whose sanctuaries were scattered throughout the country. In one of his dreams recorded on an ostracon, Hor of Sebennytos, priest of Thoth at Saqqara, alluded to the food needed to care for the 60,000 birds kept in the sanctuary (Ray 1976, p. 138). Archaeologists have estimated that the catacombs once housed almost two million mummies of birds, which represent 10,000 mummies deposited

FIGURE 1.14. "Alethe, Attendant of the Sacred Ibis" (1888). Oil on canvas (106 x 65 cm), by Edwin Longsden Long (1829–1891). BORGM 01350 (photograph reproduced with the kind permission of the Russell-Cotes Art Gallery and Museum, Bournemouth, England)

annually for the period during which the cult was practiced at this site. Therefore, the seemingly large number dreamt of by Hor might represent a reasonable estimate of the size of the sacred flock required to satisfy the ever-growing needs for offerings to dedicate to the bird cults of North Saqqara. A large team of servants and guardians of the ibises was undoubtedly required to give proper care to these birds (fig. 1.14). The same would have held true for the care of the sacred falcons and the mass production of their mummies to be deposited in catacombs.

CONCLUSION

Ducks, geese, and pigeons may not have been the most prestigious animals in the eyes of ancient Egyptians. Nevertheless, these birds were an intrinsic part of every Egyptian's life: as food on their table, as feathers in their pillows and fans, as fertilizer in the fields to secure another crop, but also as offerings on the altars of deities and deceased relatives. Birds were accessible to all, fluttering in the bushes of the gardens of the elite, or wandering in the passages and streets of every ancient Egyptian village, just as they do today. They provided nourishment, employment to fowlers and herdsmen, and appeasement to the gods and the dead in their afterlife. Birds in ancient Egypt should thus be seen as the promise of a better present, future, and forever after.

NOTES

[1] Bird migration in Egypt is not limited to inter-continental movements. The intra-African movement of avian species would have also impacted the ancient Egyptian bird population. Some birds, such as the collared pratincole (*Glareola pratincola*) and the Egyptian plover (*Pluvianus aegyptius*) travel north and east from March to September to breed. Furthermore, another influx of birds from the south up the floodplains of Africa occurs in August and September. The economic impact of these bird movements within Africa is yet to be identified. However, the arrival of these birds within Egypt could have filled the gap between the colossal fall and spring migrations. I thank John Wyatt for this information.

[2] Wendorf et al. 1980; Gautier 1988; Churcher et al. 1999; Brewer 2002.

[3] The symbolic significance of this scene is discussed in the entry for Catalog No. 13.

[4] A device for trapping birds which consists of a net kept in a furled position for release by a pull-cord. When a group of birds moves into the catching area, the net is released and is thus thrown over the birds (Weaver 1981).

[5] Houlihan 2001, p. 59; Goodman and Meininger 1989, p. 33. These authors mention that, during pharaonic times, the Delta backswamps were called the "bird tanks of pleasure." They also estimated that, from 1979 to 1986, 261,000 to 375,000 birds were caught in the Nile Delta each year, thus demonstrating the large potential of the region for fowling.

[6] Ostrich bones are only attested in the faunal assemblages of a few sites of the Nile Valley: Merimde Beni-Salame, Maadi (Boessneck 1988, pp. 19, 24), and, more recently, at Hierakonpolis (Renée Friedman, personal communication). However, no butchery marks have been recorded.

[7] Remains of eggshells have been found at most prehistoric settlements, located both in the desert and in the Nile Valley.

[8] Montet 1925, pp. 116–25; Vandier 1969, pp. 418–28; Mahmoud 1991, pp. 228–36.

[9] Gardiner and Sethe 1928, pl. 3; Wente 1990, p. 212.

[10] It is clear that the upper echelon of society included fowl in their menu; however, evidence is scarce when it comes to the rest of the population, that is, the inhabitants of farming settlements. Fish was the main source of protein, with meat and fowl presumably added on special occasions. See Malaise 1988, pp. 68–69; Ikram 1995, pp. 199–229.

[11] Colthred 1966; MacDonald and Edwards 1993; Lentacker and van Neer 1996; Hamilton-Dyer 1997.

[12] An intriguing scene in the New Kingdom tomb of Horemheb (fig. 1.12) presents a unique group of five Dalmatian pelicans (*Pelecanus crispus*) standing close together near a clap-netting scene and may be "amongst the fruit of the trappers' efforts." Eggs are also piled up in baskets near them, with grass placed on top and underneath them to prevent potential breakage. One can surmise that these eggs, just like the birds, were intended to be eaten (Houlihan 1986, pp. 12–13).

[13] For example, on the west wall, north side of the broad hall of the Theban tomb of Nakht (TT 52).

[14] There is as yet no indication in the archaeological record of Egypt that ostriches were consumed as food. However, it is possible that hunters who were able to capture one or several of these fast runners partook in a celebratory meal that featured ostrich meat (see Linseele et al. 2009).

[15] The less luxurious feathers of the many ducks, geese, and pigeons processed for food were used for pillows. Ten pillows filled with feathers and down were recently discovered gathered in a coffin in Valley of the Kings tomb 63. See Teeter 2010b, p. 4.

[16] The list of goods this inhabitant of the Western Desert brought to the Nile Valley, among which figure several types of birds, is proof that fowling could have taken place in the arid landscape of the Eastern Sahara. Scenes recording the trapping of birds have been discovered carved on rocks far from the Nile Valley and dated to the first few dynasties. At the site of Meri 02/50, southwest of the Dakhla Oasis, birds (an ostrich and some birds of prey) were depicted with their legs tied up (Hendrickx et al. 2009, pp. 201–05). At el-Kharafish, north of the Dakhla Oasis, the discovery of avian remains (bones and eggshells) belonging to migratory birds indicates that the inhabitants of this region complemented

their diet with fowl and eggs (Riemer et al. 2008). Finally, the rock carving of a clap-netting scene and the many representations of geese at a desert police station south of Dakhla Oasis "bears witness to the fowling of migrating birds being a favourite pastime." A quarry in this region was even called "Khufu's fowling place" (Kuhlmann 2002).

2. THE ROLE OF BIRDS WITHIN THE RELIGIOUS LANDSCAPE OF ANCIENT EGYPT

FOY SCALF

AVIAN ELEMENTS IN THE DIVINE ICONOGRAPHY OF ANCIENT EGYPT

The proliferative variety of animal imagery within ancient Egyptian religion continues to remain a source of astonishment and bewilderment to many viewers (Pearce 2007, pp. 242–64). Crowned beasts, human bodies with animal heads, and fantastic deities depicted with the commingled limbs of numerous creatures — what Virgil called "monstrous shapes of every species and Anubis the barker" — are commonly found in the Egyptian artistic repertoire (Smelik and Hemelrijk 1984, p. 1854). What, however, did such representations mean? For some Greco-Roman authors seeing and hearing of Egyptian practices, animal veneration was a source of ridicule, hypocritically invoked as Greeks and Romans had their own forms of animal worship, some of which were imported from Egypt.[1] Others, such as Plutarch, Diodorus, and Horapollo, while often not approving of the practice, had at least a partial understanding of the complex symbolic web woven by Egyptian philosophers. Despite the potential confusion a glance at an Egyptian religious work of art can cause, the visual metaphors employed actually have an internal consistency and logic. If it were not the case, what power would the images have either to influence people or explain their ideologies.

A primary impediment to understanding a figure such as the bimorphic Horus, shown with a human body and a falcon's head, is adopting a literal interpretation of the scene (fig. 2.1). The iconography of divine beings was a human invention, an intellectual construct developed to provide a means to express, discuss, manipulate, and understand the various physical forces within the cosmos inhabited by the people of ancient Egypt. It should be remembered that the ancient Egyptians still had intimate contact with and reliance upon the natural forces of their environment. Such forces had an assortment of traits that could be used metaphorically to embody abstract concepts or provide iconic vessels for the physical manifestation of cosmic and social characteristics. Features of flora and fauna derived from the natural world were chosen in order to communicate concepts such as ferocity, protection, or motherhood. In this view, literal readings must be abandoned. Like any artistic expression, "these are communicative devices, metaphors, in a system of formal art that aims not at realist reproduction but at the essence of being" (Quirke 2008, p. 74).

Diodorus Siculus, a historian from first-century BC Sicily, had already grasped the basic metaphorical concept. Concerning the symbolism of the falcon, he wrote:

> Now the falcon signifies to them everything which happens swiftly, hence this animal is practically the swiftest of winged creatures. And the concept portrayed is then transferred, by the appropriate metaphorical transfer, to all swift things and to everything to which swiftness is appropriate, very much as if they had been named.[2]

It is this metaphorical transfer which underpins the "imagistic" system of ancient Egypt.[3] Horus, a god whose name literally means "the one who is far

FIGURE 2.1. Bimorphic depiction of Thoth, with the head of an ibis, and Horus, with the head of a falcon, shown anointing the pharaoh Ptolemy VIII Euergetes II (170–163 BC). From the temple of Kom Ombo (photo by Foy Scalf)

away," is depicted as a falcon, which can soar high into the sky, but the falcon is not limited to Horus. Montu, a god associated with valor and combat, can also be depicted as a falcon due to the bird of prey's ferocious killing abilities. Likewise, the falcon is a common form of the solar deity Re because the flight of the falcon alludes to the flight of the sun across the sky. The complexity of the natural world and the ambivalence of its flora and fauna led to a vast amount of overlap in the iconographic canon (table 2.1).

Egyptian divine images should be understood in their multiplicity and diversity, not as monolithic entities without nuance. We should not interpret figures such as a human body with a falcon head as representing some actual entity in the universe, whose particular likeness distinguished it exclusively from every other divine being. Rather, this is one way to express a particular quality about a force in the universe which the ancient Egyptians were attempting to explain and these "hybrid representations" should be considered "a form of iconographic signs and can be compared to hieroglyphics."[4]

AVIAN ELEMENTS AMONG THE "TRANSFORMATION" SPELLS OF EGYPTIAN FUNERARY TEXTS

Because of the close association between departed humans and the divine world, the metaphors evoked by avian imagery have further significance for understanding the Egyptians' conception of the afterlife. In the Egyptian collection of mythological episodes scholars now call the Book of the Heavenly Cow, it is said that man comes into being from the tears of the sun god. The creator of this etiological myth employed a playful pun, connecting the Egyptian word for "man" (*rmṯ*) with the word for "tear" (*rmy.t*) because they contain similar consonantal roots. However, the further implication contained in this myth is that man is "consubstantial" with the gods; man is made from divine material (Ritner 2011). For the ancient Egyptian, the ultimate desire for the afterlife was to join in the company of the gods and partake in the role of the sun during the day and Osiris throughout the night. The deceased actually sought to become gods and to possess the powers of the gods, including the ability to manifest in representative animal forms and attain the qualities of the cosmic forces the images conveyed.

Just as substantial avian imagery appears within Egyptian religious art, funerary literature reserves a prominent place for birds within the so-called transformation spells. The designation "transformation" derives from the recurrence of the Egyptian verb "to become" (*ḫpr*) in the introduction to such spells (fig. 2.2). Within the traditional funerary compilations of the Pyramid Texts (PT), Coffin Texts (CT), and Book of the Dead (BD), the idea of "becoming" a particular being, including the gods themselves in addition to a variety of plant and animal forms, occupied the focus of many passages. In the Greco-Roman period, descendants of the transformation spells were used independently on papyri to form their own composition referred to as the Book of Transformations.[5] It was believed that those who employed these texts could transform into animal forms of their choosing and Book of the Dead spells were dedicated to becoming a "falcon of gold" (BD 77), "divine falcon" (BD 78), "phoenix" (BD 83), "heron" (BD 84), "*ba*-bird" (BD

TABLE 2.1. Prominent deities associated with avian iconography

Name	Avian Features
Benu	Heron
Horakhty	Falcon, Winged Sun Disk
Horus	Falcon, Winged Sun Disk
Isis	Falcon, Kite, Kestrel, Swallow
Khonsu	Falcon
Montu	Falcon
Nekhbet	Vulture
Nephthys	Falcon, Kite, Kestrel, Swallow
Qebehsenuef	Falcon Head
Re	Falcon, Winged Sun Disk
Sokar	Falcon
Thoth	Ibis

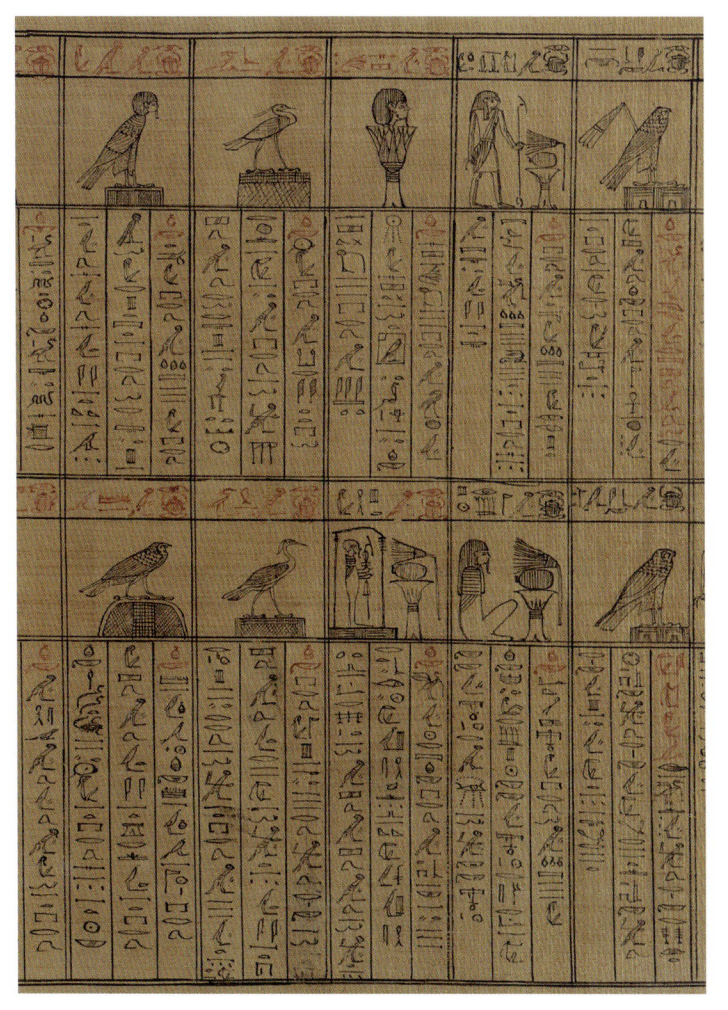

FIGURE 2.2. Spells 77–86 from Papyrus Milbank (OIM E10486), a Ptolemaic Book of the Dead papyrus belonging to Irtyuru. The vignettes show the various forms in which the deceased wished to transform himself by means of the accompanying spells (D. 17930; photo by Anna Ressman)

manifestation of the sun god as creator, who was born of an egg laid upon the primeval mound that first rose from the cosmic waters.

For the deceased individual, the *ba* often manifested in iconography as a human-headed bird (see Catalog No. 34). The bird body represented the freedom of movement of the deceased and specifically the ability to fly into the sky so that he might "share in the cosmic existence of the sun god."[6] However, as the transformation spells suggest, individuals could take innumerable forms in the afterlife. In addition to the human-headed bird, the deceased could be depicted as a falcon-headed human, attested by anthropoid coffins with falcon heads, mummies fitted with cartonnage falcon heads, and scenes on stelae showing the deceased's falcon-headed corpse lying upon a funerary bier (compare the writing of Qebehsenuef in table 2.1).[7]

85), and a "swallow" (BD 86). These animal appearances represented the gods and the powers associated therewith (fig. 2.3).

In the "spell for becoming a divine falcon" (CT 312/BD 78), Horus announces to Osiris that he will send the deceased as a messenger in his own falcon form: "I made my form as his form when he comes and goes to Busiris, for my appearance is his appearance." Later in the text, the messenger replies: "I have performed what was ordered because Horus endowed me with his *ba*." The *ba*, although often translated as "soul," represents the physical manifestation and power of the god. Thus, the *ba*s of the sun god were the many forms he could take, one of which was the phoenix, which is called the "*ba* of Re" and into which the deceased wished to transform by means of BD spell 83 (see Catalog No. 2 and fig. 2.3). The phoenix, called the *benu*-bird in Egyptian (table 2.1), was the

FIGURE 2.3. Inherkhau shown standing before the phoenix in his tomb (TT 359). The image is a supersized version of the vignette from Book of the Dead spell 83, whose introductory passage is above Inherkhau's head: "Spell for becoming the phoenix, entering and going forth by Osiris, overseer of the crew in the place of truth, Inherkhau, justified" (photo by Charles Nims)

"ONE BIRD, ONE POT": THE SACRED ANIMAL CULTS OF ANCIENT EGYPT

Avian elements were prominent in divine iconography and funerary literature, but most infamous has been the direct worship of animals within the sacred animal cults of ancient Egypt (see fig. 3.4). The veneration of selected sacred animals has a long history in Egypt extending back at least to the predynastic period as revealed by the recent excavations of the elaborate burials of fauna at Hierakonpolis.[8] The exact nature of these earliest animal cults remain an enigma because of extremely fragmentary evidence and a lack of written documents from the period to provide the indigenous perspective on these practices. Based on evidence from later historical epochs, animal cults primarily took one of two forms. In one form, an animal was considered the physical living incarnation of a particular deity on earth (Dodson 2009). There were many sacred animals associated with different gods and various cities, such as the Apis bull, a living manifestation of the god Ptah worshipped in the city of Memphis; the living crocodile, an earthly form of the god Sobek venerated throughout the Fayum; and the living falcon of Edfu, an incarnation of the god Horus. These animals, and others like them, were selected to be the representative of gods on earth, a breathing receptacle for the god's *ba* or manifest physical power, and they were well cared for, paraded during public festivals, and ornately buried. Cults of this type continued to be practiced into the Roman period and elements borrowed from Egyptian customs continued in use into the Byzantine era across the Mediterranean world (Smelik and Hemelrijk 1984, p. 1999).

The other form of animal veneration consisted of the capturing and rearing of animal species sacred to a particular deity and the mummification and burial of these species in special purpose-built necropoleis (fig. 2.4). Rather than a single chosen member, all members of these species were considered sacred to their tutelary divinity and were buried by the millions (fig. 2.5). An astonishing menagerie of fauna were treated in this manner including fish, beetles, lizards, snakes, shrews, moles, mice, ibises, hawks, falcons, dogs, and jackals. These categories of worship

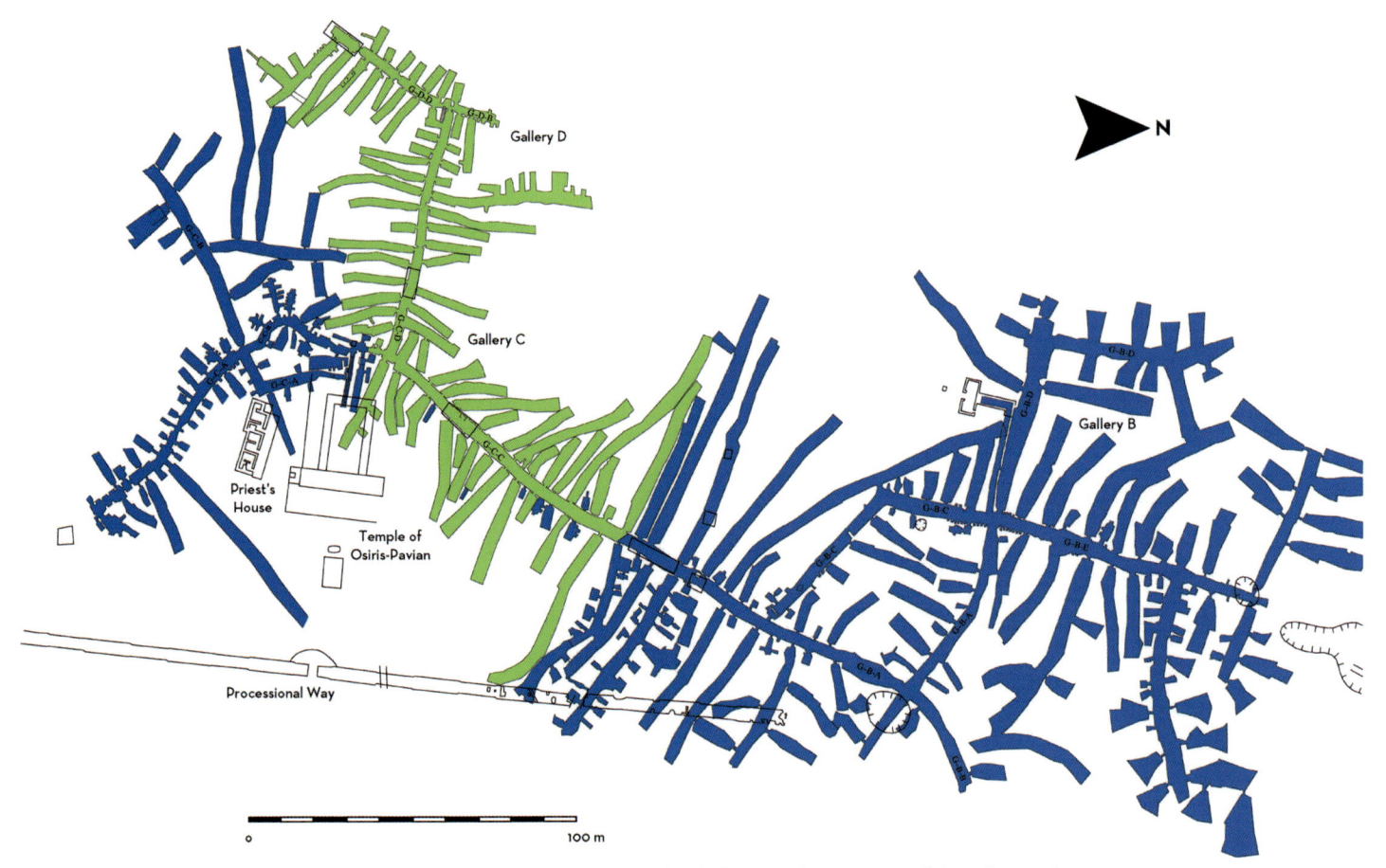

FIGURE 2.4. The subterranean animal necropolis at Tuna el-Gebel. Pre-Ptolemaic parts of the galleries shown in green (courtesy of Dieter Kessler)

2. THE ROLE OF BIRDS WITHIN THE RELIGIOUS LANDSCAPE OF ANCIENT EGYPT

FIGURE 2.5. A vulture lays before the innumerable ceramic vessels containing bird bundles stacked at the entrance to Gallery 6/5 in the Falcon Catacomb excavated at Saqqara (Davies and Smith 2005, pl. 23d)

were not mutually exclusive; the Egyptians could prepare for burial millions of falcons while still separately rearing a particular falcon which functioned as the living incarnation of the god on earth, public displays of which are known to have taken place at the temples of Edfu, Dendera, and Philae (Dijkstra 2002).

Among these cults, reverence of the ibis, sacred to the god Thoth, and the falcon, sacred to the god Horus, held special places of honor and the cults of these two birds were often administered together, as we know from the records of the personnel left behind at Saqqara, Tuna el-Gebel, Dra Abu el-Naga (Thebes), and Kom Ombo. The reverence for these birds was surely old, but our earliest indication for their mummification and burial derives from patchy evidence dated to the New Kingdom, such as a ceramic vessel with a hieratic inscription mentioning the discovery and subsequent burial of an ibis found in "the canal of Ramses I."[9] Sites dedicated to the purposes of the cult flourished throughout the land of Egypt, exploding in popularity soon after 700 BC. The exponential increase in the popularity of these animal cults followed first the Assyrian and later Persian conquests of Egypt and some scholars have interpreted the renewed vigorous participation as a nationalist response to foreign domination (Smelik and Hemelrijk 1984, pp. 1863–64). However, expansion of the sacred animal necropolis of Tuna el-Gebel continued under the Persian rulers, historical memory of whom suffered, as indicated by the tale recounted by Herodotus about how Cambyses stabbed and killed the Apis bull.

The last native kings of the Thirtieth Dynasty from Sebennytos in the Delta, who supported Egyptian religious practices through substantial building campaigns and royal sponsorship during their brief dynasty, seem to have placed particular emphasis on the animal cults. Pharaoh Nectanebo II had a royal cult dedicated to "Nectanebo-the-falcon" including priests who served statues showing the king standing beneath the breast of the Horus falcon.[10] The Macedonian rulers of the Ptolemaic dynasty (305–30 BC) sought continued employment of such traditional Egyptian symbols, including maintaining the cult of Nectanebo-the-falcon, fitting with the portrayal of Nectanebo as an ancestor of Alexander the Great in the Alexander Romance.[11] Maintenance of the sacred animal cults was important enough that the Ptolemaic sacerdotal decrees make prominent mention of royal patronage for their support. The decree preserved on the Rosetta Stone for Ptolemy V Epiphanes states that "He did many great deeds for Apis, Mnevis, and the other sacred animals of Egypt in excess of what those who came before him did. His thought concerned their condition at all times and he gave great and splendid (offerings) for their burials."[12] The language of the decrees shows how the Ptolemaic kings negotiated with the powerful priestly class in addition to presenting themselves as traditional pharaohs maintaining the cosmic order of *maat* through their religious piety.

Birds for the cult were both raised in captivity as well as captured wild. A recently published Demotic inscription on a coffin from the hawk galleries at Saqqara refers to the discovery of a dead hawk which was collected for burial (Ray 2011, pp. 271–73). Royal subsidies in the form of fields controlled by the cultic administration as part of their priestly stipend allowed them to provide feed for the birds as well as raise liquid capital by leasing the land for cultivation or selling the produce at harvest. Several members of these cultic administrations are known from objects in the Oriental Institute Museum collection. Provisioning for the living falcons in the town of

BETWEEN HEAVEN AND EARTH: BIRDS IN ANCIENT EGYPT

FIGURE 2.6. Base of the magical healing statue of Djedhor from Athribis, in which he references his job caring for the "living falcons who are in this land" (column 5 from the left). OIM E10589 (photo by Jean Grant)

Athribis during the Ptolemaic period was the responsibility of a man named Djedhor, whose statue-base inscription details how he "prepared the food of the living falcons who are in this land" (fig. 2.6). Near the town of Esna, a man named Nesshutefnut, whose Book of the Dead papyrus is now in the Oriental Institute Museum (OIM E9787), carried the title "priest of the living falcons in his tree" (fig. 2.7). Such priests had direct control over the subsidized fields and they often treated it as private property which could be bought and sold. A series of Greek receipts included not only the transfer of ownership concerning the fields, but also management of the *ibiotapheion*, the catacomb where ibis mummies were interred.

After death, either natural or induced, the birds were taken to the *wꜥb.t* "purification (room)," where they were embalmed, mummified, wrapped in linen, and many placed within ceramic jars prior to deposition in the *ꜥ.wy ḥtp* "house of rest." The Egyptians held the entire animal as sacred and elaborate wrappings suggestive of an entire bird can sometimes hold only a few feathers or bones (Catalog No. 32). From the archive of Hor, a member of the administration for the cult of the ibis and falcon at Saqqara in the Ptolemaic period, we know that reforms in the treatment of ibis mummies stipulated one bird for each vessel, but often multiple birds were deposited in a single container (Ray 1976). Short votive prayers, such as those preserved on jar fragments in the Oriental Institute Museum collection (fig. 2.8), were sometimes written on the exterior of these vessels on behalf of a patron (Scalf, forthcoming). Most inscriptions do not identify the patron by title, but in several cases we know that these donors were personnel working within the association tasked with caring for the sacred animals. The technicalities of sponsoring a burial are unknown, but a Demotic letter now in the British Museum preserves a son's promise to pay for the "burial of the ibis" if his father is relieved from illness (Migahid 1986, pp. 122–129). Unfortunately, some ambiguity persists about how participants outside of the priestly personnel contributed to the sacred animal festivities. It is unclear if royal patronage was sufficient to account for the exceptionally large cultic expenses associated with the administrative apparatus necessary for the annual processing of 10,000 birds at some sites.

The reasons why the Egyptians made such inordinate investments in their animal mummies have recently come under debate. For many years, it was common for scholars to explain that the mummies

FIGURE 2.7. The title of Nesshutefnut, *ḥm nṯr n nꜣ bik.w ꜥnḫ.w m ḫt=f* "priest of the living falcons in his tree," from his Book of the Dead papyrus in the Oriental Institute Museum (OIM E9787)

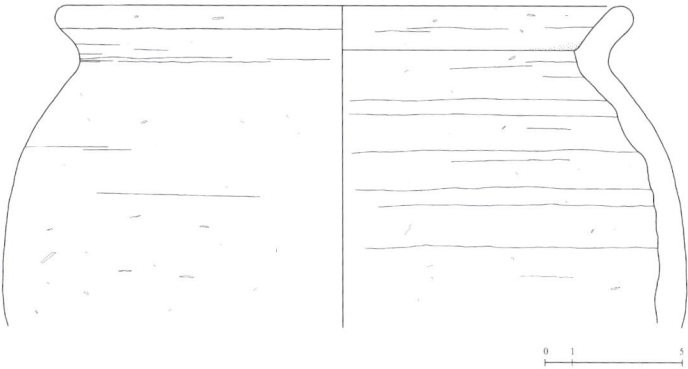

FIGURE 2.8. A fragmentary ceramic vessel that had probably been used as a container for an ibis mummy, with a Demotic votive inscription that mentions "the gods of the house of rest." OIM E19051 (D. 17991; photo by Anna Ressman; profile drawing by Natasha Ayers)

were produced for a vibrant pilgrimage industry. According to this view, travelers visiting sacred sites on festival days throughout Egypt would buy a votive offering such as a mummy and/or bronze figure and dedicate it to the sanctuary of the god. There is some evidence for outside participation but it is somewhat vague about the exact nature of the interaction. What is known primarily concerns the actions of the religious associations, groups of personnel including priests, craftsmen, and other workers who supported the cult via their trade. At sites such as Saqqara and Tuna el-Gebel, where millions of hawk and ibis mummies have been found, administering the cult was a monumental investment that involved caring for the birds, an enormous pottery industry to produce the ceramic jars, stone-cutting crews to excavate the labyrinth of burial galleries, scribes for accounting, and priests to perform the appropriate religious rites. Massive crown subsidies suggest that the royal house took a particular interest in the sacred animals. Dieter Kessler, who has worked closely with the

Tuna el-Gebel material, has argued that the practices were actually part of the royal cult itself, important in the yearly ritual renewal of the king. Likewise, he believes that only those with the appropriate authority would have had permission to handle the animal mummies, which were literally called "god" (nṯr), and enter the sacred space of the subterranean necropolis at Tuna el-Gebel.[13] Kessler's theories await further confirmation, but based on the incomplete nature of the data, it is likely that the royal house profited ideologically from their patronage of the animal cults and that the populace participated through priestly intermediaries.

Avian imagery found within the religious landscape of ancient Egypt across the millennia is an important element in the iconographic canon of divinities, as symbols of the postmortem powers of the deceased, and as living, breathing repositories evoking the divine presence on earth. Despite offending the tastes of certain foreigners visiting the country, the complex metaphorical associations created by Egyptian philosophers through the use of animal representation had an internal logic based on the empirical observation of the natural environment and the rationalizations created to explain the world around them. Just as the Egyptian hieroglyph for "god" was a flag (𓊹), whose waving denoted the invisible presence of deity, birds and their unique characteristics, provided a fertile source of imaginative religious associations that continued to be employed throughout Egyptian history.

NOTES

[1] Burkert 1985, pp. 64–66; Gilhus 2006, p. 102.

[2] Greek text and English translation in Oldfather 1967, pp. 96–97. Unfortunately, this concept was the only one applied in the attempts to decipher the Egyptian hieroglyphic script from the fifth-century explanations of Horapollo to the seventeenth-century writings of Athanasius Kircher.

[3] "Imagistic" used here in the sense of Ritner 1993, pp. 247–49.

[4] Smelik and Hemelrijk 1984, p. 1861. See also Quirke 2008, pp. 73–74; Hornung 1996, pp. 100–42.

[5] M. Smith 2009, pp. 610–49; M. Smith 1979; Legrain 1890. To this can be added the so-called Book of the Ba, published in Beinlich 2000.

[6] Assmann 2005, p. 92; M. Smith 2009, pp. 610–17.

[7] Spiegelberg 1927, pp. 28–29; Broekman 2009.

[8] Van Neer et al. 2004, p. 106; Linseele et al. 2009, pp. 119–20; R. Friedman 2011, pp. 39–40.

[9] Ray 2011, p. 221; Spiegelberg 1928, pp. 14–17.

[10] See Yoyotte 1959; de Meulenaere 1960; Holm-Rasmussen 1979; Ray 2002, pp. 121–22; Gorre 2009; Ladynin 2009, pp. 7–9. For statues showing Nectanebo II between the legs of the Horus falcon, see Metropolitan Museum of Art 34.2.1 published in Arnold 1995, pp. 44–45 (no. 50), and Musée du Louvre, Paris, E 11152. These statues can be compared to images known already in the Old Kingdom such as the statue of Khafre (Egyptian Museum, Cairo, CG 14) with Horus stretching his wings around the head of the king (see fig. 4.4 in this volume) and the alabaster statue of an enthroned Pepy (Brooklyn Museum 39.120) whose back pillar doubles as a *serekh* with Horus perched atop.

[11] The Alexander Romance refers to a collection of stories about Alexander the Great that circulated in antiquity, some of which show Egyptian connections (Jasnow 1997).

[12] Apis and Mnevis were sacred bulls deemed to be the earthly incarnations of Ptah and Re respectively (Dodson 2005, pp. 72–95).

[13] Kessler 1989, pp. 299–303; Kessler 2010, pp. 269–70.

3. AN ETERNAL AVIARY: BIRD MUMMIES FROM ANCIENT EGYPT

SALIMA IKRAM

All animals played a crucial role in the lives of the ancient Egyptians, not only in terms of the practical and quotidian, but also the spiritual; however, birds were arguably the most significant creatures in the religious sphere (see Chapter 2 in this volume; Davies and Smith 2005, p. 54). Raptors were totems or *ba*-spirits of the various forms of the sun god Re as well as of Horus, the eternal king; the phoenix-like *benu*-bird was a symbol of creation; the sacred ibis (*Threskiornis aethiopicus*) was associated with Thoth, the god of wisdom; the goddesses Nekhbet and Mut were both linked to vultures; the goddess Maat, manifestation of order and balance, was often shown as a feather; the goddesses Isis and Nephthys could transform themselves into kites (*Milvus migrans*); and the different aspects of the human soul, the *ba* (much like the modern idea of spirit) and the *akh*[1] (understood as the part of one's soul that united with the gods and the eternal stars), were respectively shown as a human-headed bird and a bald ibis (*Geronticus eremita*). Thus birds served as symbols of the gods themselves, as well as the divine essence within each individual.

Although birds played a part in the religious life of the ancient Egyptians in all eras, the importance of birds in cult practice is most apparent starting in the Late Period and continuing through the Roman period. This is manifested by the significant number of cult installations of avian deities and the millions of mummified birds that were buried as votive offerings in vast catacombs associated with them all over Egypt (see figs. 2.4–5). Although animal mummies existed throughout Egyptian history, the majority that have survived date to the later periods. There are at least four kinds of easily defined animal mummies: pets, victual or food offerings, sacred animals, and votive offerings (Ikram 2005a, pp. 1–15). Pictorial evidence indicates that pet birds existed (see fig. 1.4), though thus far no known avian mummy can unreservedly be identified as that of a pet. Poultry features prominently among victual mummies as diverse species of geese, ducks, and pigeons/doves were prepared as if to be eaten — desiccated, anointed with oils and unguents, and wrapped — then given as food offerings to sustain the deceased (fig. 3.1 and Catalog No. 40). These were most common from the New Kingdom through the start of the Twenty-first Dynasty (fifteenth to eleventh century BC) (Ikram 1995a, pp. 239–84; Ikram 2004; Ikram, in preparation). All the same, this type of mummy does not make up the majority of those produced in Egypt.

The most plentiful types of animal mummies are votive and sacred animals. The idea behind sacred animals is that the spirit of a god enters into the body of his or her totemic animal, and during its lifetime that creature is regarded as a manifestation of that god, to be revered, worshipped, and cosseted until its death. Thus an ibis or a baboon (or both), as manifestations of Thoth, would be kept at the temple and would act as a conduit for the god, particularly in an oracular role (Davies and Smith 2005; Smith et al. 2011; Ray 1976). After the animal died, it would be embalmed and buried with great pomp in a catacomb. The divine spirit would migrate from that animal's body and take

FIGURE 3.1. Victual mummy from the tomb of Yuya and Tuya (KV 46) (photo by Anna-Marie Kellen, courtesy of the Egyptian Museum, Cairo)

up residence in the body of a similar animal, recognizable to the priests by specific markings.

Votive animals, on the other hand, are actually very similar to any other kind of votive offering, such as stelae and statues, or in a more modern context, candles that are lit in churches. Presumably the votary would purchase a mummified animal, dedicate and consecrate it through the priests, and it would be kept for a time within the temple precincts. Then, during a specific festival, priests would inter it in the catacomb or "house of rest" assigned to that god, called an *ibiotapheion* in the case of ibises (Davies and Smith 2005, p. 64). Thus every year thousands of ibises of all ages, from eggs to adults, were interred, sometimes neatly stacked in ceramic vessels, each layer separated by a protective and purifying layer of sand, or else just tossed in a pile (figs. 2.6, 3.2). The idea was that the mummies would take the donor's prayers to the relevant god, in perpetuity. The donor presumably was someone who either officially or spiritually felt a connection with that god. Mummified animals might have been preferred to other ex votos, as animals were thought to be able to communicate more directly with the divine world and it was deemed more likely that the gods would attend to the prayers brought by their own creatures who had once been flesh and blood, rather than by images of stone or metal (Ikram 2005a, pp. 9–12; Charron 1990).[2]

The majority of mummified birds come from such catacombs, and are, for the most part, raptors and ibises dedicated to Re, Horus, Thoth, and the idea of divine kingship. A few representatives of other species are also found within these vast labyrinths (von den Driesch et al. 2005; Kessler 1989; Kessler and Nur el-Din 2005; Davies and Smith 2005, p. 9; Ikram, in preparation), most likely because they died within a sacred area and were interred there, rather than due to a close affiliation with the specific divinities revered at the site. In some cases, birds were not the only species wrapped in one set of bandages. At several sites some raptors have been coupled with shrews, burying the diurnal and nocturnal totems of the sun god in one mummy (Lortet and Gaillard 1903, pp. 115–16; Ghaleb, unpublished). A few ibis mummies from Abydos that have been closely examined by this author show that snails have been placed in their beaks to provide them with sustenance in the afterworld (Wade et al. 2012), with a similar example coming from Tuna el-Gebel (Lortet and Gaillard 1903, p. 123). The most curious combination of "interspecies" burials are those of priests of Thoth whose cartonnage shows a painted image of the god in avian form, roughly beneath which is placed a mummified ibis, cradled against the body of the deceased man.[3]

Additionally, some mummy bundles contain only feathers, single bones (sometimes not even of birds, but of other creatures that are wrapped to resemble birds), and portions of what have been interpreted as nest fragments (Catalog No. 32). For the cynical, these "false" mummies might be a way of cheating votaries; for the charitable, they might be a case of a part representing the whole, or else a way of keeping the mummification debris, which was itself sacred, protected and in a consecrated place (fig. 3.3).

FIGURE 3.2. Pots containing mummies in the falcon galleries in the sacred animal necropolis at Saqqara (photo by Salima Ikram, courtesy the Supreme Council of Antiquities/Ministry of State for Antiquities)

3. AN ETERNAL AVIARY: BIRD MUMMIES FROM ANCIENT EGYPT

FIGURE 3.3. Mummy bundle consisting of ibis feathers and reeds that have been tied together with strips of papyrus and then wrapped. Excavated at Abu Rawash (photo by Salima Ikram, courtesy of Michel Baud and the French Mission to Abu Rawash)

SITES OF AVIAN NECROPOLEIS

The majority of avian catacombs are for ibises, raptors, or more often, both together. The popular combination of ibis and raptor burials might be due to the fact that together these birds invoked many of the deities involved in the creation of the world, and also balanced each other, with Horus guarding the sunlit day, and Thoth protecting the moonlit nights (Ray 1976, p. 137) (see Catalog Nos. 23 and 28). Other birds also feature within these catacombs, but to a much lesser extent (Kessler and Nur el-Din 2005, pp. 152–54; von den Driesch et al. 2005, pp. 205, 216–17).

The two most famous sites with bird catacombs are Tuna el-Gebel in Middle Egypt, and the royal burial ground at Saqqara, located close to the capital city of Memphis. However, it should be noted that ibis and/or raptor mass burials are found throughout Egypt at sites such as Abukir/Canopus, Taposiris Magna, Alexandria, Quesna, Buto, Bahnasa, Abu Rawash, Arab el-Tawila, Heliopolis, Giza, Abusir al-Malik, Umm el-Baraghat, Herakleopolis, Qasr el-Banat, Zawiet Barmasha, Asyut, Akhmim, Qaw, Qus, Zawiyet el-Maitin, Roda, Sharuna, Abydos, Hu, Thebes, Gebelein, el-Gharag, Kom Ombo, Ghoran, El-Shutb/el-Borsa, Edfu, Esna, Elephantine, Bahariya, Dakhla, and Kharga (fig. 3.4). Millions and millions of birds have been buried in these locations throughout time. The catacombs of Saqqara alone are estimated to contain over 1.75 million birds (Nick Fieller and Paul Nicholson, personal communication), while those of Tuna el-Gebel boasted at least one million (von den Driesch et al. 2005, p. 214).

REARING BIRDS

To generate such a vast number of mummies these animals must have been farmed extensively, since, in the wild, ibises tend to raise only one brood a year, probably most commonly between March and August in Egypt. Thus, to some extent the sacred (*Threskiornis aethiopicus*) and glossy (*Plegadis falcinellus*) ibises must have been enticed to reside permanently in Egypt, rather than being migrant visitors (von den Driesch et al. 2005, p. 205), and could have been farmed as tamed animals in a very basic way. According to Duncan Bolton, curator of birds at Birdworld, England, sacred ibises are easy to rear (personal communication). If the priests removed the eggs or the chicks from the parents, those parents would breed again, with the possibility of up to three broods a year. Bolton also suggests that the eggs could be removed and hatched under a different species, or in an incubator.

Near Saqqara the area bordering the Abusir Lake has been posited as a possible ibis habitat (Miroslav Bárta, personal communication), and magnetometry surveys have revealed a series of installations that might have served as support for such an activity (Ian Mathieson, personal communication). Lake Dahshur, although farther south, could also have provided a site for rearing ibises that perhaps supplied the Saqqara catacombs. Similarly, a lake close to Tuna el-Gebel could have served as a bird sanctuary and/or breeding ground (von den Driesch et al. 2005). Additionally, Sami Gabra, the first archaeologist to undertake a systematic excavation of Tuna el-Gebel, discovered an area not far from the Great Temple that consisted of a garden with a large reservoir, perhaps a site to keep the birds; such a site is described in the Tebtunis Papyri (Gabra 1971, pp. 59, 156–58). Texts indicate that a group of priests were dedicated to the care and upkeep of their respective flocks (Ray 1976), even to the point of incubating eggs (Davies and Smith 2005, pp. 64–65; Ray 1976, p. 138). Certainly eggs have also been found among the mummified offerings at several ibis burial sites in Egypt (see Catalog No. 33). In addition to the large-scale ibis production, it is feasible to suggest that private individuals might have kept ibises in an ad hoc way, to provision the temples, or collected dead birds which they then donated to the temples. Inscriptions on certain bird mummy containers indicate that not all bird mummies were locally produced; devotees could

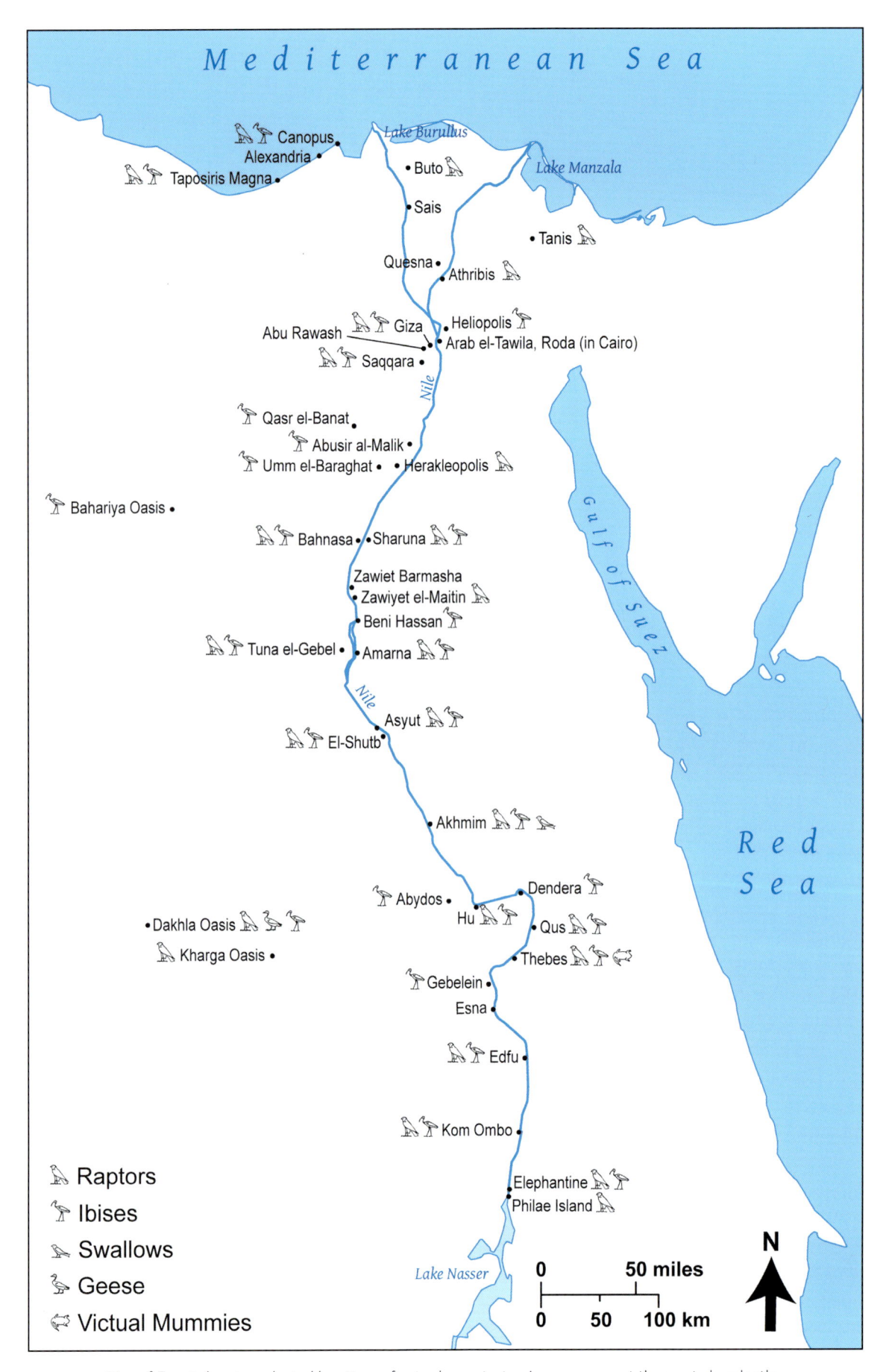

BETWEEN HEAVEN AND EARTH: BIRDS IN ANCIENT EGYPT

FIGURE 3.4. Map of Egypt showing selected locations of animal cemeteries. Icons represent the most abundantly attested mummified birds at these sites (after Nicholas Warner, in Ikram 2005, p. xvii)

send them from Lower Egypt in the north, all the way to Tuna el-Gebel in the south (Spiegelberg 1918, pp. 118–20; Spiegelberg 1928, pp. 14–17; Kessler 1989; von den Driesch et al. 2005).

MUMMIFICATION

The embalmers prepared birds in a variety of ways. Studies are still underway to attempt linking specific styles of embalming with particular time periods, geographic areas, and even ateliers. In all areas, however, it seems that mass burials and industrial-style mummification was possible as many birds show evidence that they were deliberately killed, frequently by having their neck wrung, the first step in a factory-efficient mummification process. Of course, birds that died naturally (especially chicks) were also offered. The presence of chicks in mummy bundles indicates that, if they were wild, these must have been collected and prepared in March/April. The positioning of the birds is fairly standard: raptors are positioned with their legs and talons pulled down along the body with the wings tidily folded (see Catalog No. 26); ibises generally have their long necks twisted so that the head and beak lies along the belly, although variations occur, with the head tucked under the wing (Ikram and Iskander 2002; Lortet and Gaillard 1901; idem 1903; idem 1905–09).

The modes of mummification were diverse. Gabra found that at Tuna el-Gebel some ibises were coated with hot terebinth resin and then wrapped in linen, deposited in a jar (each jar contained at least one, and more commonly two or more birds) that was then sealed. Apparently, the resin burned through the feathers, skin, and flesh of the birds, ultimately leaving a fine powder and bones (Gabra 1971, p. 111). For the ibis and falcon mummies from the catacombs at Saqqara, and for many other bird mummies, scholars suggest a similar method: dipping the birds in molten resin as so many of them were covered with a black substance that is either resin or a mixture of resin and oil (Lortet and Gaillard 1903, p. 114; Ghaleb, unpublished). There are a few examples of mummies of birds covered with a dark resinous material being gilded (Catalog No. 26 and CG 29681). Thus far this author has only noted this phenomenon in raptors, which are generally related to the cult of Re. This might be due to a variety (or a combination) of reasons. The gilding might: indicate a sacred rather than a votive mummy; emphasize the association of raptors with the sun god; be a more costly votive mummy; allude both to the solar nature of the birds and underline the idea that the act of mummification transformed the bird from a secular entity into a sacred one, as was the case with humans. According to Egyptian religious beliefs, the flesh of the gods was made of incorruptible gold, which is why human mummy masks are painted yellow or gilded, and possibly why these avian mummies were also gilded.

Other methods used to prepare bird mummies are closer to those employed for mammalian mummies: evisceration, desiccation through natron or other salts, anointment with oils, and wrapping. Sometimes the anointment step might be omitted. Several of the ibises coming from the Shunet ez-Zebib, a funerary enclosure at Abydos, examined by this author, seem to have been prepared by evisceration, desiccation, in some cases oiling, and wrapping. Many of these mummies have beautifully preserved feathers and forms.

In an effort to identify the materials used[4] in animal mummification, researchers from the Bristol Biogeochemistry Research Centre have used gas chromatography and other related tests on tissues and wrapping from two raptors and one ibis mummy. The results show that the coating of the ibis was a combination of sugar gum (maybe used to keep the bandages in place), plant oil, and wax, and the raptors were coated with oil and wax (Buckley et al. 2004). Interestingly, no coniferous resin was present in any of these examples. It should be noted, however, that the mummies that were tested did not have the dark appearance that is so common in the mummies from Tuna el-Gebel and Saqqara; clearly a vast range of techniques were used to mummify birds.

Many birds seem to have been simply prepared by desiccation through natron, without evisceration. Experimental work has shown that this is possible, but not always totally successful (Clifford and Wetherbee 2004), as the resulting product is a semi-articulated skeleton with some feathers attached. Some scholars have posited that the birds might even have been buried in pits and macerated until the feathers and flesh fell away, and then gathered up (insofar as this was possible), wrapped individually or in groups, and given as offerings (von den Driesch et al. 2005, p. 210; Kessler and Nur el-Din 2005, p. 156). This is somewhat debatable, although not impossible, as it is difficult to extract small and delicately boned single creatures from mass graves. However, it could explain why many mummies are so fragmentary. Another reason for the fragmentary nature of some of the mummies was provided early on by Lortet and Gaillard (1903, p. 115), who suggested that the birds might have been collected when dead, but at different times, and in different states of decomposition, hence portions have gone missing (see Catalog No. 31).

BANDAGES AND CONTAINERS

There are four basic forms of ibis mummies, with variations in each form: wrapped with linen bandages and deposited; wrapped and placed in a pottery jar (as Catalog No. 30), with some jars bearing simple inscriptions; wrapped and covered with plaster or cartonnage and painted; and wrapped and buried in a stone, metal, or wooden container, which could be rectangular, ovoid, or in the form of the bird that it was meant to contain (as Catalog No. 28). The last form was possibly used for sacred animals, although it is possible that this was a way in which expensive offerings were presented.

The linen bandaging of mummies is of particular interest as this is a rich source of information for dating the bundles as well as isolating and identifying ateliers. From the third century BC through the second century AD, many bird mummies sported final elaborate wrappings, akin to shrouds, consisting of bandages of darker and lighter shades of brown and beige layered to produce different patterns: wicker basket style, coffered squares or lozenges, checks, herringbones, or covered with fine linen net patterns (Catalog No. 32 and figs. 3.4–5; Ikram and Iskander 2002; Raven and Taconis 2005). Ibises in particular were often covered with a plain shroud adorned with appliquéd images of Thoth in his different forms (fig. 3.7; Ikram and Iskander 2002; Raven and Taconis 2002). Archaeologists have uncovered both raptors and ibis mummies with faces modeled in linen with painted features and appliquéed eyes; in a few examples the pupils were made of glass (Davies and Smith 2005, p. 4; Ikram and Iskander 2002, pp. 40, 93, 95, 97). Some raptor mummies had cartonnage or mud masks placed over their heads, or had their heads modeled in gesso, one example having a *wesekh*-collar and vertical band of inscription applied in gold foil (fig. 3.8; Davies and Smith 2005, p. 4; Nicholson 1995, p. 7; Ikram and Iskander 2002, pp. 13, 48, 74; Raven

and Taconis 2005, pp. 272, 274, 280). Frequently raptors are wrapped so that they resemble small human mummies with upturned feet (Ikram and Iskander 2002, p. 96); indeed, some could easily have been misidentified as mummies of infants.

Ibis mummies sometimes had heads, beaks, and headdresses elaborately modeled in linen or a combination of linen and cartonnage (figs. 3.8–9; Ikram and Iskander 2002, p. 93; Davies and Smith 2005, p. 4; Charron 1990). There are also examples of ibises that were wrapped in linen and then covered with a layer of plaster that is painted. The whole takes on the form of an "ibisoid" coffin, further enhanced with glass eyes (CG 29874). For the most part the birds are not found with any funerary jewelry, although this

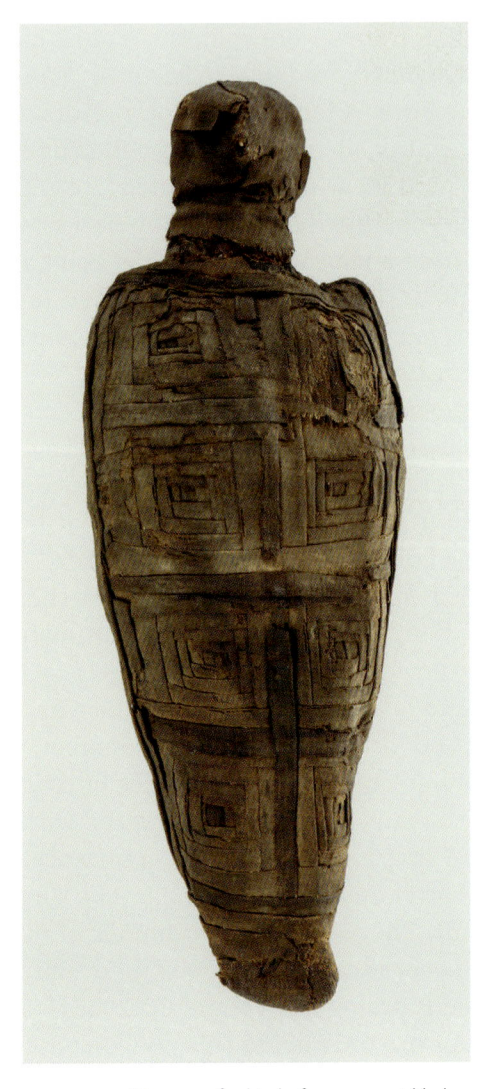

FIGURE 3.5. Mummy of a bird of prey, most likely a long-legged buzzard (*Buteo rufinus*), elaborately wrapped with a coffered square design. OIM E146 (D. 17890; photo by Anna Ressman)

3. AN ETERNAL AVIARY: BIRD MUMMIES FROM ANCIENT EGYPT

FIGURE 3.6. Ibis elaborately wrapped in linen bandages, then in a net of fine linen thread (photo by Anna-Marie Kellen, courtesy of the Egyptian Museum, Cairo; CG 29873)

FIGURE 3.7. Ibis mummy from Saqqara whose shroud is decorated with an appliquéed image of a baboon, another avatar of Thoth, in a wheeled naos (photo by Anna-Marie Kellen, courtesy of the Egyptian Museum, Cairo; CG 29871)

FIGURE 3.8. Raptor mummy with a cartonnage mask. Interestingly, the raptor inside is headless (photo by Anna-Marie Kellen, courtesy of the Egyptian Museum, Cairo; CG 29685)

author has found a blue faience *wadjet*-eye amulet in an ibis pot from Abydos, and Davies and Smith report faience amulets around a falcon mummy (2005, p. 45, FCO-534–5).

There are even more variations in the containers for mummies than there are in the modes of mummification. At many sites (e.g., Thebes, Kom Ombo, Abu Rawash) the wrapped birds are deposited in their eternal resting places as mummy bundles. However, the birds from Tuna el-Gebel and Saqqara were generally buried in jars that were then sealed, either with plaster, or with lids secured by plaster (von den Driesch et al. 2005; Nicholson 2005; Nicholson and Smith 1996). These vessels can also be used to date the deposits. A group of these vessels resemble eggs, emphasizing the idea that the birds are hatching into an eternal existence and stressing the egg as a symbol of rebirth and resurrection (e.g., Catalog No. 30). In Dakhla Oasis a group of stone "eggs" have been found, each containing several birds (ibises and raptors). Simple rectangular wood or stone boxes have also been found at the various catacombs, containing bird mummies. It is unclear if these were for the sacred animal and the ceramic vessels were for the votive offering.

At Akhmim groups of raptors have been found buried in large wooden boxes in the shape of shrines, the exterior painted with images of different divinities and funerary texts, and other groups were buried in oversize anthropoid coffins with raptor heads. In Vienna's Kunsthistorisches Museum a human-size anthropoid coffin with an ibis head contains several ibises. In addition to these wooden and cartonnage coffins there are some wooden and many cast bronze coffins, some with detailing in gold or silver, in the shape of raptors or ibises that contained a wrapped bird.

FUTURE RESEARCH

Avian mummies continue to be a rich source of information for many aspects of ancient Egyptian culture: mummification materials and technology, temple and state economy, religion, the breeding of birds, veterinary practices, bird species found in antiquity, and the changes in biodiversity. In addition to visual examinations of the mummies, scientific techniques such as radiography, CT scanning, and other imaging enable us to identify the different species, their position within the bandages, the presence of amulets, signs of disease and trauma on the skeleton, and veterinary interventions. Examination of samples of the bones, flesh, and embalming agents are also extremely useful — indeed, it is hoped that the Ancient Egyptian Animal Mummy Bio Bank, based at the University of Manchester, will be a source for such studies (see Chapter 11). Gas chromatography and mass spectrometry can help to identify different embalming agents, and elucidate both technology and trade routes through which these materials arrived in Egypt (Buckley et al. 2004; Ikram, in preparation). New DNA studies have been launched in order to establish the evolution in ibis DNA, both diachronic and geographic (Spiegelman et al. 2008). Thus, these ancient avian mummies continue to provide us with concrete evidence that allows our imagination to take flight when recreating the landscape and culture of ancient Egypt.

NOTES

[1] The term *akh*, most of the time written with the hieroglyph , representing a northern bald ibis, is frequently translated as the "the effective one" or the "blessed dead." It is a status ancient Egyptians wished to attain after death, allowing them to be united with the gods and the eternal stars. As Janák remarked (2007, p. 116; 2010, pp. 17–19), while belonging to the divine world, the *akh* retained the ability to affect the world of the living.

[2] It should be noted that not all scholars agree on the idea of mummified votive offerings. Dieter Kessler believes that these masses of mummified animals, particularly the birds, are the result of acts of piety carried out by a series of cult organizations that were related to a manifestation of state power and were a major source of income for the reigning elite and the state, rather than ex votos made by pilgrims (Kessler and Nur el-Din 2005, p. 143; von den Driesch et al. 2005, pp. 236–40). Textual evidence from the containers of some bird mummies indicates that they were buried far from where they were gathered (collected and mummified in Memphis and buried in Tuna el-Gebel, for example), rather than purchased from a local temple (Spiegelberg 1928, pp. 14–17; Spiegelberg 1918, pp. 118–20), although this might simply be a manifestation of a higher level of devotion of followers of Thoth who were far away from their local temple and wished to be remembered there for religious, social, and political reasons.

[3] Two examples are the mummy of Herakleides at the J. Paul Getty Museum in Los Angeles, JPGM 91.AP.6 (Corcoran and Svoboda 2010, esp. pp. 66–71), and the "Basel Mummy" in Basel Antiquities Museum, BSAe 1030.

[4] I am grateful to Drs. O'Connor and Adams for inviting me to participate in their project at Abydos.

FIGURE 3.9. Ibis mummy from Abydos with an elaborately constructed head; the actual skull of the bird is in within the mummy bundle (photo by Anna-Marie Kellen, courtesy of the Egyptian Museum, Cairo; CG 29868)

4. SHELTERING WINGS: BIRDS AS SYMBOLS OF PROTECTION IN ANCIENT EGYPT

RANDY SHONKWILER

The care and protection that many parent birds provide for their offspring seem to have had a great influence on Egyptian concepts of protection. Again and again in Egyptian art and texts we find birds, wings, and feathers used as symbols of protection. Protective goddesses in human or serpent form are fitted with wings, and in the Greco-Roman period we find the word *mki* "to protect" written with a vulture extending its wings as if shielding its young: 🦅.[1] The Egyptians adapted observations of birds in nature into a visual and textual language of protection.

One of the most familiar of Egyptian tomb scenes is that of the tomb owner fishing and fowling in the marshes, attested as early as the Fourth Dynasty (Binder 2000). A major component of these scenes is a papyrus thicket filled with birds (fig. 4.1). These birds are shown in various states of alarm due not only to the human hunter but also, in many tomb scenes, to the presence of genets and mongooses that raid nests to devour fledglings and eggs.[2] Some of the birds are depicted flying above the thicket in apparent disorder; some are shown attacking the genets and mongooses by pecking them, while others are represented sitting upon their nests with their eggs below them in an unusual posture, with their wings held out in front of their bodies. In the wild birds react in a number of ways to a predator approaching their nest and young. Some immediately take to the air and swoop upon and peck the predator. Some birds feign injury to distract the predator from the nest. Other birds freeze on the nest, relying on the camouflage of their plumage to hide and only burst into flight at the last moment (Burton 1985, pp. 178–79). Perhaps this was the artist's intent when representing the birds sitting on their nests. As noted above, the birds' pose with their wings in front of their bodies is unusual. Birds on their nests, even when freezing at the approach of a predator, usually have their wings folded on their backs (Evans 2010, pp. 140–41). Linda Evans has shown that this odd manner of depicting these birds derives from a form of threat display, in which a bird will raise its head and body feathers (fluffing), fan its tail, and spread its wings in order to look bigger in the same way that a cat will raise its back and puff out its fur at the approach of a dog. Not only do the spread wings make the bird look bigger, but the open wings of many birds have white or brightly colored patches that can surprise the predator or even look like the eyes of a larger creature (Burton

FIGURE 4.1. Birds in a papyrus thicket. Fishing and fowling scene from the tomb of Seankhuiptah at Saqqara (courtesy of Naguib Kanawati; from Kanawati and Abder-Raziq 1998, pl. 76)

FIGURE 4.2. Snowy owl (*Bubo scandiacus*) in a defensive posture at the approach of a territorial peregrine falcon (*Falco peregrinus*). Northerly Island, Chicago, Illinois (photos by Rick Remington)

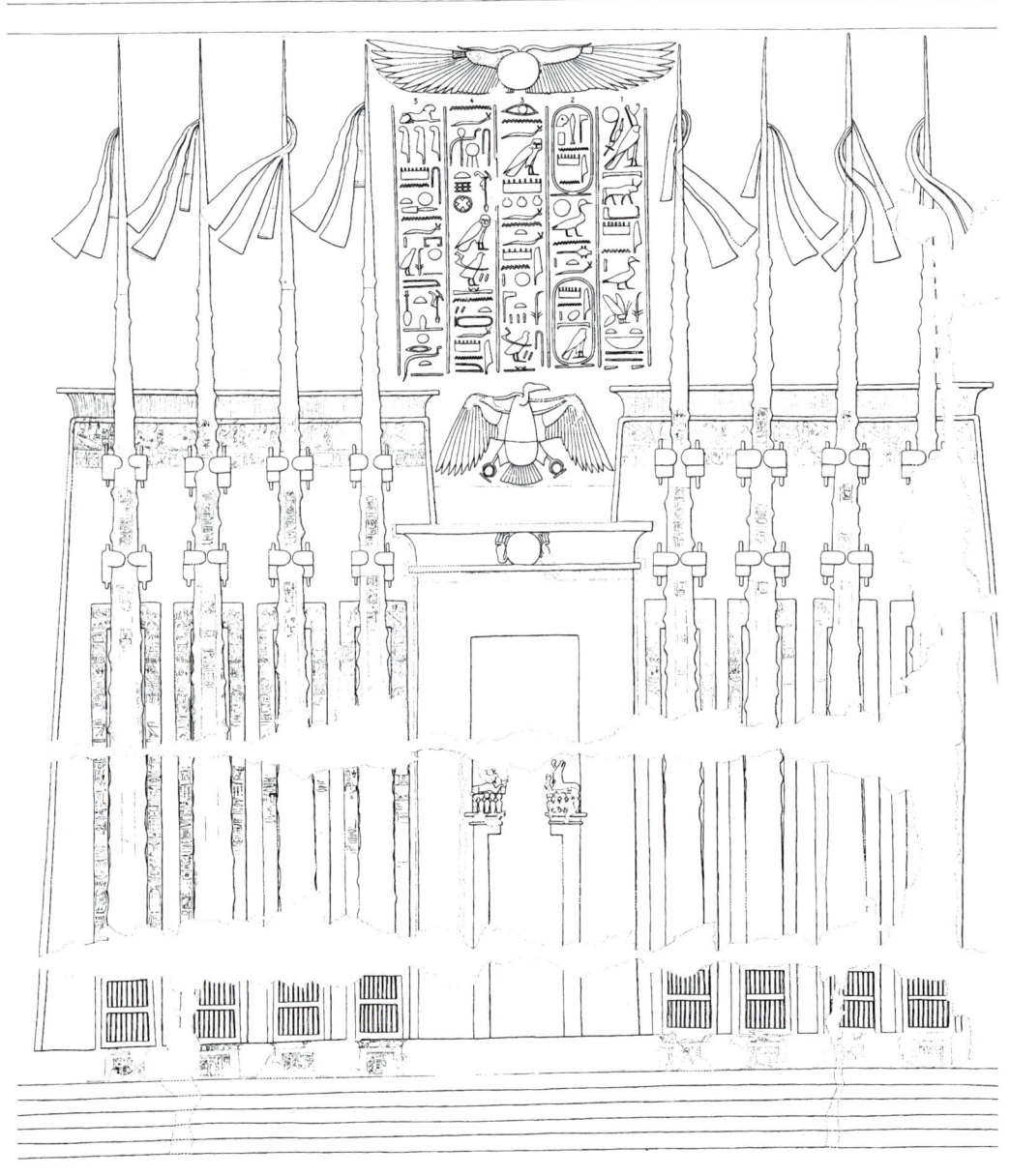

FIGURE 4.3. Vulture goddess protecting the temple of Amun-Re at Karnak (after Epigraphic Survey 1979, pl. 52)

with great fidelity in their art. Nevertheless, it is also possible to detect feelings of ambivalence toward the animals in ancient Egyptian culture. Their behavior could be both predictable and unpredictable, a situation that did not sit well with the Egyptian psyche. So while their annual migrations heralded the seasons reliably, the disorder of a flock taken suddenly to wing made them equally an ideal symbol of chaos. As such, however, birds were the very embodiment of the myriad forces of nature, for which Egyptian admiration and respect is made manifest in every carefully observed image.[27]

FIGURE 10.10. (left) Pied kingfisher (*Ceryle rudis*) hunting. Detail of a wall scene from the tomb of Hesi, Saqqara. Sixth Dynasty (reproduced with permission from Kanawati and Abder-Raziq 1999, pl. 54). (right) Pied kingfisher hovering (iStockphoto.com / © Patrick Kuyper)

NOTES

[1] Houlihan 1986. See also Germond 2001.

[2] Unidentified scavenging species adorn the obverse of the Naqada III Battlefield Palette (ca. 3300–3100 BC), while a helmeted guineafowl (*Numida meleagris*) appears on the reverse. See Patch 2011, cat. no. 123. For a different interpretation, see Chapter 9 in this volume.

[3] For example, the first and second pectorals of Sit-Hathor-Yunet from Lahun; see Aldred 1971, figs. 73–74.

[4] See Houlihan 1986, fig. 1.

[5] Houlihan 1986, fig. 148.

[6] A *rishi*-coffin, from the Arabic word for "feather," is decorated with a pair of wings wrapping the body from the shoulders to the feet; for an example, see Robins 1997, fig. 126. It has been suggested that the feather decoration, which first appeared in the Seventeenth Dynasty, may represent the enveloping wings of the goddess Isis or the goddess Nut, as explained in Chapter 5.

[7] See numerous examples in the tomb of Tutankhamun (e.g., on the second [JE 60660] and fourth [JE 60668] outer gold shrines that encased his sarcophagus).

[8] Evans 2010. For detailed zoological descriptions of the species found in Egypt, see Cramp et al. 1977–96.

[9] The different toe positions of swimming and walking birds are clearly indicated in a poultry-yard scene in the tomb of Ti (Épron et al. 1939, pl. 28), where the advancing foot of a goose exiting a bathing pool is held flat against the substrate, while his submerged foot is still pursed.

[10] The birds were provided with an abundance of food. See, for example, the tomb of Kagemni (Harpur and Scremin 2006, fig. 14).

FIGURE 10.11. (above) Goose hissing (iStockphoto.com / © Martina Berg), and (right) goose distress calling. Detail of a wall scene from the tomb of Nikauisesi, Saqqara. Sixth Dynasty (reproduced with permission from Kanawati and Abder-Raziq 2000, pl. 50)

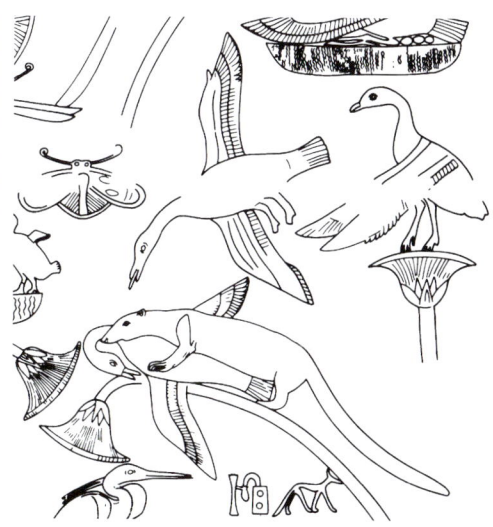

[11] Containers are depicted in poultry-yards in the tombs of Ti (Épron et al. 1939, pls. 7–8), Kagemni (Harpur and Scremin 2006, fig. 13, pl. 203), and Mereruka (Kanawati et al. 2010, pl. 83c).

[12] For example, in the tombs of Sekhemka (W. S. Smith 1978, fig. 73) at Giza, and Mereruka (Kanawati et al. 2010, pl. 82), Hesi (Kanawati and Abder-Raziq 1999, pl. 52), and Mehu (Altenmüller and Johannes 1998, pl. 23) at Saqqara.

[13] Épron et al. 1939, pls. 7, 8, and 28.

[14] Harpur and Scremin 2006, figs. 13–14.

[15] Kanawati and Abder-Raziq 1999, pl. 56.

[16] See Harpur and Scremin 2006, pls. 200–01.

[17] For example, in the tombs of Akhethotep (Ziegler 1993, pp. 132–33), Ptahhotep I (Murray 1904, pl. 11), Ti (Wild 1953, pl. 120), and Ankhmahor (Kanawati and Hassan 1997, pl. 42).

[18] Nestlings are attacked in the Fifth and Sixth Dynasty tombs of Akhethotep (Davies 1901, pls. 13–14), Nikauisesi (Kanawati

and Abder-Raziq 2000, pl. 50), Mereruka (Kanawati and Woods 2010, pls. 67, 69, and 70), Seankhuiptah (Kanawati and Abder-Raziq 1998, pls. 69–70), Hesi (Kanawati and Abder-Raziq 1999, pl. 54), Methethi (Kaplony 1976, p. 10), and Mehu (Altenmüller and Johannes 1998, pls. 9–11 and 13).

[19] Paget and Pirie 1896, pl. 21.

[20] Evans 2007.

[21] Hoffmann 1989; Evans 2011.

[22] For the impact of migratory bird species on ancient Egyptian culture, see Goelet 1983 and Janák 2007.

[23] Borchardt 1913, pl. 15.

[24] See Newberry 1893, p. 70 and pl. 33; 1900, p. 1 and frontispiece; Shedid 1994, figs. 109 and 111; and Kanawati and Woods 2010, pls. 193–94.

[25] See, for example, the tombs of Nefer and Ka-hay (Moussa and Altenmüller 1971, pl. 5), Ti (Wild 1953, pl. 115), and Kaiemankh (Kanawati 2001, pl. 31).

[26] For examples, see Evans 2010, passim, but especially pp. 193–94.

[27] The author wishes to acknowledge the Australian Centre for Egyptology, which is a division of the Macquarie University Ancient Cultures Research Centre (MQACRC), for permission to reproduce figures from their tomb reports, and also Mary Hartley, for producing the line drawings.

11. STUDYING AVIAN MUMMIES AT THE KNH CENTRE FOR BIOMEDICAL EGYPTOLOGY: PAST, PRESENT, AND FUTURE

LIDIJA M. McKNIGHT

Building on the success of the Manchester Mummy Research project, founded in 1994, the International Ancient Egyptian Mummy Tissue Bank, established in 1996, pioneered a scientific approach to the study of mummified remains (A. R. David 2008; Lambert-Zazulak 2000). Since 2003, the KNH Centre for Biomedical Egyptology has been the home of the Mummy Tissue Bank, which currently holds samples recovered from over 100 mummified human bodies from international museum collections.

The study of Egyptian mummies has been dominated by research on human remains. In many respects this was a conscious decision by the academic community, a belief that the physical remains of a human society could be more beneficial and have a greater impact on the modern world than their animal counterparts. The study of ancient Egyptian animals remains on the periphery of the discipline, generally studied in terms of isolated small-scale projects, often restricted to single museum collections and using basic scientific techniques. Numerous collections are to this day undocumented, unstudied, uncataloged, and for the most part in storage. For this reason, animal remains from Egypt represent a largely untapped resource with great research potential.

AIMS AND OBJECTIVES

As a result of this realization, the Ancient Egyptian Animal Bio Bank (hereafter Bio Bank) was established in 2010 to collate information and increase awareness of these remains (McKnight et al. 2011). The motivations for establishing the Bio Bank are numerous, yet at no point has the historical value of the mummies been compromised. The mummies studied are all immensely valuable as oracular devices within a complex religious system, regardless of their condition and appearance. For this reason, the major aim of the project was simple — to locate as many animal mummies as possible, and log information and images of them in a database in order to allow parallels to be drawn between species, chronological time period, and geographic location.

The Bio Bank database contains condition reports, visual descriptions, accurate measurements, geographical and chronological provenience, results of previous work, and copies of publications. An image bank of current photographs and radiographic images provides a non-invasive insight into the contents and constitutes an important element of the project. As custodians of the past, researchers play a vital role in the conservation and preservation of these important objects for the benefit of future generations. In essence, we are charged with providing accurate records incorporating new information gathered through modern techniques so as to improve and advance our understanding.

MATERIALS AND METHODS

DATA ACQUISITION

Since its inception, the Bio Bank has recorded and studied 215 animal mummies belonging to a wide range of species from museums in the United Kingdom. The location of specimens was approached systematically in geographical phases to ensure that the most comprehensive survey possible was conducted.

A pilot scheme covering Northern England located eighteen collections holding viable material. The museums were visited to collate information, undertake macroscopic analysis, and to assess whether the mummies were able to travel to Manchester for imaging. The aims and objectives of the project were fully described in a research proposal document and discussed during the visit to ensure that the museum staff understood our goals, what we hoped to achieve, and how.

The project is not restricted to a single taxonomic group. Avian specimens constituted 30 percent of the study group (sixty-two individuals).[1] A further

4 percent (nine specimens) have been classified as pseudo-birds — modeled to resemble bird mummies but containing no identifiable avian skeletal material.

THE BIO BANK METHODOLOGY

The emphasis of the project is on non-invasive methods of analysis that aim to provide the maximum amount of useful information on these specimens without jeopardizing their preservation. The methodology employed by the Bio Bank utilizes macroscopic techniques initially to create a record of the specimens incorporating historical information and measurements. Combining this data with imaging techniques enables a pictorial record to be created of both the exterior and interior of the mummies. These initial stages are of paramount importance and provide the most comprehensive record possible from which much can be learned.

In the case of damaged mummies or those whose condition is deteriorating due to poor environmental storage, the minimally invasive removal of microscopic samples enables information regarding the animals and their postmortem treatment to be ascertained using a number of biomedical techniques. A small number of investigations require the destruction of the sample and as such consent would only be given in cases where the same information could not be gleaned using a non-destructive method. Fortunately, once the samples have been retrieved, there are a number of techniques that enable them to be studied without facilitating their destruction, enabling them to be reused in the future.

This section provides the reader with an insight into the individual techniques that have been used so far and ones that could be utilized in specific circumstances. Examples of the results are given to illustrate the potential value of the techniques and their implication to the study of avian remains from Egypt.

MACROSCOPY

Initial macroscopic investigation of the specimen includes an assessment of the current state of preservation and detailed visual description, in addition to recording accurate dimensions, provenience, acquisition details, previous research, and publication history.

Observations on the appearance of mummies, the wrapping style and techniques, and the decorative adornments used, enable a greater understanding of the specimens and their history. Identifying trends in wrapping styles can provide correlations between provenienced and unprovenienced specimens. For example, there are distinct differences between ibis mummies originating from the two animal cemeteries of Abydos and Saqqara. Abydos specimens (fig. 11.1) tend to have elaborate bi-colored bandaging arranged in geometric patterns, occasionally with appliqué designs and false heads (Peet and Loat 1913, pls. 18–21). This wrapping style is also noted in the case of Catalog No. 32, which displays bi-colored bandaging characteristic of Abydos. Specimens from Saqqara (fig. 11.2) are often conical in shape, wrapped in plainer linens often arranged in a herringbone design, occasionally with appliqué imagery (Emery 1965, pl. 5). Many of the plainly wrapped specimens display multiple layers of pale thread wrapped around the exterior of the bundles (fig. 11.3). Radiological evaluation of specimens from the two sites has shown that those originating from Abydos tend to contain more complete skeletons in comparison to those from Saqqara, which often contain partial or disarticulated skeletal elements (figs. 11.4 and 11.5).

PHOTOGRAPHY

Digital photographs are acquired for all the specimens, acting as a conservation technique by creating a dated visual record, interpretation of which at a later date can show changes to the stability of the specimen over time. Photographs are taken from all angles provided that the specimen's condition is stable enough to allow for positioning.

RADIOGRAPHY

A collaborative partnership with the Central Manchester University Hospitals NHS Foundation Trust, to whom we are enormously grateful, provides every museum access to medical imaging facilities. Imaging is carried out on weekends, when the facilities are not being used for clinical duties. In exchange for arranging transport of the specimens to Manchester, every museum receives copies of the images (x-rays and selected CT images) for use as a teaching or display resource, or simply to enable better documentation of their collections.

11. STUDYING AVIAN MUMMIES AT THE KNH CENTRE FOR BIOMEDICAL EGYPTOLOGY

FIGURE 11.1. Mummified ibis AEABB55 from Abydos showing highly elaborate geometric wrapping techniques and a false head with the Atef crown positioned behind (© University of Manchester / photo by Stephanie Atherton)

FIGURE 11.2. Elaborately wrapped ibis mummy AEABB56 from the catacombs at North Saqqara. This specimen displays a tight herringbone design formed from pale linen and an appliqué motif to the proximal aspect depicting Thoth seated on a throne and surmounted by the Atef crown (© University of Manchester / Manchester Museum)

FIGURE 11.3. Wrapped ibis mummy AEABB164 from Saqqara displaying characteristic plain linen bandaging with multiple layers of thin thread applied concentrically around the bundle (© University of Manchester / photo by Lidija McKnight / Oriental Museum, University of Durham)

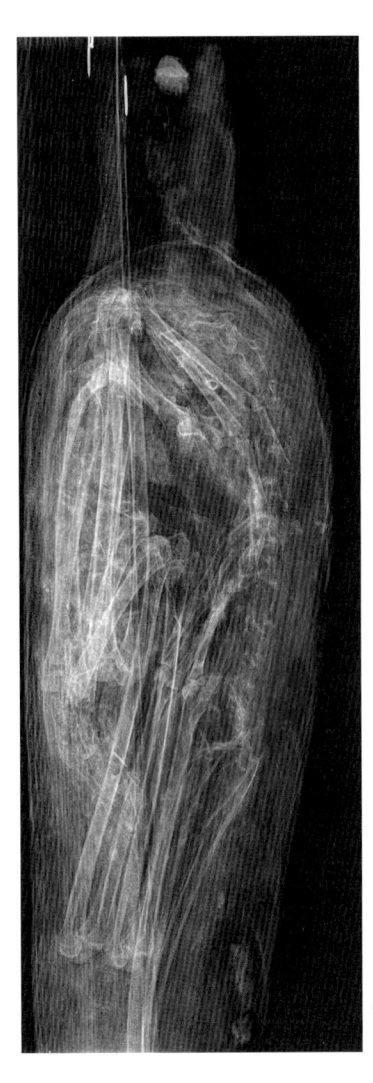

BETWEEN HEAVEN AND EARTH: BIRDS IN ANCIENT EGYPT

FIGURE 11.4. Radiograph of mummy AEABB55 showing the presence of a complete ibis skeleton within the wrappings. The skull has been detached following severance of the spinal column and has been placed between the bird's legs (© University of Manchester / Central Manchester University Hospitals NHS Foundation Trust / Manchester Museum)

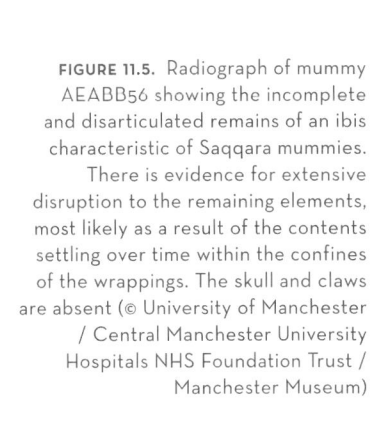

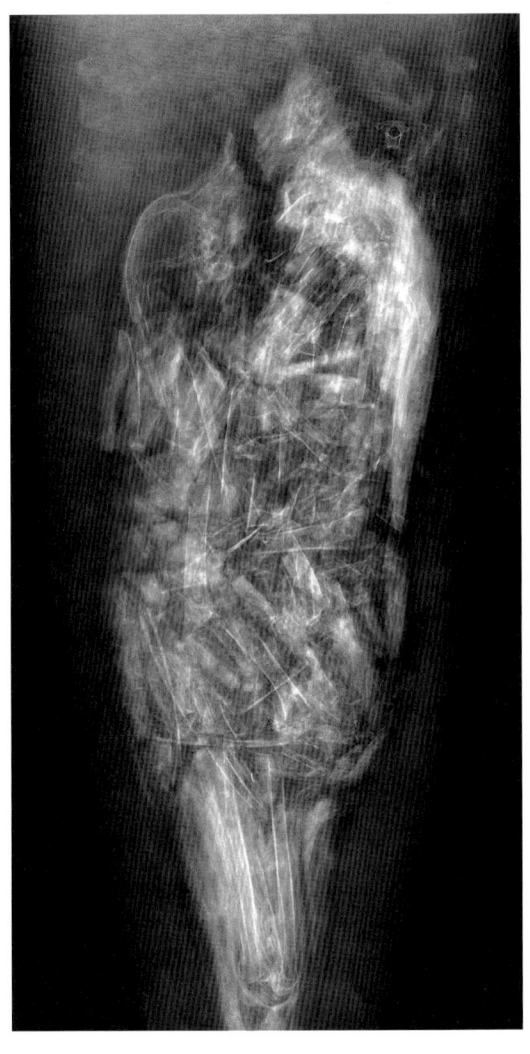

FIGURE 11.5. Radiograph of mummy AEABB56 showing the incomplete and disarticulated remains of an ibis characteristic of Saqqara mummies. There is evidence for extensive disruption to the remaining elements, most likely as a result of the contents settling over time within the confines of the wrappings. The skull and claws are absent (© University of Manchester / Central Manchester University Hospitals NHS Foundation Trust / Manchester Museum)

Institutions electing to acquire radiographic images themselves (usually either due to the distance the objects would need to travel to reach Manchester or their fragile state) are often not able to procure the full range of images. Despite this, even the most basic x-ray can give a wealth of information about a wrapped specimen. In total, 178 mummies have been imaged to date for the Bio Bank project, with further sessions planned.

Radiographic study is the preliminary research tool for the Bio Bank project for reasons outlined in previous work by the author (Owen 2000; Owen 2001; McKnight 2010). As a non-invasive technique, no physical damage is done to the specimen, but a clear image of the contents can be extrapolated relatively easily and cheaply. The value of radiography as a tool in the study of wrapped bodies is well attested as mummies have been studied using this technique for many decades (Aufderheide 2003; Ikram and Iskander 2002; Moodie 1931; Raven and Taconis 2005).

As technologies improve, the potential of the technique to achieve excellent results has increased with many artifacts studied during the early years benefiting greatly from being restudied using the enhanced methods.

The methodology employed for the Bio Bank project further combines computed radiography and computed tomography echoing previous research by the author (Owen 2000; Owen 2001; McKnight 2010). The specimens are imaged in groups of between thirty and fifty specimens to make best use of the facilities.

COMPUTED AND DIGITAL RADIOGRAPHY

The mummified specimens are imaged in dual projections (anterior-posterior and lateral) on x-ray computed radiographic (CR) and digital radiographic (DR) equipment (Philips Medical System, Best, Netherlands). A focal spot size of 0.6 mm (57kV-1mAs) was found to be sufficient for all specimens. The presence of dense radio-opaque mummification unguents encountered in mummies studied in the future may require higher radiation and exposure rates. The radiographic factors used to obtain radiographs of the mummies were adapted from those used routinely for imaging human patients; 57kV-1mAs is the preset standard for imaging the human hand.

The acquisition of images in multiple projections maximizes visibility of the internal structures. Lateral and anterior-posterior images are obtained as standard for all specimens, with oblique projections being acquired in those cases where the skeleton of the animal or other anomalies are found to be lying at an awkward position within the bundle. A major advantage of using a CR/DR system is that the images are viewable directly on screen, which allows for any repeat investigations to be carried out while the specimen is still on the radiographic table.

COMPUTED TOMOGRAPHY

Computed tomography (CT) was performed using a GE LightSpeed 32-row multi-detector CT (MDCT) scanner (General Electric, Milwaukee, USA). Helical volumetric scans were obtained using 120kVp-200 mA, a pitch of 0.969:1, rotation of 0.6 seconds giving a slice thickness of 0.625 mm.

CT eliminates the issues of magnification, blurring, and superimposition that can be problematic when using radiography alone; however, it suffers a slight reduction in spatial resolution. The methodology advocated here utilizes CR/DR as the "triage" technique, with CT being employed to add further detail (McKnight 2010).

The DICOM (Digital Imaging and Communications in Medicine) data acquired by the CT process is manipulated using GE software to allow axial images to be viewed in isolation and for reconstructions to be acquired. Individual transverse axial images allow the researcher to view defined locations in the body and can help to clarify the nature of regions of interest. Reconstructions created in any plane allow visualization of the entire specimen and volume-rendering software allows different elements and tissue types to be visualized in isolation.

The application of volume-rendering techniques utilized in medicine to aid visualization of certain tissue types can be problematic in the study of ancient mummified remains (McKnight 2010). Mummification permanently alters the composition of soft tissues; as they desiccate, they shrink and recede. Volume rendering of bone thresholds was shown to also isolate the desiccated soft tissues within the specimens that had become almost skeletal in their composition.

A major advantage of CT is the ability to identify packing materials or visceral contents, either those placed there intentionally by the embalmers or as the result of a natural process. Often CR/DR demonstrates their presence, but CT is required to add valuable information on such structures.

IS RADIOGRAPHY SAFE?

It is likely that ionizing radiation causes some detrimental effects to the stability and ability for duplication of ancient DNA (abbreviated aDNA); however, studies carried out to date have proved to be inconclusive in demonstrating the extent to which this damage occurs (Götherström et al. 1995; Grieshaber et al. 2008). Whether useful aDNA from this type of remains can be extracted is uncertain as the majority of specimens have been damaged and contaminated either as a result of the mummification procedure, the unguents used to achieve preservation, or poor storage conditions since their removal from the animal cemeteries in Egypt.

Research at the KNH Centre focuses on the application of radiographic techniques to mummified human and animal remains. The use of non-invasive imaging techniques outweighs the potential damage that may arise to the aDNA as a result of such analysis. DNA studies require the acquisition of uncontaminated tissue samples from the core of the bundle that in many cases would damage the integrity of the mummy, in which case the use of imaging has been deemed a more appropriate method.

SAMPLING

The Bio Bank has a further element that brings it in line with the original aims of the International Ancient Egyptian Mummy Tissue Bank — the acquisition and storage of tissue samples. Although they are not the primary motivation for the Bio Bank at this stage, samples form a useful addition to the information and images held on the specimens. Paradoxically, they also have a useful conservation role; in removing minute samples and storing them in optimum controlled conditions, the Bio Bank is

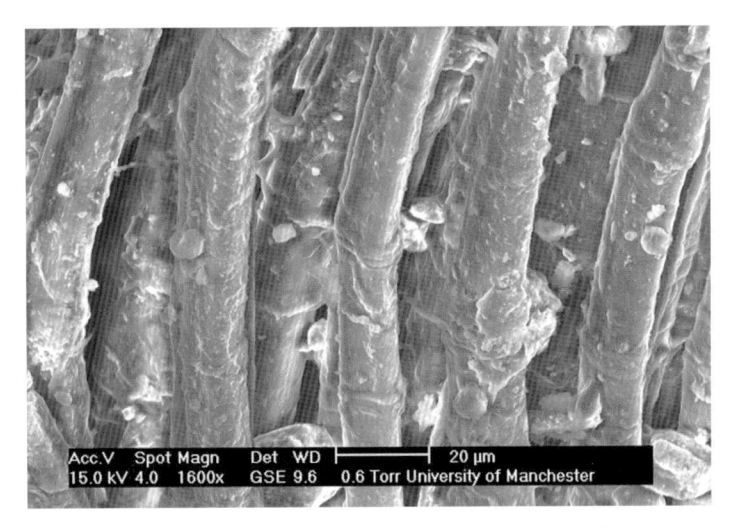

FIGURE 11.6. ESEM image of mummified ibis AEABB178 showing the bamboo-like cellular structure characteristic of flax fibers (© University of Manchester)

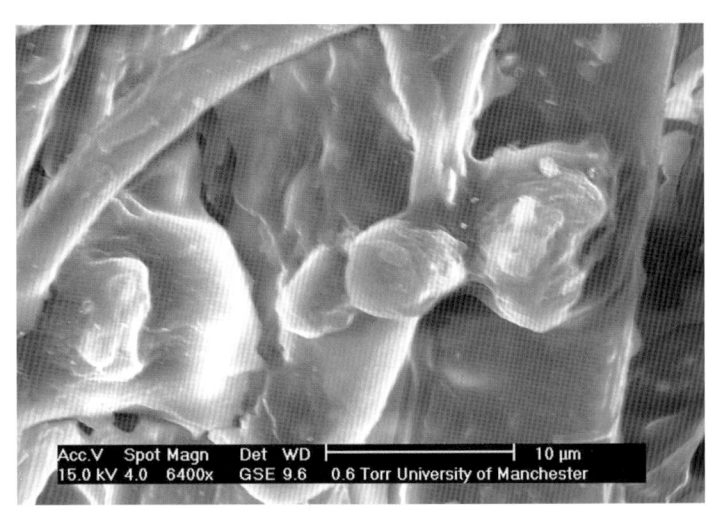

FIGURE 11.7. ESEM image of a linen sample taken from mummified ibis AEABB178 showing the presence of a coating applied to the wrappings during the mummification process (© University of Manchester)

preserving elements of these mummies for the benefit of future researchers. The mummies themselves, especially those held in small regional museums, are often stored in unsuitable environmental conditions and as a result many are showing noticeable signs of deterioration.

Samples are retrieved only from poorly preserved specimens or those with associated loose debris. In the majority of cases and because the specimens are generally wrapped, it is impossible to remove anything other than linen threads. Areas of existing damage can be exploited to remove small samples from the interior of the bundle such as bone, soft-tissue, viscera, or mummification materials such as reeds or packing.

All samples are collected using a standard dissection kit under sterile conditions to minimize the risk of further contamination and are stored in glass jars with Teflon-coated lids to prevent plasticization. Samples removed from the mummies are stored in the Tissue Bank facility at the KNH Centre alongside the human mummy material following a quarantine period. This ensures that samples are stable and are not harboring insects or fungal spores that could cause contamination.

MICROSCOPY

How the samples are studied varies depending on the type of sample available and the research question being posed. Microscopic investigation of linen samples (using white, ultraviolet, and polarized light) can identify weave patterns, evidence of textile reuse, and the presence of mummification substances. Environmental Scanning Electron Microscopy (ESEM) used alongside Energy Dispersive X-ray Spectroscopy (EDAX) can identify elements present in a sample at microscopic level. Figures 11.6 and 11.7, acquired through the ESEM analysis of samples from a mummified ibis from Abydos (AEABB178 sample 1 — linen, outer layer), demonstrate the ability of the technique to detect the presence of flax and coatings applied during the mummification process. Figure 11.8 (AEABB178 sample 2 — dark linen, inner layer) shows the EDAX spectrum for a sample removed from the inner layer of bandaging on the same specimen, highlighting calcium, chlorine, and sulfur indicating the presence of natron.

Bone and soft-tissue samples can be analyzed using histology to determine the tissue type and to detect adaptations in the tissue structure and pathology. Techniques such as Gas Chromatography-Mass Spectroscopy (GC-MS) are destructive and as such are only employed where there is a clearly defined aim and where non-destructive techniques are insufficient to answer posited questions.

In the future, it is hoped that DNA techniques might be able to shed light on the evolution of specific breeds using ancient samples removed from these mummies. This would require destruction of the samples, and presently the ability of the technique to replicate aDNA from such specimens is limited due to their often poor preservation and the postmortem treatments they received.

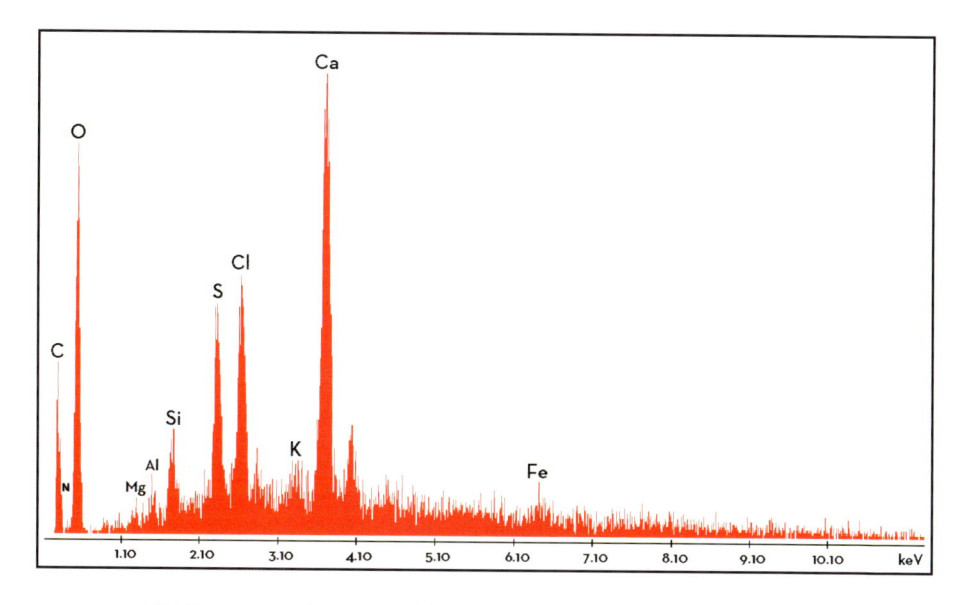

FIGURE 11.8. EDAX spectrum of mummified ibis AEABB178 showing that the composition of this substance is consistent with natron (© University of Manchester)

RESULTS AND DISCUSSION

Radiographic analysis of the seventy-one specimens believed to be mummified birds revealed that nine contained no identifiable avian skeletal material; therefore these are classified as pseudo-mummies. Of the remaining sixty-two specimens, comparative skeletal collections were used to identify species including kestrels (*Falco tinnunculus*), sparrowhawks (*Accipiter nisus*), and sacred ibises (*Threskiornis aethiopicus*). The specimens all belong to the votive category and none show signs of having been eviscerated or excerebrated. The majority of specimens containing complete skeletons had been positioned in the "standard" manner — for example, in the case of Falconiformes, the lower limbs outstretched, the wings folded in close to the body, and the head upright (fig. 11.9; see also Chapter 3).

Radiographic analysis showed that evidence for pathologies in the avian skeletal remains was low, with two reported cases of Harris lines[2] and one example of a healed fracture in the femur of an ibis (Atherton et al. 2012). This low frequency of skeletal pathologies is not entirely surprising and has been reported in other avifaunal studies at Tuna el-Gebel (von den Driesch et al. 2005, p. 226). The suspected underlying reason for this is that the birds would not have lived to such an age as to exhibit pathologies in the skeleton, due their selection for mummification purposes at a young age. However, diseases would have been prevalent in *ibiotropheia* (ibis feeding places) due to over-crowding, in-breeding, and dietary factors. Histological analysis of soft-tissue samples may well reveal pathological disease markers; however, analysis of the skeletons has not yielded much evidence of pathology, which negates the reason for invasive sampling in many of the bird mummies studied to date.

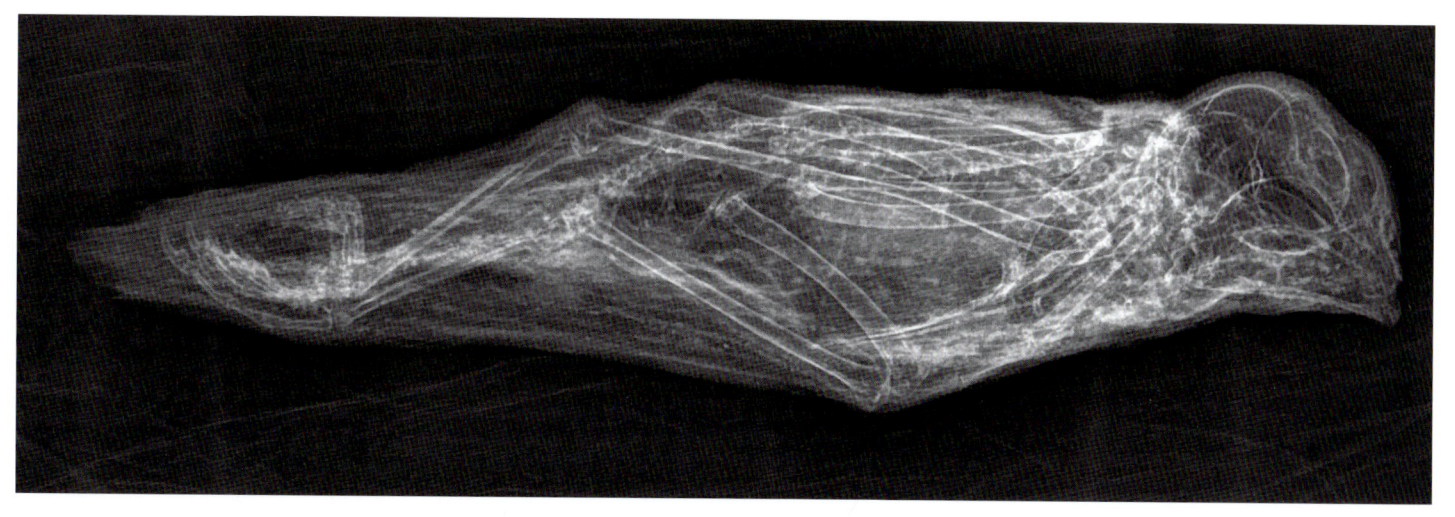

FIGURE 11.9. Lateral radiograph of the mummified Falconiforme AEABB006 from the Kendal Museum demonstrating the characteristic body position commonly seen in mummies of this kind (© University of Manchester / Central Manchester University Hospitals NHS Foundation Trust / Kendal Museum)

INTERNATIONAL COLLABORATOR — THE ORIENTAL INSTITUTE, CHICAGO

The animal mummies from the Oriental Institute of the University of Chicago form part of the Ancient Egyptian Animal Bio Bank database. Recent work by Rozenn Bailleul-LeSuer on the bird mummies has prompted medical imaging to be used to study selected specimens for the first time.

FUTURE OF ANIMAL MUMMY STUDIES

The number of mummies in the database continues to grow steadily with further imaging sessions planned for the coming months. Preliminary microscopic investigations are yielding interesting results. It is anticipated that by November 2012 the total number of specimens in the database will have increased to in excess of 444 due to the incorporation of specimens from the Museum of Fine Arts, Boston. Working with scholars from around the world will help to publicize this material and to showcase the importance of the results that can be acquired through studying it. Applications from researchers for information, images, and samples are considered on the basis of academic merit with non-destructive techniques favored whenever possible.

There is no doubt that much can be learned from the biomedical study of animal remains, both in terms of the lives and deaths of the animals themselves, and about the connection with the civilization that created them.

ACKNOWLEDGMENTS

The author would like to express sincere thanks to the participating museums, without whom this project would not have been possible. Thanks go to the radiographers at the Central Manchester University Hospitals NHS Foundation Trust for their time, patience, and expertise, in particular to Professor Judith Adams, Chair of Clinical Radiology. I am grateful to my colleagues at the KNH Centre for Biomedical Egyptology for the continual ideas and support, particularly to Stephanie Atherton; and to Rozenn Bailleul-LeSuer, Jack Green, and the staff of the Oriental Institute for their support with the project and the opportunity to be included in this publication.

NOTES

[1] Further specimens recorded for the purposes of the Bio Bank Project include canids (dogs and jackals), cats, fish, crocodiles, snakes, rodents, and monkeys. Forty specimens have been classified as pseudo-mummies containing no identifiable skeletal material.

[2] Harris lines, otherwise known as lines of arrested growth, form when bone growth is temporarily halted due to a period of ill health, malnutrition, or disease. The lines, where present, are clearly visible on radiographs as linear opacities across the width of the long bones.

12. MEDICAL CT SCANNING OF ANCIENT BIRD MUMMIES

BIN JIANG, MD, *and* MICHAEL VANNIER, MD

Computed tomography (CT) has been a valuable, non-invasive investigative tool for mummy research since it was first applied in 1975 and remains the method of choice for examining mummies (Raven and Taconis 2005, p. 32). X-ray CT using a medical CT scanner allows for non-invasive inspection and can provide detailed morphologic information about the scanned mummies. CT has been used to study ancient Egyptian bird mummies, as well as other animal mummies, most of which had been manufactured to be votive offerings to major deities such as Horus and Thoth. In the past, the detailed techniques for CT scanning of mummified animals has not been reported or discussed. The aim of this chapter is to describe up-to-date CT techniques regarding the avian mummies. These parameters are based on our experience with medical CT scanning of mummified birds which are relatively small in size, making them technically different compared with scanning human mummies.

CT SCANNING

Computed tomography has undergone tremendous progress since it was first introduced into medical practice in 1975. Today's CT scanners offer higher scanning speed (rotation time of 400 milliseconds) and isotropic (sub-millimeter) and true volume acquisition, which are appropriate for bird mummies. Before CT scanning, film-based radiography was often used to examine the contents of wrapped mummies (McMillan 1994). Although skeletal features can be adequately detected with radiography, a satisfactory characterization of wrappings, contents, and mummification techniques is not possible (Forbes 2011). The three-dimensional morphology of specimens is captured with x-ray CT, allowing detailed evaluation using computer graphics visualization tools.

TECHNIQUES FOR AVIAN MUMMY CT SCANS

For the detailed analysis of structures inside the specimen, it is essential to select a CT scanning protocol suitable for examining bird mummies with optimal image quality (see Chapter 13). Hundreds of different CT scanner protocols are used in daily clinical work. The wrapped avian mummies are usually small in size and contain materials ranging from high-density amorphous masses (desiccated tissue and cortical bone) to low-density air pockets (Forbes 2011; Gumpenberger and Henninger 2001). To delineate material characteristics of avian specimens, CT scanning was performed on the Philips Brilliance iCT 256-slice system at four different energies, including 80, 100, 120, and 140 kVp. Multi-energy CT scanning can provide additional information on the material composition of specimens, and this is important when the real components inside the wrapped bird specimens are unknown (Wade et al. 2012). Additional scanning parameters best suited to avian specimens include small field of view (25 cm), 0.7 mm slice thickness, 0.35 mm slice spacing, and 512x512 matrix. As much magnification as possible, tailored to the individual specimen, is used for image reconstruction. These parameters are comparable with those used to examine the temporal bone, where isotropic resolution of 0.35 mm can be achieved, sufficient to delineate the ossicles of the inner ear.

Each CT scan acquisition produces a set of raw projection data that includes measurements obtained from the multirow detector array. These raw data are written to a disk storage device and used for image reconstruction to produce a set of axial slices. In the examination of bird mummy specimens, the raw projection data was archived to off-line digital media. Similarly, after slice images were generated from these data, the scans were written to a digital archive. These images can be used for a wide variety of subsequent analyses without the need to rescan the specimens.

The archival storage of raw projection data is especially advantageous as new reconstruction methods are developed. For example, in the year following the scanning of our first bird mummy specimens, the CT scanner manufacturer introduced a new implementation of iterative reconstruction methods (iDose^4)[1] that provides much greater image quality from the same scanner we used to collect the raw data. We were able to reconstruct the axial images with the iterative method without the need to rescan the specimens using archived raw data.

DATASETS PRODUCED WITH MEDICAL CT SCANNERS

After reconstructed axial images were obtained, post-processing visualization and analysis become important. Two- and three-dimensional reformations were performed on a computer graphics workstation (Philips Brilliance). Multiplanar reformatted images (MPR), maximum intensity projections (MIP), volume rendering (VR), and surface shaded display (SSD) are essentially valuable for close inspection of bird mummy internal structures, for example, the bone structures and the multilayer wrapping materials. All images use a DICOM (Digital Imaging and Communications in Medicine) standard format so they can be transmitted and stored using a writable CD, DVD, or removable storage device (Hunt et al. 2012).

As a result of this work, we now have CT scans and raw data from a multitude of specimens that have been archived in digital form and these data are available for data sharing and analysis, some of which are presented in Chapter 13.

NOTE

[1] Philips Medical Systems, Inc., iDose^4 iterative reconstruction technique. Document no. 4522 962 67841 * FEB 2011.

13. CHALLENGES IN CT SCANNING OF AVIAN MUMMIES

CHARLES A. PELIZZARI, CHAD R. HANEY, ROZENN BAILLEUL-LeSUER,
J. P. BROWN, and CHRISTIAN WIETHOLT

The introduction of computed tomography (CT) in the 1970s was one of the most significant developments in medicine of the past half-century. The capability conferred on physicians was almost magical: to see the normal and pathological anatomy within a patient's body in exquisite three-dimensional detail without surgical invasion. Compared with early scanners, which required hours to acquire and reconstruct even a small number of centimeter-thick slices, today's machines can generate hundreds or even thousands of sub-millimeter slices in a matter of seconds and can virtually freeze the motion of a beating heart.

Computed tomography has had similar revolutionary impact in many other fields, with specialized systems developed for imaging tasks from the very large (examining the contents of shipping containers, for example) to the very small (verifying the structure of integrated circuits, visualizing the anatomy of insects) and everywhere in between (identifying defects in metal castings such as automobile engine blocks, characterizing the internal structure of core samples from potentially oil-bearing rock formations, inspecting checked airline baggage). For best results, each of these applications requires scanning instrumentation optimized for the respective object size, material composition, and level of detail required for the task at hand. All share the basic principle of acquiring a large set of x-ray views through the object from varying directions ("projections") and using one of several computer algorithms to reconstruct from these projections the distribution of x-ray attenuation coefficients within the object.

CT scanning is a powerful tool for investigating mummies for the same reason as in medicine — it allows us to "see" inside an object that we would very much prefer not to slice open. If anything, this motivation may be even stronger in the case of mummies than that of patients — whereas a patient can heal from exploratory surgery, a mummy would be irreparably damaged if it were cut open. Thus over the past few decades there have been a number of well-publicized projects involving CT scanning of human mummies using clinical CT scanners that have yielded fascinating and valuable information concerning the age, diet, social status, state of health, and in some cases the violent death of individuals who lived hundreds, or even thousands of years ago. Animal mummies have also been investigated through CT scanning (McKnight 2010; Wade et al. 2012; see Chapter 11 in this volume).

Typically, results of avian mummy CT scans are far less impressive than those of humans. The basic reasons for this are the small size of the specimens, typically smaller than all but the tiniest infant human patients, and the fact that bones in birds are thinner than in mammals, even for animals of comparable size. Birds, except for the very largest specimens, challenge the capabilities of even state-of-the-art medical CT scanners. To generate high-quality results when imaging birds, considerable attention must be paid to optimizing the scanning protocols used — the x-ray energy, detector slice width, reconstructed matrix size, and, very importantly, the spatial filter used in image reconstruction (see Chapter 12). In this chapter we present results acquired with several different protocols for avian mummies over a range of sizes, showing the clear differences in the quality of visualization that result.

Scanners used in the present studies are all located at the University of Chicago Medical Center. As described in the overview by Drs. Jiang and Vannier (Chapter 12), a large number of specimens from the Oriental Institute were scanned on a Philips Brilliance iCT scanner in the Department of Radiology during two sessions in August and October 2011. Additionally, several smaller specimens were scanned on a dedicated small-animal CT scanner, a Gamma Medica-Ideas FLEX Triumph microPET/SPECT/CT system.[1] The microCT is capable of imaging considerably finer detail than the clinical CT, but is limited to specimens no larger than 9 centimeters in diameter.

To illustrate the dramatic difference in detail provided by the microCT scanner, we present results for specimen OIM E42440, a common kestrel (*Falco tinnunculus*) (fig. 13.1). This is an unprovenienced bird mummy in the Oriental Institute Museum collection, which had been unwrapped in the past, before the advent of non-invasive investigative techniques.

For the first clinical scan, in August 2011, an abdomen/pelvis protocol was used with technical parameters as follows: x-ray–quality 120 kVp, image matrix 512x512, reconstructed field of view 151 mm, slice thickness/spacing 0.9/0.45 mm, standard filter. Image reconstruction was performed using clinical software on the scanner console. For the microCT scan, performed in June 2011, the x-ray quality was 70 kVp, image matrix 512x512, reconstructed field of view 88 mm, slice thickness/spacing 0.178/0.178 mm, sharp filter. Image reconstruction was performed using a locally developed filtered back-projection code. Due to the limited scan volume of the microCT, separate scans were taken of the upper, middle, and lower thirds of the mummy with some overlap, and the three volumes were merged and normalized utilizing the overlap regions. Figure 13.2 shows approximately corresponding coronal sections through the clinical and microCT scans. Obvious differences are the much finer detail that can be observed in the microCT due to its higher spatial resolution and correspondingly smaller pixel size (field of view divided by image matrix size — for the microCT 88/512 = 0.178 mm, for the clinical CT 151/512 = 0.295 mm); and the higher contrast of the microCT image due to the lower x-ray energy. The clinical CT is capable of operating at lower energy than was used in this scan, as low as 80 kVp. The contrast difference between the two scans could thus be largely overcome, but

FIGURE 13.1. Mummy OIM E42440, common kestrel (*Falco tinnunculus*) (D. 17999; photo by Anna Ressman)

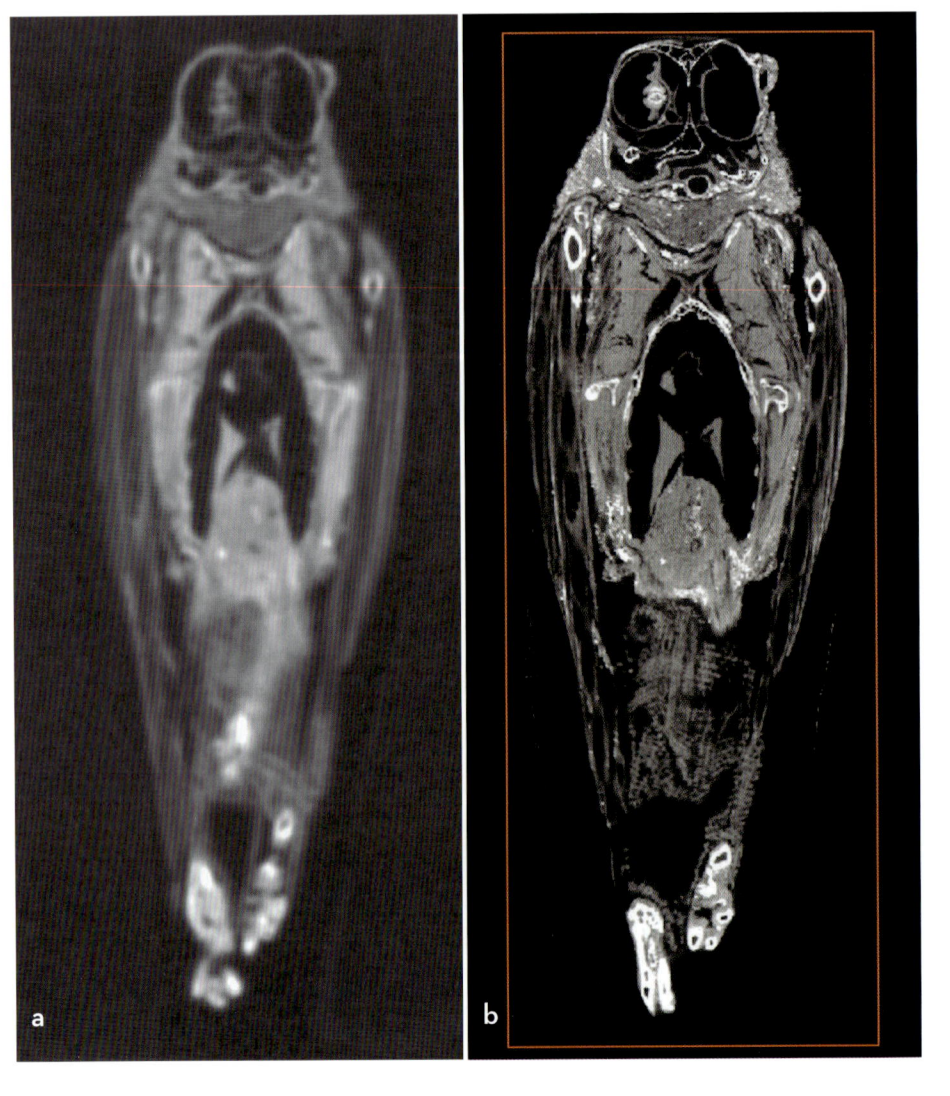

FIGURE 13.2. Mid-coronal sections through the (*a*) clinical CT and (*b*) microCT scans of OIM E42440

the resolution advantage of the microCT is such that a clinical scanner is simply incapable of revealing as much fine detail. As detailed below, with careful selection of scanning parameters, somewhat better image quality can be achieved with a clinical scanner, but whenever a specimen is sufficiently small to fit in a microCT scanner it is always advantageous to use one. An additional issue affecting the capability to detect fine detail is the so-called partial volume effect, which is due to the fact that each image voxel (the three-dimensional extension of a pixel) averages the x-ray attenuation over a small but not infinitesimal volume of the sample. When the scanner resolution is not sufficiently fine this can result, for example, in fine high-density structures such as small bones or grains of sand being averaged together with lower-density materials such as tissue or air. Since some of the distinctive adaptations of a bird's skeleton for flight include the thinning and lightening of the outer shell of its bones, the partial volume effect can prevent us from clearly identifying skeletal elements from the dehydrated soft tissues in a bird mummy. This is even more difficult when the specimen is a small bird, such as was the case with OIM E42440.

With a high-quality CT dataset in hand, qualitative and quantitative analysis of the image volume can help in identifying the type of bird contained within a mummy, its condition, and potentially its source, how it was prepared, and for what purpose it was intended. Findings of anatomical abnormalities can reveal whether a bird had a difficult, possibly violent, transition to the afterlife or whether it was carefully prepared; if it was intact and likely sacrificed for the purpose of mummification, or if it was already dead and partially decomposed when collected. Various types of visualization are useful in different contexts. One particularly simple example is a technique called multiplanar reformation, or MPR, as illustrated in figure 13.2, where the image volume has been "sliced" along a coronal or frontal plane. MPR allows perception of 3-D structures and relationships that may be difficult to appreciate from the original, transaxial slices. Another very powerful visualization technique is volume rendering, where voxels in the 3-D image volume are assigned visual properties of color and transparency based on their x-ray attenuation values, and an optical compositing algorithm is used to produce a 3-D view as if looking into the semitransparent colored volume. A volume rendered view of

FIGURE 13.3. Cutaway volume rendering of the microCT scan of OIM E42440 showing intact internal organs but a severed and reattached head (annotations courtesy of Kenneth Welle, DVM, University of Illinois at Urbana-Champaign)

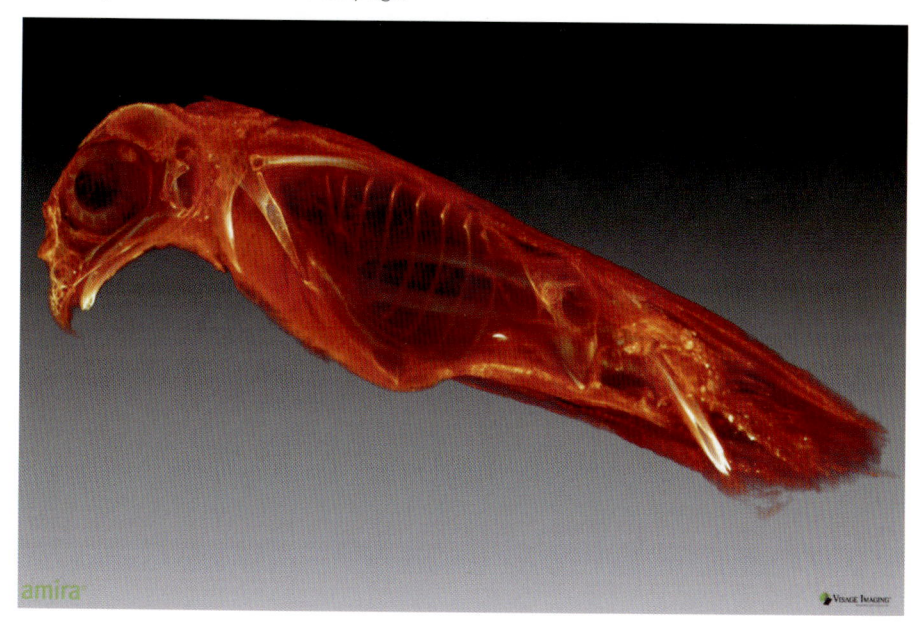

FIGURE 13.4. Cutaway volume rendering of OIM E42440

the OIM E42440 microCT dataset with half of the data cut away is shown in figure 13.3. This gives an impression similar to a multiplanar reformatting; yet what lies beyond the cut plane remains visible, as if looking at the actual 3-D object cut open instead of a single slice through the image volume. From this view we can clearly see from the intact internal anatomy that this bird was not eviscerated, and we can also see that the head has been severed from the body and reattached, confirming the impression from the photograph (fig. 13.1). This visualization was produced with Amira, a commercial scientific visualization software system developed by Visage Imaging, Inc. The high-resolution microCT image reveals details such as the internal trabecular structure of the beak and posterior skull, the well-preserved spine severed at the neck, and the presence of grit in the ventriculus. With a different location of the cutplane, as in figure 13.4, we can see the intact ribcage and, within its orbit, the sclerotic ring, a structure that provides support and protection for the eye. The diameter and depth of the sclerotic ring, along with the number of segments it contains, can be helpful in the identification of bird species.

Image processing and advanced volume rendering techniques can often allow visualization even when the specimens are degraded and CT scan data are suboptimal. It is common to encounter a mummy whose outer shape does not accurately reflect its contents. Mummy OIM E9162 gives the impression of containing a medium-size bird (fig. 13.5). However, sections through the CT volume (fig. 13.6) reveal that the package actually contains a small bird, possibly a juvenile Eurasian sparrowhawk (*Accipiter nisus*), in this case less than 200 mm in length — smaller, in fact, than the kestrel OIM E42440. The wrapped mummy is too large for the microCT scanner and was therefore scanned on the Philips scanner using the same protocol as described above. The images from the clinical scanner are poorly resolved, suffering from both partial volume effect and the decomposed state of the soft tissue and cartilage. To visualize the inner bird it proved useful in this case to segment the voxels corresponding to the void spaces, which can then be viewed as if a plaster cast had been made from the voids. By also segmenting some of the major bones it is possible to appreciate some of the geometry of this small bird (fig. 13.7). Finally, a cutaway volume rendering with the inner air voxels suppressed gives an impression of this little bird at repose within its generous wrappings (fig. 13.8).

As we have indicated, clinical CT scanners are well matched to scanning relatively large specimens. We demonstrate with three large bird mummies that clearly experienced very different treatment in their transitions to the afterlife. The first is OIM E18275, a victual mummy, prepared to be sent along as food for the departed (fig. 13.9, Catalog No. 40). The mummy rests on a wooden dish, as if ready to be carved. A section through the midsagittal region shows that while the lower part of the body cavity has been stuffed with fibrous material (most likely linen), some of the internal organs remain in the thorax and upper

FIGURE 13.5. OIM E9162 (D. 17920; photo by Anna Ressman)

13. CHALLENGES IN CT SCANNING OF AVIAN MUMMIES

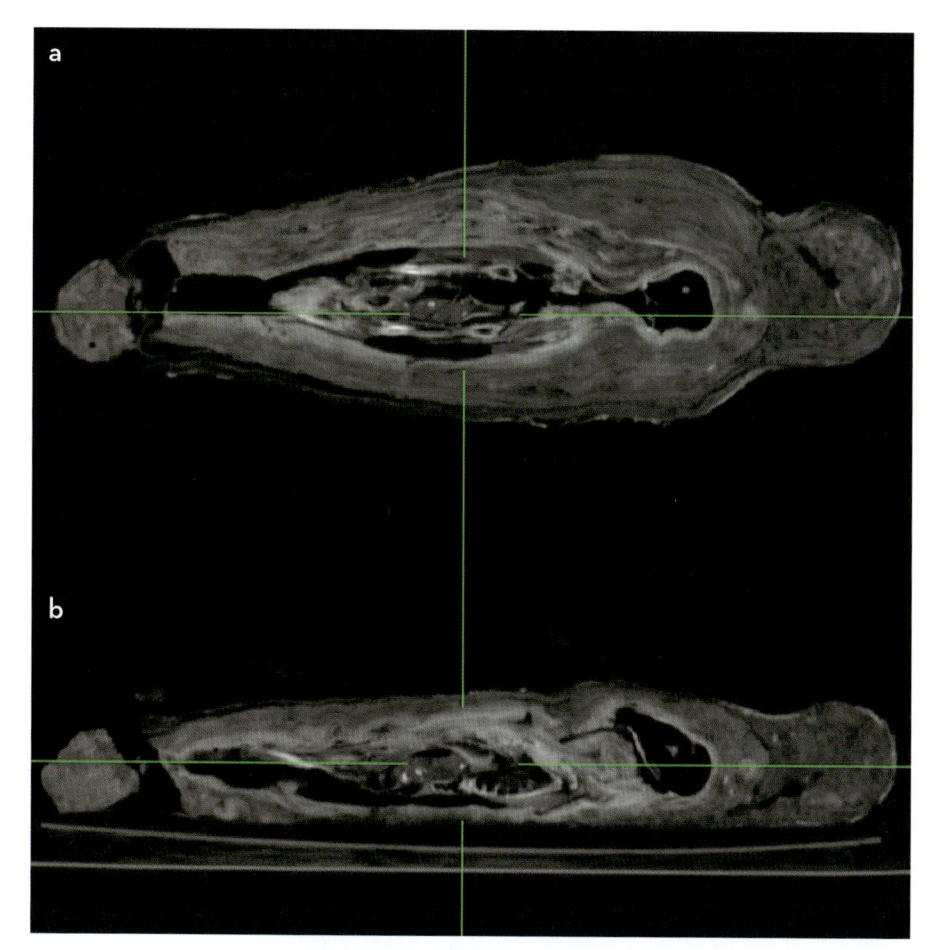

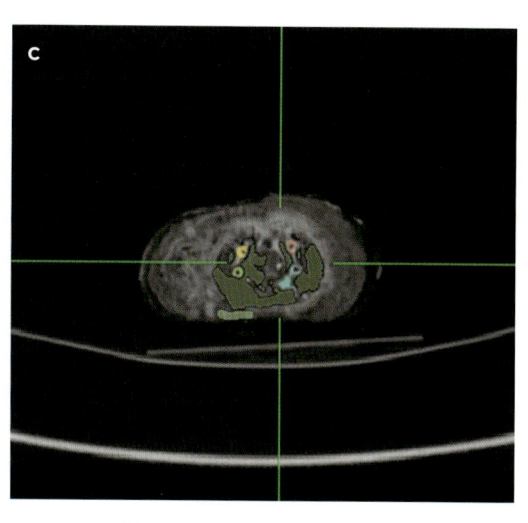

FIGURE 13.6. (a) Sagittal, (b) coronal, and (c) axial sections through the clinical CT scan of OIM E9162. Colored overlays on the axial section represent segmented regions: inner air (including decomposed tissue) and several bones

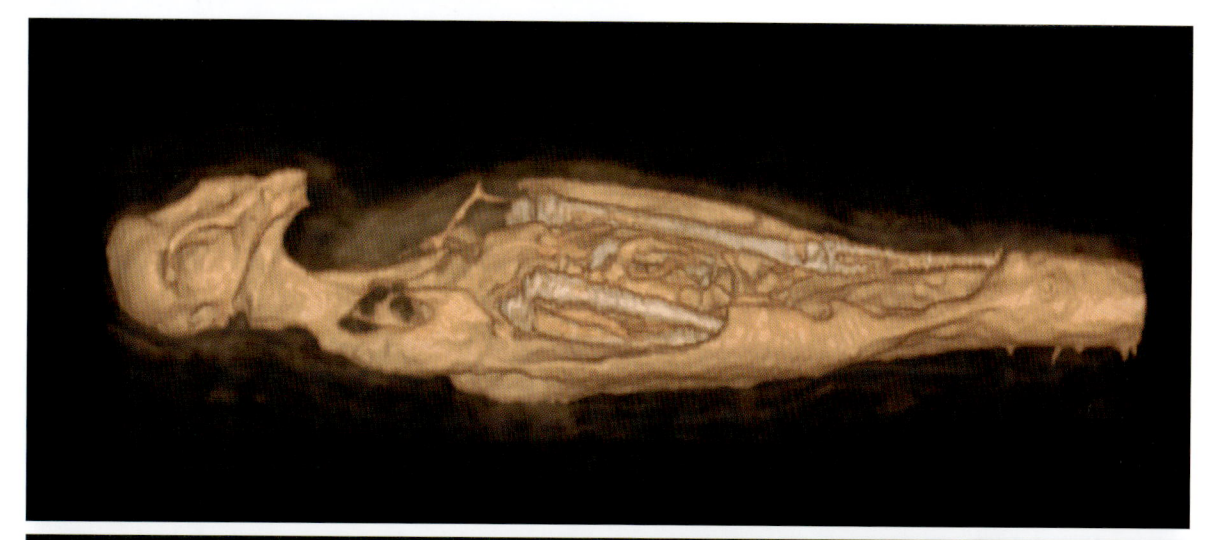

FIGURE 13.7. Visualization of the segmented inner air spaces and several bones from the clinical scan of OIM E9162

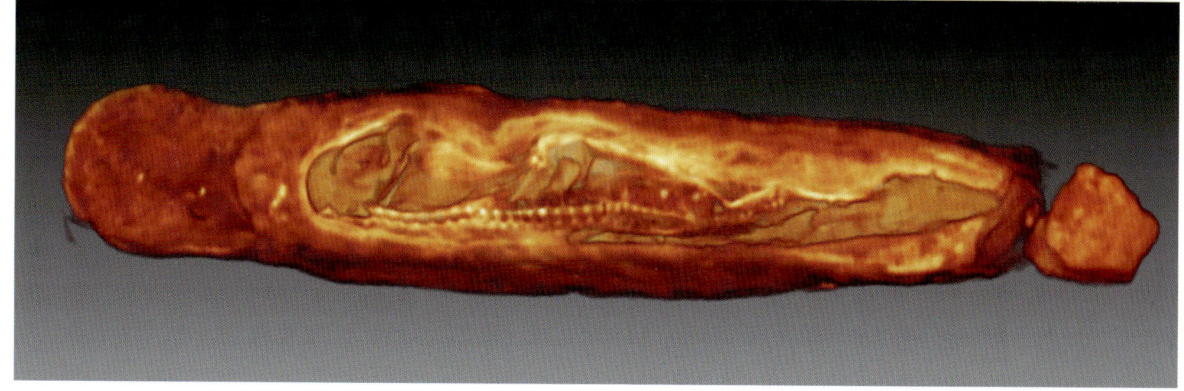

FIGURE 13.8. Volume rendered view of OIM E9162 with cut plane and inner air voxels suppressed

BETWEEN HEAVEN AND EARTH: BIRDS IN ANCIENT EGYPT

FIGURE 13.9. Victual mummy OIM E18275 on wooden case OIM E18276 (D. 17982; photo by Anna Ressman)

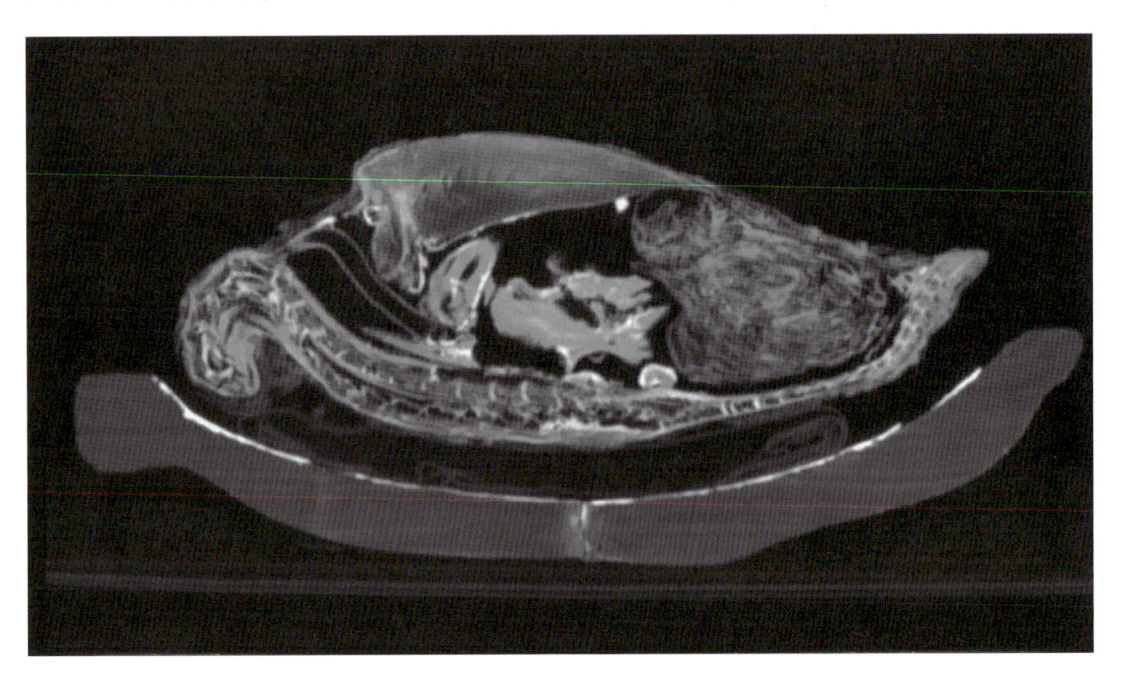

FIGURE 13.10. Midsagittal slice through the scan of OIM E18275–76 showing intact organs and fibrous stuffing

FIGURE 13.11. Three-dimensional volume rendered view of OIM E18275

abdomen (fig. 13.10). In preparation for consumption, the head, wingtips, and feet have all been removed, as seen in the volume rendered view (fig. 13.11).

Our second large bird seems to have taken quite a different route to the afterlife. This mummy, OIM E9234 (fig. 13.12, Catalog No. 31) was scanned with the protocols described above and at several different x-ray energies. The highest contrast was obtained in the scan taken at 80 kVp. From the axial slice we can see that the remains of this ibis were anything but well treated (fig. 13.13). The anterior chest wall is missing and the neck drops into the thoracic cavity. The sternum and chest wall are detached and sit askew in the back of the body cavity. Three-dimensional viewing reveals randomly oriented shards of bone in the body cavity (figs. 13.14–15). It is plausible that this bird was found already dead, possibly already partially decomposed or partially consumed by carrion eaters — this may indeed be a 2,000-year-old "road kill." Interestingly, there appears to be a bundle of small snails in the body cavity (visible in fig. 13.14). It is unlikely that so many whole snails would naturally be present in the ventriculum, since they should ordinarily be crushed in the bird's digestive system. It may have been intentionally deposited by the embalmers prior to the wrapping process as a food offering for the bird (Wade 2012; see Catalog No. 31).

Our final large bird mummy is a female sacred ibis from the collection of the Field Museum of Natural

FIGURE 13.12. OIM E9234 (D. 17925; photo by Anna Ressman)

FIGURE 13.13. Axial slice from the clinical scan of OIM E9234

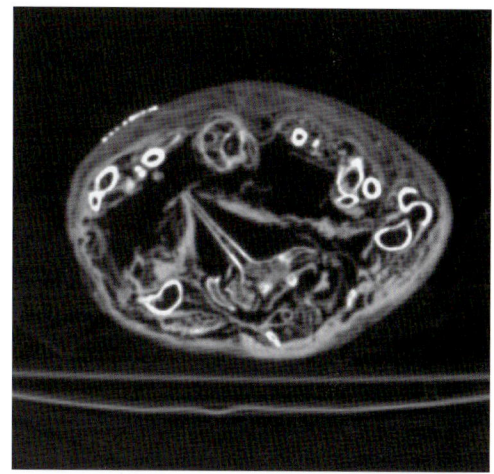

FIGURE 13.14. Oblique slices through the scan of OIM E9234 showing randomly oriented bone fragments and a cluster of snails

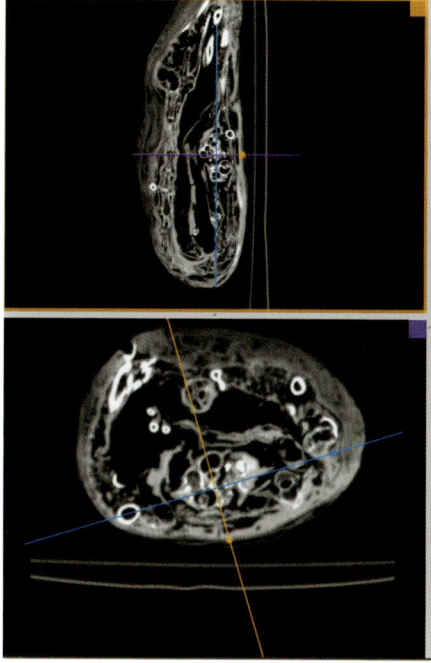

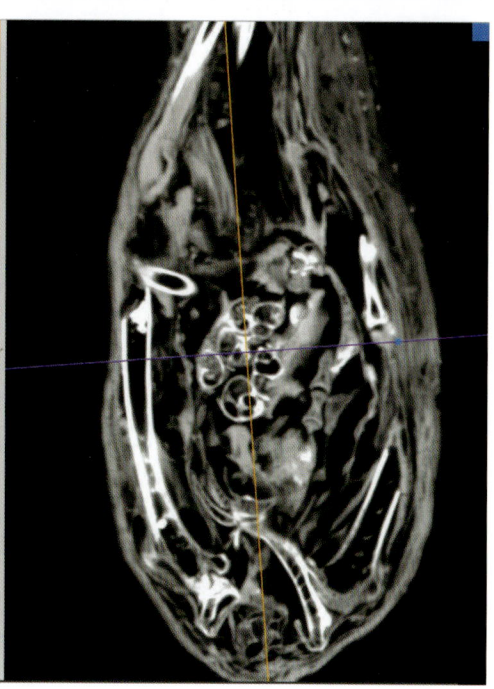

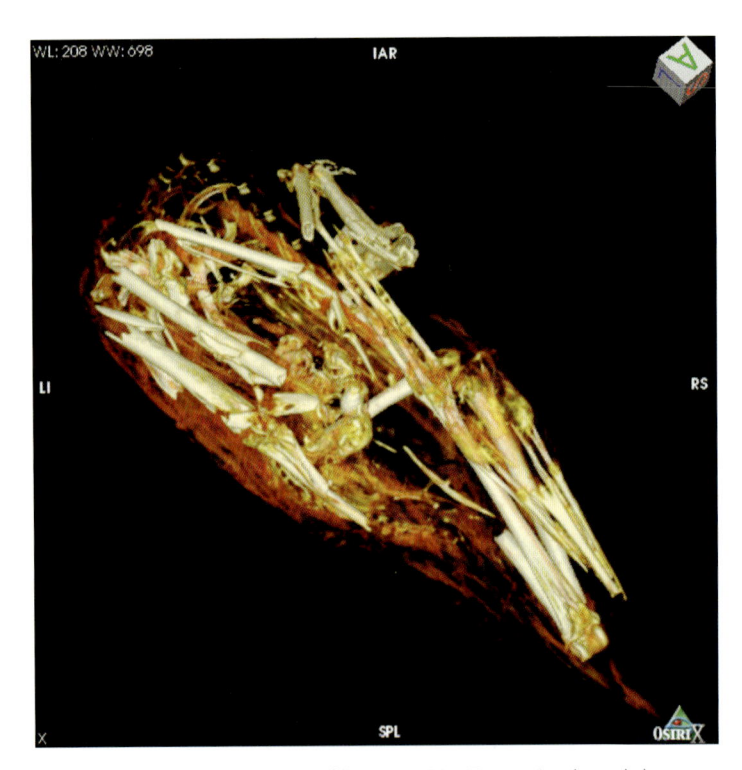

FIGURE 13.15. Volume rendering of bones in OIM E9234. Snails in abdomen visible in center

reveal somewhat more detail, including the trabecular structure of bones and the weave of the linen wrappings. While not at the same level of detail as the microCT scans of the kestrel mummy OIM E42440 presented above, these scans certainly provide a very highly resolved 3-D description of the contents of the mummy. A volume rendered view produced from the 90 kVp IAC protocol scan is sufficiently well resolved that details of fabric texture, condition, and wrapping technique can be assessed without handling the mummy (fig. 13.18). Finally, a volume rendered view with all but the highest-density materials rendered transparent shows that this specimen, unlike our other large birds, has not suffered any mutilation and its skeleton is essentially completely intact — as smooth a journey to the afterlife as a sacrificed animal could have experienced (fig. 13.19).

In conclusion, CT scanning of avian mummies is a powerful tool for understanding the practices associated with preparation and burial of these artifacts. Due to their small size and unique, lightweight skeletal structure, birds present a challenge to even state-of-the-art CT scanners. With careful optimization of scanning protocols coupled with sophisticated image processing and visualization, this technology, which was developed to diagnose modern human disease, can help us peer back through millennia into the practices of ancient cultures.

History's Zoology Department. The specimen was brought back from Egypt in the late nineteenth century, and was kindly loaned for scanning by Dr. John Bates of the Field Museum. The mummy is shown in figure 13.16 positioned on the patient support couch of the Philips Brilliance CT Big Bore 16-slice scanner in the University of Chicago Department of Radiation and Cellular Oncology, where it was scanned in March 2012. Scanning was performed with a pediatric internal auditory canal (IAC) protocol (x-ray quality 90 kVp and 140 kVp, image matrix 768x768, reconstructed field of view 227 mm, slice thickness/spacing = 0.8/0.4 mm, bone filter) and with a cervical spine (C-spine) protocol (120 kVp, image matrix 512x512, reconstructed field of view 228 mm, spice thickness/spacing = 0.8/0.4 mm, sharp filter). Corresponding slices from the IAC and C-spine protocol scans are shown in figure 13.17. Both contain finer structure than the scans using the body protocol shown earlier, and the smaller pixel size and sharper filter of the IAC protocol

FIGURE 13.16. The female sacred ibis mummy positioned on the CT scanner (photo by Charles A. Pelizzari)

13. CHALLENGES IN CT SCANNING OF AVIAN MUMMIES

FIGURE 13.17. Slices from scans of the Field Museum ibis using cervical spine (*left*) and pediatric internal auditory canal (*right*) protocols

FIGURE 13.18. Volume rendered view of the Field Museum ibis mummy. Compare detailed texture to photograph in figure 13.16

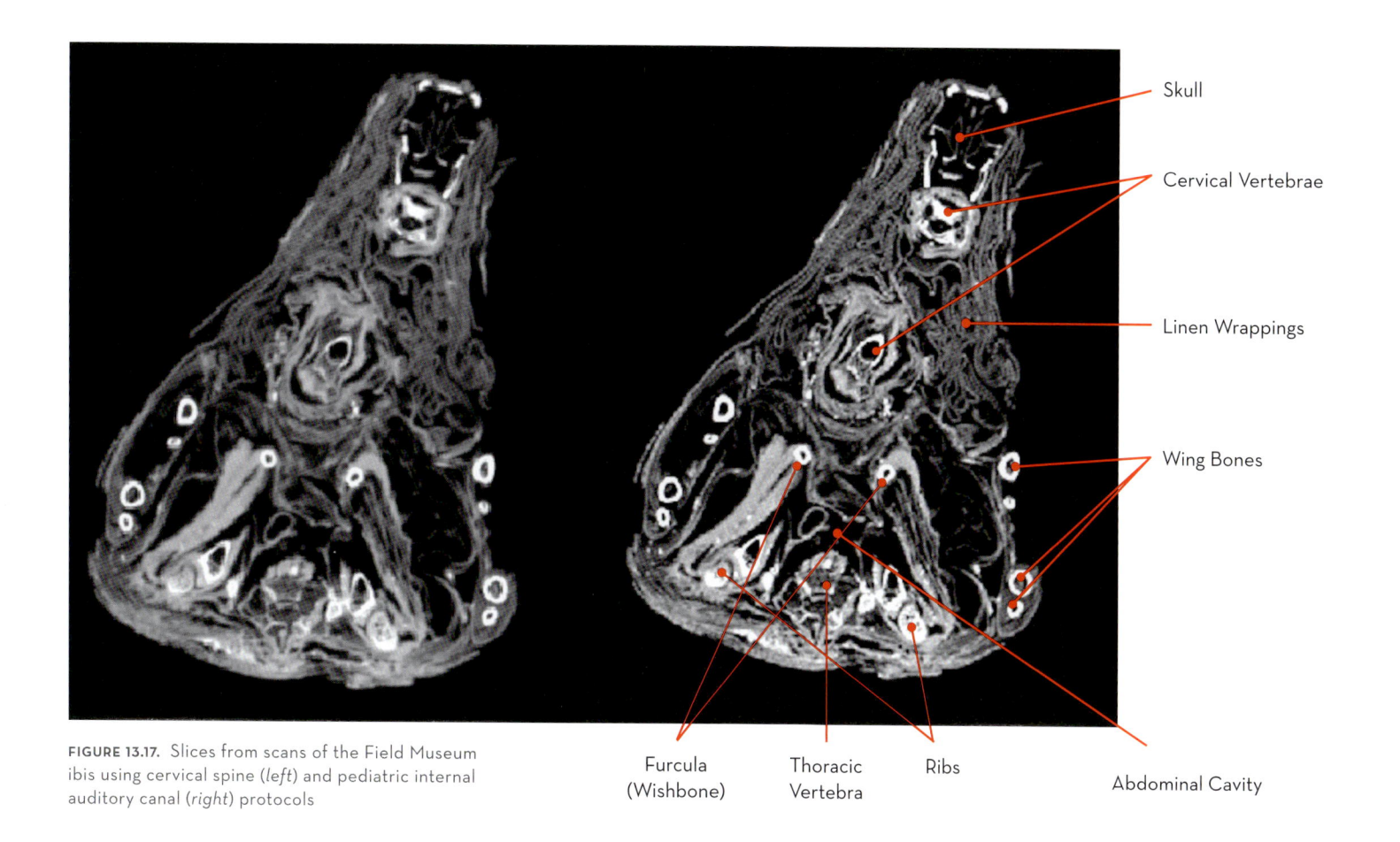

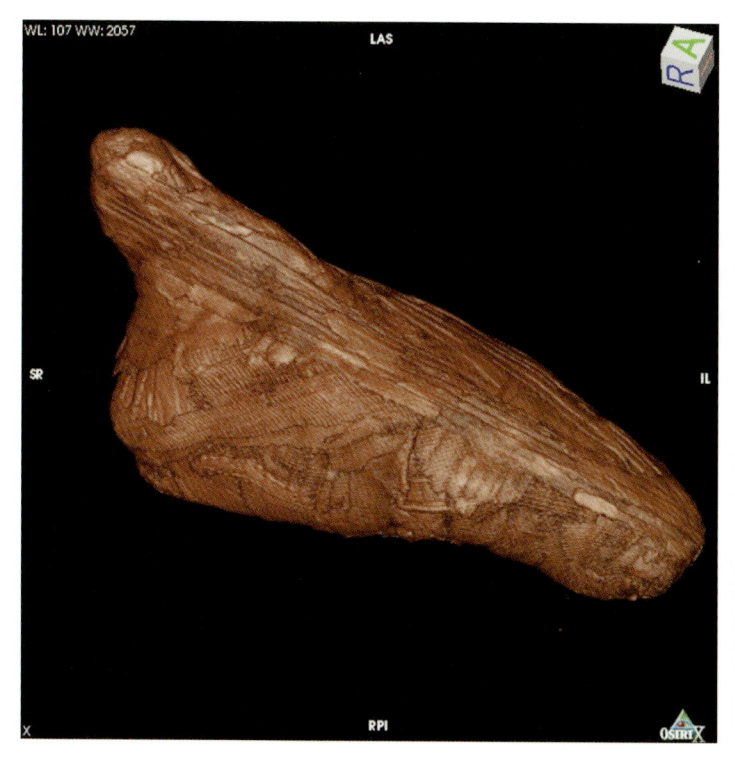

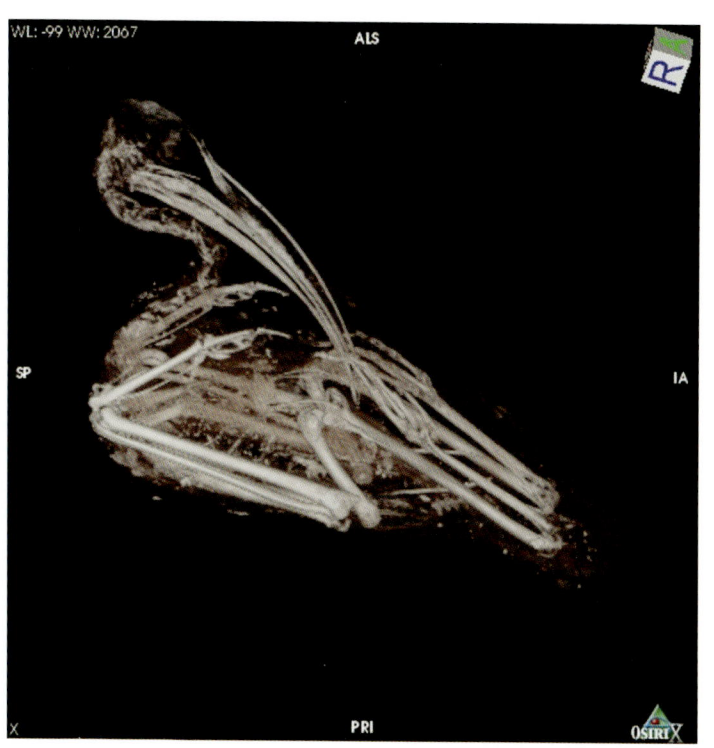

FIGURE 13.19. Transparent view of the Field Museum ibis mummy showing complete, undamaged skeleton

NOTE

[1] This work was conducted at the Integrated Small Animal Imaging Research Resource (iSAIRR), which is supported in part by funding provided by the Virginia and D. K. Ludwig Fund for Cancer Research via the Imaging Research Institute in the Biological Sciences Division of the University of Chicago.

14. TERAHERTZ PULSE IMAGING OF AN EGYPTIAN BIRD MUMMY

J. BIANCA JACKSON, GÉRARD MOUROU, JULIEN LABAUNE, *and* MICHEL MENU

Terahertz pulse imaging and spectroscopy is emerging as a non-destructive evaluation tool of high potential within the fields of art conservation and archeology (Jackson et al. 2011), in particular with mummies, as a complement or alternative to x-ray imaging techniques (Fukunaga et al. 2011). It is the combination of material characterization, time-of-flight imaging, and the penetration of optically opaque materials that gives rise to applications for subsurface imaging of many culturally significant objects. Moreover, the variety and adaptability of the many electronic, optical, and hybrid terahertz sources allows for versatile approaches to measurement (Schmuttenmaer 2004; Dragoman and Dragoman 2004; Chamberlain 2004). Resolution can be scaled from tens of micrometers to several millimeters, with the possibility of taking measurements without sample extraction, in situ and in the field. Lastly, moderate exposure to terahertz radiation poses significantly less long-term risk (Walker et al. 2002; Kristensen et al. 2010) to the molecular stability of the historical artifact and to humans than x-rays, ultra violet, or visible radiation, because it is non-ionizing. Therefore, terahertz technology provides a non-ionizing, non-invasive, non-contact, non-destructive toolset (Chan et al. 2007) for unique and priceless objects.

The terahertz (THz) region of the electromagnetic (EM) spectrum (fig. 14.1) is possibly the least understood and most complicated. EM radiation is propagated by a sub-atomic particle called a photon, which travels at the "speed of light," 3×10^8 m per second, and is defined by wavelength and frequency. The terahertz region has been arguably defined as being between 30 μm and 3 mm in wavelength, thus putting its scale on the border between the microscopic and macroscopic worlds. At frequencies between 0.1 and 10 trillion (10^{12}) cycles per second, the terahertz regime overlaps with both the microwave and far infrared regions of the spectrum. The terahertz regime also corresponds to photon energies between 0.4 and 40 eV. Lower-frequency microwave radiation has lower photon energy, therefore the waves cannot be measured directly, only collectively by the electrical bias they induce in a detector. Alternatively, infrared radiation is optical, since its photon energy is large enough that individual photons can be directly measured. Thus, terahertz radiation uniquely straddles the worlds of

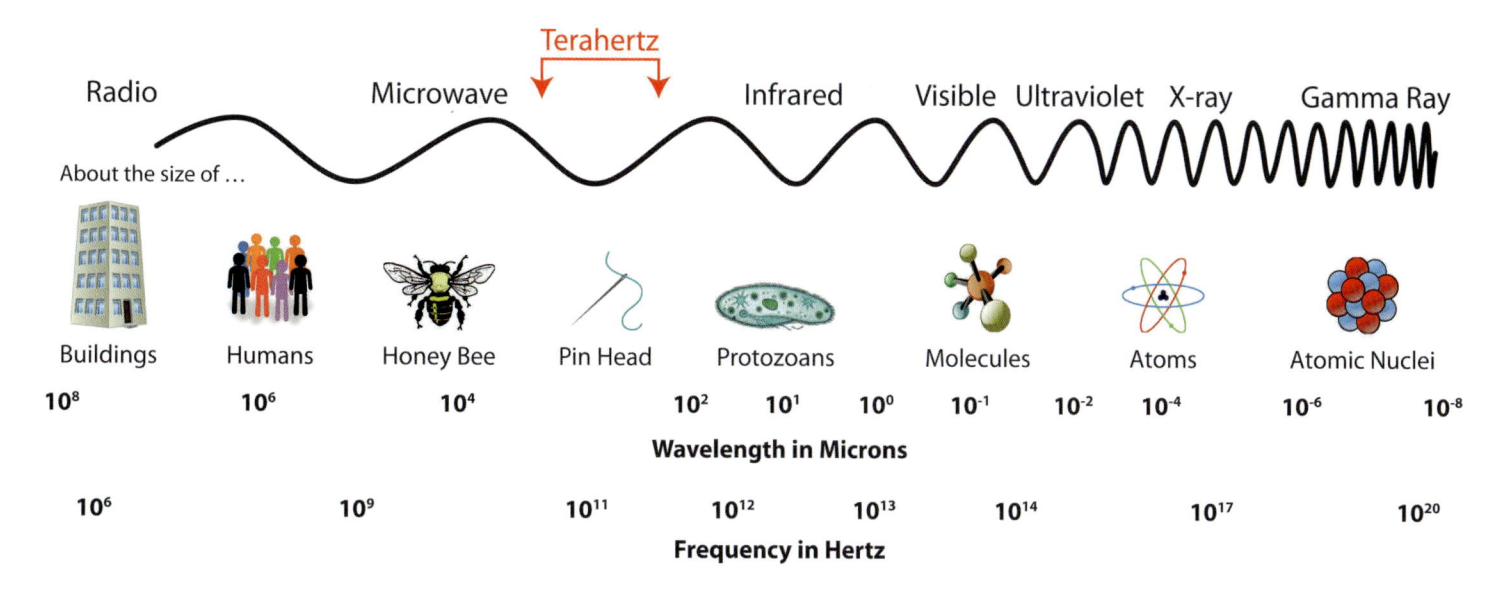

FIGURE 14.1. The electromagnetic spectrum. Regions are scaled by wavelength to common items (adapted from NASA source)

electronics and optics. Over the last couple of decades, means of producing and detecting sub-picosecond (10^{-12}) broadband pulses of terahertz radiation by integrating optoelectronic devices with ultrafast optical lasers has sparked many new forms of research, including time-domain terahertz spectroscopy and imaging. As the terahertz gap is filled, the number of terahertz applications constantly increases, including those developed for the chemical-mapping of pharmaceuticals, the non-destructive evaluation of space shuttle foam, people-safe security imaging, and atmospheric-chemical species monitoring.

Pulsed terahertz electric field measurements provide temporal and spectral information simultaneously. If the terahertz pulse transmits through materials of low electrical conductivity without large return loss or absorption, one can exploit the change in reflection of electromagnetic waves due to differences in terahertz refractive index. It then becomes possible to image the lateral spatial characteristics of materials buried beneath visibly opaque surface layers. While the wide bandwidth of the terahertz pulses can aid in spectroscopically discriminating between buried materials that exhibit different terahertz-refractive-index spectra, the short-time-duration nature of terahertz pulses can help one to isolate and distinguish depth information from different interfaces within an object.

METHODOLOGY

Our time-domain terahertz imaging system consists of computer-controlled, motorized translation stages and the Picometrix T-Ray 4000 (TR4K) commercial terahertz system. The major benefits of the system design are that the optical components are contained within a box of suitable size and weight for transport, and the fiber-coupled antennas permit rapid modification of the measurement geometry. This allows for easy on-site examinations. The mode-locked, two-stage, amplified, Ytterbium fiber laser operates with a center frequency near 1064 nm, a 100 fs pulse width, a 50 MHz repetition rate and a maximum output power of 400 mW.

The terahertz pulses were generated and then propagated through free-space using a biased, photoconductive switch antenna consisting of a photosensitive low-temperature grown gallium arsenide semiconductor with two metal electrodes deposited on its surface. The antenna is illuminated at normal incidence by the ultrafast laser pulse, thus generating electron-hole pairs into the semiconductor. A voltage bias is applied to the electrodes to generate a photocurrent. The free-space terahertz electromagnetic field emanating from the antennas is proportional to the rapid change in the photocurrent, the sub mechanisms of which determine the duration and bandwidth of the terahertz pulse.

A second photoconductive antenna is used as the terahertz receiver. The optical pulse generates photocarriers in the receiver by the same photoexcitation mechanism as when the emitter is illuminated. In this case, however, the incident electric field of the terahertz pulse causes a time-varying potential to develop across the receiver, thus serving as an applied voltage bias that induces a transient photocurrent,

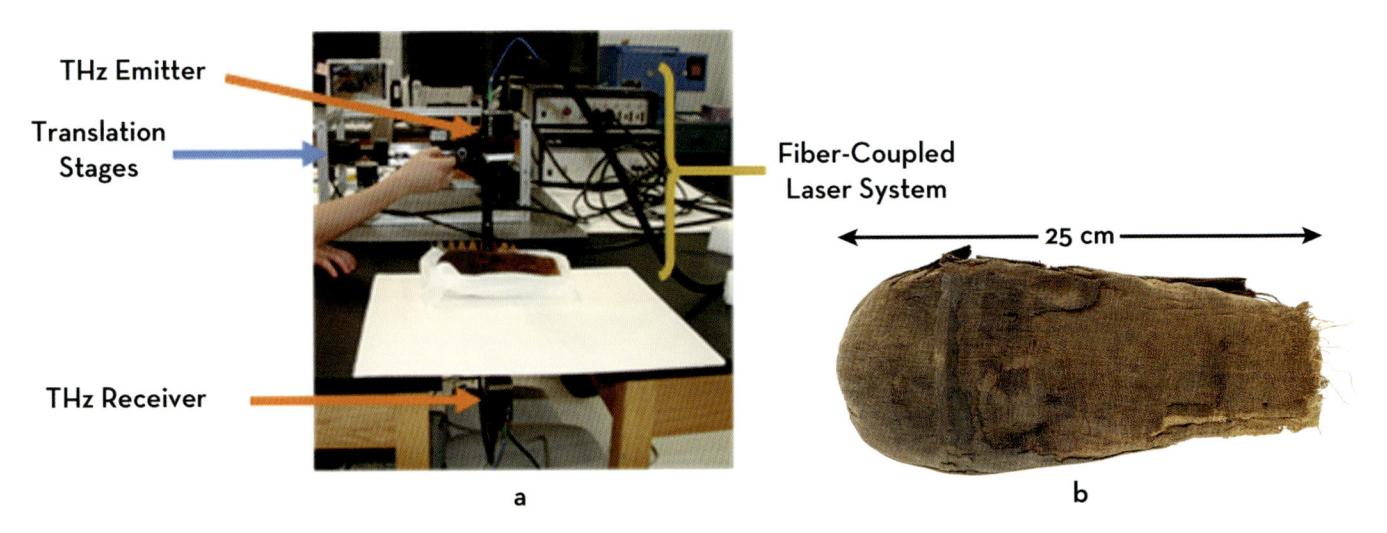

FIGURE 14.2. Photographs of (a) the experimental setup and (b) the Egyptian bird mummy OIM E9164 (mummy image: D. 17921; photo by Anna Ressman)

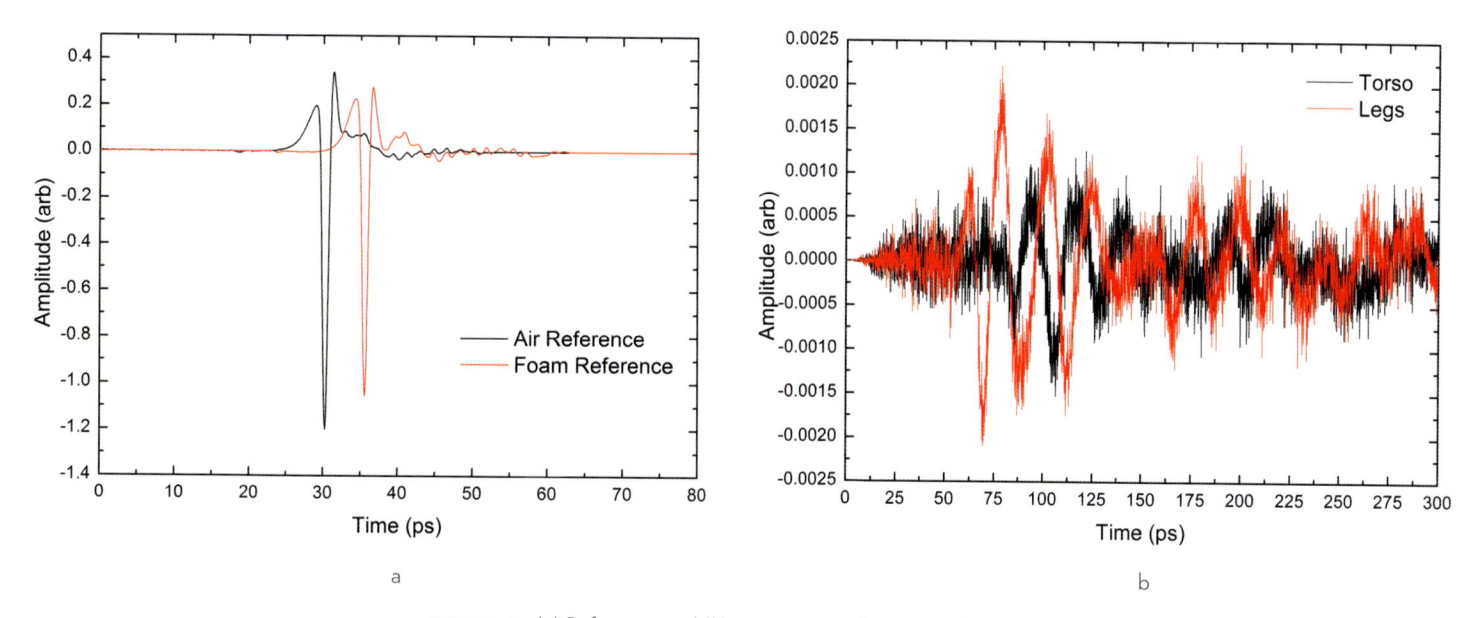

FIGURE 14.3. (*a*) Reference and (*b*) mummy time-domain terahertz signal

which is amplified and measured as an electrical signal by using a data-acquisition board and computer.

Previously, Ohrstrom and colleagues (2010) used terahertz transmission imaging to view the contents of a mummified human hand and fish. They demonstrated that, despite having coarser resolution than x-ray computed tomography (CT), it was possible with terahertz imaging to recognize differences in the desiccated flesh and it added a temporal aspect[1] nonexistent in other techniques. In our study, we examined the bird mummy OIM E9164 in the Oriental Institute Conservation Laboratory at the University of Chicago (fig. 14.2). The preference of conservators is to disturb artifacts as little as possible. We took advantage of the relatively low terahertz absorption and refractive indices of polystyrene and paper to utilize a foam board support, which permitted us to securely scan the top and bottom of the mummy in transmission with minimal consequence to the signal.

Figure 14.3a shows time-domain terahertz signals through the ambient environment and the foam support. Transmission through the upper region, or head, of the mummy was too small to discern a signal through the baseline noise. Figure 14.3b shows exemplary signals through the middle region (torso) and lower region (legs) of the bird mummy. The multiple peaks are a result of internal reflections of the

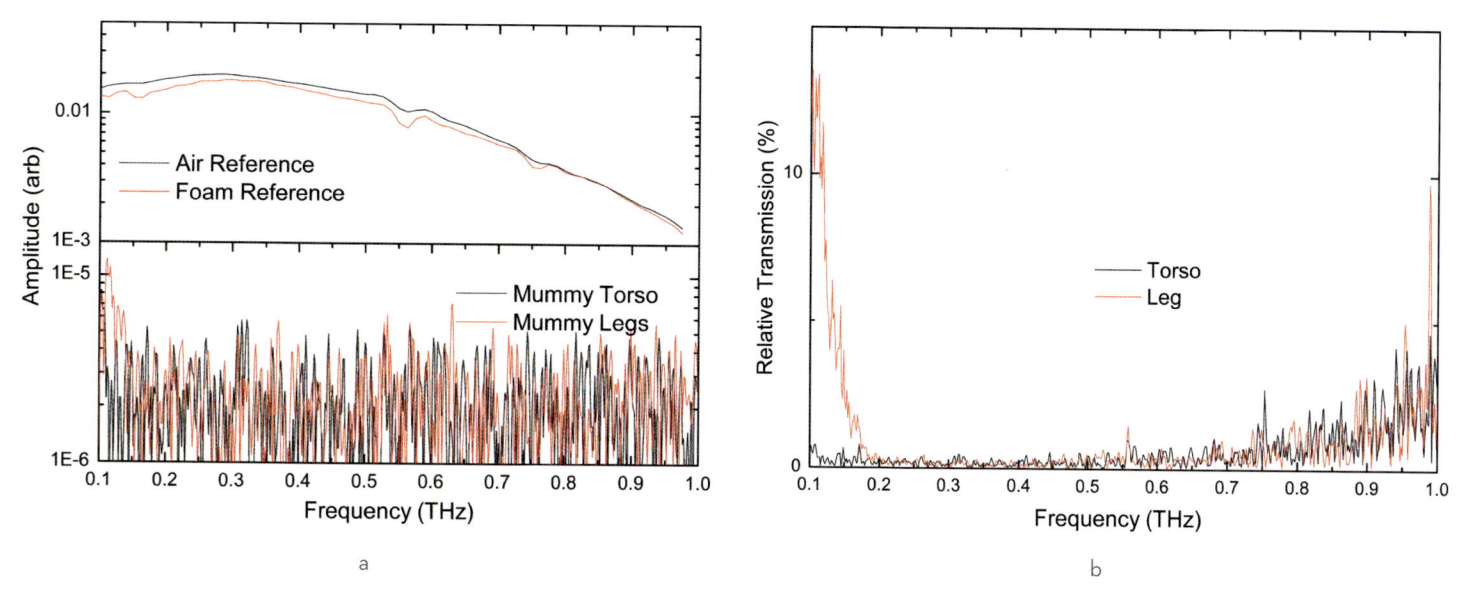

FIGURE 14.4. (*a*) Amplitude and (*b*) relative transmission frequency-domain terahertz signal

terahertz pulse as it interacts with the textile wrap, desiccated flesh, and bones of the bird.

The terahertz spectra are obtained by performing a fast Fourier transform of the time-domain signals (fig. 14.4a). Clearly, there is very little signal loss due to the foam support; however, there is a one to two order of magnitude signal loss through the mummy (fig. 14.4b) below 0.2 terahertz, while most of the higher frequencies seem to be lost due to scattering.

Two-dimensional scans of the middle and lower regions are seen in figure 14.5, and were calculated by integrating the square of the spectrum for each pixel. The white star in figure 14.5a corresponds to the exemplary pixel (that is, the extracted waveform) for the torso region, while the black star in figure 14.5b corresponds to the exemplary pixel for the leg region. The false color scales of the two regions were set equally. The spatial resolution, or power to see detail in the image, was negatively impacted by decreased bandwidth of the signal, as well as the changing spot size of the Gaussian beam through the bird. For the torso region, there is very strong absorption where the skeleton and possibly ventriculus would be (deep violet). For the leg region, the flesh and bone are less dense, resulting in better signal to noise and a more distinct figure. It is likely that the purple regions correspond to dense muscle tissue, while the orange corresponds to less dense fat, skin tissue, and bones. The clear outline of the feet, however, is the most impressive feature of this image.

CONCLUSIONS

Terahertz pulse imaging is a promising tool for the non-destructive evaluation of precious cultural artifacts, and mummies in particular. While the spatial resolution is not as detailed as x-ray imaging and there is significant signal loss as the object scale increases, there is adequate contrast between the components of the mummy for identification. Additionally, portable terahertz systems provide more flexibility in the geometry of the measurement, scale, and convenience by permitting the system to be taken to the object's location.

ACKNOWLEDGMENTS

The authors would like to thank Jack Green, Chief Curator, as well as Laura D'Alessandro and Alison Whyte from the Conservation Laboratory in the Oriental Institute at the University of Chicago, for their generosity and access. This work was supported by the European Commission's Seventh Framework Program CHARISMA (grant agreement no. 228330).

NOTE

[1] Having a temporal aspect means that it is possible to produce a 3-D image from a 2-D scan, because the internal structures affect the time-of-flight of the initial pulse and internally reflected pulse.

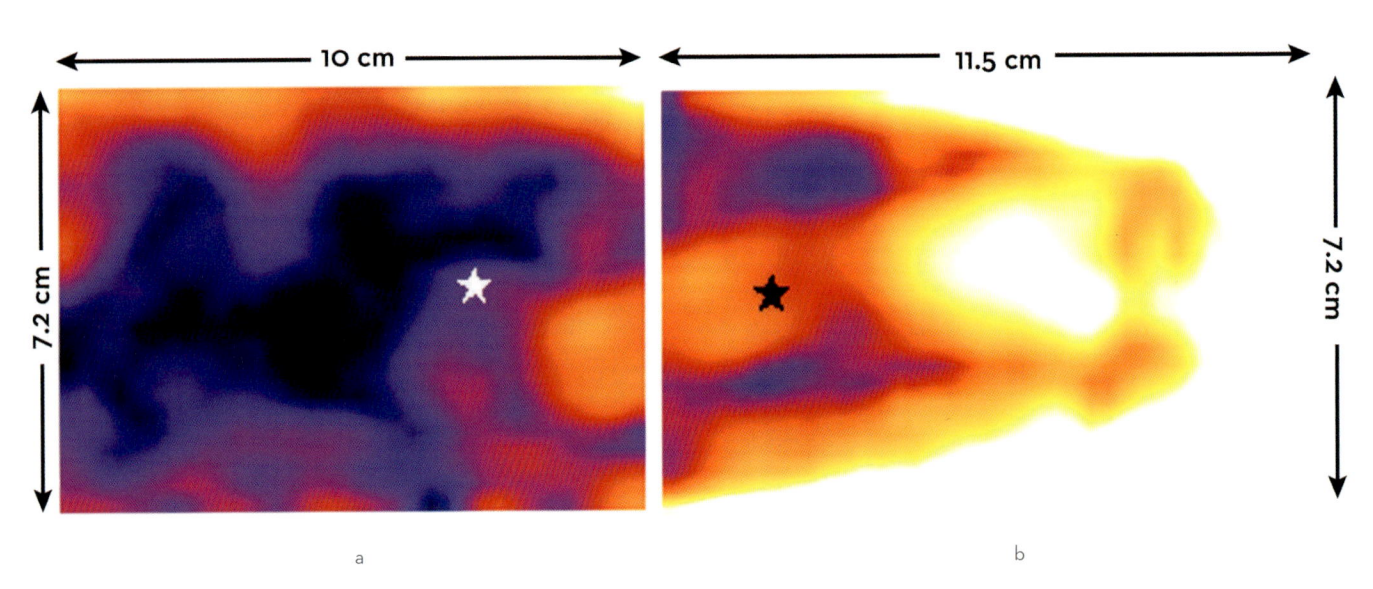

FIGURE 14.5. Terahertz transmission image of bird mummy (a) torso and (b) legs and feet (color scale: yellow = higher transmission, violet = lower transmission)

III

EPILOGUE

15. THE AVIFAUNA OF THE EGYPTIAN NILE VALLEY: CHANGING TIMES

SHERIF BAHA EL DIN

The Nile River takes its waters from the Ethiopian highlands and gently flows along the valley across the Sahara Desert and finally into the Mediterranean Sea, acting as a miraculous conduit of life between two distinct biogeographical regions. The Nile Valley is thus inhabited by a unique mixture of plants, animals and birds that either have Palearctic or African affinities, a diversity that is perhaps paralleled by its human inhabitants.

In pharaonic times, the Nile was a dynamic river whose flow fluctuated annually and across the years. Annual cycles of flooding and receding meant that the riverbanks remained largely barren and sandy or muddy during much of the year, as great fluctuations in water level did not permit any substantial vegetation to become established. During the late summer, the water level would suddenly start rising, flooding the entire valley and transforming it into a long temporary wetland. Equally, the water would retreat into the main channel of the river, leaving behind many small pools and ponds, some of which stayed wet for long periods, such as Lake Dahshur, which still remains today (fig. 15.1), though most dried quickly. In winter, the river would diminish even further, leaving behind wide sandy banks. In the Delta, where the effect of water fluctuations was dampened and where water was retained in many wetlands throughout the year, swamp vegetation and papyrus beds were formed, mingled with an extensive matrix of grassy savannah and cultivations.

The river and the Delta wetlands supported most of the birdlife. The abundance of waterbirds in particular and their significance to all aspects of life in ancient Egypt is well documented on the walls of tombs and temples. The Nile River and its largely barren banks is where many waterbirds fed and rested during migration and is where the Egyptian plover (*Pluvianus aegyptius*) thrived. The impressive fall migration of garganey (*Anas querquedula*) and other waterfowl and waders coincided with the inundation of the Nile Valley in late August and September. The hundreds of thousands of white storks (*Ciconia ciconia*) crossing the Gulf of Suez and the Eastern Desert must have had a bonanza arriving at fully swelled river with extensive wetlands surrounding it. The summer floods brought with them some occasional southern visitors like the yellow-billed stork (*Mycteria ibis*) and pink-backed pelican (*Pelecanus rufescens*). In winter, millions of waterfowl visited the extensive Delta wetlands, where they were hunted extensively, as is the case today.

Resident and breeding species included a selection of herons, ibises, and waders. Many of these species still exist today, but many have vanished from Egypt. The Egyptian plover used to be fairly widespread along the Nile River and even seen in Cairo. The marbled duck (*Marmaronetta angustirostris*) and white-headed duck (*Oxyura leucocephala*) have both disappeared during the past century, along with the famous sacred ibis (*Threskiornis aethiopicus*). Species such as the great crested grebe (*Podiceps cristatus*), coot (*Fulica atra*), and white-tailed sea eagle (*Haliaeetus albicilla*) were known to breed in the Delta wetlands, but have all stopped doing so, being found now only as winter visitors. And until recently the

FIGURE 15.1. Lake Dahshur, a glimpse of the past (all photos by Sherif Baha el Din)

chestnut-bellied sandgrouse (*Pterocles exustus*), an inhabitant of the desert edge, was thought to have been extinguished.[1]

Ecological changes, caused mainly by man and exacerbated by climatic change, have led to large and increasingly rapid shifts in the composition and distribution of avifauna in the Egyptian Nile Valley, particularly over the past few decades. The establishment of the Aswan High Dam had singularly the most significant impacts on the ecology of the Nile River in Egypt. Some of the ecological consequences are still evolving today after some fifty years since the cessation of the Nile flooding and the taming of the River. The High Dam led to the creation of Lake Nasser, a vast wetland with an extensive and complex shoreline, which is becoming an increasingly important wintering ground for Palearctic waterfowl, as other Egyptian wetlands shrink and become increasingly degraded. Egyptian geese (*Alopochen aegyptiacus*), yellow-billed kites (*Milvus aegyptius*), and Egyptian vultures (*Neophron percnopterus*) have healthy populations around the lake. Downstream from the dam, many gradual changes in the ecology of the river have taken place. The stability of the water level within the river course allowed a progressive invasion and establishment of thick reed beds and emergent vegetation along the riverbanks. The naturally barren sandy banks of the river were gradually transformed into swampy thickets.

The riverbanks now form a longitudinal band of habitat that has allowed many swamp-inhabiting species, such as the purple gallinule (*Porphyrio porphyrio*) (fig. 15.2), squacco heron (*Ardeola ralloides*), little bittern (*Ixobrychus minutus*), and purple heron (*Ardea purpurea*) to spread along the Nile, where they did not exist previously. The newly established swampy conditions were also a conduit for the northward spread of some African water birds, such as green heron (*Butorides striata*), which has managed to invade the entire Egyptian Nile Valley and even the Delta in a mere twenty years. The three-banded plover (*Charadrius tricollaris*) is gradually following suit. Being documented as a vagrant for the first time in the early 1990s, it has now been confirmed as breeding in the Aswan area.

The stability in water supply in the Nile Valley has also meant that cultivation is intensified year round and land is no longer left fallow for part of the year. This has also meant that water is available for horizontal expansion of agriculture now reaching as far as 60 kilometers west of Alexandria and almost half the way to El Arish in North Sinai. All along the Nile Valley, agriculture has been pushed east and west of the River, adding hundreds of thousands of acres of new arable land. In the meantime, an area of almost the same size has been lost to urbanization. The intensification in agricultural practices and expansion in cultivated land has lead to the loss of marginal lands which used to be home to species like the chestnut-bellied sandgrouse and the Delta subspecies of lesser short-toed lark (*Calandrella rufescens*).

FIGURE 15.3. The Senegal coucal (*Centropus senegalensis*) is a species of African affinity that still thrives and is quite adaptable to changing Egyptian landscapes, spreading quickly and with ease into newly cultivated areas

FIGURE 15.2. Purple gallinule (*Porphyrio porphyrio*) and ringed plovers (*Charadrius hiaticula*)

15. THE AVIFAUNA OF THE EGYPTIAN NILE VALLEY

It also simultaneously led to the expansion in range of many breeding species, such as the Senegal coucal (*Centropus senegalensis*) (fig. 15.3) and Senegal thick-knee (*Burhinus senegalensis*), which can be found in areas that were barren desert just a decade ago. The introduction of pesticides has led to declines in the population of birds of prey and other farmland birds such as cattle egrets (*Bubulcus ibis*).

The changes in cropping patterns has also contributed to this shift in the Nile Valley avifauna. Two decades ago cotton was a predominant crop in the Delta during the summer months. Now rice has become one of the most widely cultivated crops, transforming the Delta into a huge wetland in the summer. Furthermore, huge areas of the northern Delta have also been transformed into fish farms, which also provide alternative wetland habitat. These man-made and manipulated habitats have in fact increased opportunities for some water bird species to grow in numbers and spread, particularly herons.

The huge influx of freshwater now draining into northern Delta lakes such as Burullus (fig. 15.4) have transformed them into freshwater bodies rather than the brackish lakes they originally were. As a result, extensive reed beds and swamp vegetation took over these wetlands. A survey of Lake Burullus in spring 2012 found a large population of breeding whiskered terns (*Chlidonias hybridus*), a species that did not breed in Egypt before 1999, and huge breeding colonies of squacco herons, little egrets (*Egretta garzetta*) (fig. 15.5), night heron (*Nycticorax* sp.), and cattle egrets (fig. 15.6).

FIGURE 15.5. Little egret (*Egretta garzetta*) at Lake Burullus

A combination of climatic- and landscape-wide changes in the natural habitats of Egypt and in its surrounding regions probably has contributed to the dramatic shifts in the distributions of species like the white-breasted kingfisher (*Halcyon smyrnensis*) (fig. 15.7), which was considered a rare vagrant until the mid 1980s but is now a prominent avian inhabitant of the lower Nile Valley and Delta south to at least Minya. The establishment of the blackbird (*Turdus merula*) as one of the Nile Valley's prominent resident breeding birds (which until the 1980s was only a fairly

FIGURE 15.4. Fishermen on Lake Burullus

FIGURE 15.6. Herons and egrets are among the species that have benefited most from ecological changes in the Nile Valley. This is a part of a huge colony recently found in the middle of Lake Burullus

common winter visitor), and its spread into the isolated oases of the Western Desert is puzzling. Equally puzzling is the establishment of Spanish sparrow (*Passer hispaniolensis*) as a common breeding species in Dakhla and Farafra Oases in the middle of the Western Desert. These types of changes in range can only be explained as a meta-population response to very large ecological shifts, potentially induced by climatic change.

The widespread introduction of exotic trees, such as mango, orange, and olive trees is certainly contributing to the changes in the Nile Valley landscape. Small patches of wooded habitats can now be seen in a region that was fairly treeless in the past, originally made up of open savannah-like habitat with scattered acacias and palm trees, but with very limited availability of the dense wooded microhabitats now found in the Egyptian agricultural matrix.

There are also three dove species that are in different stages of invading the Egyptian territories. The collared dove (*Streptopelia decaocto*) started its expansion into Egypt during the 1980s, and is now a common and widespread resident almost throughout the country. The pink-headed fruit dove (*Ptilinopus porphyreus*), which was only known from the extreme south eastern corner of Egypt on the Red Sea coast, is slowly expanding its range northward along the Red Sea and has been reported along the Nile Valley and in South Sinai. Just last year African mourning doves (*Streptopelia decipiens*) were documented probably breeding at Abu Simbel, representing yet another new expansionary species extending its range into newly created habitats.

FIGURE 15.7. White-breasted kingfisher (*Halcyon smyrnensis*) in Giza

The Egyptian avifauna has been evolving over the past few millennia during and after the Pharaonic period, but probably never as fast or as dramatically as during the past century. The rate of change seems to still be accelerating due to global and local ecological changes caused by to rapid increase in human demands on natural resources. As indicated above, some of these changes seem to be positive for some avian species, but are not such good news for others. Species of semi-desert habitats, such as the coastal Mediterranean deserts and steppes (houbara bustards, coursers and larks), are particularly under threat. These habitats are the prime target for agricultural expansion and are subject to heavy overgrazing and long-term droughts. In the future, unless changes are implemented, Egypt will be dominated by those bird species that are most resilient and adaptable, such as hooded crow (*Corvus cornix*), common bulbul (*Pycnonotus barbatus*), and palm dove (*Streptopelia senegalensis*); while the more ecologically sensitive and space demanding species like houbara bustard (*Chlamydotis undulata*), Dupont's lark (*Chersophilus duponti*), and Egyptian vulture (*Neophron percnopterus*) will join other memories from the past.

NOTE

[1] In spring 2012 a small population was discovered in Minya.

IV

CATALOG

BIRDS IN CREATION MYTHS

Few of the surviving texts and images that relate the creation myths of the ancient Egyptians were composed for the sole purpose of describing how the world came into existence. In order to discover what Egyptians believed about creation, it is necessary to examine a wide variety of texts and images. What we call the "creation myths" of ancient Egypt consist of short episodes woven into larger contextual frameworks such as narrative literature, magical spells, funerary compositions, or temple scenes.

The Egyptian view of the cosmos begins with the god Nun, a personification of the primeval waters in which all the elements of creation were dissolved. From this primordial soup, the so-called creator god appeared, whom the Egyptians referred to as "the one who came into being himself." No explanation is offered for the mechanism behind his appearance. In fact, in Coffin Texts spell 75, this god explicitly states "Do not ask how I came into being from Nun." Depending on the source, this appearance occurs either independently, upon a mound, in a rising lotus, or from an egg. Through the act of masturbation, spitting, sneezing, thinking, or speaking, this god created the elements of the cosmos, which the Egyptians presented as divine personifications of water (Tefnut), air (Shu), earth (Geb), and sky (Nut). With the earth and sky separated by the air, the creator god could travel by day in the form of the sun disk, thereby laying the physical foundations for the world as the Egyptians knew it.

Within the framework of the Egyptian creation myths, birds appear on several occasions. In one telling, a goose lays an egg (see Catalog No. 1) on the mound which has risen from the primeval waters. From this egg, the sun god hatches in the form of a heron (see Catalog No. 2). This story, already present in the Pyramid Texts of the late third millennium BC, would have an important influence on the classical myth of the Phoenix. FS

1. OSTRICH EGG

Organic remains
A-Group, ca. 3100 BC
Qustul, Cemetery S, deposit 4
Excavated by the Oriental Institute, 1962–63
15.4 × 12.7 cm
OIM E21384
Oriental Institute digital images
D. 17994–95

This undecorated ostrich egg was excavated by the Oriental Institute Nubian Expedition from a deposit within Cemetery S at the Nubian site of Qustul, which lies just north of the border with Sudan.[1] Several important cemeteries from the A-Group period were excavated at Qustul, with Cemetery S containing the largest tombs equal in size and wealth to the famous Early Dynastic tombs at Abydos.[2] The egg is nearly complete with a small hole in one end through which it had been drained.[3] Similar ostrich eggshells have been discovered at other sites throughout Egypt and Nubia (and throughout the Mediterranean), some dating back into the Holocene and continuing into the pharaonic period.[4] A number of examples are decorated with desert animals and hunting scenes, paralleled in the contemporary artistic repertoire as represented on a wide diversity of media including rock art, tomb paintings, pottery decoration, and palette designs, among many others.[5] The form of the ostrich egg was so valued that craftsmen produced imitation vessels made from stone or ceramics.

The definitive meaning of such ostrich eggs has been debated. Although ostrich eggs would have filled different functions within Egyptian and Nubian life, including utilitarian roles as potential food source, beads, or containers for liquids, the deposition of such items within the sacred space of cult sites, tombs, and "royal" cemeteries implies a symbolic function tied to prestige, power, and ritual practices.[6] Religious correlations are demonstrated by several spectacular archaeological discoveries. Recent excavations of predynastic Cemetery HK6 at Hierakonpolis uncovered a large deposit of twenty-two ostrich eggshells.[7] An ostrich eggshell was discovered buried inside a jar at the Nile Delta site of Tell el-Farkha as a potential foundation deposit.[8] In a Neolithic tomb at Naqada, W. M. Flinders Petrie unearthed the remains of an individual whose missing head was replaced by a decorated ostrich egg.[9]

Support for the spiritual significance of the egg motif has been found by turning to religious literature from later periods of pharaonic history. In Book of the Dead spell 77 for "turning into

1, bottom

a falcon of gold," the deceased recites: "I have risen as the great falcon which has gone forth from his egg."[10] The passage refers to one of the mythological accounts of the creation in which a goose, referred to as the "Great Cackler" (*Ngg wr*), lays the cosmic egg from which the sun god hatches and rises up to create the visible world.[11] Through means of this text, the deceased associated himself with the sun god in the hopes of joining the solar-Osirian cycle, thereby ensuring his eternal existence in the entourage of the gods.[12] The egg, therefore, came to symbolize both birth and rebirth, an associated quality maintained into Egypt's Coptic period, when it was connected with Christ's birth and resurrection.[13] Despite the difficulties of forming an understanding based on data from millennia later, most interpreters have assumed that similar intentions motivated the utilization of these ostrich eggs within sacred landscapes during the very foundation of Egyptian and Nubian civilization.[14] FS

PUBLISHED (SELECTED)

B. Williams 1989, p. 103

NOTES

[1] B. Williams 1989, p. 103.
[2] B. Williams 2011, p. 87.
[3] Kantor 1948, p. 46; Teeter 2011b, cat. no. 5.
[4] Muir and Friedman 2011, pp. 582–88; Phillips 2009, pp. 1–2; Cherpion 2001, pp. 286–87.
[5] Kantor 1948; Hendrickx 2000; Teeter 2011b, cat. no. 5.
[6] B. Williams 1989, p. 10; Cherpion 2001, pp. 288–91; Muir and Friedman 2011, pp. 588–90.
[7] Muir and Friedman 2011.
[8] Ciałowicz 2008, pp. 31–32; Ciałowicz 2011, pp. 773–75.
[9] Petrie and Quibell 1896, p. 28; Cherpion 2001, p. 288.
[10] For text, see Lepsius 1842, pl. 28, BD 77, line 1. For translation, see T. G. Allen 1974, p. 66.
[11] For references to the "Great Cackler" (*Ngg wr*), see Leitz 2002, vol. 4, p. 367.
[12] Such is specified in more detail in BD 149, where the sun god is addressed directly: "Hail to you, this noble god in his egg, I have come before you so that I be in your following."
[13] Phillips 2009, p. 2.
[14] Muir and Friedman 2011, p. 588; Dreyer 1986, p. 97 n. 389.

2. "THREE VIGNETTES, THEBES, TOMB OF QUEEN NEFRETERE, RAMESSES II, 1292–1225 B.C."

Nina de Garis Davies, ca. 1936
Tempera on paper
42.54 x 59.69 cm
Collection of the Oriental Institute
Oriental Institute digital image D. 17885

This tempera by Nina de Garis Davies depicts a scene found on the west wall in the antechamber of the tomb of Nefertari, queen of Ramesses II, in the Valley of the Queens (QV 66). Her tomb is justly famous for the remarkable preservation and vivid colors of the painted scenes decorating its walls. Due to the delicate nature of the plaster and potential harm caused by salt, water, and temperature fluctuations, visiting the tomb is often restricted and conservators have worked diligently in an attempt to slow the rate of deterioration which has continued to plague the tomb over the last century.[1] Therefore, Davies's paintings are valuable not only for their artistic beauty, but in some cases they preserve a record of monuments now damaged or lost.

From right to left, the figures depicted are the goddess Nephthys in the form of a common kestrel, the *benu*-bird in the form of a grey heron, and the lion of yesterday.[2] The scene is well known as a portion of the vignette from Book of the Dead (BD) spell 17, which adorns the interior of Nefertari's tomb along with texts and scenes from various Book of the Dead spells and other funerary literature. BD 17 is one of the most frequently attested spells in the Book of the Dead corpus and this long vignette highlights a number of important passages, characters, and themes mentioned in the text.[3] The text itself is a complex and not completely understood compilation of interwoven narratives, glosses, and commentaries through which the tomb owners demonstrated their religious knowledge while identifying themselves as the creator god.[4]

Nephthys is shown here in the form of a kestrel with her name *Nb.t-ḥw.t* "Lady of the enclosure" written in hieroglyphs on top of her head. In the original scene she stands at the head end of a funerary bed holding the mummy of Nefertari with Isis also in the form of a kestrel at the foot end. Isis and Nephthys were the principle mourners in the collection of Osirian myths, thus by extension for the deceased, and the piercing shrieks of birds of prey were thought to represent their wailing cries. The two goddesses are referred to as "screechers" (*ḥȝ.t*) in Pyramid Text spell 535: "As the screecher comes, so the kite comes, namely Isis and Nephthys."[5] As the protectors of the deceased, Isis and Nephthys are commonly depicted as women with outstretched bird wings on the corners of New Kingdom royal sarcophagi.[6] In a composition from the end of the fourth century BC called the "Stanzas of the Festival of the Two Kites," two women who have undergone the ritual preparation of complete hair removal and had the names Isis and Nephthys written on their arms, don wigs, and carry tambourines while reciting the stanzas before Osiris.[7]

For the Egyptians and in the context of BD 17, the *benu*-bird (*bnw*) is a symbol of the rejuvenation of the deceased, shown standing next to the funerary bier flanked by the kestrels Isis and Nephthys. The stories of the Egyptian *benu*-bird formed the inspiration for the classical story of the phoenix, a bird whose mythological life cycle ends in a fiery conflagration that resulted in the renaissance of the new phoenix rising from the ashes of the old.[8] Tales involving the phoenix traveled far and wide throughout the ancient Mediterranean world. Known as the "soul (*bȝ*) of Re" or the "heart (*ib*) of Re," the *benu*-bird had a close association with the sun god and appeared on scarab-shaped amulets placed near the heart of the mummy often inscribed with BD 29B, which begins: "I am the *benu*-bird, the soul of Re, who guides the gods to the netherworld from which they go forth."[9] Through the spell of BD 83, a "spell for turning into the *benu*-bird," the deceased sought transformation into the phoenix for the purpose of rejuvenation and affiliation with the gods.

In addition to being an icon of rejuvenation, the *benu*-bird figured in certain Egyptian cosmogonic stories. In Pyramid Text spell 600, the *benu*-bird is said to appear as the creator god Atum-Khepri at the beginning of time upon the primeval mound rising from the cosmic waters (Nun), probably inspired by herons wading in the marshes and pools of the Nile.[10] This mythic episode was memorialized in the temple of the *benu*-bird in Heliopolis, where the primeval mound was symbolized by the pyramidal *benben*-stone and where the corpse of the sun god is said to reside.[11] The *benu*-bird thus represented the power (*bȝ*) of the sun god as creator and the avian imagery further reinforced the metaphor of the sun's daily "flight" across the sky. FS

PUBLISHED (SELECTED)

Davies 1936, vol. 2, pl. 93

NOTES

[1] Corzo and Afshar 1993.

[2] Davies 1936, vol. 3, pp. 180–81.

[3] Taylor 2010, p. 51; Milde 1991, pp. 31–54; Saleh 1984, pp. 14–22.

[4] Lapp 2006; Westendorf 1975; Rößler-Köhler 1979.

[5] For text, see Sethe 1908, vol. 2, p. 219. For translation, see Faulkner 1998a, p. 203; J. P. Allen 2005, p. 102.

[6] Hayes 1935.

[7] Faulkner 1936.

[8] Van den Broek 1972, pp. 14–32.

[9] For the *benu*-bird identified as the "heart of Re," see BM EA 7878 in Taylor 2010, p. 227 (no. 114).

[10] Faulkner 1998a, p. 246.

[11] Van den Broek 1972, p. 15; Assmann 2005, p. 429 n. 19.

CATALOG NO. 3

PHARAOH THE LIVING HORUS AND HIS AVIAN SUBJECTS

Bird imagery was used to represent the gods, the king, and the common man and, at the same time, to indicate their relative status. The king, the semi-divine ruler who was shown as a potentially fierce falcon or falcon-headed man, was the "Living Horus on Earth." The hieroglyphic writing of the titles that expressed his divinity incorporated a falcon and a vulture, solitary and sometimes aggressive birds. In contrast, the king's subjects were portrayed in the form of gregarious, vocal, and wary lapwings. ET

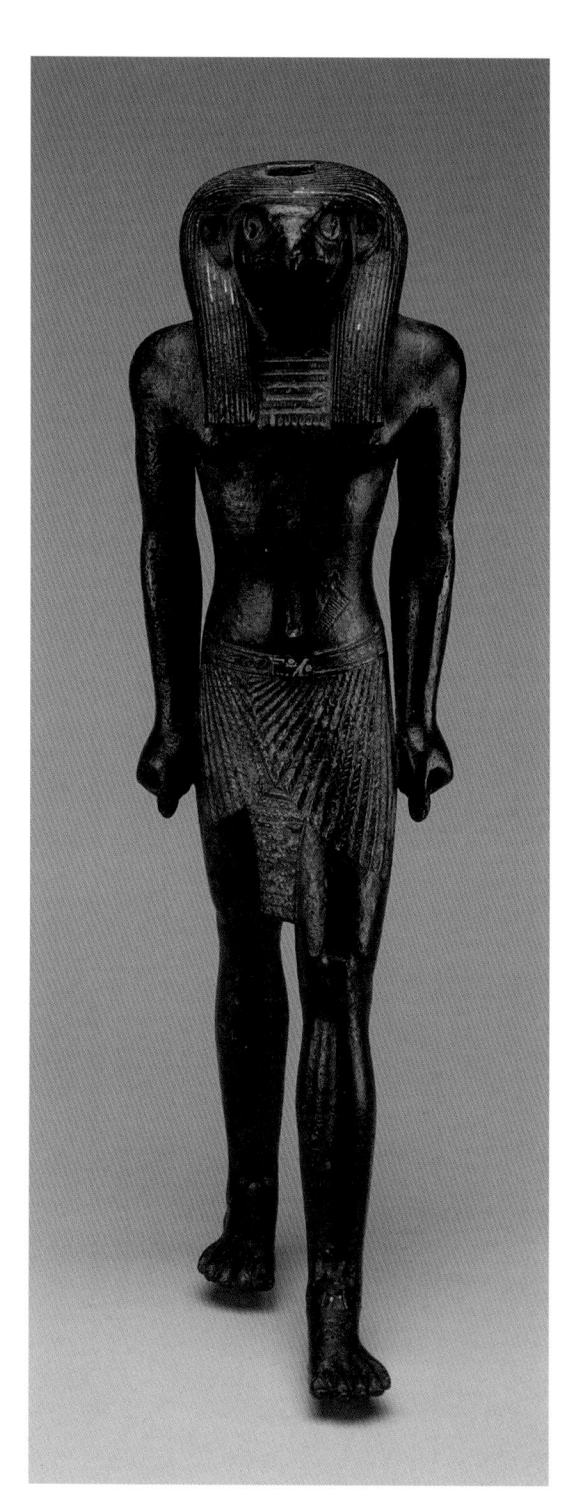

3. **STATUE OF RE-HORAKHTY**

Bronze, gilt
Third Intermediate Period–Late Period,
Dynasty 25–early Dynasty 26, ca. 722–640 BC
25.0 x 8.3 cm
Collection of the Art Institute of Chicago.
Gift of Henry H. Getty, Charles L. Hutchinson, and Robert Fleming
AIC 1894.261

This solid cast bronze figure represents Re-Horakhty ("Re, Horus of the Horizon"), one of the most prominent solar deities. Re-Horakhty is shown in his most common form, with a falcon head and a human body. His broad chest and trim muscular body are those of a being in the prime of life, and the striding posture stresses his mobility and power.

The statue's head is carefully detailed with the characteristic markings of a falcon around the eyes. The god is dressed in the pleated *shendyt*-kilt worn by kings and gods, and a lozenge-patterned belt that bears the text "Re-Horakhty, Chief of the Gods." A rectangular hole in the top of the head allowed for the attachment of a solar disk, another identifying feature of the god. He wears a pectoral made of five rows of beads, the bottom row of of which are teardrop shaped. Traces of gilt are preserved on his wig, pectoral, and in the folds of his kilt. His toenails and thumbnails have recesses to receive gilt inlay, which is well preserved on his left foot. Tenons that extend from the soles of the feet allowed the statue to be affixed to a base. The left ankle bears the impression of a butterfly-shaped cramp, indicating an ancient repair.

Re-Horakhty is among the most important members of the Egyptian pantheon. In the form of Re, he was associated with the king who, by the Fourth Dynasty (ca. 2543–2436 BC), assumed the title "Son of Re." From at least the New Kingdom, the king was described in terms that referred to the luminosity of the sun's disk: "the living image of Re," "the dazzling sun disk appearing at the head of his army," "the horizon dweller who brightens the earth ...." The king is described as one "by whose beams people see, one who brightens the Two Lands more than the sun disk."[1] The cartouche that encircles the name of kings (fig. C1) further equated them with the sun god, for the oval represents the *shen*-sign ◯, symbolizing that the king ruled all that the sun encompassed or illuminated.

Re was also a preeminent god in the mortuary sphere. The Egyptians believed that he traversed the sky in the twelve hours of the day to "die" at dusk and then traveled through the dark hours of the underworld to be "reborn" at dawn. This cycle, which represented rejuvenation and rebirth, alludes to Re-Horakhty's role as a god of eternal creation. By about the sixteenth century BC, a fundamental part of Egyptian mortuary theology was that the soul of the deceased could join the god in the endless cycle of birth, death, and rebirth, guaranteeing eternal life after death.

This funerary aspect of Re-Horakhty became very prominent about the time this statue was cast. Many elite burials of the time included a wood round-top stela that shows the deceased offering to Re-Horakhty in order that he might grant offerings of bread and beer (among other provisions) to the deceased forever.

Many of the solar gods, including Re, Re-Horakhty, and Horus, were portrayed as birds probably because their power of flight alluded to the movement of the sun across the horizon and because they dwelled in the sky. ET

PUBLISHED

T. G. Allen 1923, pp. 101–02; Roeder 1956, p. 80 (§114a), pl. 74a; Teeter 1994, pp. 24, 26

NOTE

[1] For references, and for many other examples of these epithets, see Redford 1995, pp. 169–72.

FIGURE C1. Cartouches of King Amunhotep I (ca. 1525–1504 BC), conveying that he ruled all that the sun shone upon (photo by Emily Teeter)

4. STELA OF HORUS

Limestone
Ptolemaic period, 4th–1st centuries BC
43.5 × 33.5 cm
Collection of the Field Museum of Natural History, Chicago
FMNH 31279

On this stela, a falcon, the representation of the god Horus, is shown perched atop an altar. At the top of the stela is a wide curved hieroglyph for "sky" or "heaven" ▱. Below this sign hovers the winged sun disk, the representation of the Behdetite, a form of Horus at the cities of Edfu and Tell el-Balamun (see Chapter 4). The disk is flanked by protective uraeus-snakes. Another disk with a uraeus appears behind Horus. The sky and solar symbols refer to Horus's association with the sun and his heavenly domain.

Horus and the living Egyptian king were synonymous. On this stela, the shared identity of Horus and the king is proclaimed by the double crown of Upper and Lower Egypt worn by the falcon. This association can be traced back to the decoration of ceremonial palettes of the late predynastic era (ca. 3150 BC), such as the Narmer Palette, which shows a falcon attacking the northern enemies of Egypt (see fig. 4.11). By the First Dynasty (ca. 3050 BC), the king's name was written in a frame (*serekh*) that represents the facade of the palace topped with a falcon. The Pyramid Texts (PT), the oldest compilation of royal funerary texts (ca. 2350 BC), refer frequently to the king in the form of a falcon, as a "fledgling," or "having grown wings as a falcon, feathered as a hawk" (PT 156), or that the king's "wings will grow as those of a big-breasted falcon, as a falcon seen in the evening" (PT 340), or even more explicitly, "the face of this (king) [is the face of] a falcon, the wings of this (king) are those of birds ... he [will fly] away from you ..." (PT 443).[1]

4

Later texts often refer to the king as "the living Horus upon earth." This assimilation of the king and falcon was so complete that the ruler could be shown dressed in a feathered garment (fig. 4.13 in this volume; Giza-Podgórski 1984) or with the head of a falcon (Radwan 1975, 1985). King Shoshenq II (Twenty-second Dynasty, ca. 873 BC) was buried in a silver mummiform coffin with a hawk head (Montet 1951, pp. 37–40, pls. 17–20).

This type of stela would probably have been erected in a shrine honoring the god.   ET

PUBLISHED

T. G. Allen 1936, p. 50, pl. 24; Parlasca 1974, p. 486, pl. 82a

NOTE

[1] Translations from J. P. Allen 2005, pp. 40, 134, and 150.

5

5. PLAQUE WITH ROYAL TITLE

Limestone
Late Period–Ptolemaic period, 7th–1st centuries BC
Purchased in Cairo, 1920
14.8 × 10.5 × 1.8 cm
OIM E10557
Oriental Institute digital images D. 17937–38

The vulture (probably a griffon vulture, *Gyps fulvus*) and the cobra on this plaque represent the deities Nekhbet and Wadjet, who were protectors of the king. The pair was known collectively as the "Two Ladies" (*nb.ty* in ancient Egyptian). The composition is a pun, for *nb*-baskets (⌣) that the goddesses sit on are the hieroglyph used to write the word for "lady" (⌣ *nb.t* in ancient Egyptian), while two *nb*-baskets, the dual form, is *nb.ty* (⌣) (Schott 1956, p. 56; Wilkinson 1999, p. 203).

The two deities were so strongly associated with the king that from the First Dynasty (ca. 3050 BC), the title the "Two Ladies" followed by an epithet appeared as one of the five elements that eventually made up the full ceremonial name (titulary) of the king (Callendar 2011, p. 127). Examples of the *nb.ty* name may refer directly to the king's relationship with the deities, such as "the One Who Does Truth for the Two Ladies" (Userkaf, Dynasty 5), or "the One Who Satisfies the Two Ladies" (Teti I, Dynasty 6), or the name may refer to success that was presumably the result of the goddesses' protection, for example, "the One Who Seizes All Lands" (Thutmose I, Dynasty 18). The *nb.ty* name was part of royal names until the end of the Ptolemaic period (first century BC).

In Egyptian reliefs, one or the other of the Two Ladies was frequently depicted hovering protectively over the king. In those scenes, the cobra deity assumes a hybrid form of a vulture with a cobra head, neatly solving the conundrum of a hovering snake while stressing the dominance of bird imagery (see further in Chapter 4, and fig. 4.6).

Throughout the pharaonic period, complementary pairs are a feature of Egyptian culture. This symmetry is expressed by Upper and Lower Egypt, the red crown and the white crown, and the papyrus and lily, all of which express the south-north division of the land. The Two Ladies also expressed this geographic duality, for the center of the worship of Nekhbet was at El Kab in the south, while the city associated with Wadjet was Buto in the north.

The reverse of this plaque has two patches of fish-scale-like decoration, perhaps traces of carving that was erased.

The function of these small plaques is debated. Some, especially those with sections of frames at the edge that may have served to gauge the depth of the carving (as on the left of this example), have been interpreted as sculptors' trial pieces. Other examples may possibly be votive plaques that honor a god. The Two Ladies motif is found on several other examples of this type of object.[1] ET

NOTE

[1] Among them, Metropolitan Museum of Art, New York, 11.155.12; Walters Art Museum, Baltimore, 22.36, 22.264, 22.287; Egyptian Museum, Cairo, CG 33448, 33449, 33450, 45927; and ostracon no. 33248 in the Petrie Museum of Egyptian Archaeology, London.

5, back

BETWEEN HEAVEN AND EARTH: BIRDS IN ANCIENT EGYPT

6. LAPWING TILES

Faience, glaze
New Kingdom, reign of Ramesses III
(ca. 1184–1153 BC)
Luxor, Medinet Habu, western fortified gate
Excavated by the Oriental Institute, 1931–32

a. OIM E16721
   10.1 x 9.7 x 1.8 cm
   Oriental Institute digital image D. 17978

b. OIM E15488
   6.3 x 3.6 cm
   Oriental Institute digital image D. 17482

c. OIM E16719
   10.5 x 5.6 cm
   Oriental Institute digital image D. 17977

6a

6b

6c

140

These three fragmentary faience tiles depict the lapwing in the form of the *rekhyt*-rebus. The tiles consist of white, blue, green, and red faience inlays set into a faience matrix. The *rekhyt*-rebus consisting of an adoring lapwing and the cartouche of Ramesses III is shown on one tile (OIM E16721); another depicts the wing of a lapwing above the *nb*-basket (OIM E16719); and the third contains the upper part of an adoring lapwing (OIM E15488). The three fragments are from a doorway within the mortuary complex of Ramesses III at Medinet Habu and functioned as a representation of the *rekhyt*-people within the temple, perpetually adoring the cartouche of the pharaoh.

Decorated faience tiles once adorned the base of the jambs flanking at least one doorway within this complex at Medinet Habu, with a small number still being in place during the late nineteenth century (Lewis 1882, pp. 180–81). The three fragmented tiles in this exhibit, along with many other inlays, were excavated at the western fortified gate of the temple, although their original location is undetermined. Similar tiles are also known to have come from the doorway leading from the first courtyard of the temple to the king's palace. Modifications to this doorway indicate that the decoration was originally executed in sunk relief. However, later in the king's reign, the jambs were recarved to accept the more elaborate faience inlays (fig. C2). While these tiles have since become detached, with many finding their way into various museums, the original relief decoration has survived beneath (Hölscher 1951, pp. 10, 40–44, pls. 5, 35c, 38c; Epigraphic Survey 1932, pls. 62, 66).

The tiles come in the form of the *rekhyt*-rebus, which is composed of three main elements, the most important of which is the lapwing itself, believed by many scholars to represent the "common people," "subjects" of Egypt. The lapwing squats atop a *nb*-basket (⌒), the hieroglyph meaning "all." The lapwings have human hands raised in adoration while a small star, which carries the same meaning of adoration, is placed directly in front of the birds to reaffirm this action. The whole composition thus reads "all the *rekhyt*-people adore the Lord of the Two Lands, Usermaatre-Meryamun (Ramesses III)."

Faience tiles in the form of the *rekhyt*-rebus have also been excavated from the palace of Ramesses III at Tell el-Yahudiya,[1] suggesting that the doorjambs there were also adorned with similar friezes (Lewis 1882). Additionally, the bases of two columns from the private apartments within the palace of Merenptah at Memphis contain friezes of lapwings in the form of the *rekhyt*-rebus that were originally filled with faience or a similar decorative paste.

The lapwing is one of the earliest and most easily identifiable birds in Egyptian art, being depicted both in hieroglyphs and reliefs from the protodynastic period through to the Roman period. It is still possible to identify two species of lapwing, both of which are crested, that were present in pharaonic times. The northern lapwing (*Vanellus vanellus*) can be identified by a solid breast-band (fig. C3; see also fig. 9.10). The upper wings and back of this species appear black, although in reality it is a glossed blue-green color. The northern lapwing breeds in parts of Europe, northern Asia, the Middle East, and Morocco and can still be found wintering

FIGURE C2. Fragments of the inlaid work from the palace doorway at Medinet Habu with decorated tiles depicting worshipping *rekhyt*-birds, and reconstruction of this doorway (Hölscher 1951, pls. 5, 38d)

in Egypt, particularly in the Nile Valley, the Delta, the Fayum, along the Mediterranean Sea coast west of Alexandria, in the vicinity of the Suez Canal, and the Dakhla and Siwa Oases. The black-headed plover (*Vanellus tectus*) can be identified by the lack of a breast-band (see fig. 9.11). The upper wings and back of the black-headed plover are a sandy color while the head is black, interrupted by white on the forehead, lower face, and across the rear of the head and nape. This species currently occurs only in the sub-Saharan Sahel region of North Africa, from the Atlantic Coast right through Sudan and Ethiopia to the Red Sea.

Doorways with friezes of *rekhyt*-people, either in the form of the lapwing or anthropomorphic figures, are well attested within the temples of the New Kingdom through to the Roman period, including the sites of Abydos, Karnak, Luxor, and Dendera (Griffin, forthcoming). The *rekhyt*-people are consistently represented in the form of the rebus flanking these doorways, including the doors of the sanctuary, with their arms raised in adoration (fig. C4). Contra Bell (Bell 1997, pp. 163–71; Griffin 2007), the rebuses should not be interpreted as an indicator of public accessibility but instead they should represent the metaphysical presence of the *rekhyt*-people within the temple. Additionally, the rebuses functioned as animated compositions, with the *rekhyt*-people perpetually adoring both the pharaoh and the deities residing within the temples. In doing so, the *rekhyt*-people not only guarantee their own existence, but also that of the entire cosmos, the principle concept that forms the basis of all decoration within the Egyptian temple. KG

FIGURE C3. Northern lapwing (*Vanellus vanellus*) (photo by David Cottridge)

PUBLISHED

a. Teeter 2003, cat. no. 29
b. Green et al. 2012, cat. no. 21d
c. Hölscher 1951, p. 44, pls. 35c, 38d

NOTE

[1] See, for example, British Museum, London, EA 12967 and 12979, Metropolitan Museum of Art, New York, 17.194.2336.

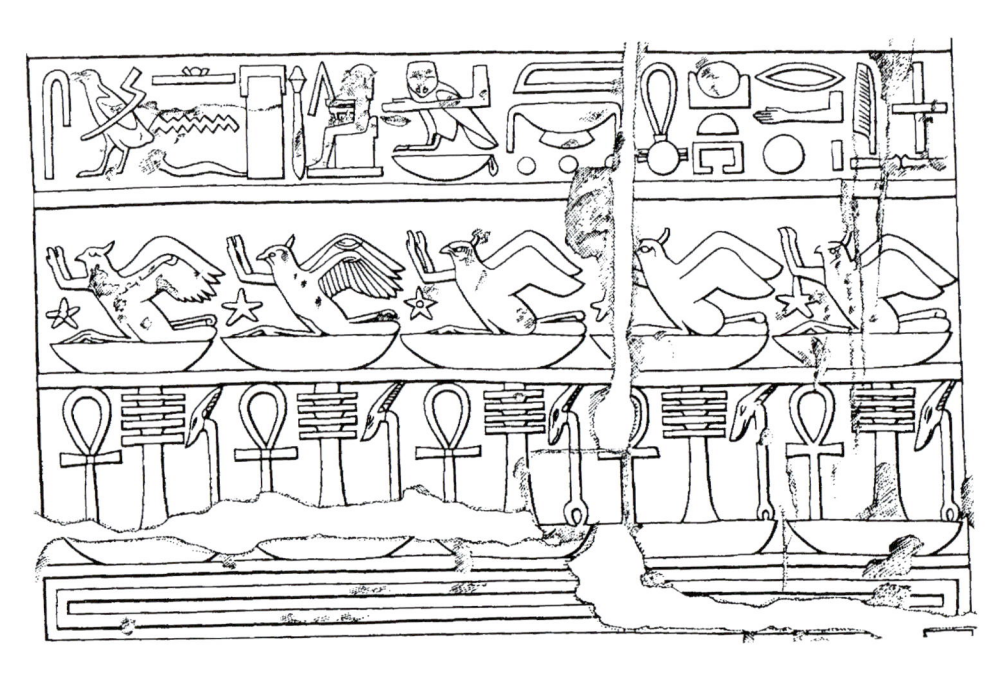

FIGURE C4. Frieze of lapwings in the form of the *rekhyt*-rebus from the southern doorjamb of the portico within the temple of Khonsu at Karnak. Reign of Nectanebo II (ca. 360-343 BC) (Epigraphic Survey 1981, pl. 131b)

CATALOG NO. 7

BIRDS AS PROTECTION IN LIFE

Personal expressions of Egyptian religion extend well beyond the better known elite funerary productions of inscribed texts, coffins, and mummification. Far more common are amulets, small-scale protective images worn by individuals of all social levels, occupations, and regions. Correspondingly, these portable witnesses of religious belief vary in material, expense, and design. Bird deities figure prominently, conveying to the possessor the vulture's destructive nature recast as motherly care (Mut), with the raptor's rending habits made defensive guardianship (Horus), and the probing skill of the wading ibis (Thoth) conferring wisdom and Truth (Maat) upon his devotee. Implements of household protection draw upon these same amuletic images for localized zones of protection, most typically the bedroom, where the sleeper is potentially vulnerable to noxious animals, night terrors, and demons of disease. Amulets and implements retained their value after the death of the owners, and were interred with them for similar protection in the afterlife. RKR

7. THOTH REBUS AMULET

Carnelian
Date uncertain, possibly post-New Kingdom to Greco-Roman period, 11th century BC to 3rd century AD
Purchased from Mohareb Todrus in Luxor, 1920
4.1 × 2.8 × 0.7 cm
OIM E10537
Oriental Institute digital image D. 17935

Represented as a striding ibis crowned by a lunar crescent and full moon, the god Thoth appears on the hieroglyph for a basket while the feather of Maat stands below his beak. By rebus, the composition of the amulet actually can be "read" as

FIGURE C5. Thoth and Maat feather on a standard

Ḏḥwty nb Mȝʿ.t "Thoth, Lord of Truth," incorporating a standard epithet of the god of wisdom.[1] The design of this amuletic pendant highlights two of the primary aspects of Thoth: his role as moon deity, through his healing the injured lunar eye (*wedjat*) of Horus, and his position as the divine scribe at the underworld court of Osiris, where he records the verdict when the heart of a deceased individual is weighed against the feather of Maat. Thoth's title on this piece is paralleled by others that stress his link to Maat during judgment.[2] Without the additions of crown and basket, this image resembles more common depictions of the god and feather placed upon a divine standard (fig. C5).[3] The combination of the Thoth ibis and Maat exists at least by the Third Intermediate Period, but may be earlier,[4] and it continues into Roman times. A date for the Chicago example is uncertain. Carnelian (Egyptian *ḫrs.t*) was considered one of the more important gemstones by the Egyptians. It was regularly used for amulets, particularly the *wedjat*-eye of Horus,[5] which may have contributed to its selection for this amulet depicting the healer of that eye. When acquired by the Oriental Institute, the figure was attached as a pendant on a string of faience beads,[6] alternating between blue and white, the latter covered in gold foil. As the string is modern, it is questionable whether these beads are part of the original arrangement. RKR

NOTES

[1] The epithet appears in a range of contexts, from the New Kingdom Book of the Dead to Late Period healing statues and Ptolemaic temple reliefs; see Boylan 1979, p. 188; Leitz 2002, vol. 3, pp. 639–42, esp. 640 §A.v (and cf. citations 169, 93, 23, 245, and 197).

[2] For the related epithets *sš Mȝʿ.t* "scribe/recorder of Truth," *wp Mȝʿ.t* and *wḏʿ Mȝʿ.t*, both indicating "who determines Truth," see Boylan 1979, pp. 53–55.

[3] See Arnold 1995, p. 30 (relief inlay); Petrie 1914, p. 49 and pl. 42:247a and d (amulets); and Daumas 1988, vol. 3, pp. 318–19, nos. 531–45 (hieroglyphs).

[4] See Andrews 1994, p. 49. Amulets in metal of a striding ibis atop a standard (without Maat) appear already in graves of the First Intermediate Period.

[5] See Harris 1961, pp. 120–21.

[6] The beads are composed primarily of silicon dioxide (quartz) with some calcium and, as colorant for the blue beads, copper. I thank Oriental Institute conservator Alison Whyte for this analysis. For discussion of terminology, see Nicholson 2000.

8. THOTH AND MAAT AMULET

Green glazed composition
Date uncertain, possibly post-New Kingdom to Greco-Roman period, 11th century BC to 3rd century AD
Gift of Alfred, E. P., and Guy Maynard, 1925
3.3 x 2.4 x 1.3 cm
OIM E12244
Oriental Institute digital image D. 17974

8

9. THOTH AND FEATHER AMULET

Green glazed composition
Date uncertain, possibly post-New Kingdom to Greco-Roman period, 11th century BC to 3rd century AD
Gift of Elizabeth F. Cheny, 1970
1.2 x 9.0 x 1.6 cm
OIM E25011
Oriental Institute digital image D. 17996

9

Images of Thoth with either the goddess Maat (Catalog No. 8) or her feather (Catalog No. 9) supporting his beak are common in statuary, amulets, hieroglyphs, and even as painted decoration on the wooden coffins of ibis mummies.[1] The ibis is typically crouching with his beak upon the feather, so that the combination produces a rebus for related titles of the god that indicate both Thoth's physical posture and his "consumption" of Truth: ḥtp ḥr Mȝʿ.t "satisfied with/resting upon Maat"[2] and ʿnḫ m Mȝʿ.t (rʿ nb) "who lives by means of Truth (every day)."[3] RKR

NOTES

[1] For examples of a crouching ibis with Maat (or feather), see Houlihan 1996, p. 161 (statuary); Andrews 1994, pp. 25 and 49 (amulets); Petrie 1914, p. 49 §247 and pl. 42 (amulets); Daumas 1988, vol. 2, p. 320, nos. 563, 565, 571, 573, and 577 (hieroglyphs); and Ikram 2005a, pl. 6:1 (opposite p. 162) (ibis coffin).

[2] Leitz 2002, vol. 5, p. 573; and Boylan 1979, p. 193.

[3] Leitz 2002, vol. 2, pp. 144–45.

10

10. APOTROPAIC KNIFE

Hippopotamus ivory
Middle Kingdom, ca. 1600 BC[1]
Purchased from Mansour Mahmoud
in Luxor, January 24, 1920
23.1 × 3.6 × 1.0 cm
OIM E10788
Oriental Institute digital image D. 17954

The apotropaic (Greek for "turning back/warding off") knife was an object common to nurseries of the Middle Kingdom.[2] Carved from a hippopotamus tusk, the ivory knives are engraved with a series of knife-wielding figures including the goddess of childbirth, Taweret, and the vulture goddess Nekhbet. Though often described as "wands," the pieces are counterparts to the knives held by the deities depicted upon them. Inscribed examples state that the divine figures provide "protection by day and protection by night." By both their material and decoration, the knives are closely associated with the hippopotamus Taweret, and thus with the protection of mothers and newborn children.

On the basis of style, the Chicago example has been assigned to Middle Egypt,[3] but the prominent use of vultures indicates influence from Upper Egypt as well.[4] Signs of ancient breakage[5] or — as here — wear suggest that they may have been used to draw protective circles in the sandy floor around a child's bed. Such knives were also included among tomb offerings, so that they might ensure the rebirth of their deceased owner. Use of the knives continued into the New Kingdom, as indicated by representations on the rear wall of the Eighteenth Dynasty tomb of Bebi at El Kab, where three female figures (one designated "nurse") hold such knives to create a protective perimeter about the tomb owner and his wife.[6]   RKR

PUBLISHED

Ranke 1936, pl. 321 (smaller example); Altenmüller 1965, vol. 1, p. 63, and vol. 2, cat. no. 31, pp. 29–30; Teeter and Johnson 2009, cat. no. 55; Teeter 2011a, fig. 72

NOTES

[1] Altenmüller 1965, vol. 2, p. 30, dated with parallels. The authenticity of the piece has been challenged by E. F. Venk (personal communication, e-mail of 3/5/12), but without evidence.
[2] For other examples, see Ritner in Silverman 1997, cat. no. 77, with further bibliography; Ritner 2008, pp. 176–77; Ritner 2006, pp. 212–13; Petrie 1927, pp. 39–43, pls. 36–37.
[3] Altenmüller 1965, vol. 1, p. 63. The central lotus bundle is also characteristic of Middle Egypt; see ibid., pp. 163–64.
[4] Altenmüller 1965, vol. 1, pp. 50, 162–63; Petrie 1927, pl. 36:7 and 10, and pl. 37:15.
[5] Altenmüller 1965, vol. 1, pp. 12–13.
[6] Ritner 2008, pp. 176–77; Ritner 2006, pp. 212–13.

FOWLING IN THE MARSHES AND AVICULTURE

Ancient Egyptians were surrounded by a large variety of bird species, whose numbers were greatly increased during the spring and fall migrations (see Catalog No. 11). In addition to wild birds, farmyard fowl such as ducks, geese, and, much later in Egyptian history, chickens, were most likely wandering in the streets and passages of every village, just as it is the case in modern Egypt. While not as frequent in the diet as fish, poultry was indeed included among the common dishes available to the majority of the population. Zooarchaeologists have uncovered evidence indicating that, as early as the late Paleolithic period, the inhabitants of the Nile region were already catching some of the migratory birds stopping in the local wetlands. Fowling continued to be common practice during the predynastic and historic periods, as demonstrated by the frequency of its representation in the tombs of the elite, thus indicating that ancient Egyptians wished to enjoy poultry in the netherworld just as they did in their lifetime. Single birds could be caught with a throwstick (see Catalog Nos. 12 and 13) or a spring trap. Clap-nets, in the expert hands of fowlers, allowed for the capture of large numbers of waterfowl in the marshes of the country (fig. C6). When hunting was no longer sufficient to provide the fowl needed for all the religious and funerary offerings, as well as the kitchens of the ancient Egyptians, birds were gathered in farmyards and reared in captivity, which eventually led to the domestication of the greylag goose (*Anser anser domesticus*) (see Catalog No. 14). When settling in Egypt in the fourth century BC, the Greeks, and later the Romans, brought with them their culinary taste for pigeons and doves. Large dovecotes then became landmarks in the countryside and remain so to this day. RBL

FIGURE C6. Clap-netting scene in the Middle Kingdom tomb of Khnumhotep II, at Beni Hassan (Rosellini 1834, pl. 7; special thanks to the Special Collections Research Center of the University of Chicago Library)

11. "BIRDS IN AN ACACIA TREE"

Nina de Garis Davies, 1932
Tempera on paper
46.36 x 55.9 cm
Collection of the Oriental Institute
Oriental Institute digital image
D. 17882

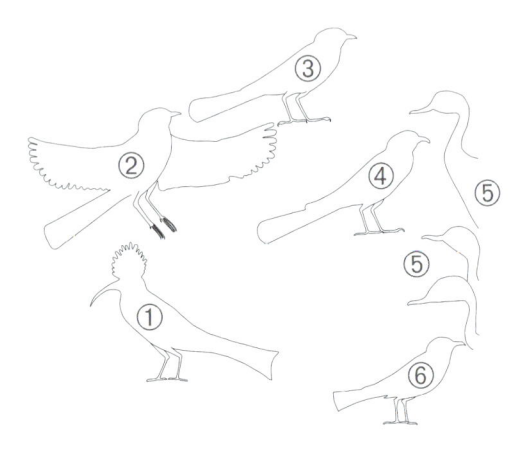

FIGURE C7. Legend to Catalog No. 11. (1) Hoopoe (*Upupa epops*), (2) immature and (3) adult masked shrike (*Lanius nubicus*), (4) red-backed shrike (*Lanius collurio*), (5) drake pintails (*Anas acuta*), (6) redstart (*Phoenicurus phoenicurus*)

Nina de Garis Davies, in the company of her husband Norman, dedicated the season of 1931–1932 to working in the Middle Kingdom elite tombs of Beni Hassan. Her main goal was to copy the large and imposing fishing and fowling scene that occupies the east wall in the tomb of Khnumhotep II (ca. 1878–1837 BC).[1] When writing his report for the *Metropolitan Museum of Art Bulletin*, Norman de Garis Davies declared that, as a whole, the scene is "a fine example of Middle Kingdom painting and as regards certain details is of quite superlative merit and attractiveness." One of the charming details de Garis Davies undoubtedly had in his mind is the composition reproduced so faithfully by Nina, "Birds in an Acacia Tree," which was chosen as the cover illustration for this report (Davies 1933). It is but a part of a much larger clap-netting scene painted above the doorway leading into the shrine. The main protagonist of the scene is the tomb owner, seated behind a screen and holding the rope that has closed the clap-net, previously installed on a pond and now filled with a variety of waterfowl. On either side of the pond, the artists who decorated the tomb included some unique and very attractive details such as two acacia trees filled with colorful songbirds,[2] either roosting, unaware of the chaos taking place in the pond, or taking flight. Nina de Garis Davies focused her attention on the larger of the two trees,[3] depicted standing behind the fowler's screen and growing on the edge of the pond whose water is symbolized by black zigzag lines, seen in the bottom right corner of the scene pictured here.

As elegantly described by Davies herself, this acacia tree is "shown flowering instead of seeding, the sweet-scented little yellow balls being distributed amongst the delicate pale-green foliage decoratively arranged around the brownish stems" (Davies 1936, vol. 3, p. 23). Perching[4] on its branches are a hoopoe (*Upupa epops*),[5] an adult male masked shrike (*Lanius nubicus*), and a red-backed shrike (*Lanius collurio*), all birds that are commonly observed in such an environment (fig. C7). A humoristic touch or mark of inattention was left by one of the tomb painters: the male common redstart (*Phoenicurus phoenicurus*) was painted as if standing on the back of a drake pintail (*Anas acuta*), instead of perching on a branch. Another bird, an immature masked shrike, is depicted in flight, perhaps joining the other birds and ready to also settle on a branch or, as suggested by Linda Evans in Chapter 10, this flying bird may be trying to intimidate and chase the other masked shrike from its territory.

Although the artists were constrained by the principles of Egyptian art, which gives an overall stiffness to the scene,[6] they exploited the palette of colors at their disposal and attempted to represent the colorful plumage and characteristic features of these bird species as accurately as possible. Their efforts have allowed us to readily identify these birds, which, except for the hoopoe, are rarely attested in Egyptian art. The more frequent occurrence of the hoopoe in art can easily be explained by its status as a breeding resident in the country. Ancient Egyptian artists had the opportunity to carefully examine all year long this attractive bird, with its black-tipped erect crest and long, slender curved bill. On the other hand, the two species of shrikes and the redstart, represented here in their breeding plumage, are passage migrants, only briefly stopping in Egypt. The accurate representation of many of the characteristic fieldmarks of these birds testifies to the talents of observation of the artists at work in this tomb, who had but rare chances to see these bird species in their surroundings. The immature shrike can be differentiated from its adult counterpart by the presence of black markings on its flanks. The redstart, whose cinnamon-colored tail gives the bird its name,[7] is also beautifully rendered.[8]

This remarkable scene, as well as many of the other wall paintings in the tombs of Beni Hassan, can now be admired in the new color publications that were issued after the removal of the dark "curious natural film," as described by de Garis Davies, that had accumulated over the millennia (Shedid 1994; Kanawati and Woods 2010). However, prior to these recent publications, Nina Davies's work was the standard reference, along with that of F. L. Griffith, for scholars wishing to view the scenes in color. When comparing her tempera to these new photographs, one cannot but gain a greater appreciation for the accuracy of her work despite the challenges she had to face, such as poor lighting and the presence of a "grey mist" over the wall paintings.[9] RBL

PUBLISHED (SELECTED)

Davies 1933, cover; Davies 1936, vol. 1, pl. 9; vol. 3, pp. 23–24

NOTES

[1] Tomb no. 3 in Beni Hassan.

[2] I thank John Wyatt for identifying precisely the bird species in this scene.

[3] The other acacia tree is reproduced in color as the frontispiece to Griffith 1900.

[4] It is interesting to note that none of the roosting birds are represented as grasping the branch they are perched on. Their long toes, instead of being wrapped around the branch, are simply painted flat, as if standing on the ground. This is also the standard pose of birds in the hieroglyphic writing system.

[5] John Wyatt, personal communication: "It is possible that this is the representation of an African hoopoe (*Upupa africana*), rather than the Eurasian hoopoe (*Upupa epops*) because of the overall color and crest markings."

[6] These birds have been described as resembling stuffed specimens in a museum. See Frankfort 1929, p. 23, which compares this scene with the marsh representations in the wall paintings at Amarna. However, this severe description is not shared by the majority of Egyptologists; many have described this scene in the most laudatory terms: "the group [of birds] ... is exceptionally charming" (Davies 1933, p. 24); "one of the most charming pieces of observation on the part of an ancient painter and a fine instance of the naturalistic impulse that remains constant near the surface in all Egyptian works" (Smith and Simpson 1998, p. 112).

[7] "Start" comes from Old English "steort" and Middle English "stert," which designates the tail of an animal.

[8] For a detailed description of these bird species, see Houlihan 1986, pp. 118–19, 126–28, 134–35.

[9] Davis wrote on the back of this tempera: "Beni Hasan 12th Dynasty. The wall has rather more grey mist (a result of salt coming through the colours) but slight damping shows the colours as bright as I have painted. Nina de G. Davies 1932" (Carswell 1978, cat. no. 6).

12

12. FOWLING THROWSTICK

Wood
Dynasties 17 and 18(?), ca. 1575–1400 BC
Purchased in Akhmim(?), 1894–95
56.5 × 6.2 × 0.5 cm
OIM E370
Oriental Institute digital image D. 17898

The hyper-arid climate of Egypt and the location of many cemeteries at the desert margins are all favorable conditions for the preservation of organic material. As a result, a large array of weapons made of wood has been discovered in tombs. They complement the evidence provided in representations of hunters and fowlers, which frequently feature in funerary and religious iconography. Among these weapons is the throwstick, attested in the archaeological record as early as the Naqada III period (Ritner in Teeter 2011b, p. 242). The numerous scenes that depict the king and members of the elite bringing down geese and ducks by means of a throwstick (fig. C8; also see Catalog No. 13) have led Egyptologists to conclude that these weapons were for the most part used to catch waterfowl. Several shapes are represented in these scenes, many of which resemble the hieroglyph) (later)).[1] The design of OIM E370 is closer to that of a modern boomerang. Some similar artifacts have been discovered in Theban elite tombs of the Seventeenth and early Eighteenth Dynasties (ca. 1570–1400 BC), most famously in the tombs of Senenmut and King Tutankhamun, among an arsenal of hunting weapons (Hayes 1959, pp. 211–12; Carter 1927–33, vol. 3, pp. 141–42 and pls. 76–77; see Ritner in Teeter 2011b, p. 242 n. 5).

This throwstick was carved from the center of a log of hardwood and fashioned so as to have a slight curvature and tapered edges. The wider, thicker, and heavier end of the stick would have been grasped by the hunter. When hitting prey at high speed, this simple apparatus would have been a powerful and most likely deadly weapon. It has been suggested that fowling with this type of weapon was a leisure activity of elite men who could thus demonstrate their ability to strike such fast-moving targets as flying birds. It would have constituted a good training exercise for members of the military, allowing them to develop their dexterity and reflexes.[2]

The Egyptian elite are not the only people depicted handling throwsticks. Some hunters on predynastic palettes[3] and in tomb representations, such as that of Khety from the Eleventh Dynasty,[4] are shown wearing feathers in their hair and grasping a throwstick in their hand. Such a headdress is later attributed in Egyptian art to Nubian and Libyan warriors (Teeter 2010b, p. 3). Ancient Libyans are known to have hunted ostriches using these simple weapons, as clearly stated in a hymn to Mut: "Let us take for her feathers of the back(s) of ostriches, which the *tmhy.w*-Libyans slay for you with their throw sticks, their straps being of leather ..." (Darnell in Friedman et al. 1999, p. 28).

It is difficult to say how widespread the use of the throwstick was. It is not the most efficient method of capturing birds, since a successful hit requires great skill and a thorough knowledge of the prey's behavior to anticipate its movement. Its presence in funerary contexts could suggest that it had become a status symbol for ancient Egyptians,[5] a reminder of the hunting skills of those able to enjoy a life of leisure, but also a proof of their military might. RBL

NOTES

[1] Gardiner numbers T14 and T15. See Decker and Herb 1994 for an overview of fowling scenes. Examples of such style of fowling stick are Metropolitan Museum of Art, New York, 12.182.67; Museum of Fine Arts, Boston, 12.1242, from the Middle Kingdom; and Metropolitan Museum of Art, New York, 19.3.166 and 36.3.204, from the Seventeenth and Eighteenth Dynasties.

[2] The presence of other fowling implements, such as bronze stunning bolts and arrows with blunt tips, in elite tombs of the New Kingdom may be further proof of this theory, as explained by Hermann Genz (2007). Bronze stunning bolts are attested in Egypt only during the New Kingdom. Arrows with blunt tips, also referred to as wooden bumper arrows, may have been used in Egypt as early as the First Dynasty and are also found in tombs of the Eighteenth Dynasty (Staley et al. 1974, pp. 355–56).

[3] In particular the Hunter's Palette from the Naqada III period (Patch 2011, cat. no. 115).

[4] Metropolitan Museum of Art, New York, 26.3.354-3 from the tomb of Khety (TT 311) at Deir el-Bahari, on the west bank of Thebes, dated from the reign of Mentuhotep II (ca. 2009–1959 BC).

[5] Throwsticks, either as actual weapons or as models, have been recovered in the tombs of almost every king of the Eighteenth Dynasty and early Nineteenth Dynasty (Loeben 1987, p. 146).

FIGURE C8. Tomb owner Menna fowling in the marshes with his family. He seemingly has many throwsticks at his disposal, since several have already hit their targets above the papyrus thicket. Two designs of fowling sticks can be identified: type 1, resembling the hieroglyph), further adorned with a snake design, and type 2, similar to OIM E370. Thebes, tomb of Menna (TT 69) (Davies 1936, vol. 2, pl. 54)

NINA DE GARIS DAVIES'S FACSIMILES FROM THE PAINTED TOMB-CHAPEL OF NEBAMUN

Nina de Garis Davies executed a series of tempera facsimiles of fragmentary wall paintings held at the British Museum. These had been removed in the early 1800s from the Theban tomb of Nebamun, a scribe and grain accountant in the granary of the divine offerings of Amun; the tomb location, however, was not recorded and is now lost. The style, choice of scenes, and color palette, as well as the draftsmanship employed in these scenes, have led art historians to surmise that the walls of this tomb were painted during the New Kingdom by the same artist or group of painters who worked in the tombs of Nakht (TT 52) and Menna (TT 69) (Kozloff 1992, p. 272), suggesting that Nebamun lived during the reigns of Thutmose IV and Amenhotep III (ca. 1400–1353 BC) (Parkinson 2008, p. 41). RBL

13

13. "FOWLING IN THE MARSHES"

Nina de Garis Davies, ca. 1932
Tempera on paper
97 x 83 cm
Collection of the Oriental Institute
Oriental Institute digital image D. 17883

Nina de Garis Davies successfully captured and conveyed the mastery of the artist who executed this fowling scene in the tomb-chapel of Nebamun.[1] The tomb owner, in the company of his wife Hatshepsut and his daughter, dominates the scene, not only because of his larger scale and his active stance, but also because of his luminous skin color. With his left foot forward on the wooden deck of his papyrus skiff, he is ready to hurl a snake-headed throwstick toward the birds flushed from a papyrus thicket. He brandishes three cattle egrets (*Bubulcus ibis*) with his right hand, which most likely symbolize the decoys often used in fowling expeditions to attract wild birds flying by (Parkinson 2008, p. 124). A remarkable polychrome inscription painted around Nebamun and his wife describes the scene; it is further summarized in a short column of black hieroglyphs written before Hatshepsut:

> Taking enjoyment; seeing the good things and the deeds of the god of the trap, the works of the Marsh goddess, Sekhet, by the one praised by the mistress of hunting, by the scribe and grain accountant [in the granary of Amun in the estate of Amun, Nebamun, justified] and his [beloved] wife, [mistress of the house], Hatshepsut. (Manniche 1988, p. 151)

The protagonists are taking part in this expedition in the marshes elegantly dressed and adorned. Nebamun, with a wig typical for men of this period, is wearing a short white loincloth covered with a longer but thinner overkilt. Holding onto his left leg, and looking toward her mother, a daughter of the couple, depicted naked and with a side-braided lock typical of youth, is adorned with a gold collar with a floral border, armlets and wristlets, as well as a pendant in the shape of a lotus flower. The most elegant of the party is undoubtedly Hatshepsut, with an elaborate wig topped by a perfume cone and lotus blossoms. She wears a pleated full-flowing garment that reveals her form.[2] Her costume is further adorned by gold earrings, collar, and wristlets. With a bouquet of lotus flowers kept close against her chest, she holds a sistrum and *menat*-necklace, ritual implements used to celebrate the cult of Hathor, the goddess of fertility and sexuality, commonly associated with marshes.

The tomb artists applied the same delicate mastery in representing the flora and fauna as they did the protagonists in the scene. To the left of the scene, a thick clump of papyrus, with buds shown opening in full bloom as they rise toward the sky, is filled with vibrant activity. An overzealous cat (*Felix silvestris libyca*), perched on two stems, has caught three birds: a wagtail (*Motacilla* sp.)[3] is imprisoned by the cat's hind paws; his front claws hold onto another songbird,[4] while he simultaneously bites into the wing of a pintail duck (*Anas acuta*). As the skiff is getting closer to the papyrus thicket, an Egyptian goose (*Apolochen aegyptiaca*)[5] appears to be guarding its prow (fig. C9). Painted with its beak open, it seems to be honking and sending further alert to the surrounding birds. The texture of the plumage is rendered with small red strokes and the eye ring is indicated by black dots. The artist did not fail to paint the bill's serration and dark tip. The characteristic black spot on its chest is represented in profile.

Roosting in the midst of crescent-shaped nests, each holding two eggs, a little egret (*Egretta garzetta*), a juvenile African finfoot (*Podica*

FIGURE C9. Egyptian geese (*Apolochen aegyptiaca*) (photo by Jonathan Rossouw)

FIGURE C10. Legend to the birds in front of Nebamun. (1) Little egret (*Egretta garzetta*), (2) juvenile African finfoot (*Podica senegalensis*), and (3) little bittern (*Ixobrychus minutus*)

senegalensis), and a little bittern (*Ixobrychus minutus*) (see fig. C10) have not felt threatened enough to fly away, although several ducks have already taken wing. Another songbird, just before Nebamun, attempts to avoid the deadly throwstick. The air is not just filled with birds, but also with fluttering butterflies, all African monarchs (*Danaus chrysippus*), with delicate orange and black wings elegantly rendered. Finally, the waters are just as teaming with life: in the midst of lotus blossoms and water weeds, many species of fish are swimming below the waterline.[6]

The many studies dedicated to elucidating the meaning of this composition offer several interpretations for the scene. As the caption recapitulates, it may depict a pleasant recreational time spent in the marshes that the elite wished to further enjoy in the hereafter. The tomb owner, in his best garb, shows his ability to skillfully throw his weapon to kill birds, which could become tasty sustenance in the afterlife. Other scholars argue that only a symbolic reading of the scene is plausible: while Nebamun is ridding the world of the forces of chaos symbolized by the wild birds of the marshes, his wife Hatshepsut is depicted in an attractive and erotic fashion, celebrating the cult of Hathor in the primeval environment of the marshes from which the world emerged and is reborn every year after the Nile flood fertilizes the black land of Egypt.[7] However, as R. Van Walsem rightly suggested, the two interpretations are not mutually exclusive. Both readings of recreational provisioning of food and the sexual symbolism scattered in the scene are "part of the complete range of messages that are transmitted by different (pictographic) language games in such themes" (2005, p. 79). RBL

PUBLISHED (SELECTED)

Davies 1936, vol. 2, pl. 65, vol. 3, pp. 125–27; Parkinson 2008, pp. 122–32 (on the original fragment)

NOTES

[1] I thank John Wyatt for identifying precisely the bird species in this scene. Original fragment now in the British Museum (EA 37977; 83.0 x 98.0 cm). The British Museum owns eleven fragments from the tomb of Nebamun, most of which were purchased in 1823. See Strudwick 2006, pp. 170–77; Parkinson 2008.

[2] I thank Aleksandra Hallmann for her advice on the clothing worn by the various figures in this scene.

[3] Houlihan (1986, p. 126) and Parkinson (2008, pp. 127–28) suggest that the bird is a white wagtail (*Motacilla alba*). The facial pattern supports this identification, but the back appears to be all black, thus making the African pied wagtail (*Motacilla aguimp*) an alternative possibility. However, some details validating these suggestions are missing, such as the breast-band, thus making straightforward identification challenging (John Wyatt, personal communication).

[4] Shrike species have been proposed.

[5] This bird, sacred to Amun, survived the iconoclastic frenzy of the followers of Akhenaten, which is not the case in many other Theban tombs, such as that of Nakht (TT 52).

[6] This fowling scene was complemented on the other side of the papyrus clump by the traditional spearing of two fish. The end of the spear can be seen in the left-hand corner of the scene, as it enters the water. The fragments depicting Nebamun fishing tilapia and lates fish in the company of his son were in the Benzion collection, then the Egyptian Museum, Cairo; their present location is unknown. See reconstruction of the scene in Parkinson 2008, fig. 137.

[7] The lotus flower is a common symbol of rebirth found throughout Egyptian funerary iconography, whose role is to multiply the chances of the deceased to live anew in the hereafter. The erotic undertone is also to be seen in the goose, often metaphorically used in love poetry to portray the lover taken in the snares of the girl he is attracted to. The cat doubly acts as an apotropaic character, defeating the enemies of the sun god during the hours of the night, but also as a sensual creature associated with Hathor. See Hartwig 2004, pp. 103–06, for a detailed review of the "fishing and fowling" motif in funerary contexts, and Parkinson 2008, p. 132, for the detailed interpretation of Nebamun's fowling scene.

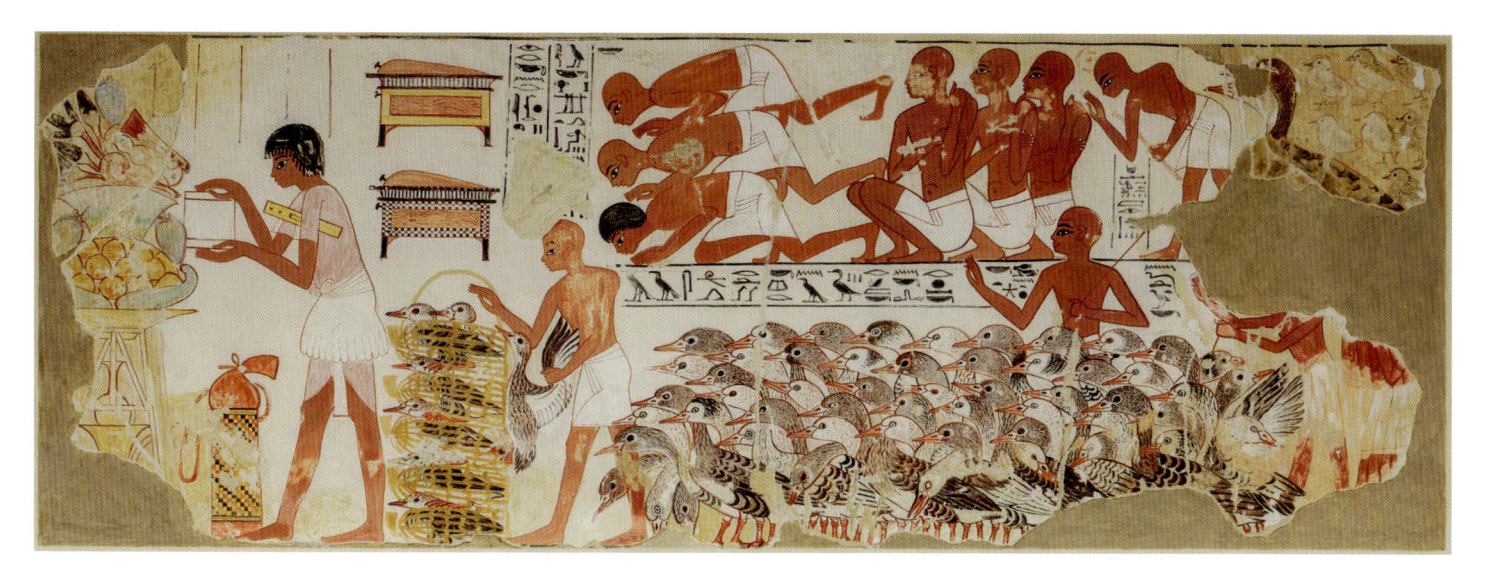

14. "FARMERS DELIVER THEIR QUOTA OF GEESE"

Nina de Garis Davies, 1932
Tempera on paper
41.28 x 114.30 cm
Collection of the Oriental Institute
Oriental Institute digital image D. 17884

In this tempera, Davies partly reproduced the presentation of geese[1] to the tomb owner, Nebamun, who is depicted on another fragment detached from this scene, seated on a stool and wearing the elaborate garb indicative of his status in society.[2] At the left of the present fragment,[3] a pile of food offerings, with fruits and vegetables topped by a bouquet of lotus flowers, has been placed in a bowl on a wooden stand before the tomb owner to provide him with sustenance while inspecting the flocks of his estate. A metal ewer and bowl would have allowed him to wash his hands. Standing to the right of the wooden stand, a scribe, equipped with his leather kit bag, the wooden chests holding the papyrus rolls keeping track of the accounts, and his scribal palette tucked underneath his arm, has opened a roll of papyrus with the intention to read it to Nebamun. However, the text, which would have been painted above him, was never written — the vertical text columns have been left blank. This scribe, wearing a wig, kilt, overkilt with scalloped edges, and a diaphanous tunic suggestive of his status,[4] is followed by workers of more humble status, depicted at a smaller scale with simpler clothing more fitting for their occupation. Except for one man, the eight characters shown behind the scribe all have shaved heads. The wig of the remaining worker may have been a mark of his higher status, distinguishing him as their overseer. They are all represented showing respect and greeting their master, either by kissing the ground, holding their right hand to their heart while clasping their left shoulder with their left hand, or simply raising their right hand and bowing their head.

While no caption in this facsimile describes the activity — the extant text records the various speeches and calls expressed by these servants of Nebamun (Guglielmi 1973, pp. 155–56) — it is clear that the object of this gathering was the presentation of the flocks from Nebamun's aviaries.[5] Numerous birds have already been placed in baskets from which their heads and webbed feet stick out. Some of these crated waterfowl display a small knob on their bill, an indication that they might be immature or female knob-billed ducks (*Sarkidiornis melanotos*). A female pintail duck (*Anas acuta*), being held by its wing, is going to join others in the top crate.

The main tableau of the scene is the elaborately and vibrantly painted flock of geese. The artist cleverly represented the movement and confusion of the flock by overlapping the birds, depicting them looking in various directions. Some of them, in the foreground, can be seen pecking at the ground, having spotted some providential food; a few of them look back toward the herdsmen. Most of the birds are keeping their head up in a thick flock, and the artist varied the colors of the plumage to avoid monotony: some have gray heads with black highlights; others have white heads with red highlights. A few birds have black patches in the front or back of their heads; even their eye color varies: either gray, black, or red. The covert feathers in their wings are depicted by scalloped lines, followed by straight lines for the secondary and primary wing feathers. Their scaly legs with their thick knees are outlined in red and painted yellow. The lower section of the scene, which would have included their webbed feet, has not survived.

The presentation of birds to the tomb owner is already attested as part of the Old Kingdom funerary repertoire: a variety of birds — ducks, and geese, as well as doves, pigeons, and cranes — are often labeled with a hieroglyphic caption and are led under the supervision of a herder (see Chapter 1). The scene in the tomb of Nebamun is unique in a few respects. First, this artist was successful not only in representing a visually appealing scene, but it also seems that he wanted to convey the sense of cacophonous activity that would have been inevitable with such a gaggle of geese honking all together. A few geese herders are attempting to keep some order with their long wooden sticks — one is represented in their midst, while two more are closing behind the flock to prevent any bird from escaping. Furthermore, this is the only depiction of goslings shown in such a setting.[6] These goslings closely follow their parents and have thus most likely hatched in captivity. Note that this group of parent geese and goslings is separated from the rest of the flock and is painted on a different register. This scene has been interpreted as proof that the domestication of the greylag goose (*Anser anser domesticus*) had taken place by this time, further conveyed by the variety of colors in the plumage of the many geese from Nebamun's estate.[7] This lively representation is of special interest not only because of its undeniable artistic qualities, but also because it reveals that a large number of workers were involved in the management of Nebamun's flocks, from the scribe keeping count of the birds to the herders in charge of feeding and maintaining them.   RBL

PUBLISHED (SELECTED)

Davies 1936, vol. 2, pl. 67, vol. 3, pp. 128–29; Parkinson 2008, pp. 92–105 (on the original fragment)

NOTES

[1] I thank John Wyatt for identifying precisely the bird species in this scene.

[2] The fragment held at the British Museum, EA 37978, includes an additional register with a second flock of geese being registered by a seated scribe. Two servants are also depicted carrying baskets, possibly filled with eggs.

[3] For a reconstruction of the whole tableau, see Parkinson 2008, fig. 101.

[4] I thank Aleksandra Hallmann for her advice on the clothing worn by the various figures in this scene.

[5] Parkinson 2008, p. 97 and fig. 7: in the faded register Davies chose not to copy, a caption recorded on a tracing from the nineteenth century of this scene mentions that the goose herd "(will) make an inspection of birds at the turning year."

[6] Goslings or ducklings are also depicted in the New Kingdom Theban tomb of Horemheb (TT 78), but in baskets among other offerings to the deceased. See Brack and Brack 1980, pl. 34a. For the most part, young birds are represented in marsh scenes, nestled in a nest built on a papyrus clump, under the supervision of their parents, or threatened by a marauding mongoose or genet.

[7] According to A. Gautier, variations in the skin, fur, and plumage in domesticated animals are numerous and in general allow us to differentiate them directly from their wild counterparts (1990, p. 49).

BIRD MOTIFS IN ANCIENT EGYPTIAN ARTS AND CRAFTS

Every year, during fall and spring, the Egyptian wetlands became overcrowded with huge flocks of waterfowl migrating back and forth between Sub-Saharan Africa and Eurasia. As Pascal Vernus remarked, during the flood, Egypt was a "gigantic duck pond" (Vernus and Yoyotte 2005, p. 358). Some of these birds opted to stay in Egypt for the duration of the winter to benefit from the warm temperatures. Egyptian artists thus had innumerable models from which to draw inspiration, as well as the leisure to perfect their art and abilities. Thus, Irtisen, one of the few artisans known by name, from the reign of the Eleventh Dynasty king Mentuhotep II (ca. 2009–1959 BC), claimed to be able to represent different types of birds: "I know the posture of the male statue and the appearance of the female, the attitude of eleven birds [of prey] ..." (Stela Louvre C 14; Barbotin 2005, pp. 56–57).

The painted walls of tombs give us a glimpse of the colorful variety of birds that were encountered in the Egyptian marshlands, among which ducks and geese are the most abundant. These waterbirds were especially imbued with complex symbolism. The throngs of waterfowl became a literary metaphor for bustling multitudes, and on temple and tomb walls they came to be identified as creatures outside of the area of control of the king. For the ruler of the Two Lands who was responsible for reinstating and maintaining *maat*, that is, order and balance in the country, the forces embodied in the birds had to be brought under control and managed. The king, in the company of deities, became the fowler capturing these wild birds in his clap-net.

Bird imagery could be interpreted in other ways. The predictable biannual arrival of flocks of birds covering the wetlands with variegated colors was also viewed as a promise of regeneration and rebirth in the afterlife, thus explaining their very frequent inclusion on the tomb walls of the offering chapels of the Egyptian elite. The inclusion of ducks and geese in these scenes of daily life may have served several purposes. At a pragmatic level, they provided tasty food for the afterlife, and their presence also guaranteed the deceased's rebirth.

The challenges of capturing these elusive winged creatures, always ready to take flight and escape when feeling threatened, may have been the inspiration of the poetic association of a lover with a goose that the young lady tries to ensnare in her net or trap (Derchain 1975; Peterson 1987; Schlichting 1994; Teeter 2010a, pp. 164–66). This imagery was also transferred to the decoration on more mundane objects, such as vases, bowls, and cosmetic boxes (Peterson 1987, p. 25). Thus, in a marshland setting, the depictions of ducklings and goslings, when carefully held in the arms of a young woman (fig. C11), were filled with multilayered symbolism. On the one hand, this may be an allusion to the moment of creation, when the duckling hatches from the egg on the primeval mound that had emerged from the watery Nun, thus guaranteeing the promise for a new life. But it can also refer to the young bird as being the young man whose love has been captured by the beautiful and elegant maiden,[1] a discrete reference to the sexual potential of the deceased in the afterlife (Derchain 1975, p. 64).

Birds fluttering in the marshes also were common motifs on palace walls (for example, those of

FIGURE C11. Young woman holding a duckling. Detail from "Fowling in the Marshes," Thebes, tomb of Nakht (TT 52) (Davies 1936, vol. 1, pl. 47)

Amenhotep III at Malkata, and of his son, Akhenaten, at Amarna), appearing as the vision of an ideal landscape with the wildlife of the wetlands, whose watery expanses brought freshness into the arid desert where these palaces were located.

As a source of food, a symbol of wild and vibrant forces, or a reference to rebirth and love, it is this rich symbolism, in addition to a simple appreciation for a graceful motif drawn from nature, which may have further motivated ancient Egyptian artists to include this motif so frequently and in so many different contexts, from the walls of tomb-chapels and palaces, as well as in objects used daily in the houses of the ancient Egyptian elite (fig. C12).

For the sake of simplicity, in the following entries the bird depicted is referred to as a duck. However, the stylized form of the motif in many cases does not allow such a precise identification, and any species of ducks and/or geese may be intended.[2]   RBL

NOTES

[1] Robins 1990, p. 47. The role of the woman in this context is to allude to sexuality, potential fertility, and her role in childbirth.

[2] Adler 1996, pp. 64–69 suggests that, depending on the type of artifact, ducks (*Anas* sp.), geese (*Anser* sp.), swans (*Cygnus* sp.), and mergansers (*Mergus* sp.) are possible models used by artists.

FIGURE C12. Gold vases decorated with bird motifs. Wall painting from the Theban tomb of Sobekhotep (TT 63; ca. 1397–1388 BC) (Davies 1936, vol. 1, pl. 43)

15. STONE JAR IN THE SHAPE OF A DUCK

Red breccia
Naqada III, ca. 3200–3100 BC
Purchased in Cairo, 1920
29.0 × 19.0 × 10.0 (rim diameter) cm
OIM E10859
Oriental Institute digital image D. 17969

Birds enter the iconographic repertoire of the inhabitants of the Nile Valley at least as early as the Late Palaeolithic period, 15,000 years ago, as demonstrated by the presence of *Anatidae* (ducks, geese, and swans) in the Qurta petroglyphs (Huyge and Ikram 2009, pp. 162–64). Artists of the predynastic period also adapted this motif and included it in the design of slate palettes of the late Naqada I–Naqada II period, on which eye pigments were ground, either by carving the top edges as a

FIGURE C13. Goose swimming in the water (iStockphoto.com / © Pavle Marjanovic)

pair of bird heads, or by giving the object a stylized avian form.[1] Ivory combs destined to adorn the hair of women in ancient Egypt could also be delicately carved in the shape of ostriches or ducks (Patch 2011, pp. 58–59). Birds and cosmetic implements thus seem to be already closely connected in prehistoric Egypt. The repertoire of avian art also included three-dimensional objects, especially vases in the shape of ducks, either in clay[2] or in stone.

This red breccia duck-shaped vase is one of the rare examples of zoomorphic stone vessels dated to the Naqada III period.[3] It is testimony to the talent of the stone-workers of this period, who were able to carve and manipulate this hard and colorful stone to give it an exquisite modeling.[4] It represents a swimming duck, whose extended neck and slightly tilted tail indicate that it is crossing the waters (fig. C13), and one does not need much imagination to see the ripples it would create behind it as it swims in the Nile River or the marshes of the valley.

Its round head is summarily shaped, with two small eye depressions, which may have been originally filled with inlays. The short wide beak is delicately incised to delineate the upper and lower mandibles, but the nostrils are not marked. Similarly, the artist chose not to indicate the bird's plumage. Two pierced tubular handles may have been used to keep the vase suspended, perhaps in a domestic setting. The provenience of this exquisite item is unknown. However, most of the artifacts from the predynastic period come from a funerary context. It is thus possible that the vase had been deposited in the tomb of an elite member of society. It cannot be excluded that it had beforehand been used in a house, perhaps to contain oils and ointments.[5] It has also been suggested that the symbolic value attached to the animal represented in the shape of the vessel, in this case the waterfowl as a symbol of fertility and rebirth, "may have imbued its contents with magical qualities of strength or healing" (Dreyfus 2005, p. 242). RBL

PUBLISHED

Glubok 1962, p. 48; Marfoe 1982, p. 21; Teeter 2011b, cat. no. 46

NOTES

[1] For example, the guineafowl palettes; see Germond 2001, p. 23, fig. 18; Stevenson 2009, pp. 2–4, figs. 2, 5, 7; Patch 2011, cat. nos. 29 and 30.

[2] For example, duck-shaped bowl from the Naqada IC period, Museum of Fine Arts, Boston 09.379 (Patch 2011, cat. no. 31); Decorated Ware in the shape of a duck from the Naqada II period, Petrie Museum of Egyptian Archaeology UC 15354 (Graff 2009, p. 380).

[3] Another impressive example is the ibis/flamingo vase, Ägyptisches Museum und Papyrussammlung, Staatliche Museen zu Berlin, 24100 (Patch 2011, cat. no. 33); another duck-shaped vessel is in the British Museum, EA 35306.

[4] Breccia, being such a hard stone, is abandoned after the Old Kingdom in favor of Egyptian alabaster (calcite).

[5] Diana Craig Patch suggests that Ägyptisches Museum 24100 may have been a donation to a temple rather than a funerary item, in part because of the vase's size and the elegant carving in such a hard stone (Patch 2011, cat. no. 33). One can also wonder if the shape of the container may be a clue as to its original content, that is, this duck-shaped vessel may have been intended to contain bird fat. However, this is merely a hypothesis and is impossible to verify based on the nature of the evidence. One can surmise, however, that the quality of the vessel indicates that it was most likely used to store a valuable commodity. Furthermore, as noted by Renée Dreyfus, "many [of the animal vases] are also beautifully crafted, exhibiting the practical skill, artistic sensibility, and humor of the artists who made them. Indeed, it seems quite likely that these vases were valued as much for their visual appeal as for their usefulness" (2005, p. 242).

16. COSMETIC DISH DECORATED WITH DUCK MOTIFS

Blackened steatite
New Kingdom, most likely Dynasty 18, ca. 1539–1292 BC
7.7 × 7.2 × 1.6 cm
Collection of the Art Institute of Chicago. Gift of Charles L. Hutchinson, Henry H. Getty, and Norman W. Harris
AIC 1894.610

During the New Kingdom, particularly in the Eighteenth Dynasty, decorative art reached a high level of refinement testifying to the technical advances and mastery of the craftsmen, who had become proficient in manufacturing exquisite objects in many different media.[1] They often strove to combine functionality and visual appeal in articles of daily life, often drawing inspiration from floral and faunal motifs. Waterfowl, which regularly filled the sky and the waters of the Nile Valley, was a favorite design in their iconographic repertoire. This charming cosmetic dish was most likely manufactured during this period. A block of soft steatite was carved into the shape of what at first glance appears to be two ducks. Their heads, with carefully incised details, are turned back so that their necks curve to the side along the edges and frame the top of the dish. The artist only hinted at the birds' plumage, by including a ring at the base of each of their necks and a few indentations around it. Only one leg is represented for each bird, with the splayed webbed feet summarily depicted and no indication of a hind toe. The section of the bowl that would have included the tail has been broken away. Most of the underside's surface is covered with zigzag lines in low relief, a traditional

FIGURE C14. Sleeping duck on the water (iStockphoto.com / © Liang Zhang)

graphic representation of water in ancient Egyptian art.

As seen with Catalog No. 15, the duck motif was often incorporated in objects related to hygiene and the care of the body, important to all Egyptians, men and women alike.[2] This small cosmetic dish, which could be held in the palm of a hand, may have been used to mix unguents and perfumes, to prepare hydrating salves for the skin, or to prepare oil and pigments as paint that protected one's eyes from the glare of the sun or from the sting of insects. Many of these exquisite articles were discovered in tombs of the elite who wished to use them in the afterlife. Abrasions and other markings suggest that they had also been used during the life of the deceased before being placed in the tomb (Fay 1998, p. 32).

Art historians have pondered the meaning of the avian motif on these objects and how it relates to the private life of ancient Egyptians (Hornung and Staehelin 1976, pp. 135–37; Robins 1990). Was it purely aesthetics that motivated artists to copy these attractive and delicate motifs from nature? Was there some erotic undertone conveyed by the duck and the cosmetics used both for hygiene and adornment? Ducks and waterfowl, present in large numbers in the wetlands of the Delta and the Nile Valley, are also a common symbol of regeneration and rebirth. Furthermore, many of the New Kingdom duck-shaped dishes are in the form of a trussed waterfowl, an intriguing motif for a cosmetic item.[3] Their discovery in funerary assemblages has led scholars to conclude that their role would have been manifold: the deceased was provided with food in the afterlife in the form of trussed birds ready for consumption, and he was also guaranteed renewed sexual vigor and thus rebirth, which is implied by the presence of the waterfowl, inhabitant of the marshes, the quintessential place for creation and domain of the goddess Hathor.

But are the birds depicted on the Art Institute bowl in fact trussed fowl?[4] Their wings are not visible, thus hinting that they may have been removed. Their heads could be interpreted as lying to the side, as is often depicted in piles of offerings destined to appease the gods and the dead. However, how does one explain the presence of water, in the form of zigzag lines? Comparative studies on similar cosmetic dishes[5] reveal that feathers and wings are in some cases carefully carved on the surface of the bowl, thus refuting the hypothesis that these birds are shown ready for consumption. Hermann's suggestion that ducks with their head turned back are depicted as sleeping[6] may be applied to the motif carved on this bowl. In fact, all evidence suggests that the sculptor of this dish was attempting to depict only one duck, resting on a pond with its image reflected in the calm waters (fig. C14). This conclusion may be more appealing to our modern tastes and sensitivities than the use of trussed poultry for cosmetic items. RBL

PUBLISHED

T. G. Allen 1923, p. 95

NOTES

[1] See in particular Roehrig 2005, pp. 191–259; Kozloff et al. 1992, pp. 331–451; Markowitz and Lacovara 1999.

[2] Such a motif for cosmetic spoons is already attested for the early dynastic period (ca. 2900–2545 BC) and remains popular for the entire pharaonic era. See Patch 2011, cat. no. 164.

[3] Fay 1998, pp. 28–29. See, for example, Museum of Fine Arts, Boston, 72.43006; Metropolitan Museum of Art, New York, 40.2.2a and b, 40.2.3; Brooklyn Museum, 11.665.

[4] In his study of vessels with duck motif, Wolfgang Adler identified the birds depicted on similar objects as being dead (Adler 1996).

[5] See von Bissing 1904, pl. 8, CGC 18561 and 18562; item no. 4169 in the Egyptian Collection of Hilton Price (1908); bowl in the collection of E. and M. Kofler-Truniger, Luzern (Paszthory 1992, fig. 4).

[6] Hermann 1932.

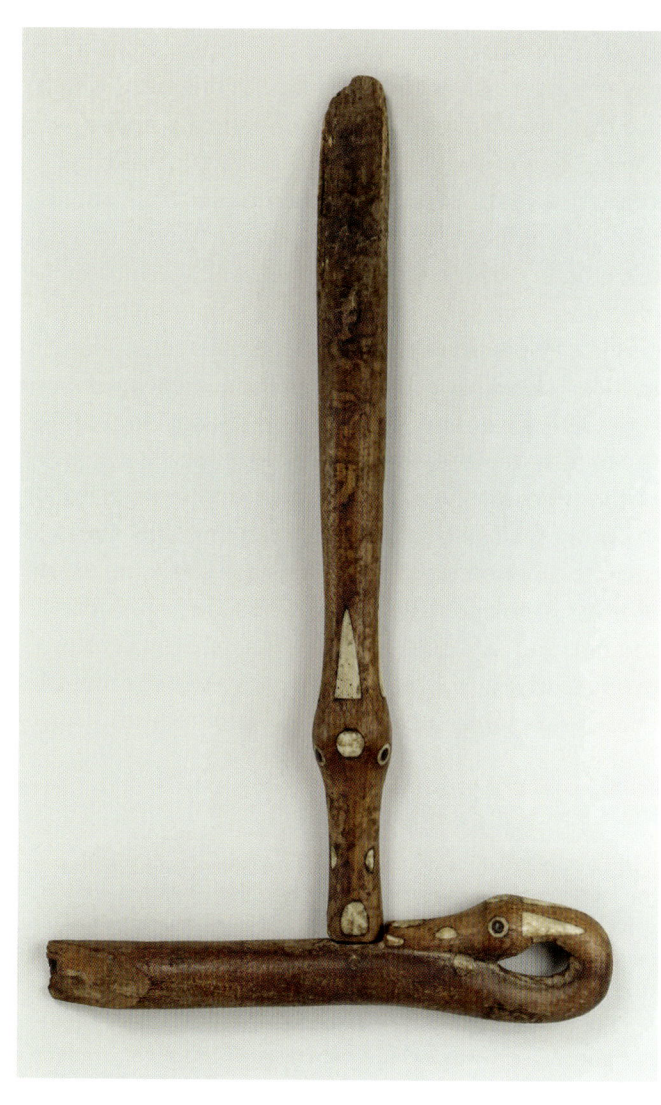

(ca. 1980–1760 BC). Folding stools were originally designed for practical purposes, so as to be easily stored and transported in military camps. They were then adapted by the elite and became a status symbol (Romano 2001). This trend may have started during the reign of Thutmose III, whose numerous military campaigns and conquests in the Levant and Nubia are recorded on the walls of Karnak Temple in Thebes. Folding stools were most likely used on a regular basis during these campaigns by military officials who accompanied the king and brought the design back home. They later became popular for the members of the New Kingdom elite, in particular during the Eighteenth Dynasty, as attested by the frequency of its representation in Theban tombs of this period, and by the discovery of intact stools in the tombs of Kha and Meryt (TT 8) and King Tutankhamun (Baker 1966, pp. 134–35; Killen 1980, pp. 40–43; Museum of Fine Arts, Boston 1982, cat. no. 41).[1]

Two types of folding stools incorporate the duck motif. The stool with four duck heads biting onto a plain base rail is the most common and is considered the classic representation of the style. The second type is characterized by four duck heads carved onto the ends of the folding legs joined to base rails, whose ends are also decorated with duck heads turned backward (fig. C15) (Wanscher

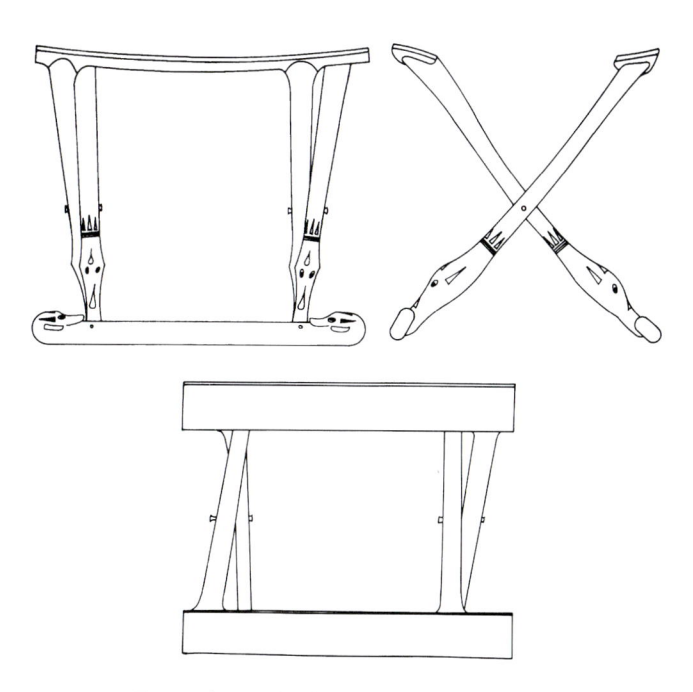

17

17. FRAGMENTS OF A STOOL WITH DUCK HEADS

Nakkeru wood (*Cordia myxa*), ivory, ebony
New Kingdom, ca. 1539–1077 BC
Purchased in Cairo, 1920
A: 26.0 × 2.6 × 5.2 cm;
B: 35.0 × 3.0 × 3.0 cm
OIM E11198A–B
Oriental Institute digital image D. 17971

Stools were the most common type of seating in ancient Egypt and were included among the furnishings of all Egyptian households. These two wooden fragments, carved with ducks' heads, used to be part of a cross-legged folding stool, a piece of furniture first attested in the Middle Kingdom

FIGURE C15. Frame of a wooden folding stool. BM EA 29284, from the tomb of Ani, Thebes, Eighteenth Dynasty (after Killen 1980, fig. 41)

1980, pp. 20, 55–61, 64–66).[2] The stool from which fragments OIM E11198A–B came belonged to the latter group and thus included a total of eight duck heads in its design. The two pairs of legs would have swiveled around a bronze rivet. They were joined to the base rail by a system of mortise and tenon, secured by a short dowel, and positioned in such a way that the end of the leg met the bill of the base's duck. Each head is inlaid with three triangular pieces of ivory,[3] most likely intended to imitate the plumage and markings of the bird. Two additional circular ivory inlays were inserted at the top of the head and the tip of the bill. Two small semi-circular inlays represent the bird's nostrils. Finally, the eye rings are indicated by small circles of ivory, with an ebony iris. This style of folding stool also included two rectangular seat rails onto which a flexible piece of leather was attached, and which could collapse when the stool was folded. Sitting could be made more comfortable by the use of linen cushions filled with feathers from waterfowl or pigeons.

Cedar or other imported wood was favored for the manufacture of these seats, most likely because of the status associated with imported material. These fragments are said to be of Nakkeru wood (*Cordia myxa*), native to Egypt, probably treated with wax or resinous oils to protect its natural surface (Wanscher 1980, p. 38). If local wood was indeed used in the fabrication of this stool, one can surmise that it might have belonged to a lesser official, or was used as a regular item of the house and was later placed in the tomb as part of the funerary assemblage.

Other folding stools from this period are decorated with lions' paws, associating the power and strength of the animal with that of the owner of the stool and granting dignity to the person seated upon it. Another common motif of footrests used by royalty are the nine bows or bound enemies, which are thus under the feet and symbolically under the control of the king. Similarly, by choosing the attractive motif of a duck's head to decorate these types of folding stool, the artist may have implied the mastery of the stool's owner over the forces of chaos symbolized by the birds, which he could display by placing his foot on the base rails. The motif of the duck with its head turned backward can represent a sleeping duck, as seen in Catalog No. 16. It can also depict a slaughtered bird, as clearly seen in the hieroglyph [4] standing for the word *snd*, meaning fear, in this case the fear that one wants to impose on enemies to maintain *maat*. The inclusion of these stools in funerary assemblages reinforces the notion that, for the tomb owner to obtain the promise of a new life, he must master the forces of chaos and maintain his power of procreation. RBL

NOTES

[1] The combination of the dry climate of the Theban region and the location of the tombs in the limestone cliffs of the west bank have contributed to many of these organic and perishable materials remaining essentially intact to this day (Wanscher 1980, p. 12).

[2] In the Theban tomb of Ken-amun (TT 93), such a stool with eight duck heads was included among the goods to be brought to the royal treasury, along with a footstool (Davies 1930, pl. 17). Complete examples of this style of folding stool are: British Museum, London, EA 29284, from the tomb of Ani; Metropolitan Museum of Art, New York, 12.182.49 and X.387; Royal Ontario Museum, Toronto, 914.2.1; and Musée du Louvre, Paris, AF 1849 and AF 6350.

[3] The ivory could either be from elephant or hippopotamus tusks.

[4] See Hermann 1932, p. 87.

18. LADLE

Bronze
Coptic period, 3rd–9th centuries AD
Purchased in Abydos(?), 1894–95
32.0 × 3.7 × 3.5 cm
OIM E70
Oriental Institute digital images
D. 17886–87

18, detail

Ladles were common utensils in the ancient world, used to draw liquid from deep jars storing water, oil, or wine (Oliver 1977, p. 43). This bronze ladle has a very simple, yet elegantly proportioned form, with a small egg-shaped bowl. Its long handle, rising vertically, bends at the top to form a hook that would have allowed the ladle to hang on the rim of a large container. The end of this hook is shaped like the head of a duck. The details of the bird's head are only summarily rendered, with grooves indicating the eye sockets and meeting at the base of a flat and broad bill. This design constitutes the only decoration on the utensil.

Similar duck-headed implements are attested in Egypt as early as the Twenty-first Dynasty with a silver ladle discovered in the tomb of King Psusennes (ca. 1051–1006 BC).[1] They remained popular until the Greco-Roman period and were adopted by the Coptic community, used both in daily life during banquets, and in the celebration of the cult, with which the communion could be served (Benazeth 1992, pp. 66–67).

This style of ladle thus had a long history and a wide geographic distribution. Called *kyanos* in Greek and *simpulum* in Latin, it was a popular item in Etruria during the fifth century BC,[2] in Greece during the fourth through third centuries BC,[3] and also in imperial Rome (27 BC–AD 476).[4] It was commonly used to draw wine, which would subsequently be poured through a strainer, also adorned with the same avian motif on its handle. Duck-headed ladles were also excavated in Nubian cemeteries of the Meroitic period (ca. 300 BC–AD 400).[5] The motif of the backwards-turned duck head decorating metal objects can be traced at least to the late Middle Kingdom (ca. 1700 BC) in the Levantine port of Byblos (Montet 1928, p. 185, cat. no. 706). It continues to be popular in Syria-Palestine in the

New Kingdom as evidenced by the beautiful gold ornament composed of two duck heads framing a head of the goddess Hathor, uncovered in the tomb of King Idanda at Qatna (ca. 1340 BC).[6] It should be noted that the principle of using a duck head as a hook also occurs during the New Kingdom in Egypt as beautifully illustrated by the gold necklaces holding the heart scarabs belonging to the three foreign wives of King Thutmose III (ca. 1479–1425 BC).[7] The ends of the thick golden wire are modeled as thin bird heads, delicately incised with the features of an *Anatidae* (goose, duck, or swan). It remains uncertain whether Syrian goldsmiths accompanying the foreign queen introduced the pattern in Egypt, or whether it simply constitutes another adaptation of a very common design during Eighteenth Dynasty Egypt, that is, the motif of the duck with its head turned backward, as shown in Catalog Nos. 16 and 17.[8] Nevertheless, one can only marvel at the success of this simple design, which was used with only limited modification[9] for more than two millennia all around the Mediterranean basin and in Nubia.[10] Because of the widespread distribution of this item, it is challenging to assign any significance to the use of the duck motif other than pure aesthetic appeal of a graceful design. One can also surmise that, since this implement was used both in a culinary context and as part of rituals, the notion of fowl as food and offering may have been the inspiration and justification for the endurance of this decoration motif. RBL

NOTES

[1] Montet 1951, pp. 99, 102, fig. 41. The name of the king is carved on the bowl. Montet also recorded finding a bronze ladle in a Late Period house at the site of Tanis; Petrie (Petrie and Mackay 1915, p. 35, pl. 30:3) discovered a ladle for the most part similar to OIM E70 in a tomb he estimated to be dated from the Twenty-third through Twenty-fifth Dynasties.

[2] For example, British Museum, London, 1868.0606.4 excavated near Bolsena, Italy.

[3] See Crosby 1943; Delemen 2006, p. 263, fig. 11.

[4] See Harcum 1921, p. 41, fig. 3; p. 43, fig. 4. Some of the ladles have handles with hinges or a joint, for example, Roman bronze *simpulum* Metropolitan Museum of Art, New York, 1988.11.1, dated to the second century AD.

[5] For example, British Museum 51474, excavated in Faras, in the Meroitic cemetery (grave 1092); Museum of Fine Arts, Boston, 23-3-702, excavated at Meroe.

[6] I thank Jack Green for bringing this fascinating material to my attention.

[7] Metropolitan Museum of Art 26.8.91, 144, 145 (Lilyquist 2003, cat. nos. 16–18, and fig. 103).

[8] Hermann (1932, p. 100) refers to several metal spoons from the Eighteenth Dynasty, one of which was excavated at Amarna and is now in the Ägyptisches Museum und Papyrussammlung, Berlin, 22149 (pl. 11a). Scenes of offerings and gifts in the tombs of Ken-amun (TT 93) (Davies 1930, pl. 18) and Rekhmire (TT 100) (Davies 1935, pl. 18) also display spoons with their handle terminating with a duck head. Lilyquist (1998, p. 27), when describing the duck-head motif, differentiates "between passive (dead, trussed, sleeping, or resting) and active waterfowl (birds with head up, oriented frontally or turned back." She assigns the active bird with head turned back as being of Canaanite origin. The lack of detail of the bird's head on this ladle does not allow us to say if it depicts an active or passive duck.

[9] The shape of the bowl can vary and is usually shallower in Greek models; the stem of the handle can also be rectangular, with a slight flare at the shoulder.

[10] The waterfowl motif as an adornment for metal implements also spread eastward, possibly from Egypt, as evidenced by a silver spoon with a delicately curved handle terminating with a duck head turned backward, discovered in Iran at the site of Pasargadae dated to the second half of the Achaemenid period (ca. mid-fourth century BC). I thank Jack Green for this information.

BIRDS IN THE WRITING SYSTEM

The hieroglyphic writing system is one of the most attractive, but also most intriguing, features of ancient Egyptian culture. For more than 3,500 years, rows and columns of small figures were written on papyri and carved and painted on temple and tomb walls, stelae, and official monuments.[1] The early Egyptians who devised this writing system drew their inspiration heavily from their surroundings and from the natural world. Among the approximately 800 signs in regular use until the Ptolemaic period, birds are well represented, with sixty-five different signs incorporating numerous species of birds, in a variety of positions and activities, as well as parts of birds.[2] These are all gathered in sections G and H of Alan H. Gardiner's sign-list in his *Egyptian Grammar* (Gardiner 1957, pp. 467–74 and 545) (fig. C16). Most of the birds are depicted in profile, in a stylized fashion, in accordance with the canon of Egyptian art. But one bird, the owl, stands out for it is one of the few hieroglyphs represented facing the viewer, since that is, after all, its most characteristic, expressive, and impressive point of view (fig. C17). Either painted with vibrant colors or carved with minute details, some hieroglyphic representations can be considered ornithological masterpieces, displaying the talents of both the scribe and the sculptor at their best.

As stated by Peter Kaplony (1972, p. 3), "the Egyptian is with his whole being a visual person, a friend of images, not only in art, but also in speech and script."[3] Hieroglyphs are not simply components of the Egyptian writing system, such as letters in the Roman alphabet. Each sign is a miniature image, whose efficacy could be unleashed magically, just like any other artistic representation depicted on walls. In a funerary context, "where fear conquers reality" and where "deepest fears, reality and magic commingle,"[4] the signs of animals deemed to be potentially dangerous for the deceased were modified and attempts were made to render them harmless. At times, only part of the animal is depicted, such as the head, and this section stood for the whole. For example, in some Middle Kingdom version of the funerary collection of spells known as the Coffin Texts, 𓄿 is written for 𓅂, 𓅓 for 𓅐, and so forth (Lacau 1914, p. 41). In other instances, signs are mutilated and parts of the animal's body are removed, such as legs and feet; for example, 𓅮 for 𓅭 (Picardo 2004, p. 14). Weapons, especially knives and arrows, could be added, piercing the animal sign. Even seemingly inoffensive birds such as a quail chick suffered this kind of graphic mutilation.[5] "Due to its iconicity, the hieroglyphic sign is kept oscillating between the word and the world" (Goldwasser 1995, p. 80).[6]

A selection of three limestone plaques with the relief decorations of a quail chick, a house martin, and a falcon, as well as a small sculpture in the round of an owl's head, showcase the talents of ancient Egyptians in representing bird hieroglyphs. These objects, unfortunately with no provenience, are labeled sculptors' models, or votive plaques, and are dated from the Late Period to early Ptolemaic period (see also Catalog No. 5). For several decades art historians have debated whether these are models and practice pieces executed at sculptors' workshops (Young

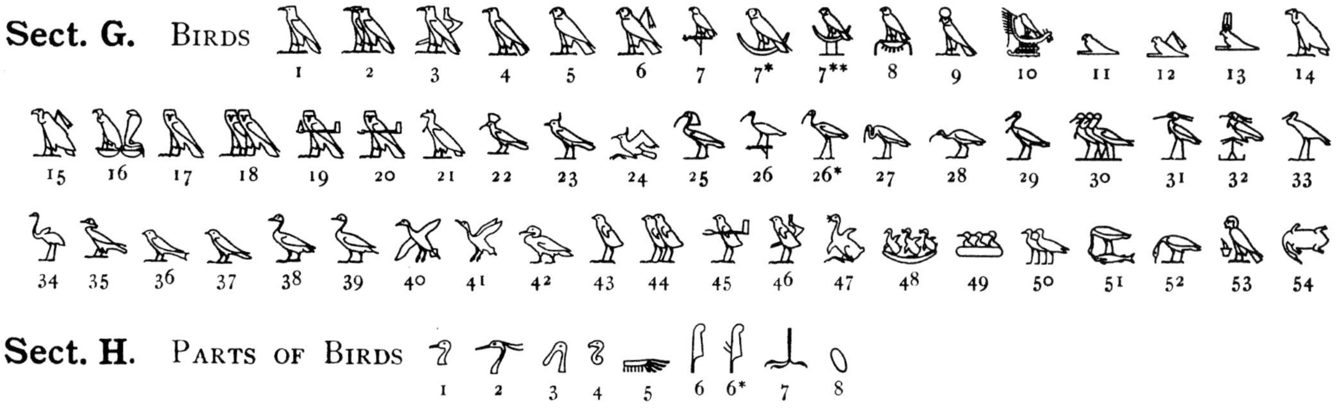

FIGURE C16. Sections G (birds) and H (parts of birds) from Gardiner's sign-list (Gardiner 1957, p. 545)

FIGURE C17. Owl hieroglyph painted on a wooden coffin (from Davies 1936, vol. 1, pl. 6)

1964; Tomoun 2005), or whether they are votive offerings deposited in temples by fervent worshippers (Bothmer 1953). No consensus has yet been reached (Hill 2009). RBL

NOTES

[1] For the emergence of hieroglyphic writing and its development in ancient Egypt, see the section on the Egyptian language in Woods 2010. The last known hieroglyphic inscription was carved at the temple of Isis on Philae Island in AD 394.

[2] Mammals and parts of mammals account for eighty-seven signs; amphibious animals and reptiles, sixteen signs; fish and parts of fishes, seven signs; invertebrates and lesser animals, seven signs.

[3] The author's translation of the German.

[4] Goldwasser 1995, p. 79 and n. 46.

[5] Lüscher 1990, pp. 64–65.

[6] For more on birds, and animals in general, in the Egyptian writing system, see Vernus and Yoyotte 2005, pp. 62–75.

19. PLAQUE SHOWING A QUAIL CHICK

Limestone
Late Period–early Ptolemaic period, 664–150 BC
Purchased in Cairo, 1919
12.0 x 13.2 x 1.3 cm
Collection of the Art Institute of Chicago, Museum Purchase Fund
AIC 1920.256

19

A quail chick (*Coturnix coturnix*), meant to represent the letter *w*,[1] is delicately executed in low relief on this small limestone block. It is shown looking to the right, standing on a projecting platform that forms the lower right-hand corner of this square plaque. The L-shaped projection present in the upper left corner has been interpreted as a device of the sculptor to indicate the depth of the relief (Young 1964, p. 248). James H. Breasted, who purchased this plaque in 1919 on behalf of Charles Hutchinson, president of the Art Institute of Chicago, described his acquisitions as follows: "Some of the pieces are very fine because they are permanent model studies on which the artist spent much time."[2] The quality of this piece leads one to assume that this is the work of a master craftsman who is demonstrating the extent of his talent by attempting to reproduce in stone the characteristic features of the tiny chick. He did not spare any effort in carefully carving in deeper relief the short beak, placing emphasis on the gape at its base, usually more visible in hatchlings than in adult birds. The modeling of the legs and feet is remarkable. The carving of the fragile bones and joints, the disproportionately large feet and long claws typical of young birds appear so anatomically accurate that one wonders if the artist, eager to improve his skills, had an actual bird at his disposal for close examination.

The bird on this relief is not a recent hatchling, but rather a fledgling. The presence of primary feathers that are starting to grow on the underdeveloped wings indicates that the chick is at least a few weeks old. The engraving is so fine

FIGURE C18. Head of a quail chick hieroglyph on a fragment of relief from the temple of Mentuhotep II (ca. 2009–1959 BC) at Deir el-Bahari, Thebes. OIM E9189 (D. 17922; photo by Anna Ressman)

that the shaft of each feather, or rachis, as well as the barbs attached to it can easily be identified. Nevertheless, most of the chick's body is still covered with down, which the artist has alluded to by pecking the smooth surface of the limestone all over the breast, side, and head of the bird. He did not fail to depict the typical black markings of a quail chick, shown as small ovoid outlines scattered on the bird's plump body, and in particular the eye streak and the circular design on the bird's ear covert. Such markings are often added in paint in many hieroglyphic inscriptions (fig. C18). The only possible inaccuracy in this representation is the rendering of the long black stripes present on the chick's plumage on either side of its spine (fig. C19), which confusingly appear here as a large feather all along the bird's back.[3] This does not take away by any means from the overall quality of this piece.   RBL

PUBLISHED

T. G. Allen 1923, pp. 44 (ill.), 46; Marfoe 1982, p. 20

NOTES

[1] Gardiner G43. Houlihan 1986, p. 77: "The hieroglyph can be recognized during the early dynastic period, but it is not until the beginning of Dynasty IV that we can firmly establish the identity of the bird as being a young Common Quail."

[2] Letter from J. H. Breasted to Ch. Hutchinson, Cairo, December 4, 1919.

[3] In some other examples of such representations, the dorsal stripe is represented by striations, rather than the feather motif depicted on this piece. See Metropolitan Museum of Art, New York, 11.155.11.

FIGURE C19. Painted hieroglyphic inscription with quail chick signs (Davies 1936, vol. 1, pl 18)

20

20. PLAQUE SHOWING A HOUSE MARTIN

Limestone
Late Period–early Ptolemaic period, 664–150 BC
Purchased in Cairo, 1920
12.0 × 9.8 × 1.4 cm
OIM E10555
Oriental Institute digital image D. 17936

This limestone plaque is decorated with the raised relief of a house martin (*Delichon urbicum*)[1] that, as a hieroglyph, stands for the biliteral sign *wr*. The small bird faces to the right and is shown at rest on a raised platform that forms part of the frame. Like Catalog No. 19, the upper left corner still retains an inverted L-shaped projection.[2]

Despite the damages the plaque has suffered (it had been broken into three pieces and then restored) and the dark stains,[3] it is still possible to admire the care the sculptor took to represent this charming bird. The principal morphological features of the bird are readily identifiable. The short neck and beak and long folded wings are represented in profile, while the slightly forked tail is carved from the most characteristic point of view, that is, from the top. The face with its short pointy beak so adept at catching insects in flight, and the short legs and feet with long sharp claws are carefully modeled. The sculptor took great care to carve the individual feathers on the wings and tail of the bird. He differentiated the covert feathers at the base of the wing, regularly depicted in four rows, from the longer secondary and primary wing feathers, which overlap each other. All these features are carved with such minute detail that one can easily identify the shafts and vanes of individual feathers. The smaller contour feathers of the chest and flanks are simply rendered by small pecks in the stone.

The challenge of identifying the precise species of this bird is rendered more difficult by the absence of color. Is it a martin or a swallow? The answer can be found in the many painted hieroglyphs that are extant in tomb-chapels, such as that of Nefertari in the Valley of the Queens. Nefertari was the Great Royal Wife (ḥm.t ny-swt **wr.t**) of Ramesses II, and her title that incorporates this hieroglyph is written in color in her tomb (fig. C20). The bird's wings and tail are painted blue-green, as is the crown of the head. The cheeks, chin, chest, and flanks are white. These are the characteristic colors of the house martin's plumage (Houlihan 1986, p. 125).[4] A dark spot is added at the top of the chest. This detail is included in this model, rendered by a few slanted incisions etched on the otherwise clean breast. This marking may be borrowed from the sand martin (*Riparia riparia*), which can be recognized at a distance by the presence of a brown collar underneath its white throat.

Another bird hieroglyph is often confused with ,[5] the "wr-bird," as Egyptologists frequently refer to the sign of the house martin, if the scribe or sculptor did not distinctly represent the forked tail. It is ,[6] considered to depict a house sparrow (*Passer domesticus*), depicted with a rounded tail. These two hieroglyphs may be graphically very similar, but their connotations and meanings are essentially opposite. While the basic meaning of "wr-bird" is "great," the sparrow written by itself as an ideogram can be read nḏs, meaning "small." It is also a common determinative following words expressing smallness, inferiority, evil, and so many other negative notions that it has motivated Egyptologists to call it the "bad bird" (David 2000). Sparrows could be a nuisance to the ancient Egyptian farmer, gathering in large flocks, pilfering the grain in the fields, and causing serious damage to crops (Houlihan 1986, p. 137). As a painted hieroglyph, it is often depicted in red, a color with many negative associations (Ritner 1993, p. 147 n. 662). RBL

FIGURE C20. House martin hieroglyph, from the tomb of Nefertari (VQ 66) (from Davies 1936, vol. 2, pl. 91)

NOTES

[1] For the color variation in the representation of this sign and the possible species of bird represented, see Chapter 9.

[2] See Metropolitan Museum of Art, New York, 07.228.9 in Arnold 2010, cat. no. 78, for a similar rendering of a martin, albeit with less detailed carving.

[3] The stains may be the results of burial or biological processes, or from exposure to high temperatures in a fire. They are deeply ingrained in the stone and cannot be removed. I thank Alison Whyte, conservator at the Oriental Institute Museum, for her analysis.

[4] The natural color of the house martin is a darker blue than that painted in the tomb of Queen Nefertari. As Pascal Vernus noted, the color of hieroglyphs can also reflect the symbolic value attributed to the animal. In this case, the bluish green refers to the notion of renewal and rejuvenation associated with this bird (Vernus and Yoyotte 2005, p. 65).

[5] Gardiner G36

[6] Gardiner G37

21. PLAQUE SHOWING A FALCON

Limestone
Late Period–early Ptolemaic period, 664–150 BC
Purchased in Paris, 1919
19.3 × 18.6 × 2.1 cm
OIM E9802
Oriental Institute digital image D. 17929

On this square limestone fragment, the standing figure of a falcon, with its long and pointy wings, is represented facing left. Half a sun disk is carved behind it.[1] As a hieroglyph, the falcon sign stands for the biliteral sign ḥr. It is more commonly used as an ideogram to be read "falcon," in particular the divine falcon Horus. When represented on a standard, the falcon hieroglyph acts as general determinative for divinity (fig. C21).

The sunk relief carved on this plaque is a traditional representation of both the hieroglyph and the god Horus in his avian form. The falcon is shown at rest, with its long wings folded along its sides. The round head and body are in profile, and the tail, as with all bird representations in Egyptian art, is shown as seen from above. In inscriptions where colors have survived, the back and head of the bird are painted blue and green, whereas its chest is speckled with black dots.

The author of this relief engraved the limestone with details frequently represented by brushstrokes in wall paintings. The short hooked bill of this falcon, adapted to quickly kill its prey, the supraorbital ridge, and deep set eye give a

FIGURE C21. Falcon on a standard, with an ostrich feather, as representation of the Goddess of the West (from Davies 1936, vol. 1, pl. 6)

fierce look to this predatory bird. The dark moustachial stripes below the eye, so characteristic of the facial features of the god Horus and common to most species of falcons, are surprisingly barely visible. On the other hand, the various kinds of featherings are carefully marked in a stylized and repetitive fashion. Five rows of alternating scallops stand for the upper wing coverts and scapulars on the bird's shoulder. They are followed underneath by the longer secondary and primary feathers, which enable falcons to rise high up in the sky and gather speed when diving toward their prey. Finally, the barred tail and underparts featured in peregrine (*Falco peregrinus*) and lanner (*F. biarmicus*) falcons are also indicated by individually carved rows of feathers. For unknown reasons, only one of the legs is carved in detail. However, both feet with their powerful talons are present.

Most scholars who conducted a close and detailed examination of the various depictions of the Horus falcon have come to the conclusion that no single species was used as a model by the ancient Egyptians who designed this motif. Features from several varieties of large falcons were seemingly selected and gathered so as to form a composite design, later adopted by generations of scribes and artists. The possible candidates that served as models to the Egyptian artists are the hobby (*Falco subbuteo*), lanner (*F. biarmicus*), peregrine (*F. peregrinus*), and Eleanora's (*F. eleonorae*) falcons (Houlihan 1986, p. 48).[2] The conventional representation of the Horus falcon remained virtually unchanged for several millennia, starting in the First Dynasty with the exquisite relief of the falcon standing on the *serekh* of King Wadji (ca. 2822–2815 BC)[3] and is found on monuments during the Roman period.

The falcon is one of the most frequently represented animals on ancient Egyptian monuments, both in iconography, as the depiction of one of the many gods with which the bird can be identified, and as the symbol of the living king on earth (fig. C22; see Catalog No. 4). As noted above, it is also a common hieroglyph, either written alone or combined with other elements. Eight different signs in the sign-list compiled by Gardiner include the falcon motif (see fig. C16: G5–10). RBL

NOTES

[1] The different cut marks used on half of the block seem to indicate that the relief may have originally been larger. The irregular cutting on the top and left sides may be ancient, while the right and bottom sides, with smooth edges, may have been done in modern times. A similar relief is in the Egyptian Museum, Cairo (CG 33456). In this case the sun disk is flanked by a uraeus serpent. See Tomoun 2005, cat. no. 143.
[2] Arielle Kozloff believes that only the lanner falcon was chosen as model for the representation of the god Horus; see Chapter 5.
[3] Musée du Louvre, Paris, E 11007.

FIGURE C22. Falcon representation as both the god Horus, with a sun disk behind him, and as a hieroglyph (*below, circled*), in a monumental inscription from the second court of the temple of Medinet Habu (from Epigraphic Survey 1963, pl. 389)

22. HEAD OF AN OWL

Limestone, pigment
Late Period–early Ptolemaic period, 664–150 BC
Purchased in Oakland, California, 1948
10.8 × 10.5 × 6.3 cm
OIM E17972
Oriental Institute digital image D. 17981

The head of the owl hieroglyph, standing for the letter *m*, is here represented in the round in a strikingly naturalistic fashion. The bird depicted is undeniably the barn owl (*Tyto alba*). The artist beautifully represented the characteristic heart-shaped facial disk with its conspicuous circle of short brown feathers, indicated by a scalloped outline, with small holes perforated above the eyes to imitate the black and white speckles. Grooved lines are carefully incised and faithfully reproduce in stone the white bristly feathers covering the bird's face, overlapping above the beak to form a small protuberance similar to a human nose. These feathers partly dissimulate the beak, whose tip sharply curves down toward the edge of the disk. Red paint was chosen by the artist to render the golden-buff color of the crown, nape, back, and scapulars, speckled with small back dots, just like the living bird (fig. C23).[1]

The owl hieroglyph is designed such that the bird, whose body is depicted in profile, is shown as if peering over its shoulder and staring at the viewer with its dark piercing eyes.[2] While this model with its rounded head is representative of the owl hieroglyph during the Ptolemaic period (Houlihan 1986, p. 110), the painted hieroglyph in low relief from the temple of King Mentuhotep II (ca. 2009–1959 BC) at Deir el-Bahari is closer in style to the motif followed

FIGURE C23. Barn owl (*Tyto alba*) (iStockphoto.com / © Jason Crader)

175

FIGURE C24. Owl hieroglyph on a fragment from the temple of Mentuhotep II (ca. 2009–1959 BC) at Deir el-Bahari, Western Thebes. OIM E8854 (D. 17914; photo by Anna Ressman)

for millennia by generations of scribes and artists (fig. C24). While the coloring of the bird is characteristic of the barn owl — white breast, here stippled by black dots; light brown back, wings, and tail; yellow beak and feet — the owl hieroglyph also exhibits ear tufts, a feature absent from the barn owl. Ludwig Keimer, who dedicated most of his scholarship to the study of the natural world surrounding the ancient Egyptians, proposed that two species of owls should be identified in the many representations of the sign. On the one hand, the eagle owl (*Bubo bubo ascalaphus*) can be recognized by the presence of distinct "ears" in the writing of the sign in cursive hieroglyph, either shown as a standing 𓅓 or squatting 𓅖 bird, and in one form of the sign written in hieratic 𓅓 (fig. C25). On the other hand, the barn owl is the model for the hieratic sign 𓅓, also used to write the phoneme *m*.[3] Keimer concluded that, just as it was the case with the falcon hieroglyph (Catalog No. 21), the ancient Egyptians most likely designed a composite sign encompassing the most characteristic features of several families of owl, combining the piercing black eyes and plumage of the barn owl with the ear tufts of most owl species in the *Strigidae* family

(1951, p. 79). It is not surprising that many of the features chosen to design the bird sign are those exhibited by the barn owl. These birds do not shun human presence and they flourish in Egyptian temples, where they find perfect roosting sites and a good supply of prey in the form of rats and mice as well as sparrows and turtledoves (Houlihan 1986, pp. 109–12).

Note, finally, that the owl hieroglyph is the only bird sign whose feet do not exhibit a hind toe. RBL

PUBLISHED

Marfoe, 1982, p. 31; Houlihan 1986, p. 109, fig. 158

NOTES

[1] See Metropolitan Museum of Art, New York, 07.228.11 in Arnold 2010, cat. no. 77, for a similar rendering of an owl's head in raised relief.

[2] Owls are often observed on a high perch turning their head to and fro, observing their surroundings and attempting to detect the softest sound, which could reveal the presence of a potential prey. Their skeleton is adapted so that they can turn their head and neck 270 degrees to the right and to the left, without moving the rest of their body.

[3] Keimer 1951, p. 59. Gardiner himself refers to the work of Keimer, as well as of Newberry (1951), when describing the sign in his *Egyptian Grammar*: "according to Keimer the hieroglyphs show several members of the family of *Strigidae*. Newberry states that the sign as here printed [𓅓] depicts the Barn owl (*Tyto alba alba*)" (1957, p. 469).

FIGURE C25. Eagle owl (*Bubo bubo ascalaphus*) (iStockphoto.com / © Leopardinatree)

BIRDS IN THE RELIGIOUS LIFE OF ANCIENT EGYPTIANS

Religion penetrated every facet of ancient Egyptian life, from international politics to the family household. So thoroughly were religious beliefs assumed that the Egyptian language even lacked a word for "religion." The ancient Egyptian religious system focused on a plethora of gods and goddesses, which at their core represented the cosmic and social forces in the universe. Worship of these deities involved a variety of rituals, many of which would have structured the patterns of everyday life. In death, Egyptians sought the company of the gods, thereby becoming powerful spirits to whom the living could appeal for redress of earthly grievances. Egyptian culture was entirely infused with this religiosity, offering ample opportunity for intimate contact with divinity in many ways.

Birds formed a regular feature in the Egyptian natural environment and were therefore embedded into standard religious iconography. Statues (Catalog Nos. 3, 23, and 25), temple reliefs, and amulets (Catalog Nos. 7–9) often depict divinities with avian features or in complete avian form. These features evoked for the viewer the identity of the deities and alluded to their characteristic power, such as flight or ferocity. The average Egyptian experienced his daily religion through household shrines, amulets, stelae, and the local priesthood. Although inner temple shrines and divine statues would have been restricted from the average person's gaze on a daily basis, festivals and processions gave them opportunities to witness and participate in important public rituals.

In addition to adapting avian characteristics into iconography, priests dedicated themselves to the cults of living birds which served as animate vessels for divinity. Selected birds, such as the falcon of Horus at Edfu, would have been raised as the earthly incarnation of the god. Few birds were chosen for this service, but those that were had well-maintained lives filled with public appearances and elaborate burials at death (see Catalog No. 28). However, the majority of mummified bird remains derive from mass burials related to the cults of sacred animals (Catalog Nos. 30–32). Many animals were revered because of their association with a particular deity, such as the ibis with Thoth and the falcon with Horus. Millions of such birds were captured wild or domestically raised, mummified, and interred as an offering to their tutelary god in subterranean necropoleis. FS

FIGURE C26. A Ptolemaic king makes an offering before Horus and an enshrined falcon referred to in the text as the "living falcon upon the *serekh*," from the temple of Horus at Edfu (photo by Stefano Vicini)

FALCON CULTS

23 *(caption)*

23, detail of top *(caption)*

23. STATUE OF HORUS

Serpentine (metal beak is a modern restoration)
Third Intermediate Period–Late Period, Dynasties 25–26, ca. 722–525 BC
Purchased in Cairo, 1919
59.6 × 23.4 × 55.9 cm
OIM E10504
Oriental Institute digital images D. 17932–34

This large statue of a falcon represents the god Horus.[1] The mottled color of the stone gives the impression of the subtle variation in the color of the feathers of a real bird. The face lacks the characteristic feathery markings that surround a falcon's eye. The pupils have been detailed with a gold-colored material with a black center. The modern metal cap on the beak was probably added to remedy a break.[2] The flat surface of the top of the head suggests that it originally wore a crown, most probably the double crown that stressed the association of Horus and the living king (see Catalog No. 4).[3] The bird's wing tips are crossed in the back over the tail feathers. The statue is not inscribed.

More than thirty statues of falcons of this approximate size are known, almost all of them made of basalt rather than serpentine, a stone that was most commonly used in the Twenty-fifth and Twenty-sixth Dynasties. Some falcon statues wear the double crown of Upper and Lower Egypt, others wear no crown, and yet others have lost whatever crown they originally wore. These statues are related to the cult of the king as indicated by the use of the double crown and also by a small figure of the king who stands between the falcon's legs or in front of his breast on some examples from the Thirtieth Dynasty (Ladynin 2009; see also see Chapter 2 in this volume).

Only two falcon statues (in addition to those still standing in the temple of Edfu) have a sure provenience,[4] in both cases, coming from a temple context. On that basis, it seem likely that the

23, detail of head

Chicago falcon was commissioned as a cult statue of the god Horus that was set up in a shrine or temple as the physical image of the god-king. These statues were the recipients of offerings to sustain and honor him.[5]

However, the Oriental Institute falcon has a channel that was laboriously drilled in the interior of the statue from the beak to the top of the head and from the top of the head down to the tail. The most plausible explanation for this feature is that it enabled the statue to transmit sound, probably for use as an oracle, and traditionally this has been the function ascribed to this statue. A sculpture representing the falcon god Re-Horakhty and another of the deified queen Arsinoe have similar interior channels, and they too have been cited as examples of auditory oracles. Other examples of oracles thought to transmit sound or noise include a statue of a bull excavated at Kôm el-Wist (near Alexandria), whose base was hollowed and connected to a bronze tube that may have relayed the voice of a priest to the petitioner. Similar ways of allowing unseen priests to become involved in oracles have been noted at Greco-Roman temples at Karanis and Siwa (Frankfurter 1998, pp. 150–51, 157). However, all these examples are at least three centuries later than the Chicago falcon.

Voice oracles, as opposed to the New Kingdom and Third Intermediate Period oracles that gave their decision by the movement of the divine image, are not clearly attested before the Greco-Roman era (332 BC–AD 395). Uncertainty in dating the advent of auditory oracles is created by difficulties interpreting texts that refer to the voice of the god being heard or to the god "speaking," both of which could actually refer to the report given by the priest who oversaw the oracle rather than a pronouncement of the oracle itself (McDowell 1990, pp. 109–10). Such claims can also refer to someone "hearing" the voice of the god during a dream (Frankfurter 1998, pp. 158–59). The hollowing out of the statue may then reflect its reuse as a voice oracle centuries after it was carved. ET

PUBLISHED

Bothmer 1967/68; Marfoe 1982, p. 23, fig. 11; Wilson and Barghusen 1989, no. 14; Teeter 2003, cat. no. 48; Teeter and Johnson 2009, cat. no. 15, Teeter 2011a, fig. 45

NOTES

[1] Two examples of these statues are inscribed and both refer to the god as a form of Horus (Christie's London, December 16, 1982, no. 192; Mekkawy and Khater 1990, p. 88).

[2] Another falcon excavated at Buto had what may be a similar treatment: "The beak is surrounded by an engraved frame which seems to be a space for fixing a decorative beak to hide the breakage in the beak itself. Remnants of rusted materials have been found inside these frames" (Mekkawy and Khater 1990, p. 87). It is impossible to tell what the condition of the Chicago statue's beak is under the brass cover.

[3] When acquired by the Oriental Institute in 1919, the falcon wore a brass double plumed headdress copied from the Hierakonpolis falcon. This modern embellishment was removed in the late 1990s.

[4] The two falcon statues with known provenience come from Buto, one from the temple area (Mekkawy and Khater 1990) and the other from "just a little north of the axis of the temple" (Petrie 1905, p. 38, pl. 43:7–8). Two in the Freer Gallery of Art, Washington, DC (F1909.140 and 141), are said to have come from Abukir/Canopus. Several examples (Museo del Sannio, Benevento, 253, 254, 255, 269, and Capitoline Museum, Rome, 31) were excavated from secondary contexts in Italy.

[5] In the Thirtieth Dynasty, the cult of the falcon officially fused with that of the king as attested by the titulary of Nectanebo that refers to him as "King of Upper and Lower Egypt, the Falcon Who Came Forth from Isis" (Yoyotte 1959, p. 60), and by priestly titles that refer to clerics who served the statue of the king-falcon (de Meulenaere 1960; Holm-Rasmussen 1979; Ladynin 2009, pp. 25–26).

24. ORACLE TEXT

Baked clay, pigment
New Kingdom, Dynasty 20(?), ca. 1186–1069 BC
Purchased in Egypt, 1939
5.5 x 7.0 cm
OIM E18876
Oriental Institute digital image D. 17986

Most oracles in ancient Egypt during the New Kingdom and Third Intermediate Period took the form of a statue of a deity that was carried in a litter or on a ceremonial boat on the shoulders of priests. Questions could be submitted to an oracle either orally or through writing.[1] This example of an oracle text, written in hieratic (cursive hieroglyphic script) on a bit of broken pot, asks the god "Shall I bring (hire?) Tabaket (or "the maidservant")? Will she become effective for me?" The judgment of the god was probably indicated by the movement of the god toward ("yes") or away from ("no") the petitioner or the message, or by "becoming heavy" and causing the priests to sink down. ET

PUBLISHED

Černý, 1972, p. 68 (no. 95), pl. 25 (no. 95); Teeter and Johnson 2009, cat. no. 16; Teeter 2011a, fig. 44

NOTE

[1] For a summary of the evidence, see McDowell 1990, pp. 108–14.

25. COFFIN DECORATED WITH A FALCON AND TWO DEITIES

Bronze
Late Period, Dynasties 26–31, 664–332 BC
Purchased in Cairo, 1920
11.3 x 5.0 x 12.2 cm
OIM E10604
Oriental Institute digital images D. 17941 and 17939

This coffin for the remains of an animal mummy is in the form of a platform with an altar detailed with a cavetto cornice. A falcon, wearing the double crown of the solar god Horus, stands atop the altar. Before him are two figures. The seated one wears a false beard and an ostrich feather, identifying him as Shu, the god of air. The lion-headed female wears a sun disk and uraeus. Although there are a variety of goddesses who assume this form, the pairing with Shu suggests that she is his sister Tefnut. According to the Heliopolitan tradition of the creation of the world, the siblings were the first generation of gods created by Atum. Their appearance on this coffin may allude to them being part of the retinue of the sun god who protected him during his daily circuit (Coffin Text spell 80; Assmann 1995, p. 52) and who assisted with his birth each morning. The pair also represents the

25

two concepts of eternity, cyclic and linear time, Shu being called "eternal recurrence" (*nḥḥ*) and Tefnut "eternal sameness" (*dt*) (Coffin Text spell 80).

A poorly preserved inscription on the front and right side of the base calls for "Horus-of-Pe to give all life and health eternally ... to Pa-irr-aw-ib(?)."[1]

Most examples of this style of container no longer hold their original contents. The falcon on top of the box suggests that it was intended to hold a tiny bird mummy, and indeed, remains of birds have been recovered from similar examples excavated at North Saqqara (Davies and Smith 2005, p. 89, FCO 150, 153). However, the excavators of that site reported that some of the coffins contained not the body of a bird, but "scraps of mummified fauna, usually shrew mice." These were initially interpreted as being food offerings for the falcon god of the temple (Smith 1974, p. 54). Further research has suggested that the shrew was not given this elaborate burial because it was food, but due to its association with the sun god (Brunner-Traut 1965, 1984; Ikram 2005b; Davies and Smith 2005, p. 55).

The shrew, a nocturnal animal, was probably associated with the nightly travels of the sun god that led to his rebirth at dawn, and in Book of the Dead spell 145 the shrew appears as the guardian of the twenty-first door of the underworld (Brunner-Traut 1984, col. 1161; T. G. Allen 1960, pp. 240, 243 n. dd). It was also sacred to Horus-Khentyenirty "Horus Keen of Sight" of Letopolis (Brunner-Traut 1965, p. 154). This association was probably a reference to the shrew's night vision despite its tiny eyes, and the sharp vision of the hawk during the day, together referring to the duality and at the same time the totality of night and day. Nearly sixty bronze containers topped with a figure of one or more shrews were recovered from the sacred falcon catacombs at North Saqqara (Davies and Smith 2005, pp. 52, 61, 134), further stressing the close relationship between the two animals. One of those shrew coffins was inscribed in honor of "Horus Lord(?) of Letopolis" (Davies and Smith 2005, p. 61).

Animal burials became an important part of cult activity in the first millennium BC (Kessler 1989; see Chapter 2 in this volume). Similar small bronze coffins topped with a falcon have been recovered from many sites throughout Egypt. An example from North Saqqara bears a brief inscription similar to that on the Chicago example, asking the god for blessings, "(May) Horus-of-Pe give life to Ankhkhratnoufi, son of Ankhtakelot, born of Amenpsotem(?)." Another dedication text from Saqqara takes the form of a message from the falcon to the dedicator, "[Recitation by] the falcon (for) Pedionouri, son of Pediosiri" (Davies and Smith 2005, p. 88, pl. 37). These texts that include personal names suggest that the animal mummy containers were brought to the temple and catacomb by individuals who gave them to the priests for deposition as part of a ritual demonstrating their devotion to the god. ET

25, front view

NOTE

[1] I thank W. Raymond Johnson for helping me puzzle out the text and Brian Muhs for suggestions about a possible (admittedly tentative) reading of the personal name. I also thank Foy Scalf for his general observations on this object.

FALCON CULTS AT AKHMIM

During his honeymoon in Egypt in 1894–95, James H. Breasted purchased several mummies, among them Catalog Nos. 26 and 27. It is recorded that he acquired them in the region of Akhmim and sent them to A. E. Cyril Fry in Cairo, who forwarded them to the Haskell Oriental Museum, the predecessor of the Oriental Institute Museum, at the University of Chicago. The Upper Egyptian city of Akhmim, known as Chemnis in Egyptian and Panopolis in Greek, witnessed an "unsystematic archaeological exploitation beginning in the last two decades of the 19th century" (M. Smith 2002, p. 233). A great number of artifacts were excavated, most of which have no recorded context or exact provenience. Many of them later appeared on the antiquities market, a fate shared by the mummies Breasted purchased during his trip. The presence of animal mummies at Akhmim is not surprising. The cults of sacred animals, especially birds, were of special significance in this city during the Greco-Roman period, and mummies of ibises, birds of prey, and swallows have been discovered in the nearby cemetery of el-Hawawish (Kessler 1989, pp. 21–22). Evidence suggests that several forms of the god Horus were worshipped in this region of Upper Egypt: Horus Who Pleases the Heart; Horus the Great, Lord of Letopolis, also known as Haroeris; and Horus Pillar of His Mother, also known as Harmoutes (Scharff 1927, pp. 89–90; Chauveau 1986, pp. 42–44; Smith 2002, pp. 241–42). One may assume that the two mummified birds of prey, Catalog Nos. 26 and 27, were originally buried in the cemetery of Akhmim after having been dedicated to these local forms of the falcon god. RBL

26

26. MUMMIFIED EAGLE

Organic remains, gold
Greco-Roman period, 332 BC–AD 395
Purchased by J. H. Breasted, possibly at Akhmim, 1894–95
70.0 × 18.7 × 14.0 cm
OIM E150
Oriental Institute digital image D. 17892

Prior to the common practice of applying non-invasive radiographic techniques to ancient Egyptian mummies to identify the contents hidden within the wrappings, the linen bandages were often removed and the contents of the mummy exposed. This specimen suffered such a destructive treatment and, unfortunately, no record was kept of the procedure. It is likely that the linen bandages were discarded, destroying valuable information

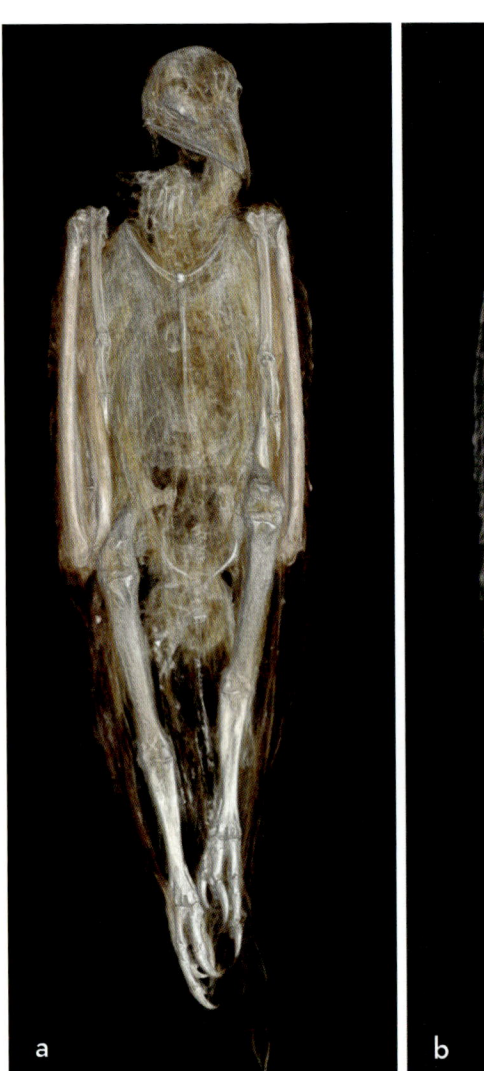

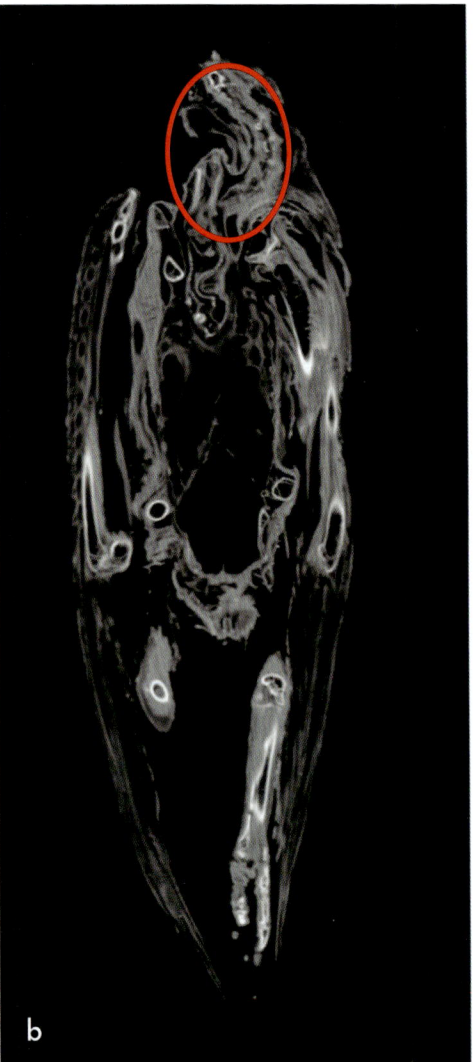

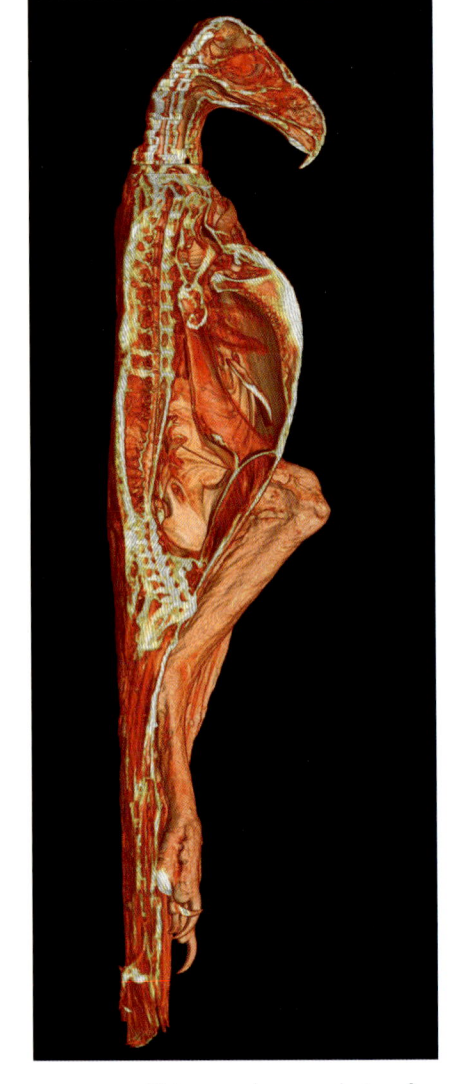

FIGURE C27. (a) Volume rendering of OIM E150 showing the awkward position of the neck and the otherwise good condition of the skeleton (segmented and rendered in Volume Graphics VG Studio Max 2.2; courtesy of J. P. Brown, Anthropology Imaging Lab, The Field Museum of Natural History); (b) Coronal CT slice of OIM E150 showing the severed cervical vertebrae (circled)

FIGURE C28. Cutaway volume rendering of OIM E150 showing the absence of viscera in the abdominal cavity (segmented and rendered in Volume Graphics VG Studio Max 2.2; courtesy of J. P. Brown, Anthropology Imaging Lab, The Field Museum of Natural History)

about the methods employed to prepare this bird mummy (see Chapter 11). Only a few small fragments of linen are still visible on the beak, neck, wings, and feet.

This large bird is a remarkable specimen. After having been generously covered with embalming material (resin and oil), the bird's head, chest, legs, and wings were covered with thin gold leaf. The reason for this luxurious treatment is unknown and rarely attested,[1] although gilding applied to mummy wrappings and casings has been recorded for the remains of sacred animals such as the Apis bull and the ram of Mendes. Should we then consider that these may be the remains of a special member of the sacred flock dedicated to Horus the falcon which may have benefited from a prestigious burial? Or did a wealthy worshipper request the manufacture of such a lavish votive offering with the hope of improving his chance to be heard by the falcon god? (See Chapter 3.) The loss of the external wrappings and the lack of provenience data prevent us from reaching a conclusion.

In preparation for this exhibit, the bird was CT scanned to obtain more information about the embalming treatment that preceded the gilding and wrapping. Its skeleton is in perfect condition, with no visible fractures. The bones are fully calcified and belong to an adult bird. Its legs are in a flexed

CATALOG NO. 26

position, with the tarsometatarsus and feet resting on the bird's tail (see Appendix). The large wings have been folded tightly against the body. The neck is in a very awkward position, which may attest to the bird having been dispatched by having its neck broken (fig. C27a and b). No viscera remain in the abdominal cavity; only air sac membranes or peritoneal membranes are visible (fig. C28).[2] Based on measurements,[3] this bird is probably a tawny eagle (*Aquila rapax*) (fig. C29).   RBL

NOTES

[1] Another mummy purchased by Breasted, OIM E151, also exhibits gilding on the beak, as does Egyptian Museum, Cairo, CG 29681.

[2] My thanks to Dr. Kenneth Welle, veterinarian at University of Illinois, for identifying these features.

[3] Measurement of the tarsometatarsus: 9.63 cm; head: length, 11.0 cm; height, 4.8 cm.

FIGURE C29. Tawny eagle (*Aquila rapax*) (iStockphoto.com / © StuPorts)

27

27. MUMMIFIED BUNDLE IN A WOODEN COFFIN

Greco-Roman period, 332 BC–AD 395
Purchased by J. H. Breasted, possibly at Akhmim, 1894–95

Mummy
Organic remains, linen
24.7 × 8.0 × 6.9 cm
OIM E154A

Wooden coffin in the shape of a falcon
Wood and pigment
45.8 × 10.1 × 10.4 cm
Cavity for mummy: 25.0 × 4.7–7.4 cm
OIM E154B

Oriental Institute digital images
D. 17895 and 17897

Most falcon mummies buried in catacombs and animal cemeteries were placed in jars.[1] Some benefited from more exclusive funerary assemblages, such as stone sarcophagi or wooden coffins;[2] others were wrapped with elaborate designs[3] and shaped as small human mummies. Bandages were at times covered with stucco and painted with the face of a hawk.[4]

FIGURE C30. Tentative reconstruction of OIM E154B (original drawing by Angela Altenhofen)

27, side view

This bundle was placed in a wooden coffin made of a single piece of wood carved in the shape of a falcon. Despite having suffered some damage and missing some of its components, this coffin is of special interest because of the rarity of similar artifacts in the archaeological record. Some of the facial features, such as the supraorbital ridge, the eyes, and a section of the beak, can be identified. Wings are summarily modeled on each side. The coffin was roughly hollowed out to produce a small rectangular cavity destined to become the final burial place of a mummified bird. A lid, now missing, was most likely used to conceal the cavity's content. It seems that the wooden body was fully covered with gesso and subsequently painted; only a few dark and red sections of this painted decoration are extant. Samples of surface residues, including a red pigment, were removed and analyzed using a JEOL scanning electron microscope with energy dispersive spectroscopy (SEM-EDS) at the Department of Geophysics, University of Chicago. Among other elements, the samples were found to contain significant amounts of lead.[5]

The majority of wooden sarcophagi for sacred animals are rectangular. Like the ibis statue (Catalog No. 28), this rare falcon-shaped coffin[6] reproduces the form of the content it was expected to hold. Holes in its head and legs indicate that a headdress and two legs, perhaps of metal or wood, further adorned this object. In 1907, L. C. Lortet discovered a complete falcon coffin with its mummified content in the Valley of the Monkeys on the west bank of Thebes.[7] That coffin is made entirely of wood. The falcon is shown wearing a double crown held in place with a peg inserted into the top of the head. It stands on a rectangular wooden base. Lortet's find from Thebes gives a glimpse at the style of wooden falcon coffins to which OIM E154B may have belonged (fig. C30).

A small mummy, wrapped in plain and coarse reddish linen bandages, is still present within the cavity. The coffin with its mummified content was CT scanned. The lead pigments applied to the wooden body are easily seen on CT scan images, appearing as a very bright outer layer surrounding the coffin (figs. C31–32). The mummy can be seen to fit very tightly in the cavity, and was probably

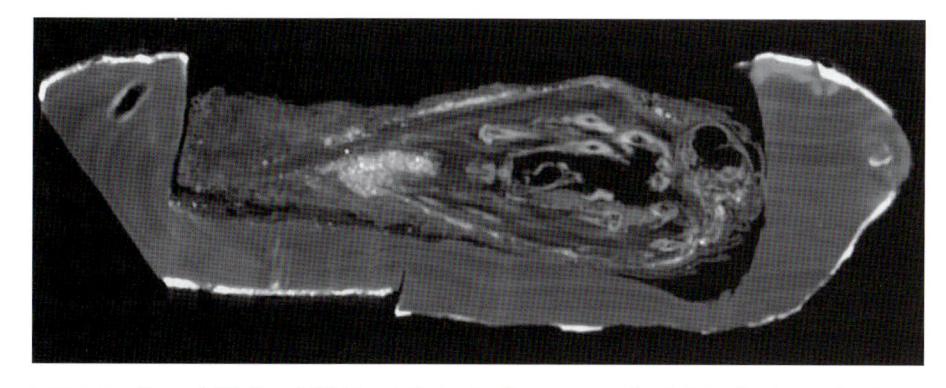

FIGURE C31. Coronal CT slice of OIM E154A–B showing the presence of embalming fluids mixed with sand within the wrappings and against the bird's remains

manufactured specifically for this coffin. The bird's head is tilted up and placed to the side, as if it were looking over its shoulder. During the embalming process, a thick layer of resin and bitumen, mixed with some sand, was applied to the bird remains (fig. C31). The presence of this dense embalming material renders the visualization and creation of 3-D images of the bird's skeleton challenging and the precise identification of the bird more difficult. The bird appears to have been eviscerated, with some remaining soft tissues having settled in the abdominal cavity. Its legs are bent and held close to the body, an unusual pose for the mummy of a raptor, whose legs and talons are frequently pulled down along the body (see Chapter 3). The bird's long tail and wings, combined with the measurements of the tarsometatarsus, indicate that this is probably a small member of the *Falco* genus, such as a Eurasian hobby (*F. subbuteo*), a merlin (*F. columbarius*) that might have been caught when migrating through Egypt, or, more likely, a common kestrel (*F. tinnunculus*), which is a resident species of the Nile Valley.[8] RBL

NOTES

[1] See Davies and Smith 2005, pls. 12–16, 20–23.

[2] Davies and Smith 2005, figs. 11–22, pls. 18–19.

[3] For example, OIM E146 and E155 with diamond designs on the wrappings' outer layer; also Egyptian Museum, Cairo, CG 29881.

[4] For example, OIM E116 and E119, also said to be from Akhmim; also de Moor et al. 2008, pp. 108–09, inv. 1024 in the Katoen Natie collection, Antwerp.

[5] I thank conservator Alison Whyte for conducting the experiment and analyzing the data.

[6] Six similar objects are known to me: Egyptian Museum, Cairo, CG 29793 and 29794, from Akhmim; Smithsonian Museum of Natural History, 423000, found in Akhmim by Maspero. It is also missing its legs and headdress (J. Krakker, personal communication); National Museum in Krakow, MNK XI-486, purchased in Akhmim in 1884 (D. Gorzelany, personal communication); and Musée des Confluences, Lyon, 90000834 (D. Emmons, personal communication); Musée Auguste Grasset de Varzy, inv. VA5 (Matoïn and Loffet 1997, pp. 29–31).

[7] Lortet and Gaillard 1905–09, p. 36, fig. 32, now in the Musée des Confluences, Lyon, 90000834. For a color photograph, see Emmons 2010, p. 80.

[8] Measurement of the tarsometatarsus: 3.74 cm. The bird's bones are not fully calcified, indicating that this is a juvenile. I thank Steve M. Goodman for bringing this to my attention.

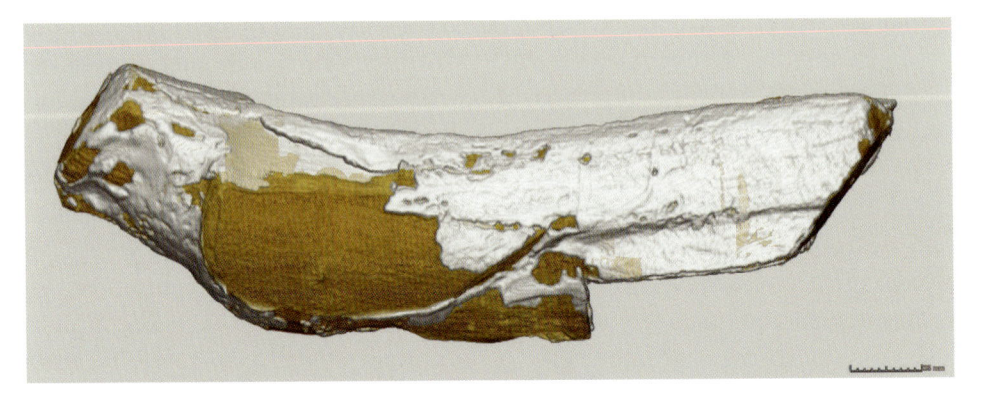

FIGURE C32. (*top*) Volume rendering of the wooden coffin and (*bottom*) the small mummy inside the cavity (segmented and rendered in Volume Graphics VG Studio Max 2.2; courtesy of J. P. Brown, Anthropology Imaging Lab, The Field Museum of Natural History)

IBIS CULTS

28

28. COFFIN FOR AN IBIS

Wood, gesso, silver, gold, rock crystal, pigment
Ptolemaic period, 332–30 BC, with modern restoration
Possibly from the ibis cemetery at Tuna el-Gebel
Ibis: 58.7 (tip of tail to beak) x 38.2 cm; 55.8 cm (circumference of body)
Wooden base: 42.8 x 20.2 x 3.2 cm
Collection of the Brooklyn Museum, Charles Edwin Wilbour Fund, 49.48

This magnificent composite statue representing a crouching ibis is a true masterpiece not only of Egyptian craftsmanship, but also of animal art. As a manifestation of the lunar god Thoth, the ibis is depicted in this figure with its silver legs, restored in modern times, bent at the knee and the tibiotarsal joints as if preparing to incubate its eggs in a nest (fig. C33). This "brooding" position might be a direct allusion to the version of the Hermopolitan creation myth in which the self-created god Thoth lays the cosmic egg upon the primeval mound that had emerged from the watery Nun (Tobin 2001, p. 470). Hermopolis Magna, located in Middle Egypt, was considered to be the site of this primeval hill and became the chief sanctuary of the ibis god. With the rise in popularity of sacred animals during the Late Period onward, the temple dedicated to Thoth the ibis at Hermopolis became the setting for public ceremonies and festivals (Kessler and Nur el-Din 2005, pp. 129–30). It was possibly at the occasion of these festivals that processions took place, during which priests in charge of the cult transported the numerous mummies dedicated to the deity from the temple area to the necropolis of Tuna el-Gebel. These votive offerings were then deposited in the vast complex of subterranean galleries, which gradually expanded during the 700 years of cultic activity at the site (see fig. 2.4).

This statue is not simply a fine representation of the ibis god; it is primarily a coffin destined to receive the remains of a sacred ibis (*Threskiornis aethiopicus*) (fig. C34). The body of the coffin is composed of a single piece of wood covered with gold leaf on a foundation of gesso. The characteristic black-tipped primary and secondary feathers, gathered over the ibis's rump when the bird does not deploy its wings, are indicated by black paint applied over the gilt. A large oval section in the back of the statue can be detached to reveal a cavity hollowed out in the wooden body. X-ray images of the statue have confirmed

FIGURE C33. Nesting ibis. Detail from a marsh scene in the mastaba of Mereruka (Sakkara Expedition 1938, part I, pl. 19)

FIGURE C34. Sacred ibis (*Threskiornis aethiopicus*) in flight (photo by Jonathan Rossouw)

that it contains the mummified remains of an ibis. The long neck and curved bill of a seemingly complete adult bird can be clearly identified in figure C35. The mummified ibis, which fits tightly into the coffin's recess, appears to have its neck stretched ventrally along the body, its two wings folded against its sides, and its legs bent against its abdomen.

Since this statue is also a sarcophagus, the crouching ibis can also be identified with the god Osiris-Ibis, "in its visible form of a resting ibis" (Kessler and Nur el-Din 2005, p. 130).[1] A representation of Osiris, the god of the dead, in a brooding position may appear to be a contradiction, but ancient Egyptians may have intended for it to be a graphic metaphor for death being simply a temporary state taking place in the sarcophagus, also called the "egg" (swḥ.t) in Egyptian, with the promise of a rebirth by hatching anew from this very egg.

While most mummified ibises were buried more modestly, at times piled up in reused tombs or placed in clay coffins (see Catalog No. 30), the bird deposited in this statue benefited from special treatment (see Chapter 3). Are these the remains of a sacred bird chosen during its lifetime to embody the god Thoth on earth, which had been kept in the god's temple and taken into processions? Or is it simply a more expensive ex voto for a wealthy worshipper? The lack of inscriptions and context for the discovery of this artifact leaves these questions unresolved.

The wooden gilded body with its mummified content, as well as the base on which the figure is positioned, have been dated to the Ptolemaic period. However, such a conclusion cannot be drawn so readily for the silver components of the statue. Composite statues of crouching ibises are attested in many museums.[2] They are for the most part composed of a wooden body with legs and head of bronze. A variety of scientific experiments conducted on a selection of these objects have

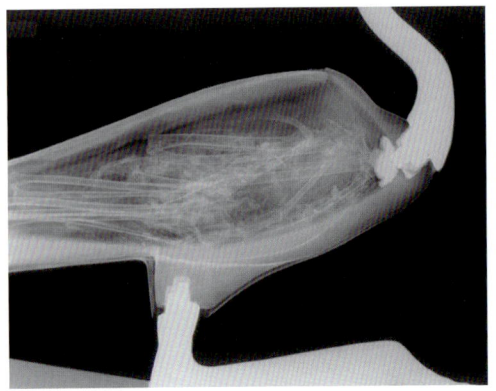

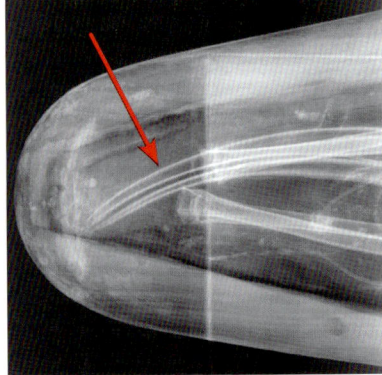

FIGURE C35. (*left*) Lateral radiograph of the coffin's wooden body showing the bird's skeletal remains; (*right*) radiograph of the wooden bird's rump showing the curved beak of the mummified ibis (*at arrow*)

revealed that, in multiple cases, the metal sections were in fact a modern addition to an ancient wooden body (Schorsch 1988).[3] It is thus possible that the elaborately modeled silver parts of this statue were manufactured rather recently, perhaps not long before the statue was acquired by the Brooklyn Museum in 1949. The choice of silver was judicious on the part of the craftsman. The live sacred ibis, in addition to the dark markings on its feathers, is easily identified by its bare black head and neck, black curved bill, as well as black legs and feet. These silver parts of the statue, at first shiny, can quickly acquire a dark tarnish in contact with the atmosphere, a coloring which would further highlight the living bird's features. These features are rendered in a highly naturalistic fashion. The ridges of the bill, the vertebrae visible under the skin of the naked neck, even the external ear openings have been carefully modeled by the silversmith. A necklace was also incised at the base of the neck. The scaly skin of the legs and feet, a remnant of the bird's reptilian ancestry, is also carefully rendered, as are the creases in the skin at the bend of the leg. The final touch is the presence of beautiful rock crystal eyes outlined with gold. RBL

PUBLISHED

Riefstahl 1949; Glubok 1962, p. 15; Bowman 1986, p. 182, fig. 111; Houlihan 1986, p. 29, fig. 36; Spanel in Fazzini 1989, cat. no. 91; Fazzini et al. 1999, p. 140

NOTES

[1] Numerous statues, figurines, and amulets in the shape of an ibis display the bird in this crouching position. Amulets: see Catalog Nos. 8 and 9 in this volume. Statues: Virginia Museum of Fine Arts, Richmond, 65.52; British Museum, London, EA 49424, Egyptian Museum, Cairo, JE 88734; Metropolitan Museum of Art, New York, 56.18, 43.2.2. Figurines: Walters Art Museum, Baltimore, 54.2152; Princeton University Art Museum, Princeton, 48.11; Cleveland Museum of Art 1940.667; Al-Ashmunein magazine inv. 1132; Mallawi Museum 278 (Nasr el-Dine 2010), and Metropolitan Museum of Art, New York, 23.6.4 and 04.2.460.

[2] The Oriental Institute also holds such a statue in its collection, which was donated to the museum in 1968 (OIM E25390). However, the authenticity of this artifact has not been verified.

[3] The metal components, especially the bronze ibis heads, have been available on the antiquities market at least since the end of the nineteenth century and can still be purchased to this day. Such a head was auctioned on May 7, 2012, for $8,000–$12,000 (http://www.antiquetrader.com/featured/online-auction-sells-more-than-250-antiquities-with-guaranteed-authenticity).

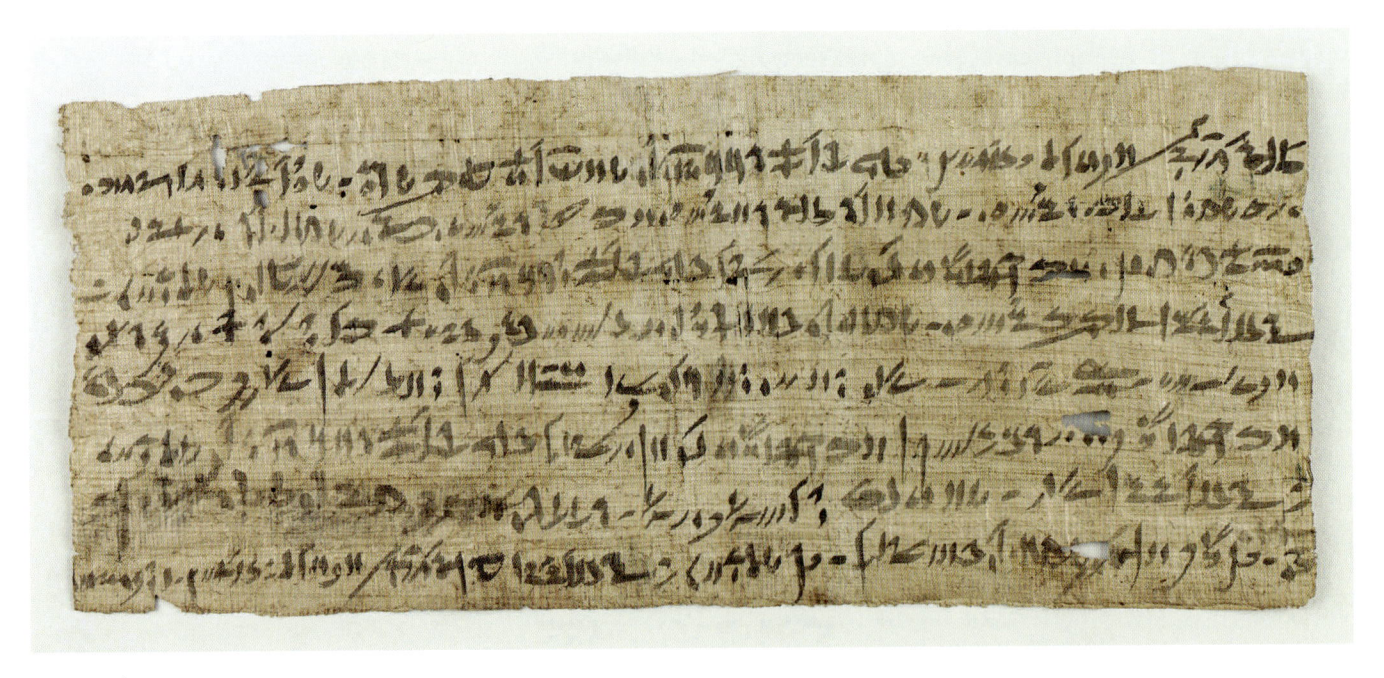

29, recto

29. DEMOTIC LETTER TO "THE IBIS, THOTH"

Papyrus, ink
Late Period, Dynasty 27, reign of Darius I,
between June 25, 502 BC, and July 24, 502 BC
Probably Hermopolis, Tuna el-Gebel
Purchased in Cairo, 1950; donated to the Oriental Institute by Alan Gardiner via George Hughes, 1956
27.0 x 11.5 cm
OIM E19422
Oriental Institute digital images D. 17992-93

In ancient Egypt, people commonly sought out powerful individuals for the redress of legal, social, or personal grievances. Such individuals could be human or divine, alive or dead. Imploring departed relatives as intermediaries for real-world difficulties (an art which has been termed "necromancy") has a long history in Egypt with direct evidence stretching back into the Old Kingdom.[1] Letters written to gods, such as this papyrus addressed to "the ibis, Thoth," are direct descendants of similar texts previously presented to the powerful spirits (ꜣḫ) of deceased individuals.[2] In fact, petitions of this kind from the Greco-Roman period were sometimes addressed to Imhotep, the famous architect of the Third Dynasty king Djoser who became deified after his death and who was honored in a shrine carved into the cliffs of Hatshepsut's mortuary temple at Deir el-Bahari.

The letter preserved on papyrus OIM E19422 was written in the Demotic script in eight lines on the recto and one line on the verso. It was composed in the reign of Darius I (522–486 BC) during the first period of Persian rule following the conquest of Egypt by Cambyses in 525 BC. It was written by a man named Efou (ꜣIw=f-ꜥw), son of Hornufechebe (Ḥr-nfr-ḫby), who worked as part of the administration of a cult of the ibis, bird sacred to the god of writing and wisdom Thoth. The letter was presumably rolled up and placed somewhere in the galleries of ibis burials within the necropolis of Tuna el-Gebel as the papyrus's excellent state of preservation suggests.

The single line of text on the verso of this appeal preserves an address identifying it as "a plea of the servant Efou, son of Hornufechebe, before the ibis, Thoth, twice great, lord of Hermopolis, the great god." The addressee is none other than a god of national importance, for Hermopolis was the most sacred city of Thoth in Egypt. Ibises from surrounding cities were sent for burial in the underground galleries of the animal necropolis and pilgrims traveled to pay their respects before this eminent deity. It is no accident that Efou writes to Thoth. As he tells us, he left his former work to perform services within the cult of the ibis. Efou probably rendered his duties to a smaller ibis

29, verso

cult outside of Hermopolis because he mentions that he has no supervisor before whom he could bring his appeal. Whether or not this statement is hyperbole can no longer be known. He then lists a series of injustices committed against him as well as the ibis cult, alleging that one Psentehe, son of Montuhotep, has stolen from him and the ibis cult, had his assistants harmed, and appropriated his stipend. As the source of his livelihood, Efou would have taken the theft of his income quite seriously. What truth may have been in these claims, we do not know, but the mention of crimes perpetrated against the very cult of the god addressed could not have hurt Efou's case. Efou does not seek for the god to harm Psentehe, but only asks to be protected from the latter's malice. FS

RECTO

A plea of the servant Efou, son of Hornufechebe, before Thoth, twice great, lord of Hermopolis: My great lord, O may he pass the lifetime of Pre. From the month of Mecheir of regnal year 11 up to today, I perform the service of the ibis. I abandoned my (former) work. More than it, I prefer the work which pertains to the ibis. I have no supervisory personnel. If the heart is stout, then they will be protected before Thoth, twice great, lord of Hermopolis. I pray on account of Psentehe, son of Montuhotep. He does not perform the service of the ibis except for eating its food. And he does not allow a guard over it either. He steals from me by force. Since year 17, he stole my money and my wheat. He had my servants harmed. He stole from me all that I have. About the burnt offerings, his heart is obstinate. If the heart is stout, then they will be protected before Thoth, twice great, lord of Hermopolis. As for Psentehe, son of Montuhotep, he has stolen from my life. He has cast me out of my portion. As the law, he acts for himself. Many things depart through his hand, which pertain to the ibis. Let me be protected from Psentehe, son of Montuhotep. Written by the servant Efou, son of Hornufechebe, in the month of Phamenoth of regnal year 20.

VERSO

A plea of the servant Efou, son of Hornufechebe, be[fore the ib]is, Thoth, twice great, lord of Hermopolis, the great god.

PUBLISHED (SELECTED)

Hughes 1958; Migahid 1986, pp. 38–44; Endreffy 2009, p. 244

NOTES

[1] Ritner 2002; idem 2008, p. 184; Gardiner and Sethe 1928.

[2] For example, the letter from a man to his deceased relative, who is referred to as a "powerful spirit" (*3ḥ*), preserved on OIM E13945, published in Woods 2010, cat. no. 81.

IBIS CEMETERY AT ABYDOS

Abydos was a prominent site in the sacred landscape of Egypt for several millennia, originally as cemetery of the first Egyptian kings and later as main cult center of the god Osiris. Numerous animal cemeteries have emerged from the sand during the past century and a half of active excavation at the site, testifying to Abydos's involvement in the popular phenomenon of sacred animal cults during the Late Period and Greco-Roman times (O'Connor 2009, p. 121; Ikram 2007). Of all the mummified animals found thus far, ibises are the most numerous. They were deposited in various sections of the site as votive offerings to the god Thoth. In 1913, one of these ibis cemeteries, dated to the Roman period, was discovered and thoroughly excavated by L. S. Loat of the Egypt Exploration Fund (EEF) (Loat 1914; Peet 1914; Whittemore 1914). The following year, the EEF sent a selection of mummified bundles from this cemetery to the Haskell Oriental Museum, predecessor of the Oriental Institute Museum. Among the material were Catalog No. 31 in its clay coffin, and Catalog No. 32 as well as some ibis eggs (Catalog No. 33), discovered alongside the bundles. RBL

30. BIRD COFFIN

Pottery, gypsum plaster
Roman period, 30 BC–AD 395
Excavated at Abydos
Gift of the Egypt Exploration Fund, 1913–1914
Pot: 45.0 x 19.0 cm
OIM E9233A
Lid: 22.5 x 13.5 cm
OIM E9233B
Oriental Institute digital image D. 18004

The majority of the mummies discovered by L. S. Loat at Abydos were found inside large cylindrical jars manufactured with unbaked clay, deposited haphazardly amid Old Kingdom tombs, and later concealed by drifting sand (Peet and Loat 1913, p. 40; Loat 1914, p. 40). Some of these vessels were filled with up to 100 mummified bundles. Additionally, some pear-shaped coffins of baked clay, such as the Chicago example, were found stacked in groups in their midst (fig. C36).

This type of clay coffin was manufactured in stages. The process of making a closed-form vessel begins with the creation of a simple cylinder or vase form. The narrower end of the coffin, where the tail of the bird lies, would originally have been the base of the vessel and was left intentionally thick to support the vessel while it was being formed. The potter raised the vessel walls slightly above the final desired height, then wrapped his hands around the top and began to slowly choke the walls inward. The choking process caused small folds in the clay, thickened the wall, and decreased the overall diameter. After two or three choking attempts, the potter might have compressed the clay wall with a wooden "rib" tool (a flat, rounded rectangular piece of wood) or by using his hands. This step smoothed out the folds and strengthened the clay. The choking process continued until the form was completely closed at the top. Once the opening was sealed, the interior of the vessel contained a pocket of air and pressure could then be applied to the outside to shape the vessel or smooth out any throwing marks, without the form collapsing.

At this stage, the pot was removed from the wheel, flipped upside down, and placed in a chuck on the wheel. The excess clay was then trimmed away to form a rounded bottom. After trimming, the vessel was allowed to dry until the clay was leather-hard. The opening on the side was then cut and left in place to dry for firing. The dried coffins were placed in the kiln, likely leaning against the kiln walls and against each other, resting on their base or "tail" ends with the lids in place to ensure a good fit during the firing.

Once firing of the coffin was complete, a mummified bundle — in this case OIM E9234 (Catalog No. 31) — was deposited inside and the lid replaced, the edges of which were sealed with a generous amount of gypsum plaster (see fig. C37).

The even wall thickness of this coffin denotes a fairly skilled potter, although the unfinished rough edges at the lid opening signal a fast production method and lack of concern for parts that would remain hidden. Cracking at the corners of the lid opening occurred due to a loss of structural integrity when the lid was cut out from the form.

Each major animal cult center most likely benefited from the services of specialized pottery workshops dedicated to the manufacture of vessels designed to be filled with the remains of mummified animals. A few pear-shaped clay coffins have also been identified in the subterranean galleries of Tuna el-Gebel, but they appear to have been used at this site for only a short period of time (von den Driesch et al. 2005, fig. 3:MS 1a1). BZ/RBL

FIGURE C36. View of the ibis cemetery at Abydos. A pile of pear-shaped ibis coffins is in the foreground (Peet and Loat 1913, pl. 16:5)

FIGURE C37. Hermetically sealed jars, each containing a single ibis (Whittemore 1914, pl. 38)

31

31. MUMMIFIED IBIS

Organic remains, linen
Roman period, 30 BC–AD 395
Excavated at Abydos
Gift of the Egypt Exploration Fund,
1913–1914
34.5 × 13.6 × 9.6 cm
OIM E9234
Oriental Institute digital image
D. 17925

As stated by Thomas Whittemore (1914, p. 248), who commented on the ibis mummies discovered at Abydos by Loat, "contrary to expectation, the birds in these small sealed jars were always plainly, and usually carelessly wrapped." This description adequately applies to this mummified ibis. Wide bands of brown linen were used for the final layer of bandages, and no effort was made to weave a fancy pattern such as that found on Catalog No. 32. Embalming material used during the process of mummification seeped through the different layers of wrappings and accumulated on one side of the bundle, possibly hinting at its original position in the coffin. Half of the outer layer is now black and damaged in a few places, giving a glimpse of the bird hidden underneath.

The examination of the contents of a significant number of ibis mummies, either by unwrapping them,[1] or more recently by using x-ray and CT scan imaging,[2] revealed that there are two methods of positioning the birds within the linen bandages. Either the neck is extended and placed centrally upon the bird's abdomen, or it is curved into an S-shape so that the head stands high and the beak is tucked underneath a wing (see Chapter 3). Each position gives the mummy a distinct shape. The pear shape of this specimen suggests that the bird inside is arranged in the first position, that is, with its neck extended and placed on its chest.

This mummy was recently CT scanned (see Chapter 13), which revealed that it contains the remains of an incomplete bird. The neck of the bird is indeed extended and placed in a ventral position. However, the beak was severed close to the head before the wrapping process. Was it intentional on the part on the embalmers in order to give the mummy the desired shape and to allow it to fit into the coffin? It is also possible that this bird was found lying dead, already in a state of decay.[3] Only one leg remains and it looks as if every bone has been shattered. The abdominal cavity is devoid of organs, but a packet filled with the shells of freshwater snails has been placed in the stomach cavity, perhaps wrapped in linen. As stated by Pelizzari and colleagues, it is unlikely that these are the remains of the bird's last meal; if such were the case the shells would not be intact, having been crushed in the crop and/or gizzard. This discovery seems to confirm the recent hypothesis proposed by Wade and colleagues (2012), namely, that ibises were provided with food for their journey in the afterlife.[4] Linen padding was added to give the bundle the desired shape, and large bands of coarse linen form the outer layer.

Based on the measurement of the remaining intact bones,[5] this mummy contains the remains of an adult male sacred ibis (*Threskiornis aethiopicus*). RBL

NOTES

[1] For example, Lortet and Gaillard 1905–09; Gaillard and Daressy 1905; Peet and Loat 1913, p. 40.

[2] Ikram and Iskander 2002; Ikram 2005a; McKnight 2010; Wade et al. 2012.

[3] Textual evidence from the hawk catacombs at North Saqqara mentions the discovery of a dead bird subsequently embalmed and mummified (see Chapter 2). Also, it has been surmised that the high frequency of remnants of bird carcasses in the mummies examined at Tuna el-Gebel implied that "it was the duty of the cult servants of the ibis organisation to collect every dead bird or part thereof in or near their homesteads" (von den Driesch et al. 2005, p. 210).

[4] The shells of freshwater snails (*Cleopatra bulimoides*) have also been identified in the stomach content of several mummies at Tuna el-Gebel (von den Driesch et al. 2005, p. 228).

[5] The only intact tarsometatarsus measures 11.4 cm.

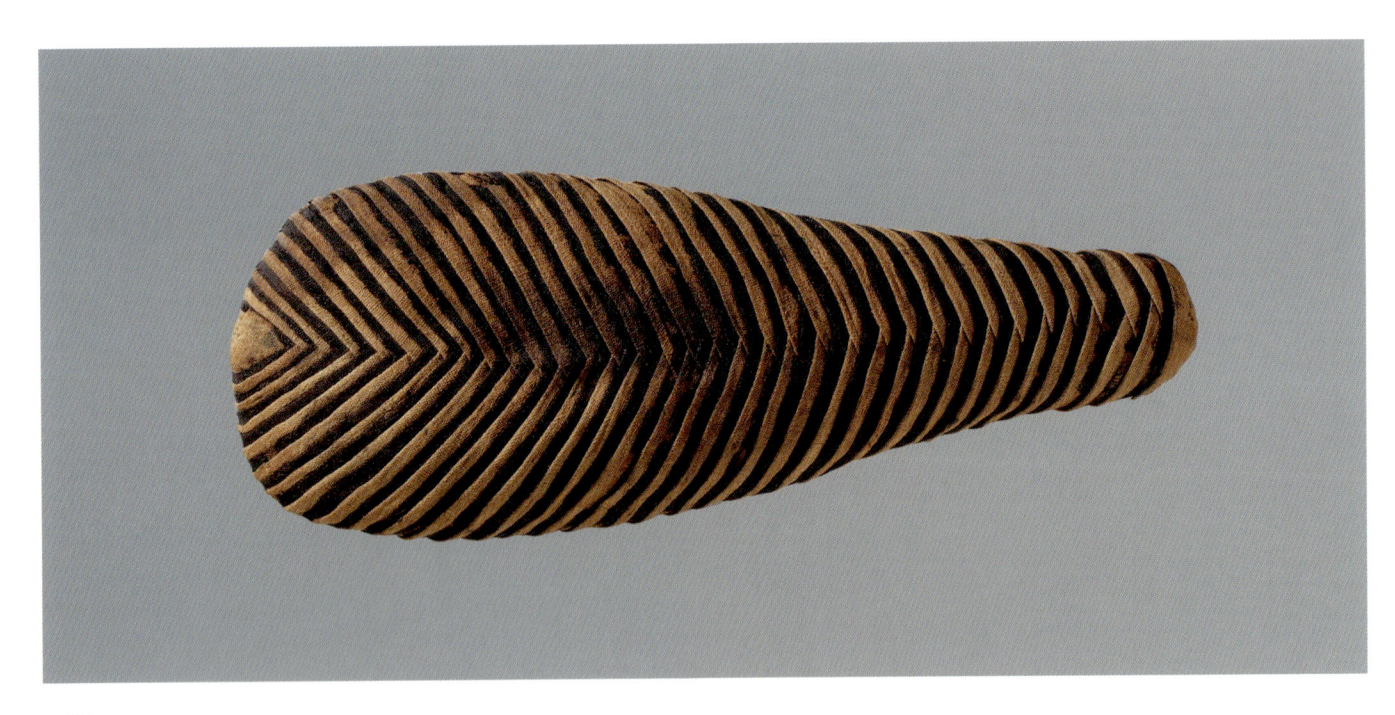

32. MUMMIFIED BUNDLE

Organic remains, linen
Roman period, 30 BC–AD 395
Excavated at Abydos
Gift of the Egypt Exploration Fund, 1913–1914
30.5 × 11.5 × 5.0 cm
OIM E9237
Oriental Institute digital image D. 17928

When removing the sun-dried bricks sealing the large jars of the ibis cemetery of Abydos, L. S. Loat was impressed by the quality of the decoration on many of the mummified bundles. He reports:

> The contents had been preserved with bitumen and then carefully wrapped in linen bandages, the outer covering being in most cases quite a work of art, accomplished by the use of narrow strips of black and brown linen, arranged in such a way as to form a wonderfully varied series of geometrical and other patterns; in fact, from this one cemetery

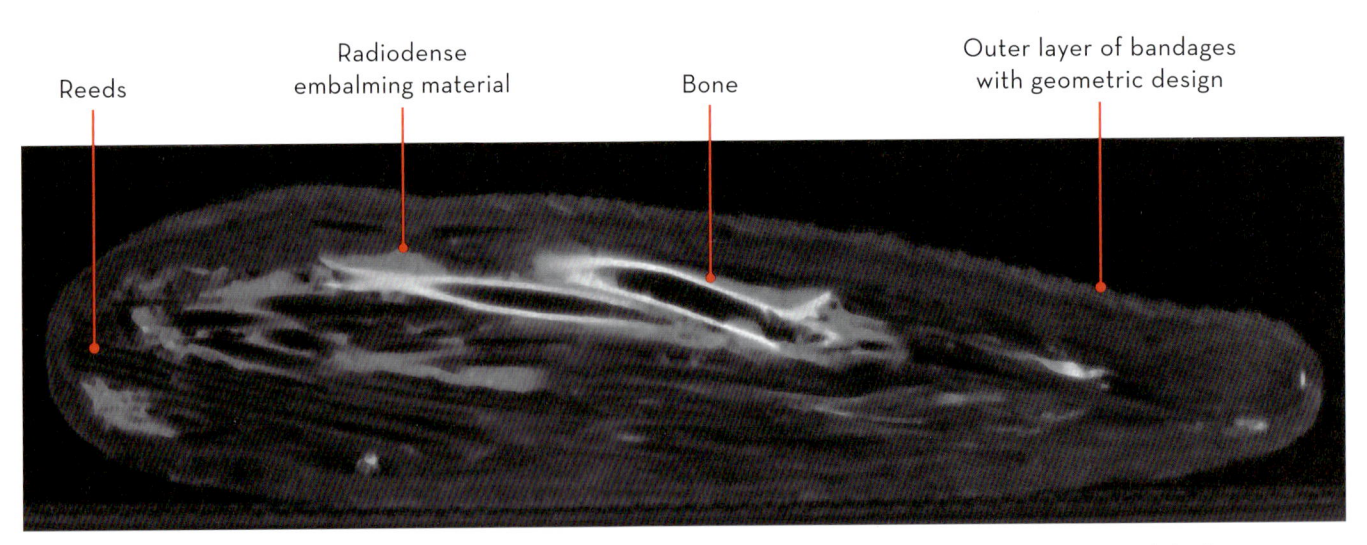

FIGURE C38. Midsagittal CT slice of OIM E9237 showing reed shafts, dense embalming material (light gray), and bone sections (white)

alone at least a hundred different designs were recorded. (Peet and Loat 1913, p. 40)

Mummy OIM E9237 is deserving of such a laudatory comment. The outer layer of bandages is composed of sixty-six thin strips of brown and black linen alternately overlapping so as to achieve a remarkably regular chevron pattern. The strips are joined in the back with threads, which were covered with a wide band of brown linen to further secure the strips and to give the bundle a tidy finishing touch.

While this mummy is beautifully preserved, it is also extremely fragile. When handling these artifacts, Loat had noticed that "the linen was somewhat brittle from age and the effect of the bitumen used in the preservation — the black linen more especially so, owing no doubt to the dyeing, the fibre crumbling in many cases to powder at the slightest touch" (Peet and Loat 1913, p. 41). He applied some varnish to stabilize the surface. The mummies were then packed in cotton wool muslin and shipped to England, and later Boston, before arriving to Chicago. Despite the precautions taken, some of the black strips of this mummy bundle remain very brittle and continue to require extreme care, as they tend to disintegrate if the mummy is handled.

Because of its fragile state, this mummy was very carefully packed by the conservation staff of the Oriental Institute Museum in order to be CT scanned (Whyte 2012). Previously, this mummy was thought to contain the remains of an ibis, most likely positioned with its neck extended and beak on its belly. CT scans revealed that this carefully prepared bundle is filled for the most part with reeds and/or feathers, as well as a few long bones, the whole being covered with radiodense[1] material to hold the various components together and to give it the appropriate shape (figs. C38–39). As mentioned by Salima Ikram, such incomplete mummies have been interpreted by some scholars as ancient forgeries, manufactured by servants of the cult desirous to maximize their profits by making several mummies from a single bird (see Chapter 3). Egyptologists now tend to believe that, since everything connected with these birds was sacred, the fragments of nest material, eggs, feathers, and remains of birds dying on the site could represent a part for the whole, and thus held the same power as would a mummy containing a complete specimen. Based on this reasoning, if the demand for votive mummies was higher than the supply of birds, servants of the cults could have manufactured bundles with bird parts and still have satisfied votaries with effective offerings. RBL

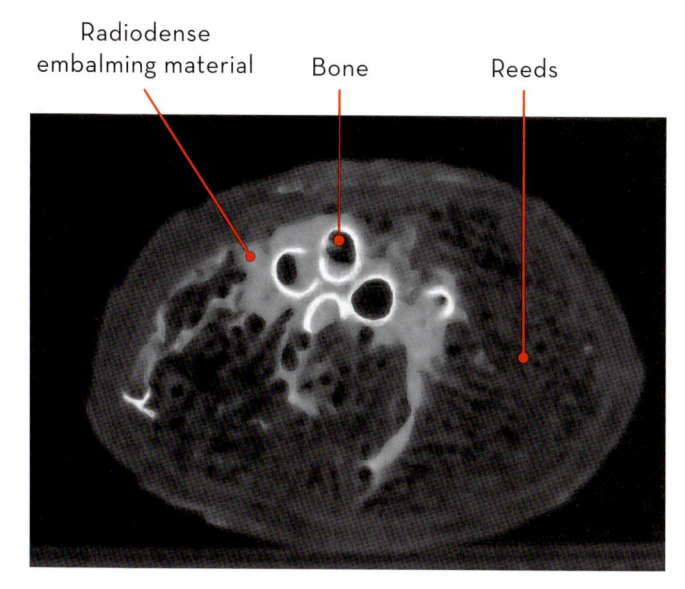

FIGURE C39. Axial CT slice of OIM E9237

PUBLISHED

Teeter and Johnson 2009, cat. no. 18

NOTE

[1] A radiodense substance is resistant to the passage of x-rays and is identified on radiographic images as opaque and white.

33 IBIS EGGS

Organic remains
Roman period, 30 BC–AD 395
Excavated at Abydos
Gift of the Egypt Exploration Fund, 1913–1914

33a

33b

a. 6.0 x 4.0 cm
   OIM E9235
   Oriental Institute digital image
   D. 17926

b. 6.4 x 3.8 cm
   OIM E9236
   Oriental Institute digital image
   D. 17927

Ibises at all stages of development are found at the Abydos animal cemetery, from eggs and embryos to full-grown adults, like Catalog No. 31. Eggs were either interspersed between mummy bundles in large vessels or deposited separately in small jars.

These two intact sacred ibis eggs were most likely discovered in such jars (Whittemore 1914, p. 248). Some of the eggs had been carefully wrapped in linen. Scarab beetles placed upon these wrapped eggs were thought to protect and "preside over the hatching process," so as to guarantee a renewable supply of birds in the afterlife (Ikram 2007, p. 425). The perfect state of preservation of the two eggs in the Oriental Institute collection raises the question whether they too had originally been protected by linen bandages but were unwrapped by the archaeologists eager to uncover the contents of the package.

There are many potential reasons for the presence of eggs in the cemetery. It has been suggested that every creature present within the sanctuary and all material associated with the flock of sacred birds was imbued with the same sacred qualities. Servants of the cult of the ibis would have regularly gathered feathers, remnants of nests, and abandoned eggs in addition to the remains of all other creatures that had died in the temple precinct. All these items would have eventually been deposited in the catacombs along with the mummies of complete birds. The discovery of a bundle containing a broken egg with a well-developed embryo in gallery D of Tuna el-Gebel has led the zooarchaeologists working at this site to wonder "whether the eggs have been removed intentionally from those ibis nests containing more than one egg, since normally only one individual will survive," thus allowing the remaining chick to benefit from the full attention of its parents and potentially having a greater chance to survive to adulthood (von den Driesch et al. 2005, p. 218). **RBL**

CATALOG NO. 34

BIRDS IN DEATH AND THE AFTERLIFE

Just as birds were part of daily life in Egypt they also had important roles in the afterlife. In many respects they played the same roles as they did in the world of the living. They provided food, and bird deities provided protection.

The bird deities usually involved in the protection of the dead are vulture goddesses (Nut, Nekhbet, Wadjet) and falcon gods (Horus, Sokar, Re). Falcon gods were especially important, because there was often a certain level of identification of the deceased with these gods. The king was protected by and identified with Horus in both life and death (Catalog No. 37) and he also became one with the sun god (Re, Re-Horakhty) and funerary gods such as Sokar (Catalog No. 35) in the afterlife. The protection of these deities was also extended to non-royalty. The sons of Horus, one of which took the form of a falcon, protected the internal organs (Catalog No. 36). Like many other cultures, Egyptians conceived of some of their spiritual forms to be bird-like. One of these was the *ba*, which is most often depicted as a human-headed bird (Catalog No. 34). The body of the ba usually takes the form of a falcon.

Egyptians depended on the living to provide for them after death through funerary cults but they also took measures should the cult fail. They provided for their needs by the magic of images, such as tomb paintings and models. As fowl was a favorite dish, there were scenes of the capture of wild birds and the care of domestic stock. Models of the butchering (Catalog No. 38) and cooking of birds would magically allow the same processes to occur in the afterlife. The use of victual mummies (Catalog No. 40) created a continuous source of food. But these images and models often had a double purpose as the capture and killing of fowl acted magically to control chaos and to destroy evil forces (Catalog No. 38; see also Catalog No. 39). RS

34. ***BA*-BIRD STATUETTE**

Wood, pigment
Late Period, Dynasties 25-30, ca. 750-350 BC
Dendera
Gift of the Egypt Exploration Fund, 1897-1898
6.9 x 7.1 x 2.8 cm
OIM E4461
Oriental Institute digital images D. 17908-09

Small statuettes in the form of a bird with human head representing the *ba* (*b3*) of the individual developed over the course of the New Kingdom, became increasingly common in the Late Period, and continued to be used in a modified form into the Meroitic period in Nubia (fourth century BC–fourth century AD).[1] They were often made of wood and brightly painted. The

34

Oriental Institute example is somewhat exceptional for its well-preserved paint, as the color decoration on many similar figures has faded away, and also for its unusual wig style.[2] The face is painted gold, the wings are given elaborate patterns of blue and dark blue, and the underside of the tail is red. A beautiful example from the mid-Eighteenth Dynasty burial of Yuya (KV 46) portrays the deceased with a black wig, red face and feet, yellow underbelly, white legs, green wings, and blue tail.[3]

The original placement of this figurine is unknown, but depictions of the *ba* are known from other elements in the funerary assemblage. A wooden statuette found in the tomb of Tutankamun (KV 62) depicts the king lying on a funerary bed with a figure of his *ba* crossing wings with a falcon figure over his torso.[4] A similar model made of black stone showing the *ba*-bird sitting next to the mummy was manufactured for a non-royal individual named Re from the Eighteenth Dynasty.[5] These objects suggest that *ba*-statuettes were placed near the corpse, perhaps over the chest, as accoutrements applied to the coffin or sarcophagus,[6] following the instructions in the rubric for Book of the Dead spell 89, the "spell for causing the *ba* to join to his corpse," which states: "Recitation over a *ba* of gold filled with precious stones, which a man placed (on) his chest."[7] In fact, actual gold amulets representing the *ba* have been discovered in both royal and private burials.[8] Alternatively, the *ba*-statuettes could have been simply left freestanding within the tomb or attached to a stela by a wooden dowel, a hole for which is preserved in the base of this example.[9]

Within ancient Egyptian philosophical tradition, human beings had several aspects to their existence including *ba* (𓅽 *b3*), *ka* (𓂓 *k3*), corpse (𓄣 *ẖ3.t*), name (𓂋𓈖 *rn*), and shadow (𓇋𓏏 *šw.t*).[10] Each of these elements symbolized the various relationships and abilities of the individual, both within this world and in the hereafter. The *ba*, most often represented as a bird with human head, was of paramount importance for it represented the individual's power of mobility.[11] In particular, the power of flight, symbolized through the metaphor of the bird body, allowed for the deceased to travel in the company of the sun god during the daily solar cycle. Corresponding to the *ba*'s airy existence is the corpse, which was destined for the netherworld, thereby complementing the solar-Osirian cycle with which everyone hoped to associate. Upon death, recitations during the funerary rituals sought to ensure that the *ba* rise in the sky and the corpse descend into the netherworld.[12] Separation of the *ba* and corpse was not permanent for the *ba* would reunite nightly with the corpse (as specified in Book of the Dead spell 89). The alighting of the *ba* onto the corpse is depicted in a miniature limestone sarcophagus model from the late New Kingdom which shows the *ba* seated upon the torso of the mummy with outstretched wings.[13] Regeneration occurred through this reunion, just as the sun god Re's reunion in the netherworld with Osiris provided the necessary conditions for his daily renewal, setting the divine precedent for Egyptian conceptions of existence in the afterlife. FS

NOTES

[1] Earlier pair and trio statues from the Old Kingdom have been assumed to fulfill a similar role, but this is far from certain. See Žabkar 1968, p. 76; Vandier 1958, pp. 85–88. An overview of the Meroitic *ba*-statues can be found in Török 2009, pp. 422–24, and Silverman 1997, pp. 306–07.

[2] See Lacovara and Trope 2001, cat. no. 7; von Droste et al. 1991, cat. nos. 111–14. A similar wig is depicted on a *ba*-statuette in the decoration of Theban Tomb 78 (Brack 1980, pl. 17).

[3] Egyptian Museum, Cairo, CG 51176 (JE 95312), Quibbel 1908, p. 63; Bongioanni et al. 2001, p. 495.

[4] Bongioanni et al. 2001, pp. 284–85; Wiese and Brodbeck 2004, pp. 120 and 194–95.

[5] Egyptian Museum, Cairo, CG 48483, Newberry 1937, pp. 372–73, pl. 30; Hornung and Bryan 2002, p. 204.

[6] A falcon statuette of similar shape and manufacture occupies this position on the famous Roman-period coffin of Soter (British Museum, London, EA 6705), as pictured in Riggs 2005, figs. 87–88.

[7] This rubric is found in the famous papyrus of Ani, now in the British Museum (British Museum, London, EA 10470.17). For photos, see Faulkner 1998b, pl. 17.

[8] Bleiberg 2008, p. 115; Andrews 1994, p. 68; Fazzini 1975, p. 126. Bronze statuettes are also attested; Roeder 1956, p. 399 and pl. 56.

[9] Bács et al. 2009, p. 137; Riggs 2003, p. 193. Stela 54343 in the British Museum preserves a *ba*-statuette attached to the top (Munro 1973, pl. 20).

[10] Zandee 1960, pp. 19–20; Assmann 2005, pp. 89–90.

[11] Žabkar 1968.

[12] Assmann 2005, pp. 90–96.

[13] Egyptian Museum, Cairo, CG 48501, Newberry 1937, p. 380, pl. 30. Cf. also CG 51107 from KV 46, Quibbel 1908, p. 49. pl. 27.

35. STATUETTE OF A FALCON

Wood, gesso, pigment
Dynasty 22, ca. 943–746 BC
Luxor, the Ramesseum
Gift of the Egyptian Research Account, 1896
8.6 × 12.5 cm
OIM E972
Oriental Institute digital images D. 17901 and 17904

35

35, back

This statuette represents the god Sokar in the form of a mummified falcon. This form of falcon, called ḥm or šm (𓉔𓅱), represented a cult image (Wilson 1997, p. 178; Affholder-Gérard and Cornic 1990, p. 44, no. 4). Though made for private use, this falcon imitates with paint the ornamentation of a cult image. It is shown wearing a menat (or menit) necklace with alternating red and green bands representing beads and a large counterpoise on the back painted black. This ornament was associated with the goddess Hathor and came to be a symbol of fertility, life, and rebirth.[1] Yellow paint on the body and base probably imitates gold leaf. The red on the back and wings represents red linen, which was associated with Osiris and rebirth (Corcoran 1995, pp. 55–57).

During the Late Period, small statuettes like this one were placed on the lids of coffins and sarcophagi (Ikram and Dodson 1998, pl. 31; Affholder-Gérard and Cornic 1990, p. 44, nos. 4–5). Others are found in association with wooden statuettes of Ptah-Sokar-Osiris in mummified human form. On the extended bases of these

203

statuettes of Ptah-Sokar-Osiris one often finds a falcon of this type covering a small cavity. Within this cavity was a Book of the Dead papyrus or a small grain-mummy meant to germinate representing new birth (Taylor 2001, pp. 212–13, fig. 156; Graindorge 2001, p. 306). Some coffins of the Third Intermediate Period have an image painted on the breast representing Sokar or Sokar-Osiris as an ꜥḥm-falcon.[2]

The god Sokar was originally a funerary and protective god of the Memphis necropolis (Bonnet 1952, p. 723; Graindorge 2001, p. 305). He was identified with Osiris and the sun god as early as the Old Kingdom, as indicated in the Pyramid Texts (ca. 2300 BC) (Bonnet 1952, pp. 724, 727; cf. PT 620, 1429, 2069). In the Middle Kingdom, Sokar assumes a role in the transfiguration at death and in the opening of the mouth ceremony (Graindorge 2001, p. 305). He was joined with the Memphite creator god Ptah as Ptah-Sokar, who was associated with the fertility and production of the soil. As Sokar-Osiris he becomes the nocturnal incarnation of the sun god. In the fourth and fifth hours of the Book of That Which Is in the Underworld, also called the Amduat, he enables the sun to complete its course and be reborn in the morning (ibid., pp. 305–06). The entity Ptah-Sokar-Osiris represents creation-metamorphosis-rebirth (ibid., p. 306).

Metamorphosis leading to rebirth is perhaps what this small mummiform falcon with its head emerging from the wrappings represents. During the Late Period, and especially in Greco-Roman times, the deceased could be called the "Sokar-Osiris" before their name in the same way that departed people had been called the "Osiris such-and-such" for centuries (Spiegelberg 1927, p. 27). People were also called pꜣ ꜥḥm (feminine tꜣ ꜥḥm.t) the "Falcon such-and-such," which Spiegelberg interpreted as "one who has transformed into a falcon" (ibid., pp. 28, 31; D'Auria et al. 1988, p. 242). During the same time period, the deceased is portrayed on stelae as a mummy with a falcon head and the coffins of both royalty and non-royalty were made with falcon heads, which likely represents the deceased as Sokar (Spiegelberg 1927, pp. 28–29; Ziegler 1987, p. 94). Both the Coffin Texts (de Buck 1938, pp. 206–53) and the Book of the Dead (Faulkner 1998b, pl. 25) include spells for "being transformed into a divine falcon" (see D'Auria et al. 1988, p. 242), while the human ba-spirit is depicted as a human-headed bird with the bird portion usually taking the form of a falcon (Bonnet 1952, p. 77). In the Greco-Roman period the ba-spirit of deities is frequently described as a falcon that alights upon the god's cult image (see Daumas 1958, p. 100; Kurth 1998, p. 199). The human-headed ba-bird became nearly interchangeable with the falcon in the Late Period as representing the ba-spirit (Spiegelberg 1927, p. 29; Wilson 1997, pp. 293–94). The union of the ba with the body is often portrayed with the ba-bird resting on the corpse. Small falcons on top of coffins and sarcophagi may represent Sokar as guarding the transforming mummy below it but, at the same time, represent the deceased at the union of the ba-spirit with the corpse. For more details on the ba-bird, see Catalog No. 34.   RS

NOTES

[1] See von Beckerath 1982; Bonnet 1952, pp. 450–51; Leclant 1961, pp. 266, 271–74.

[2] Taylor 2001, p. 235, fig. 173; Koefoed-Petersen 1951, p. 27, pl. 53; Andrews 1984, pp. 16–17, fig. 51; Affholder-Gérard and Cornic 1990, pp. 14, 75, 77, no. 53.

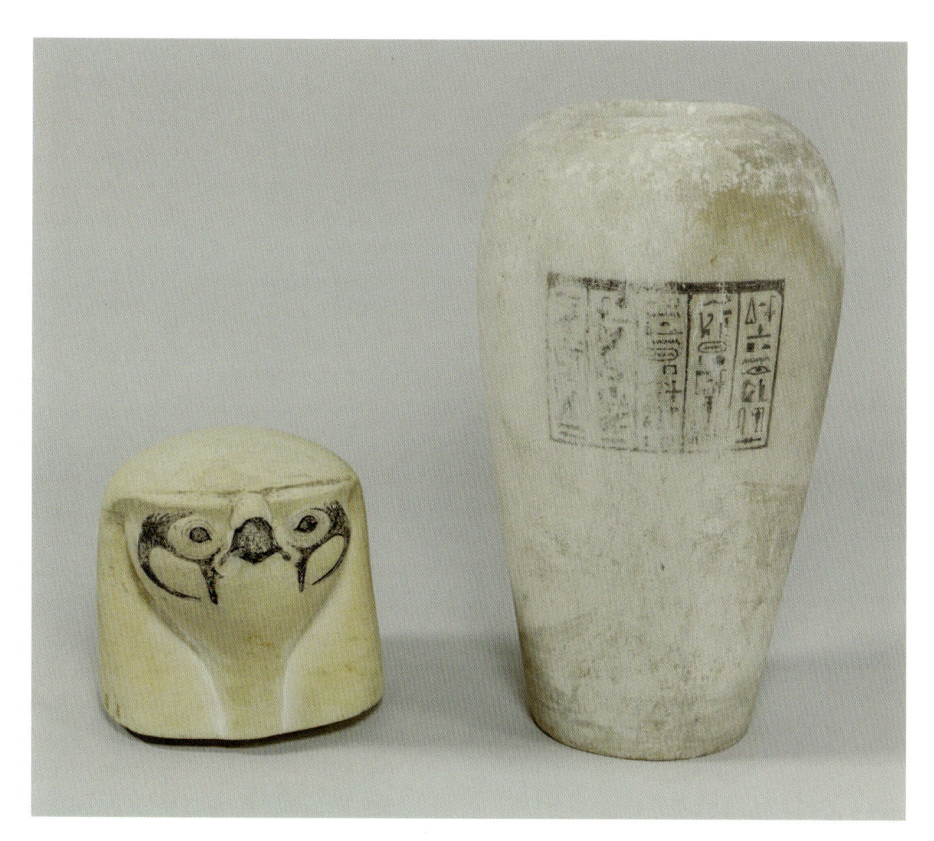

36. CANOPIC JAR AND STOPPER

Limestone and pigment
Dynasty 22, ca. 943–746 BC
Luxor, the Ramesseum
Gift of the Egyptian Research Account, 1896
Jar: H: 27.0; Diam. of opening: 8.2; Diam. base 10.0; Max. Circ. 52.0 cm; Top: H: 11.0; W of base: 13.0; W from beak to back of head: 15.0 cm
OIM E969A–B
Oriental Institute digital image D. 17899

The faint inscription on this jar identifies its owner as the "priest of Amun-Re Padimut," who was the son of the priest Hori. Canopic jars were intended to hold and preserve the internal organs of the deceased. The word "canopic" derives from ancient Greek writers who state that the mythological Greek hero Kanopos, helmsman of King Menelaeus during the Trojan War, was worshipped in the city Canopus in the form of a human-headed jar. Since some canopic jars have human-headed stoppers, early Egyptologists named these jars after this Greek hero in a case of mistaken identity, and the name stuck (Dodson 2001a, p. 231). Many canopic jars of the Twenty-second Dynasty were solid dummies, as at that time the organs were placed back in the body, but the jars had become such a standard element of burial that they were still included among the grave goods (ibid., p. 234). This jar, however, has been hollowed out from the top. Canopic jars traditionally number four and are associated with the four sons of Horus, identifiable from the New Kingdom on by their heads: human-headed Imsety, who guarded the liver; baboon-headed Hapy, who guarded the lungs; jackal-headed Duamutef, who guarded the stomach; and falcon-headed Qebehsenuef, who guarded the intestines (ibid., p. 232). In Book of the Dead spell 137, the four sons of Horus are requested to spread their protection over the deceased just as they did for Osiris (Dodson 2001b, p. 562).

Falcon-headed Qebehsenuef is the deity (or genius) depicted by this stopper and is mentioned in the text on the jar. The stopper shows the stylized markings used to depict falcons with the moustache stripe below the eye and the black line that outlines the cheek. The falcon head is supplied with the wig worn by falcon gods when they are shown with the body of a human. The sons of Horus were also identified with the four cardinal directions, with Qebehsenuef representing the west. Along with Duamutef, Qebehsenuef was linked to the most ancient city of Upper Egypt, Hierakonpolis, whereas Imsety and Hapy were linked to the most ancient city of Lower Egypt, Buto (Dodson 2001b, p. 562; Drenkhahn 1980). RS

37, view a

37, view b

37. CALCITE JAR

Egyptian alabaster (calcite)
Dynasty 5, reign of Unis (ca. 2321–2306 BC)
Purchased in Cairo, 1929
26.2 × 18.7 (rim diameter) cm
OIM E13947
Oriental Institute digital images D. 17975–76

This large globular jar is inscribed with two large falcons shown from the front with spread wings. Both falcons hold *shen*-rings ◯ in each foot, representing eternity and protection. Between the falcons is an inscription that is bordered by the hieroglyph for the sky (⎓) above and *was*-scepters (⎔) to each side. The inscription gives the full titulary of Unis, the last king of the Fifth Dynasty: "The King of Upper and Lower Egypt, the Son of Re Unis, given life forever. The Horus Uadjtawy; (the Two Ladies) Uadjemnebty; Golden Horus Uadj, given life forever."

There are a small number of inscribed globular vases from the late Fifth and early Sixth Dynasty with similar decoration. Most notable is a calcite vase in the Louvre (E 32372; see Ziegler 1999; Ziegler 1997, pp. 461–64, 471–74, figs. 2–4). This vase is smaller and rounder (taking the form of an Egyptian *nw*-vase); it has a single falcon in the same pose as the Oriental Institute vase, with its wings stretching around to the opposite side of the vase. Stretching from each foot of the bird to the opposite side are two cobras with flared hoods (called uraei). Ankh signs extend from each cobra to a cartouche with the name of Unis, which represents the renewal of life for the king (Ziegler 1997, p. 463). Two fragments of a similar vase found at Byblos bear the name of Unis inscribed horizontally and surmounted by a falcon's wing, which the excavator identified as belonging to a winged sun disk (Ziegler 1999). The falcon of the Louvre vase with the two uraei is conceptually similar to a winged sun disk with two uraei. Both the falcon and the winged sun disk are forms taken by Horus the Behdetite, but without being named it is uncertain that these falcons represent this particular form of Horus. A globular alabaster vase found in a mastaba at Edfu bears around its rim the name and titles of King Teti, the first king of the Sixth Dynasty (Bruyère et al. 1937, p. 35, pl. 17). A lotus bloom decorates the bottom of that vase and two birds with outstretched wings decorate the sides. The birds are without heads and the excavators interpreted them as vultures (Bruyère et al. 1937, p. 35) but their long rectangular tails identify them as falcons.[1]

An interesting parallel to these vases is an inscribed ostrich egg found at the modern village of Balat in the mastaba of Khentika, a Sixth Dynasty governor of Dakhla Oasis (Egyptian Museum, Cairo, JE 98774; see Castel et al. 2001, pp. 279–92, figs. a–d). The egg was not found in the burial of the governor himself but with that of a female relative. The egg is decorated with a falcon with outstretched wings similar to that of the Louvre vase but without the cobras. A *shen*-ring decorates the opening. The egg was provided with an alabaster base and a neck that fit on top, as well as a greywacke disk that acted as a stopper or lid; the overall effect of these gave the egg the appearance of a globular vase. The falcons on these vessels both represent the king and Horus and were intended to provide protection for the contents of the jar. The *shen*-rings in their talons signal that this protection is eternal. Those found in private monuments were likely presents from the king to his high officials (see Ziegler 1999, p. 362). Jars of this type may have held ointments considered essential in the afterlife (Ziegler 1997, p. 462; Bourriau 1984, col. 364).   RS

NOTE

[1] A similar vase was found in the tomb of the nomarch Izi, who lived in the time of Teti. It is decorated with two uraei separated by a vertical ankh (see Ziegler 1999, p. 361).

38

38. MODEL KNIFE AND GOOSE HEAD

Limestone, pigment
Old Kingdom, Dynasties 5–6, ca. 2435–2118 BC
Purchased in Cairo, 1920
13.6 × 7.0 × 2.4 cm
OIM E10644
Oriental Institute digital image D. 17943

Limestone "serving" statues[1] first appeared in elite mastaba tombs at Giza during the Fourth Dynasty and became widespread during the Fifth and Sixth Dynasties in the cemeteries of the Memphite necropolis. The role of these models was to fulfill the needs of the tomb owner after his death, and thus supplemented the daily life activities carved and/or painted on tomb-chapel walls. The ancient Egyptians believed that both models and representations would magically become effective in the afterlife for eternity. James H. Breasted acquired such a group of "serving" statues, a set of twenty-five figures, which would have allowed their original owner, cemetery official Ny-Kau-Inpu, to further enjoy food, drink, and music in the afterlife.[2] One of these figures has been interpreted as being a miniature limestone butcher's block.

This small rectangular model, with squared corners on one side and rounded ones on the other, is carved with the raised-relief representation of a goose's head and a flint knife and is painted with a gray wash. Details of the bird's anatomy, such as its eye and the nostril on its beak, have been added with black paint. As attested by the traditional offering formula, fowl was a favorite dish for ancient Egyptians and readily available (see Chapter 1). The examination of victual mummies also discovered in tombs (see Catalog No. 40) reveals that, to be ready for immediate consumption in the next life, birds left as offerings first had to be processed: the head, legs, and wing tips were cut, the bird was eviscerated, and its feathers plucked. In this case, the presence of this model in the tomb of Ny-Kau-Inpu would have ensured that his poultry was going to be butchered and ready for consumption in the hereafter. It may have been placed alongside the statuette representing a butcher slaughtering a bound calf[3] and may have been accompanied by a small alabaster offering in the shape of a trussed duck.[4] Some tombs also included a model depicting the actual cooking of the birds: a cook could be seen roasting a bird — a duck, goose, or dove — over a brazier of hot coal kept at the right temperature with a fan.[5]

In addition to ensuring that the deceased's table would never lack poultry, the depiction of a decapitated bird also symbolically represented the annihilation of the tomb owner's enemies. A New Kingdom dream interpretation book thus reveals that to see oneself killing a goose was a good sign, since it meant that one's enemies would be exterminated.[5] With such a model placed in his tomb, the deceased was guaranteed to experience a peaceful and pleasurable afterlife. RBL

PUBLISHED

Breasted, Jr., 1948, p. 44, pl. 98b upper scene; Teeter 2003, p. 21, Teeter 2011a, fig. 52

NOTES

[1] Some of the characters involved in menial tasks are not simply servants. Some are identified as being the sons and daughters of the deceased. I thank Emily Teeter for bringing this information to my attention. See Roth 1995, p. 57 n. 22.

[2] Tooley 1995, p. 8; Teeter 2003, p. 21: the models from the tomb of Ni-Kau-Inpu are believed to be the largest single deposit of such artifacts for the Old Kingdom.

[3] OIM E10626 (Emberling and Teeter 2010, fig. 4.9).

[4] For example, Museum of Fine Arts, Boston, 21.2816.

[5] Egyptian Museum, Cairo, CG 245; see Tooley 1995, p. 35, fig. 31.

[5] Vernus and Yoyotte 2005, p. 401. Decapitated ducks or geese are also represented in tomb offering scenes. See Brack and Brack 1980, pl. 69. On decapitation of enemies, see Ritner 1993, pp. 168–71.

39. MODEL OF A FEMALE OFFERING BEARER

Wood, stucco, pigment
Late First Intermediate Period–
Middle Kingdom, ca. 2050–1760 BC
Purchased in Cairo, 1919
Height 41.8 cm
OIM E10744
Oriental Institute digital images
D. 17945 and 17947

39, detail

FIGURE C40. Golden oriole (*Oriolus oriolus*) (photo by John Wyatt)

39

During the Sixth Dynasty (ca. 2305–2118 BC), wood started to be used to manufacture "serving" models, perhaps in order to lower the costs of fabrication and also to accelerate production. Wood fully superseded the use of stone during the First Intermediate Period. Most of the extant wooden models date to the Middle Kingdom, and are no longer restricted to the Memphite necropolis, such as was the case in the Old Kingdom. Such artifacts have been discovered in elite tombs all along the Nile Valley, thus attesting to the rising prosperity of the provinces (Tooley 2001, p. 424). Wooden statuettes of offering bearers are, along with miniature boats, the most common category of models. In particular, individual female offering bearers are a standard feature of funerary assemblages of this period and have been found throughout Egypt. Comparative studies of model sets indicate that offering-bearer statuettes are frequently larger and made with more care than the other models depicting daily activities. In some cases, they are executed as carefully as the statues of the tomb owner, and thus appear to be of higher importance than the other models. They are indeed believed to be the personification of the deceased's estates, formerly depicted on the tomb-chapel walls of the Old Kingdom elite (Roehrig 1988, p. 103; Ziegler and Bovot 2001, p. 141).

This statuette of a young woman is a typical offering-bearer model from the late First Intermediate Period or early Middle Kingdom. It is composed of at least six pieces, most likely joined together with pegs: the base, into which the feet are fixed; the body; the bird; the basket; and finally the two arms. Most of the joints are hidden underneath a layer of stucco that fully covers this figure. Depicted in an active stance with her left foot forward, the woman balances a rectangular basket of flour on her head with her left hand while grasping a small bird with her right hand. Her skin is painted yellow with further details added in black, such as the delineation of her fingers and toes, large eyes and eyebrows, and her jewelry, consisting of bracelets and anklets. She is dressed with a long white skirt held by two wide straps that cover her breasts. Finally, she wears a short white wig and around her forehead is a red filet tied in the back. Apart from her eyes, no other facial feature is enhanced by additional color. The lack of emphasis on her mouth may have been intentional, so as to prevent her from consuming any of the food brought forth for the deceased (Capel and Markoe 1996, p. 92).

The small yellow songbird this woman is holding by its legs is most likely a golden oriole (*Oriolus oriolus*), or *gnw* in Egyptian. Details, such as the bird's eyes and tail feathers, are added with black paint. The craftsman who designed this statuette chose an unusual species of bird for the woman to hold, for ducks and geese are by far the most common birds destined to become offerings. Throughout Egyptian history, waterfowl are depicted in innumerable scenes from tombs and temples being brought forth by processions of offering bearers, who hold them firmly by their wings or in their arms. In some instances, songbirds, especially pigeons and doves, known under the Egyptian term *mnw*, are listed among the goods the deceased expected to receive as offerings. While orioles were most likely consumed by the ancient Egyptians, just as they are occasionally eaten today (Houlihan 1986, p. 131), they are rarely included in offering lists. These bright yellow birds with black wings (fig. C40) figure prominently in orchard scenes, where they are depicted flocking in trees to feed on sycamore figs (see fig. 10.1). To prevent them from damaging their fruit crops, ancient Egyptians captured them individually using spring traps, or in larger numbers by casting a net over the tree in which they had gathered. The birds, when attempting to fly away, would become entangled in the fine mesh of the net and would only be freed by the fowlers as they placed them into cages for later consumption (see Chapter 1).

This statuette was most likely manufactured in a modest workshop focused on quantity rather than quality,[1] for the production does not exhibit the bright and varied colors, the wealth of details, and complex arrangements apparent on other models of the early Middle Kingdom, such as those from the tomb of Meket-Re in Thebes (Winlock 1955). RBL

NOTE

[1] See Freed and Doxey on the models of Djehuty-Nakht from Deir el-Bersheh, most of which were "executed with a minimum of detail and care. [...] A general approximation of form was believed to be sufficient for models to function properly in the afterlife" (2009, p. 152).

40

40. VICTUAL MUMMY AND CASE

Early Dynasty 18, ca. 1539–1390 BC
By exchange with the Metropolitan
Museum of Art, 1950

Mummy
Organic remains, linen
26.0 × 11.1 × 9.8 cm
OIM E18275

Case
Wood (possibly sycamore), plaster,
resin or bitumen
33.1 × 15.8 × 5.7 cm
OIM E18276

Oriental Institute digital image D. 17983

Ancient Egyptians were quite resourceful when it came to securing their supply of fowl in the afterlife. First of all, it was expected that family members and a mortuary priest would regularly bring fresh offerings to the tomb and celebrate the mortuary cult. In case such supplies were insufficient or no longer provided, numerous representations of food procurement and long lines of offering bearers were included in the iconographic repertoire of the tomb-chapel. They would become effective after being magically activated during the opening of the mouth ceremony. These scenes were complemented by the placement of the "serving" and food models within the burial chamber (see Catalog Nos. 38 and 39). The wealthier members of ancient Egyptian society could further include victual remains in their funerary assemblage. During the Old Kingdom, limestone food cases, whose shapes mirror their content, have been found in mastabas of the Memphite necropolis.[1] The practice of depositing food encased in sealed containers continued during the New Kingdom, especially in the Theban area. These funerary provisions consisted of not only bread, fruits, and grain, but also mummified meat such as cuts of beef[2] and poultry (ducks, geese, and doves) placed in wooden cases.[3]

This victual or food mummy was excavated from a tomb at Deir el-Bahari in Thebes, dated to the early Eighteenth Dynasty, during the 1918–19 expedition of the Metropolitan Museum of Art.[4] It was found in its wooden dish, which is shaped as a trussed bird and coated with white plaster. The inside of this container is also coated with some radiodense material that is clearly visible on CT scan images, probably some resin or bitumen (fig. C41). The cover, which would have been held in place by means of dowels and linen wrappings, is missing.[5]

A mummified bird had been deposited in this case, destined to provide nourishment for the deceased in his afterlife. CT scan imaging has revealed that the bird had been processed by having all its feathers removed, its head and a portion of the neck cut off, its legs severed in the middle of the tibiotarsus, and the wing tips removed at the humerus/radius-ulna joint. The presence of dense material, which has accumulated along the spine, most likely indicates that the bird was partly eviscerated, then treated with some resins and oils to further prevent decay.[6] Some organs were left in situ or replaced: it is indeed possible to identify the lungs, heart, and liver on CT scan images.[7] The abdominal cavity was then filled with a large ball of linen (see also fig. 13.11, in this volume).

Finally, the butchered and embalmed bird was covered with a single layer of linen bandages, with the neck and the wing bones wrapped separately from the body. Where the linen has decayed, bones can be seen protruding. Measurements of the humerus (ca. 13 cm) and the femur (6.3 cm) suggest that these are the remains of a white-fronted goose (*Anser albifrons*) or a lesser white-fronted goose (*Anser erythropus*). RBL

NOTES

[1] For example, Museum of Fine Arts, Boston, 13.3480; Metropolitan Museum of Art, New York, 37.6.2a–b, 37.6.4a–b.

[2] Ikram 1995, pp. 239–84; Ikram and Iskander 2002; Ikram 2005a, pp. 214–17.

[3] Goodman 1987; the nineteen bird victual mummies excavated in a Theban tomb of the early New Kingdom included geese (greylag, *Anser anser*; white-fronted, *Anser albifrons*; bean, *Anser fabalis*), pintail ducks (*Anas acuta*), garganeys (*Anas querquedula*), and turtledoves (*Streptopelia turtur*).

[4] Personal communication with Morena Stefanova, Metropolitan Museum of Art. See Lansing 1920, p. 7.

[5] For a complete example, see Metropolitan Museum of Art, New York, 30.3.21a–b.

[6] Scanning Electron Microscopy (SEM) analysis of victual mummy remains has demonstrated that some mummies were desiccated with natron (Ikram 2005a, p. 26); others had dried naturally (Goodman 1987, p. 71).

[7] Many thanks to Dr. Kenneth Welle, DVM, who helped me identify these organs. Gaillard and Lortet, who examined a large number of victual mummies from the Egyptian Museum in Cairo by unwrapping them and studying their contents, discovered that, in JE 24052, the gizzard, liver, and heart had been embalmed, wrapped, and replaced in the abdominal cavity (1905, pp. 97–98, 108–09). It is not possible for me to say at this point if the organs present in OIM E18275 were also wrapped with linen.

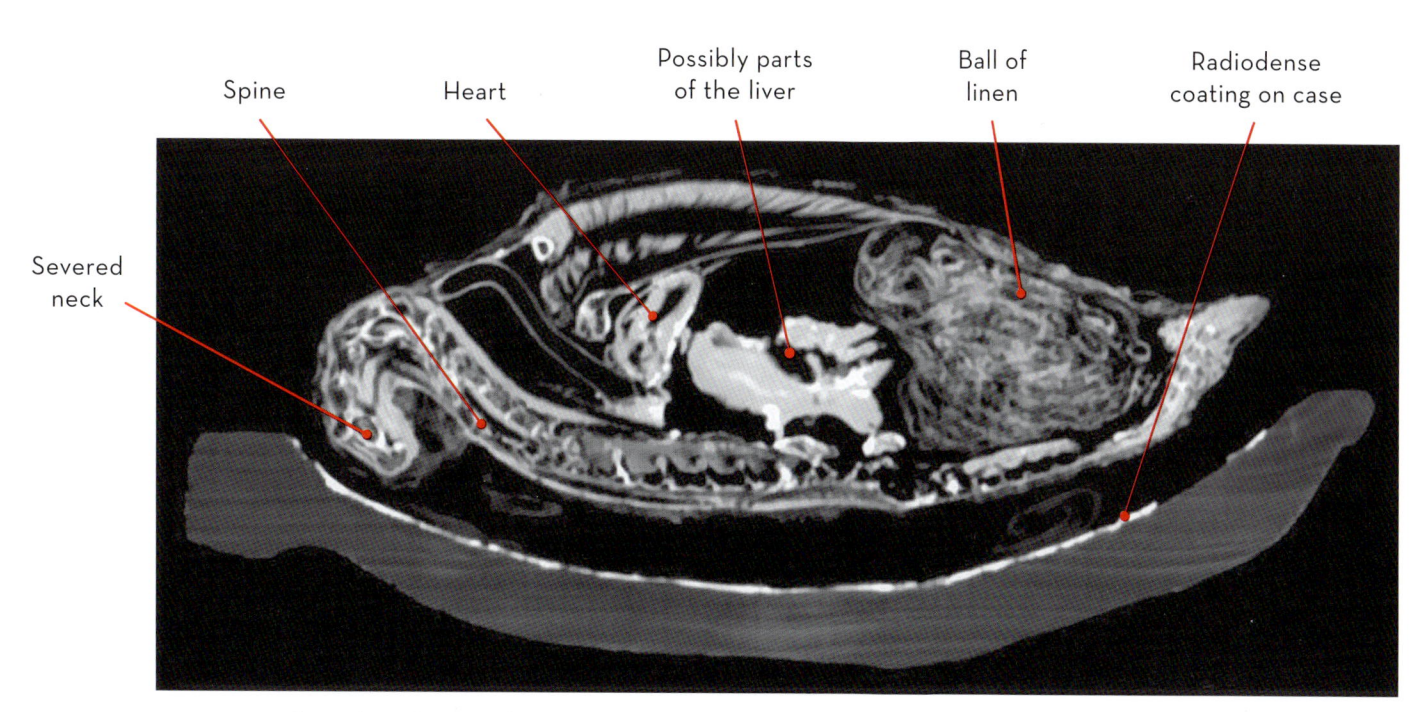

FIGURE C41. Midsagittal CT slice through OIM 18275-76 showing some anatomical features of the bird, as well as the linen filling in the abdominal cavity

APPENDIX: BIRD ANATOMY

After Proctor and Lynch 1993, pp. 59, 119. Drawings by Patrick J. Lynch. © Yale University Press

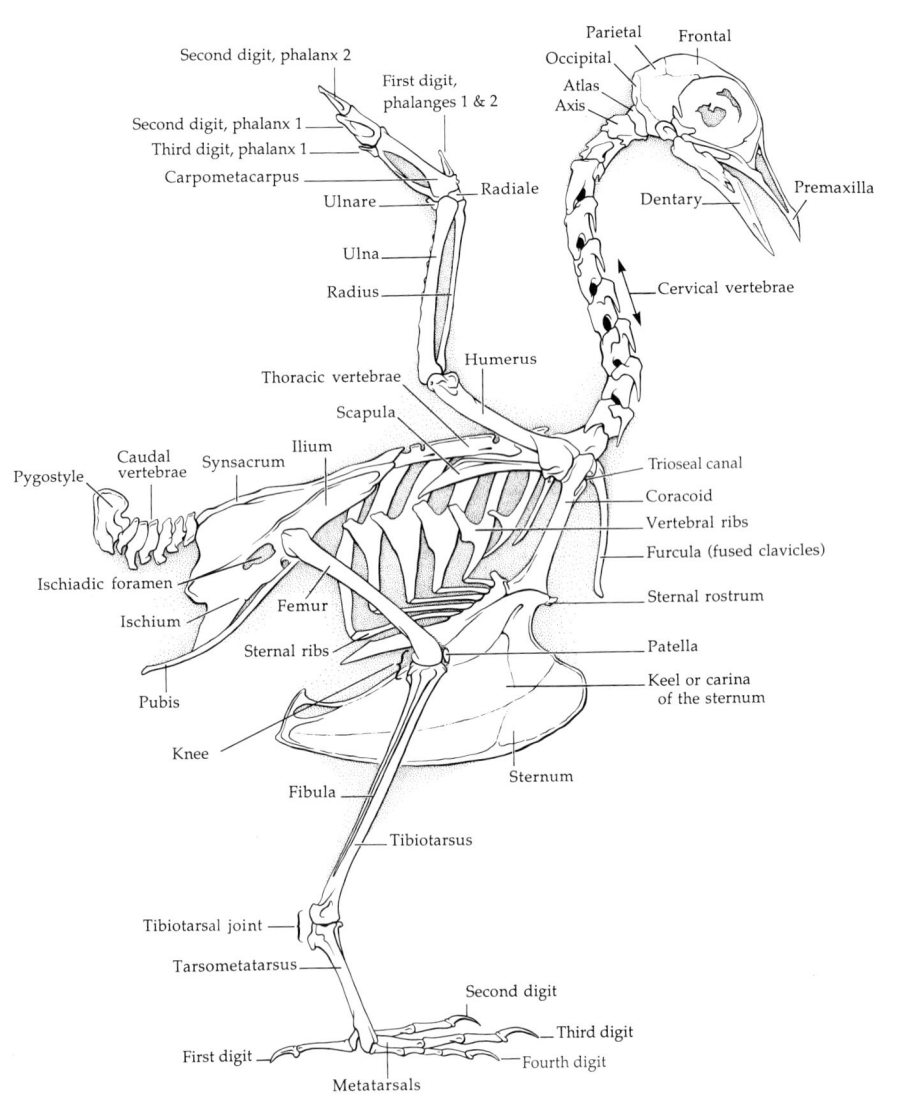

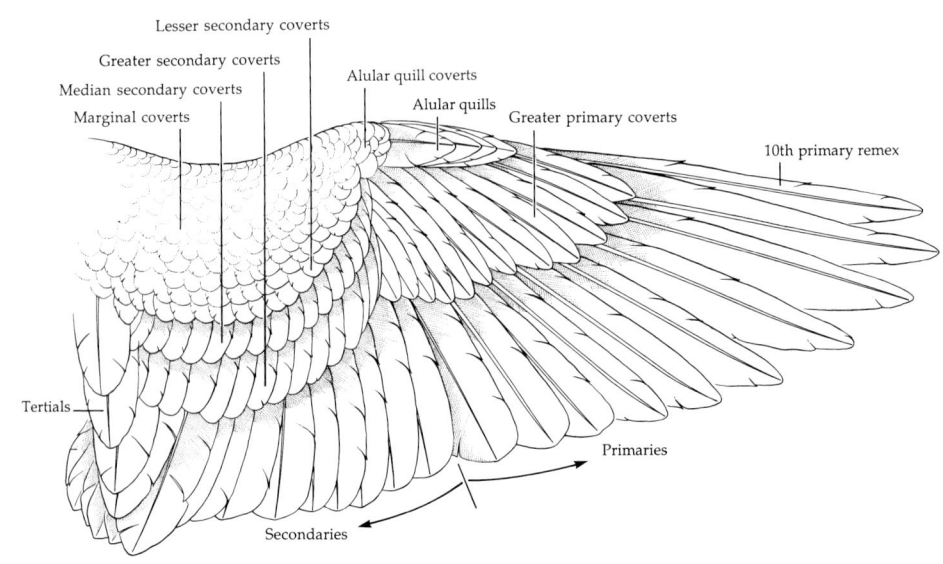

CONCORDANCE OF MUSEUM REGISTRATION NUMBERS

Registration Number	Catalog / Figure Number	Description
ART INSTITUTE OF CHICAGO		
1894.261	Catalog No. 3	Statue of Re-Horakhty
1894.610	Catalog No. 16	Cosmetic dish decorated with duck motifs
1920.256	Catalog No. 19	Plaque showing a quail chick
BROOKLYN MUSEUM		
49.48	Catalog No. 28	Coffin for an ibis
FIELD MUSEUM OF NATURAL HISTORY		
31279	Catalog No. 4	Stela of Horus
THE ORIENTAL INSTITUTE MUSEUM		
C209	fig. 4.11	Cast of the Narmer Palette
E70	Catalog No. 18	Ladle
E146	fig. 3.5	Bird mummy
E150	Catalog No. 26	Mummified eagle
E154	Catalog No. 27	Mummified bundle in a wooden coffin
E370	Catalog No. 12	Fowling throwstick
E969A–B	Catalog No. 36	Canopic jar and stopper
E972	Catalog No. 35	Statuette of a falcon
E4461	Catalog No. 34	*Ba*-bird statuette
E5234	fig. 9.5	Naqada II Decorated Ware pot
E8854	fig. C24	Owl hieroglyph on a fragment
E9162	fig. 13.5–8	Bird mummy
E9164	fig. 14.2	Bird mummy
E9189	fig. C18	Relief fragment
E9233A–B	Catalog No. 30	Bird coffin
E9234	Catalog No. 31, figs. 13.12–15	Bird mummy
E9235	Catalog No. 33	Ibis egg
E9236	Catalog No. 33	Ibis egg
E9237	Catalog No. 32	Mummified bundle
E9787	fig. 2.7	Book of the Dead papyrus of Nesshutefnut
E9802	Catalog No. 21	Plaque showing a falcon
E10486	fig. 2.2	Papyrus Milbank
E10504	Catalog No. 23	Statue of Horus
E10537	Catalog No. 7	Thoth rebus amulet
E10555	Catalog No. 20	Plaque showing a house martin
E10557	Catalog No. 5	Plaque with royal title
E10589	fig. 2.6	Statue base of Djedhor from Athribis
E10604	Catalog No. 25	Coffin decorated with a falcon and two deities
E10644	Catalog No. 38	Model of knife and goose head
E10744	Catalog No. 39	Model of a female offering bearer
E10788	Catalog No. 10	Apotropaic knife
E10859	Catalog No. 15	Stone jar in the shape of a duck
E11198A–B	Catalog No. 17	Fragments of a stool with duck heads
E12244	Catalog No. 8	Thoth and Maat amulet
E13722	fig. 8.7	Silver Ptolemaic coin
E13947	Catalog No. 37	Calcite jar
E15488	Catalog No. 6b	Lapwing tile
E16719	Catalog No. 6c	Lapwing tile
E16721	Catalog No. 6a	Lapwing tile
E16734	fig. 8.6	Lamp in the shape of a peacock
E17972	Catalog No. 22	Head of an owl
E18275–76	figs. 13.9–11, Catalog No. 40	Victual mummy and platter
E18876	Catalog No. 24	Oracle text
E19051	fig. 2.8	Ceramic vessel
E19422	Catalog No. 29	Demotic letter to "the ibis, Thoth"
E21384	Catalog No. 1	Ostrich egg
E25011	Catalog No. 9	Thoth and feather amulet
E42440	fig. 13.1–4	Unwrapped mummy of a common kestrel
D. 17882	Catalog No. 11	"Birds in an Acacia Tree"
D. 17883	Catalog No. 13	"Fowling in the Marshes"
D. 17884	Catalog No. 14	"Farmers Deliver Their Quota of Geese"
D. 17885	Catalog No. 2	"Three Vignettes, Thebes, Tomb of Queen Nefretere, Ramesses II, 1292–1225 B.C."

CHECKLIST OF THE EXHIBIT

Introduction

Ostrich Egg (OIM E21384)

"Birds In an Acacia Tree"

The Exploitation of Birds

Fowling Throwstick (OIM E370)

"Farmers Deliver their Quote of Geese"

"Fowling in the Marshes"

Birds, Pharaoh, and His Subjects

Plaque with Royal Title (OIM E10557)

Lapwing tiles (OIM E15488, E16719, E16721)

Statue of Re-Horakhty (AIC 1894.261)

Stela of Horus (FMNH 31279)

Birds and Protection

Thoth Rebus Amulet (OIM E10537)

Apotropaic Knife (OIM E10788)

Thoth and Maat Amulet (OIM E12244)

Thoth and Feather Amulet (OIM E25011)

Birds as Decorative Motifs

Ladle (OIM E70)

Stone Jar in the Shape of a Duck (OIM E10859)

Fragments of a Stool with Duck Heads (OIM E11198A-B)

Cosmetic Dish Decorated with Duck Motifs (AIC 1894.610)

Birds and Hieroglyphs (or "in the scribal training")

Plaque Showing a Quail Chick (AIC 1920.256)

Plaque Showing a Falcon (OIM E9802)

Plaque Showing a House Martin (OIM E10555)

Head of an Owl (OIM E17972)

Bird Cults

Mummified Eagle (OIM E150)

Mummified Bundle in a Wooden Coffin (OIM E154 A–B)

Bird Coffin (OIM E9233 A–B)

Mummified Ibis (OIM E9234)

Ibis Eggs (OIM E9235, E9236)

Mummified Bundle (OIM E9237)

Statue of Horus (OIM E10504)

Coffin Decorated with a Falcon and Two Deities (OIM E10604)

Oracle Text (OIM E18876)

Demotic Letter to "The Ibis, Thoth" (OIM E19422)

"Three Vignettes"

Coffin for an Ibis (Brooklyn Museum 49.48)

Birds in Death and the Afterlife

Canopic jar and Stopper (OIM E969 A–B)

Statuette of a Falcon (OIM E972)

Ba-Bird Statuette (OIM E4461)

Model of Knife and Goose Head (OIM E10644)

Statue of a Female Offering Bearer (OIM E10744)

Calcite Jar (OIM E13947)

Victual Mummy (OIM E18275)

Case for Victual Mummy (OIM E18276)

LIST OF BIRDS

African jabiru; *see* saddle-billed stork
African mourning dove (*Streptopelia decipiens*)
African pied wagtail (*Motacilla aguimp*)
bald ibis; *see* northern bald ibis
barn owl (*Tyto alba*) — fig. C23
bean goose (*Anser fabalis*) — fig. 1
black crowned crane (*Balearica pavonina*)
black ibis; *see* glossy ibis
black kite (*Milvus migrans*) — fig. 10.9a
black stork (*Ciconia nigra*) — fig. 9.12
black-headed plover (*Vanellus tectus*) — fig. 9.11
blackbird (*Turdus merula*)
cattle egret (*Bubulcus ibis*) — fig. 15.6
chanting goshawk (*Melierax musicus*)
chestnut-bellied sandgrouse (*Pterocles exustus*)
collared dove (*Streptopelia decaocto*)
collared pratincole (*Glareola pratincola*)
common bulbul (*Pycnonotus barbatus*)
common crane (*Grus grus*) — fig. 1.9
common kestrel (*Falco tinnunculus*) — figs. 13.1–4; Catalog No. 2
common kingfisher (*Alcedo atthis*) — fig. 9.3
common quail (*Coturnix coturnix*) — figs. 1.5, C18–19; Catalog No. 19
common redstart (*Phoenicurus phoenicurus*)
common shelduck (*Tadorna tadorna*) — fig. 9.2
common teal (*Anas crecca*) — fig. 1
coot (*Fulica atra*) — fig. 1.1
cormorant (*Phalacrocorax* sp.) — fig. 10.4
courser (family *Glareolidae*)
crag martin (*Ptyonoprogne rupestris*)
Dalmatian pelican (*Pelecanus crispus*) — fig. 1.12
demoiselle crane (*Anthropoides virgo*) — fig. 1.9
domestic chicken (*Gallus gallus*)
dove (*Streptopelia* sp.)
Dupont's lark (*Chersophilus duponti*)
eagle owl (*Bubo bubo ascalaphus*) — fig. C25
Egyptian goose (*Alopochen aegyptiacus*)
Egyptian plover (*Pluvianus aegyptius*)
Egyptian vulture (*Neophron percnopterus*)
Eleanora's falcon (*Falco eleonorae*)
Eurasian golden oriole (*Oriolus oriolus*) — fig. C40
Eurasian hobby falcon (*Falco subbuteo*)
Eurasian sparrowhawk (*Accipiter nisus*) — figs. 13.5–8
Eurasian teal (*Anas crecca*)

European turtledove (*Streptopelia turtur*)
garganey (*Anas querquedula*)
goose (*Anas* sp.)
glossy ibis (*Plegadis falcinellus*)
great cormorant (*Phalacrocorax carbo*)
great crested grebe (*Podiceps cristatus*)
greater flamingo (*Phoenicopterus ruber*) — fig. 9.5
green heron (*Butorides striata*)
grey heron (*Ardea cinerea*) — figs. 1.2, 10.3, 10.6
greylag goose (*Anser anser*)
griffon vulture (*Gyps fulvus*) — fig. 5.7; Catalog No. 5
hawfinch (*Coccothraustes coccothraustes*)
helmeted guineafowl (*Numida meleagris*)
hooded crow (*Corvus cornix*)
hoopoe: Eurasian (*Upupa epops*); African (*Upupa africana*) — figs. 1.3–4, 10.1; Catalog No. 11
houbara bustard (*Chlamydotis undulata*)
house martin (*Delichon urbicum*) — Catalog No. 20
house sparrow (*Passer domesticus*)
kingfisher (family *Alcedinidae*)
knob-billed duck (*Sarkidiornis melanotos*) — fig. 9.1
lanner falcon (*Falco biarmicus*) — fig. 5.1
lappet-faced or Nubian vulture (*Torgos tracheliotos*) — figs. 5.4–6
lesser short-toed lark (*Calandrella rufescens*)
lesser white-fronted goose (*Anser erythropus*)
little bittern (*Ixobrychus minutus*) — Catalog No. 13
little egret (*Egretta garzetta*) — fig. 15.5
long-legged buzzard (*Buteo rufinus*) — fig. 3.5
mallard (*Anas platyrhynchos*)
marabou stork (*Leptoptilos crumeniferus*)
marbled duck (*Marmaronetta angustirostris*)
masked shrike (*Lanius nubicus*) — figs. 10.9b; Catalog No. 11
merganser (*Mergus* sp.)
merlin (*Falco columbarius*)
night heron (*Nycticorax* sp.)
Nile goose (*Chenalopex aegyptiaca*)
northern bald ibis (*Geronticus eremita*) [formerly known as the waldrapp, hermit ibis, or crested ibis]
northern lapwing (*Vanellus vanellus*) — figs. 9.10, C2; Catalog No. 6
ostrich (*Struthio camelus*) — figs. 1.6, 9.4
painted snipe (*Rostratula benghalensis*)

palm dove (*Streptopelia senegalensis*)
peregrine falcon (*Falco peregrinus*) — fig. 4.2
pied avocet (*Recurvirostra avosetta*)
pied kingfisher (*Ceryle rudis*) — frontispiece; figs. 9.3, 10.10
pigeon (*Columba* sp.)
pink-backed pelican (*Pelecanus rufescens*)
pink-headed fruit dove (*Ptilinopus porphyreus*)
pintail duck (*Anas acuta*) — Catalog Nos. 11, 13, 14
purple gallinule (*Porphyrio porphyrio*) — fig. 15.2
purple heron (*Ardea purpurea*)
red-backed shrike (*Lanius collurio*) — Catalog No. 11
red-bellied barn swallow (*Hirundo rustica savignii*)
red-breasted goose (*Branta ruficollis*) — figs. 9.8–9
red-necked grebe (*Podiceps grisegena*) — figs. 9.6–7
redstart (*Phoenicurus phoenicurus*) — Catalog No. 11
ringed plovers (*Charadrius hiaticula*) — fig. 15.2
rock martin (*Ptyonoprogne obsoleta*)
ruff (*Philomachus pugnax*) — fig. 9.13
sacred ibis (*Threskiornis aethiopicus*) — figs. 1.14, 13.16–19, C34
saddle-billed stork (*Ephippiorhynchus senegalensis*)
sand martin (*Riparia riparia*)
secretarybird (*Sagittarius serpentarius*)
Senegal coucal (*Centropus senegalensis*) — fig. 15.3
Senegal thick-knee (*Burhinus senegalensis*)
snowy owl (*Bubo scandiacus*) — 14.2
Spanish sparrow (*Passer hispaniolensis*)
squacco heron (*Ardeola ralloides*)
owl family — *Strigidae*
swan (*Cygnus* sp.)
tawny eagle (*Aquila rapax*) — fig. C29
three-banded plover (*Charadrius tricollaris*)
turtledove; *see* European turtledove
whiskered tern (*Chlidonias hybridus*)
white stork (*Ciconia ciconia*)
white-bellied or Abdim's stork (*Ciconia abdimii*)
white-bellied barn swallow (*Hirundo rustica*)
white-breasted kingfisher (*Halcyon smyrnensis*) — fig. 15.7
white-fronted goose (*Anser albifrons*) — fig. 1
white-headed duck (*Oxyura leucocephala*)
white-tailed sea eagle (*Haliaeetus albicilla*)
white wagtail (*Motacilla alba*)
yellow-billed kites (*Milvus aegyptius*)
yellow-billed stork (*Mycteria ibis*)

BIBLIOGRAPHY

Adler, Wolfgang
1996 "Die spätbronzezeitlichen Pyxiden in Gestalt von Wasservögeln." In *Kāmid el-Lōz, Volume 16: 'Schatzhaus'-Studien*, edited by Rolf Hachmann, pp. 27–119. Saarbrücker Beiträge zur Altertumskunde 59. Bonn: Rudolf Habelt.

Affholder-Gérard, Brigitte, and Marie-Jeanne Cornic
1990 *Angers, Musée Pincé: collections égyptiennes*. Paris Inventaire des collections publiques françaises 35. Paris: Éditions de la Réunion des Musées Nationaux.

Aldred, Cyril
1971 *Jewels of the Pharaohs: Egyptian Jewelry of the Dynastic Period*. New York: Praeger.

Allen, James P.
2005 *The Ancient Egyptian Pyramid Texts*. Writings from the Ancient World 23. Atlanta: Society of Biblical Literature.

Allen, Marti Lu
1895 The Terracotta Figurines from Karanis: A Study of Technique, Style, and Chronology in Fayoumic Coroplastics. PhD dissertation, University of Michigan.

Allen, Thomas George
1923 *A Handbook of the Egyptian Collection of the Art Institute of Chicago*. Chicago: University of Chicago Press.
1936 *Egyptian Stelae in the Field Museum*. Anthropological Series 24/1. Chicago: The Field Museum.
1960 *The Egyptian Book of the Dead: Documents in the Collection of the Oriental Institute Museum at the University of Chicago*. Oriental Institute Publications 82. Chicago: The Oriental Institute. Reprinted in 2010.
1974 *The Book of the Dead, or Going Forth by Day: Ideas of the Ancient Egyptian Concerning the Hereafter as Expressed in Their Own Terms*. Studies in Ancient Oriental Civilization 37. Chicago: University of Chicago Press.

Altenmüller, Hartwig
1965 Die Apotropaia und Die Götter Mittelägyptens. PhD dissertation, Ludwig-Maximilians-Universität zu München, Rottweil/Neckar.
1974 "Bemerkungen zur Kreiselscheibe Nr. 310 aus dem Grab des Hemaka in Saqqara." *Göttinger Miszellen* 9: 13–18.
2010 *Einführung in die Hieroglyphenschrift*. 2nd edition. Hamburg: Helmut Buske.

Altenmüller, Hartwig, and Dieter Johannes
1998 *Die Wanddarstellungen im Grab des Mehu in Saqqara*. Archäologische Veröffentlichungen 42. Mainz: Philipp von Zabern.

Andrews, Carol
1984 *Egyptian Mummies*. Cambridge: Harvard University Press.
1994 *Amulets of Ancient Egypt*. London: British Museum Press.

Arnold, Dorothea
1995 "An Egyptian Bestiary." *The Metropolitan Museum of Art Bulletin* 52/4: 3–64.
2010 *Falken, Katzen, Krokodile: Tiere im alten Ägypten aus den Sammlungen des Metropolitan Museum of Art, New York, und des Ägyptischen Museums, Kairo*. Zürich: Museum Rietberg.

Assmann, Jan
1978 "Eine Traumoffenbarung der Göttin Hathor: Zeugnisse 'Persönlicher Frömmigkeit' in thebanischen Privatgräbern der Ramessidenzeit." *Revue d'Égyptologie* 30: 22–50.
1995 *Egyptian Solar Religion in the New Kingdom: Re, Amun and the Crisis of Polytheism*. London, New York: Kegan Paul International.
2005 *Death and Salvation in Ancient Egypt*. Ithaca: Cornell University Press.

Atherton, Stephanie D.; Lidija M. McKnight; Don R. Brothwell; and Rosalie David
2012 "A Healed Femoral Fracture of *Threskiornis aethiopicus* (Sacred Ibis) from the Animal Cemetery at Abydos, Egypt." *International Journal of Palaeopathology*, May 16, 2012. Available online at: http://www.sciencedirect.com/science/article/pii/S1879981712000319

Aufderheide, Arthur C.
2003 *The Scientific Study of Mummies*. Cambridge: Cambridge University Press.

Aufrère, Sidney H.
2009 "Les alphabets dits 'égyptiens' et 'cophtes' de Fournier le Jeune (1766) et la 'guerre des polices' au XVIIIe siècle. En marge de la redécouverte de l'écriture hiératique." In *Verba manent: Recueil d'études dédiées à Dimitri Meeks par ses collègues et amis*, edited by Isabelle Régen and Frédéric Servajean, pp. 29–49. Cahiers "Égypte Nilotique et Méditerranéenne" 2. Montpellier: Université Paul Valéry (Montpellier III).

Bács, Tamás A.; Zoltan I. Fábián; Gábor Schreiber; and László Török; editors
2009 *Hungarian Excavations in the Theban Necropolis: A Celebration of 102 Years of Fieldwork in Egypt*. Budapest: Department of Egyptology, Eötvös Loránd University.

Badawy, Alexander
1978 *Coptic Art and Archaeology: The Art of the Christian Egyptians from the Late Antique to the Middle Ages*. Cambridge: MIT Press.

Baha El Din, Sherif M.
1992 "Notes on Recent Changes in the Status of Breeding Herons in the Egyptian Nile Valley and Delta." *Bulletin of the Ornithological Society of the Middle East* 29: 12–15.
1999 *Directory of Important Bird Areas in Egypt*. Cairo: BirdLife International and the Palm Press.

Bailey, Donald M.
2008 *Ptolemaic and Roman Terracottas from Egypt*. Catalogue of the Terracottas in the British Museum 4. London: British Museum Press.

Baines, John
1990 "Trône et dieu: aspects du symbolisme royal et divin des temps archaïques." *Bulletin de la Société Française d'Égyptologie* 118: 5–37.
1995 "Origins of Egyptian Kingship." In *Ancient Egyptian Kingship*, edited by David P. Silverman and David O'Connor, pp. 95–156. Probleme der Ägyptologie 9. Leiden: Brill.

Baker, Hollis S.
1966 *Furniture in the Ancient World: Origins and Evolution, 3100–475 BC*. New York: Macmillan.

Barbotin, Christophe, and Didier Devauchelle
2005 *La voix des hiéroglyphes: promenade au Département des antiquités égyptiennes du Musée du Louvre*. Paris: Musée du Louvre.

Beaux, Nathalie
1990 *Le cabinet de curiosités de Thoutmosis III: plantes et animaux du "Jardin Botanique" de Karnak*. Orientalia Lovaniensia Analecta 36. Leuven: Peeters.

Beinlich, Horst
1991 *Das Buch vom Fayum*. Ägyptologische Abhandlungen 51. Wiesbaden: Harrassowitz.
2000 *Das Buch vom Ba*. Studien zum altägyptischen Totenbuch 4. Wiesbaden: Harrassowitz.

BIBLIOGRAPHY

Bell, Lanny
1997 "The New Kingdom 'Divine' Temple: The Example of Luxor." In *Temples of Ancient Egypt*, edited by Byron E. Shafer, pp. 127–84. Ithaca: Cornell University Press.

Benazeth, Dominique
1992 *L'art du métal au début de l'ère chrétienne*. Paris: Éditions de la Réunion des Musées Nationaux.

Binder, Susan
2000 "The Tomb Owner Fishing and Fowling." In *Egyptian Art: Principles and Themes in Wall Scenes*, edited by Kim McCorquodale and Leonie Donovan, pp. 111–28. Prism Archaeological Studies 6. Giza: Prism Publications.

Bleiberg, Edward
2008 *To Live Forever: Egyptian Treasures from the Brooklyn Museum*. Brooklyn: Brooklyn Museum.

Boessneck, Joachim
1960 "Zur Gänsehaltung im alten Ägypten." In *Festschrift der Wiener tierärztlichen Monatsschrift Herrn Professor Dr. Josef Schreiber zum 70. Geburtstag gewidmet*, edited by Erwin Gratzl, pp. 192–206. Vienna: Urban & Schwarzenberg.
1988 *Die Tierwelt des alten Ägypten*. Munich: C. H. Beck.

Bongioanni, Alessandro; Maria Sole Croce; and Laura Accomazzo, editors
2001 *The Illustrated Guide to the Egyptian Museum*. Photographs by Araldo De Luca. Cairo: American University in Cairo Press.

Bonnet, Hans
1952 *Reallexikon der ägyptischen Religionsgeschichte*. Berlin: Walter de Gruyter.

Borchardt, Ludwig
1913 *Das Grabdenkmal des Königs Saḥurāʿ*, Volume 2: *Die Wandbilder*. Ausgrabungen der Deutschen Orient-Gesellschaft in Abusir 1902–1908. Leipzig: J. C. Hinrichs.

Bothmer, Bernard
1953 "Ptolemaic Reliefs, IV. A Votive Tablet." *Bulletin of the Museum of Fine Arts* 51.286: 79–84.
1967/68 "The Nodding Falcon of the Guennol Collection at the Brooklyn Museum." *The Brooklyn Museum Annual* 9: 75–76.

Bourriau, Janine D.
1984 "Salbgefäße." In *Lexikon der Ägyptologie*, edited by Wolfgang Helck and Wolfhart Westendorf, vol. 5, cols. 362–66. Wiesbaden: Harrassowitz.

Bowman, Alan K.
1986 *Egypt after the Pharaohs, 332 BC–AD 642: From Alexander to the Arab Conquest*. Berkeley: University of California Press.

Boylan, Patrick
1979 *Thoth, the Hermes of Egypt: A Study of Some Aspects of Theological Thought in Ancient Egypt*. Chicago: Ares Reprints. Reprint of 1922 version.

Brack, Annelies, and Arthur Brack
1980 *Das Grab des Haremheb: Theben Nr. 78*. Archäologische Veröffentlichungen 35. Mainz am Rhein: Philipp von Zabern.

Breasted, James Henry
1930 *The Edwin Smith Surgical Papyrus*. 2 volumes. Oriental Institute Publications 3 (text) and 4 (plates). Chicago: University of Chicago Press.

Breasted, James Henry, Jr.
1948 *Egyptian Servant Statues*. New York: Pantheon Books.

Brewer, Douglas
2001 "Animal Husbandry." In *The Oxford Encyclopedia of Ancient Egypt*, edited by Donald B. Redford, vol. 1, pp. 89–94. New York: Oxford University Press.
2002 "Hunting, Animal Husbandry and Diet in Ancient Egypt." In *A History of the Animal World in the Ancient Near East*, edited by Billie Jean Collins, pp. 427–56. Handbuch der Orientalistik, Erste Abteilung, Nahe und der Mittlere Osten 64. Leiden: Brill.

Broekman, Gerard P. F.
2009 "Falcon-headed Coffins and Cartonnages." *Journal of Egyptian Archaeology* 95: 67–81.

Brunner-Traut, Emma
1965 "Spitzmaus und Ichneumon als Tiere des Sonnengottes." *Nachrichten von der Akademie der Wissenschaften in Göttingen* 7: 123–63.
1971 "Ein Königskopf der Spätzeit mit dem 'Blauen Helm.'" *Zeitschrift für ägyptische Sprache und Altertumskunde* 97: 18–30.
1984 "Spitzmause." In *Lexikon der Ägyptologie*, edited by Wolfgang Helck and Wolfhart Westendorf, vol. 5, cols. 1160–61. Wiesbaden: Harrassowitz.

Bruyère, B.; J. Manteuffel; K. Michałowski; and J. Sainte Fare Garnot
1937 *Fouilles franco-polonaises*, Rapports 1: *Tell Edfou 1937*. Cairo: Institut français d'archéologie orientale.

Buchberger, Hannes
1986 "Vogel." In *Lexikon der Ägyptologie*, edited by Wolfgang Helck and Wolfhart Westendorf, vol. 6, cols. 1046–51. Wiesbaden: Harrassowitz.

Buckley, Stephen A.; Katherine A. Clark; and Richard P. Evershed
2004 "Complex Organic Chemical Balms of Pharaonic Animal Mummies." *Nature* 431 (September 16): 294–99.

Burkert, Walter
1985 *Greek Religion*. Cambridge: Harvard University Press.

Burn, Lucilla
1991 *The British Museum Book of Greek and Roman Art*. London: British Museum Press.

Burton, Robert
1985 *Bird Behavior*. New York: Alfred A. Knopf.

Butzer, Karl W.
1976 *Early Hydraulic Civilization in Egypt: A Study in Cultural Ecology*. Prehistoric Archeology and Ecology. Chicago: University of Chicago Press.

Callendar, Vivienne G.
2011 "Curious Names of Some Old Kingdom Royal Women." *Journal of Egyptian Archaeology* 97: 127–42.

Calverley, Amice M.
1933 *The Temple of King Sethos I at Abydos*, Volume 1: *The Chapels of Osiris, Isis and Horus*, edited by Alan H. Gardiner. Chicago: University of Chicago Press.

Caminos, Ricardo A.
1956 *Literary Fragments in the Hieratic Script*. Oxford: Griffith Institute.

Capel, Anne K., and Glenn E. Markoe
1996 *Mistress of the House, Mistress of Heaven: Women in Ancient Egypt*. New York: Hudson Hills Press in association with Cincinnati Art Museum.

Carswell, John
1978 *Artists in Egypt: An Exhibition of Paintings and Drawings by Artists Employed by the Oriental Institute in Egypt, 1920–1935*. Chicago: The Oriental Institute.

Carter, Howard
1927–33 *The Tomb of Tut-Ankh-Amen, Discovered by the Late Earl of Carnarvon and Howard Carter*. 3 volumes. London: Cassell.

Castel, Georges; Laure Pantalacci; and Nadine Cherpion
2001 *Le mastaba de Khentika: tombeau d'un gouverneur de l'oasis à la fin de l'ancien empire*. Balat 5. Fouilles de l'Institut français d'archéologie orientale du Caire 40. Institut français d'archéologie orientale 864. Cairo: Institut français d'archéologie orientale.

Černý, Jaroslav
1972 "Troisième série de questions adressées aux oracles." *Bulletin de l'Institut français d'archéologie orientale* 72: 49–69.

BIBLIOGRAPHY

Chamberlain, J. Martyn
    2004   "Where Optics Meets Electronics: Recent Progress in Decreasing the Terahertz Gap." *Philosophical Transactions. Series A, Mathematical, Physical, and Engineering Sciences* 362: 199–211.

Champollion, Jean-François
    1835–45   *Monuments de l'Égypte et de la Nubie*. 4 volumes. Paris: Firmin Didot frères.

Chan, W. L.; J. Deibel; and D. M. Mittleman
    2007   "Imaging with Terahertz Radiation." *Reports on Progress in Physics* 70: 1325–79.

Charron, Alain
    1990   "Massacres d'animaux à la Basse Époque." *Revue d'Égyptologie* 41: 209–13.

Chauveau, Michel
    1986   "Les cultes d'Edfa à l'époque romaine." *Revue d'Égyptologie* 37: 31–43.

Cherpion, Nadine
    2001   "L'oeuf d'autruche du mastaba III." In *Balat V: le mastaba de Khentika; tombeau d'un gouverneur de l'oasis à la fin de l'ancien empire*, edited by Georges Castel, Laure Pantalacci, and Nadine Cherpion, pp. 279–94. Fouilles de l'Institut français d'archéologie orientale du Caire 40. Cairo: Institut français d'archéologie orientale.

Churcher, C. S. Rufus; M. R. Kleindienst; and H. P. Schwarcz
    1999   "Faunal Remains from a Middle Pleistocene Lacustrine Marl in Dakhleh Oasis, Egypt: Palaeoenvironmental Reconstructions." *Palaeogeography, Palaeoclimatology, Palaeoecology* 154: 301–12.

Ciałowicz, Krzysztof M.
    2008   "Gazelles and Ostriches from Tell El-Farkha." *Studies in Ancient Art and Civilization* 12: 21–34.
    2011   "The Early Dynastic Administrative-Cultic Centre at Tell El-Farkha." In *Egypt at Its Origins* 3, edited by Peter N. Fiske and Renée F. Friedman, pp. 763–800. Orientalia Lovaniensia Analecta 205. Leuven: Peeters.

Clement, Paul A., and Herbert B. Hoffleit
    1969   *Plutarch's Moralia*, Volume 8: *612 B-697 C*. Loeb Classical Library 424. Cambridge: Harvard University Press.

Clifford, William, and Matthew Wetherbee
    2004   "Piecing Together the Secrets of Mummification." *KMT, A Modern Journal of Egyptology* 15/2: 64–65.

Coltherd, J. B.
    1966   "The Domestic Fowl in Ancient Egypt." *Ibis* 108/2: 217–23.

Cooney, John
    1941   *Pagan and Christian Egypt: Egyptian Art from the First to the Tenth Century AD*. Brooklyn: Brooklyn Museum.

Corcoran, Lorelei H.
    1995   *Portrait Mummies from Roman Egypt (I-IV Centuries AD) with a Catalog of Portrait Mummies in Egyptian Museums*. Studies in Ancient Oriental Civilization 56. Chicago: The Oriental Institute.

Corcoran, Lorelei H., and Marie Svoboda
    2010   *Herakleides: A Portrait Mummy from Roman Egypt*. Los Angeles: J. Paul Getty Museum.

Corzo, Miguel Angel, and Mahasti Z. Afshar, editors
    1993   *Art and Eternity: The Nefertari Wall Paintings Conservation Project, 1986-1992*. Santa Monica: Getty Conservation Institute.

Cramer, Maria
    1957   "Elf unveröffentlichte, koptisch arabische Codices der Österreichischen Nationalbibliothek zu Wien. Ihre inhaltliche und paläographische Wertung." *Études de Papyrologie* 8: 113–45.
    1964a   *Koptische Buchmalerei: Illuminationen in Manuskripten des christlich-koptischen Ägypten vom 4. bis 19. Jahrhundert*. Recklinghausen: Verlag Aurel Bongers.
    1964b   *Koptische Paläographie*. Wiesbaden: Harrassowitz.

Cramp, Stanley; C. M. Perrins; Duncan J. Brooks
    1977–96   *Handbook of the Birds of Europe, the Middle East and North Africa: The Birds of the Western Palearctic*. 9 volumes. Oxford: Oxford University Press.

Crosby, Margaret
    1943   "A Silver Ladle and Strainer." *American Journal of Archaeology* 47/2: 209–16.

Darby, William J.; Paul Ghalioungui; and Louis Grivetti
    1977   *Food: The Gift of Osiris*. 2 volumes. London: Academic Press.

D'Auria, Sue; Peter Lacovara; and Catharine H. Roehrig
    1988   *Mummies and Magic: The Funerary Arts of Ancient Egypt*. Boston: Museum of Fine Arts.

Daumas, François
    1958   *Les mammisis des temples égyptiens*. Annales de l'Université de Lyon 32. Paris: Société d'Édition "Les belles lettres."
    1959   *Les mammisis de Dendara*. Cairo: Institut français d'archéologie orientale.
    1988   *Valeurs phonétiques des signes hiéroglyphiques d'époque gréco-romaine*. 4 volumes. Montpellier: Université Paul-Valéry (Montpellier 3).

David, Arlette
    2000   *De l'infériorité à la perturbation: l'oiseau du "mal" et la catégorisation en Égypte ancienne*. Göttinger Orientforschungen. 4. Reihe, Ägypten 38:1. Wiesbaden: Harrassowitz.

David, A. Rosalie
    2008   "The International Ancient Egyptian Mummy Tissue Bank." In *Egyptian Mummies and Modern Science*, edited by Rosalie A. David, pp. 237–46. Cambridge: Cambridge University Press.

Davies, Nina de Garis
    1936   *Ancient Egyptian Paintings*. 3 volumes. Chicago: University of Chicago Press.

Davies, Nina de Garis, and Alan H. Gardiner
    1926   *The Tomb of Ḥuy, Viceroy of Nubia in the Reign of Tut'Ankhamūn*. Theban Tomb Series 4. London: Egypt Exploration Society.

Davies, Norman de Garis
    1901   *The Mastaba of Ptahhetep and Akhethetep at Saqqareh*, Part 2: *The Mastaba. The Sculptures of Akhethetep*. London: Egypt Exploration Fund.
    1930   *The Tomb of Ḳen-Amūn at Thebes*. The Metropolitan Museum of Art Egyptian Expedition 5. New York: Arno Press.
    1933   "The Work of the Graphic Branch of the Expedition." *Metropolitan Museum of Art Bulletin* 28/4: 1, 23–29.
    1935   *Paintings from the Tomb of Rekh-Mi-Re' at Thebes*. Edited by the Egyptian Expedition. Publications of the Metropolitan Museum of Art 10. New York: Metropolitan Museum of Art.

Davies, Sue, and Harry S. Smith
    2005   *The Sacred Animal Necropolis at North Saqqara: The Falcon Complex and Catacomb, Archaeological Report*. Excavation Memoirs 73. London: The Egypt Exploration Society.

de Buck, Adriaan
    1938   *The Egyptian Coffin Texts*, Volume 2: *Texts of Spells 76-163*. Edited by Adriaan de Buck and Alan H. Gardiner. Oriental Institute Publications 49. Chicago: University of Chicago Press.

de Meulenaere, Herman
    1960   "Les monuments du culte des rois Nectanébo." *Chronique d'Égypte* 35/69–70: 92–107.

de Moor, Antoine; Chris Verhecken-Lammens; André Verhecken; and Hugo Maertens
    2008   *3500 Years of Textile Art: The Collection in HeadquARTers*. Tielt: Lannoo; Woodbridge: ACC Distribution.

de Rochemonteix, Maxence, and Émile Chassinat
    1984   *Le temple d'Edfou*, Volume 1. 2nd revised edition. Edited by Didier Devauchelle and Sylvie Cauville. Mémoires publiés

BIBLIOGRAPHY

par les Membres de la Mission archéologique française au Caire 10. Cairo: Institut français d'archéologie orientale.

Decker, Wolfgang, and Michael Herb
1994 *Bildatlas zum Sport im alten Ägypten: Corpus der bildlichen Quellen zu Leibesübungen, Speil, Jagd, Tanz und verwandten Themen.* 2 volumes. Leiden: Brill.

Delemen, Inci
2006 "An Unplundered Chamber Tomb on Ganos Mountain in Southeastern Thrace." *American Journal of Archaeology* 110/2: 251–73.

Derchain, Philippe
1975 "La perruque et le cristal." *Studien zur Altägyptischen Kultur* 2: 55–74.

Dijkstra, Jitse H. F.
2002 "Horus on His Throne: The Holy Falcon of Philae in His Demonic Cage." *Göttinger Miszellen* 189: 7–10.

Dodson, Aidan
2001a "Canopic Jars and Chests." *The Oxford Encyclopedia of Ancient Egypt*, edited by Donald B. Redford, vol. 1, pp. 231–35. Oxford: Oxford University Press.
2001b "Four Sons of Horus." *The Oxford Encyclopedia of Ancient Egypt*, edited by Donald B. Redford, vol. 1, pp. 561–63. Oxford: Oxford University Press.
2005 "Bull Cults." In *Divine Creatures: Animal Mummies in Ancient Egypt*, edited by Salima Ikram, pp. 72–105. Cairo: American University in Cairo Press.
2009 "Rituals Related to Animal Cults." In *UCLA Encyclopedia of Egyptology*, edited by Jacco Dieleman and Willeke Wendrich, pp. 1–8. Los Angeles: University of California, Los Angeles. Available online at: http://escholarship.org/uc/item/6wk541n0

Dragoman, D., and M. Dragoman
2004 "Terahertz Fields and Applications." *Progress in Quantum Electronics* 28/1: 1–66.

Drenkhahn, Rosemarie
1980 "Kebehsenuef." In *Lexikon der Ägyptologie*, edited by Wolfgang Helck and Wolfhart Westendorf, vol. 3, col. 379. Wiesbaden: Harrassowitz.

Dreyer, Günter
1986 *Elephantine 8: Der Tempel der Satet.* Archäologische Veröffentlichungen 39. Mainz am Rhein: Philipp von Zabern.

Dreyfus, Renée
2005 "Animal Vases." In *Hatshepsut: From Queen to Pharaoh*, edited by Catharine H. Roehrig, pp. 242–45. New York: The Metropolitan Museum of Art; New Haven: Yale University Press.

Du Bourguet, Pierre
2002 *Le temple de Deir al-Médîna.* Mémoires publiés par les membres de l'Institut français d'archéologie orientale du Caire 121. Cairo: Institut français d'archéologie orientale.

Eder, Walter, and Johannes Renger
2007 *Chronologies of the Ancient World: Names, Dates, and Dynasties.* Brill's New Pauly Supplements. Leiden: Brill.

Emberling, Geoff, and Emily Teeter
2010 "The First Expedition of the Oriental Institute, 1919–1920." In *Pioneers to the Past: American Archaeologists in the Middle East, 1919–1920*, edited by Geoff Emberling, pp. 31–84. Oriental Institute Museum Publications 30. Chicago: The Oriental Institute.

Emery, Walter B.
1965 "Preliminary Report on the Excavations at North Saqqâra 1964–5." *Journal of Egyptian Archaeology* 51: 3–8.

Emmons, Deirdre
2010 *L'Égypte au Musée des confluences: de la palette à fard au sarcophage.* Lyon: Musée des confluences.

Endreffy, Kata
2009 "Reason for Despair: Notes on Some Demotic Letters to Thoth." *Studies in Egyptology in Honour of M. A. Nur El Din*, edited by Basem Samir el-Sharkawy, vol. 3, pp. 241–52. Cairo: Dar al Kuttub.

Epigraphic Survey
1930 Medinet Habu 1. *Earlier Historical Records of Ramses III.* Oriental Institute Publications 8. Chicago: University of Chicago Press.
1932 Medinet Habu 2. *Later Historical Records of Ramses III.* Oriental Institute Publications 9. Chicago: University of Chicago Press.
1934 Medinet Habu 3. *The Calendar, the "Slaughterhouse," and Minor Records of Ramses III.* Oriental Institute Publications 23. Chicago: University of Chicago Press.
1963 Medinet Habu 6. *The Temple Proper, Part 2: The Re Chapel, the Royal Mortuary Complex, and Adjacent Rooms, with Miscellaneous Material from the Pylons, the Forecourts, and the First Hypostyle Hall.* Oriental Institute Publications 84. Chicago: University of Chicago Press.
1979 The Temple of Khonsu 1. *Scenes of King Herihor in the Court with Translations of Texts.* Oriental Institute Publications 100. Chicago: The Oriental Institute.
1981 The Temple of Khonsu 2. *Scenes and Inscriptions in the Court and the First Hypostyle Hall.* Oriental Institute Publications 103. Chicago: The Oriental Institute.
2009 Medinet Habu 9. *The Eighteenth Dynasty Temple, Part 1: The Inner Sanctuaries.* Oriental Institute Publications 136. Chicago: The Oriental Institute.

Épron, Lucienne; François Daumas; and Georges Goyon
1939 *Le tombeau de Ti.* Volume 1. Cairo: Institut français d'archéologie orientale.

Erman, Adolf, and Hermann Grapow
1926–82 *Wörterbuch der ägyptischen Sprache.* 7 volumes. Leipzig: J. C. Hinrichs; Berlin: Akademie-Verlag.
1935–53 *Wörterbuch der ägyptischen Sprache: Die Belegstellen.* 5 volumes. Leipzig: J. C. Hinrichs; Berlin: Akademie-Verlag.

Evans, Linda
2007 "Fighting Kites: Behaviour as a Key to Species Identity in Wall Scenes." *Journal of Egyptian Archaeology* 93: 245–47.
2010 *Animal Behaviour in Egyptian Art: Representations of the Natural World in Memphite Tomb Scenes.* Australian Centre for Egyptology: Studies 9. Oxford: Aris & Phillips.
2011 "Userkaf's Birds Unmasked." *Journal of Egyptian Archaeology* 97: 246–50.

Faulkner, Raymond O.
1936 "The Bremner-Rhind Papyrus—I. A: The Songs of Isis and Nephthys." *Journal of Egyptian Archaeology* 22/2: 121–40.
1998a *The Ancient Egyptian Pyramid Texts.* Oxford: Clarendon Press. Reprint of the 1969 edition.
1998b *The Egyptian Book of the Dead: The Book of Going Forth by Day.* 2nd revised edition. Edited by Eva von Dassow. San Francisco: Chronicle Books.

Fay, Biri
1998 "Egyptian Duck Flasks of Blue Anhydrite." *Metropolitan Museum Journal* 33: 23–48.

Fazzini, Richard A.
1975 *Images for Eternity: Egyptian Art from Berkeley and Brooklyn.* Brooklyn: Brooklyn Museum.
1988 *Egypt Dynasty XXII–XXV.* Iconography of Religions 16. Leiden: Brill.
1989 *Ancient Egyptian Art in the Brooklyn Museum.* New York: Thames & Hudson.

Fazzini, Richard A.; James F. Romano; and Madeleine E. Cody
1999 *Art for Eternity: Masterworks from Ancient Egypt.* Brooklyn: Brooklyn Museum of Art in association with Scala Publishers.

Forbes, Neil A.
2011 "Advanced Imaging Diagnostics in Avian Veterinary Practice." *Parrots* 10: 34–35.

BIBLIOGRAPHY

Frankfort, Henri
    1929   *The Mural Painting of El-'Amarneh*. London: Egypt Exploration Society.
    1933   *The Cenotaph of Seti I at Abydos*. Egyptian Exploration Society Memoir 39. London: Egypt Exploration Society.

Frankfurter, David
    1998   *Religion in Roman Egypt*. Princeton: Princeton University Press.

Freed, Rita E., and Denise M. Doxey
    2009   "The Djehutynakhts' Models." In *The Secrets of Tomb 10A: Egypt 2000 BC*, edited by Rita E. Freed, pp. 151–77. Boston: Museum of Fine Arts.

Friedman, Florence Dunn
    1995   "The Underground Relief Panels of King Djoser at the Step Pyramid Complex." *Journal of the American Research Center in Egypt* 32: 1–42.
    1998   *Gifts of the Nile: Ancient Egyptian Faience*. New York: Thames & Hudson.

Friedman, Renée F.
    2011   "Hierakonpolis." In *Before the Pyramids: The Origins of Egyptian Civilization*, edited by Emily Teeter, pp. 33–44. Oriental Institute Museum Publications 33. Chicago: The Oriental Institute.

Friedman, F. Renée; Amy Maish; Ahmed G. Fahmy; John C. Darnell; and Edward D. Johnson
    1999   "Report on Field Work at Hierakonpolis: 1996–1998." *Journal of the American Research Center in Egypt* 36: 1–35.

Fukunaga, Kaori; Emilia Cortes; Antonino Cosentino; Isabel Stünkel; Marco Leona; Irl N. Duling; and David T. Mininberg
    2011   "Investigating the Use of Terahertz Pulsed Time Domain Reflection Imaging for the Study of Fabric Layers of an Egyptian Mummy." *Journal of the European Optical Society — Rapid Publications* 6/11040: 1–4.

Gabra, Sami
    1971   *Chez les derniers adorateurs du Trismégiste*. Bibliothèque Arabe 119. Cairo: al-Haiʿa al-Miṣrīya li't-Taʾlīf wa'n-Našr.

Gaillard, Claude, and Georges Daressy
    1905   *La faune momifiée de l'antique Égypte*. Catalogue général des antiquités égyptiennes du musée du Caire, nos. 29501–29711, ET 29751–29834. Cairo: Imprimerie de l'Institut français d'archéologie orientale.

Gardiner, Alan H.
    1944   "Horus the Beḥdetite." *Journal of Egyptian Archaeology* 30: 23–60.
    1957   *Egyptian Grammar: Being an Introduction to the Study of Hieroglyphs*. 3rd edition. London: Griffith Institute.

Gardiner, Alan H., and Kurt Sethe
    1928   *Egyptian Letters to the Dead, Mainly from the Old and Middle Kingdoms*. London: Egypt Exploration Society.

Gaudard, François
    2009   "Le P. Berlin 8278 et ses fragments. Un 'nouveau' texte démotique comprenant des noms de lettres." In *Verba manent: recueil d'études dédiées à Dimitri Meeks par ses collègues et amis*, edited by Isabelle Régen and Frédéric Servajean, pp. 165–69. Cahiers "Égypte Nilotique et Méditerranéenne" 2. Montpellier: Université Paul Valéry (Montpellier 3).

Gautier, Achilles
    1980   "Contribution to the Archaeozoology of Egypt." In *Prehistory of the Eastern Sahara*, edited by Fred Wendorf and Romuald Schild, pp. 317–43. Studies in Archaeology. New York: Academic Press.
    1987   "Fishing, Fowling, Hunting in Late Paleolithic Times in the Nile Valley in Upper Egypt." *Palaeoecology of Africa* 18: 429–40.
    1988   "L'exploitation saisonnière des ressources animales pendant le paléolithique supérieur dans la vallée du Nil égyptien." *Anthropozoologica* Numéro spécial 22: 23–26.
    1990   *La domestication: et l'homme créa ses animaux*. Paris: Éditions Errance.

Genz, Hermann
    2007   "Stunning Bolts: Late Bronze Age Hunting Weapons in the Ancient Near East." *Levant* 39: 47–69.

Germond, Philippe
    1981   *Sekhmet et la protection du monde*. Ægyptiaca Helvetica 9. Geneva: Éditions de Belles-Lettres.
    2001   *An Egyptian Bestiary: Animals in Life and Religion in the Land of the Pharaohs*. London: Thames & Hudson.

Ghaleb, Barbara
    unpub.   Report on the Zooarchaeological Remains from the Sacred Animal Necropolis at Saqqara.

Gilhus, Ingvild
    2006   *Animal, Gods, and Humans: Changing Attitudes to Animals in Greek, Roman and Early Christian Ideas*. New York: Routledge.

Giza-Podgórski, Tomasz
    1984   "Royal Plume Dress of XVIII Dynasty." *Mitteilungen des Deutschen Archäologischen Instituts, Abteilung Kairo* 40: 103–21.

Glubok, Shirley
    1962   *The Art of Ancient Egypt*. New York: Atheneum.

Goelet, O.
    1983   "The Migratory Geese of Meidum and Some Egyptian Words for 'Migratory Bird.'" *Bulletin of the Egyptological Seminar* 5: 41–48.

Goldwasser, Orly
    1995   *From Icon to Metaphor: Studies in the Semiotics of the Hieroglyphs*. Orbus Biblicus et Orientalis 142. Göttingen: Vandenhoeck & Ruprecht.

Goodman, Steve M.
    1987   "Victual Egyptian Bird Mummies from a Presumed Late 17th or Early 18th Dyn. Tomb." *Journal of the Society for the Study of Egyptian Antiquities* 17: 67–77.

Goodman, Steve M., and Peter L. Meininger, editors
    1989   *The Birds of Egypt*. Oxford: Oxford University Press.

Gorre, Gilles
    2009   "'Nectanébo-le-faucon' et la dynastie lagide." *Ancient Society* 39: 55–69.

Götherström, Anders; C. Fischer; K. Lindén; and K. Lidén
    1995   "X-Raying Ancient Bone: A Destructive Method in Connection with DNA Analysis." *Laborativ Arkeologi* 8: 26–28.

Graff, Gwenola
    2009   *Les peintures sur vases de Nagada I–Nagada II: nouvelles approches semiologiques de l'iconographie prédynastique*. Leuven: Leuven University Press.

Graindorge, Catherine
    2001   "Sokar." In *The Oxford Encyclopedia of Ancient Egypt*, edited by Donald B. Redford, vol. 3, pp. 305–07. Oxford: Oxford University Press.

Grandet, Pierre
    1994–99   *Papyrus Harris I, BM 9999*. 3 volumes. Bibliothèque d'Étude 109/1–2, 129. Cairo: Institut français d'archéologie orientale du Caire.

Grapow, Hermann
    1924   *Die bildlichen Ausdrücke des Ägyptischen von Denken und Dichten einer altorientalischen Sprache*. Leipzig: J. C. Hinrichs.

Green, Jack; Emily Teeter; and John A. Larson
    2012   *Picturing the Past: Imaging and Imagining the Ancient Middle East*. Oriental Institute Museum Publications 34. Chicago: The Oriental Institute.

Greishaber, Britta M.; Daniel L. Osborne; Alison F. Doubleday; and Frederika A. Kaestle
    2008   "A Pilot Study into the Effects of X-Ray and Computed Tomography Exposure on the Amplification of DNA from Bone." *Journal of Archaeological Science* 35: 681–87.

BIBLIOGRAPHY

Griffin, Kenneth
2007 "A Reinterpretation of the Use and Function of the Rekhyt Rebus in New Kingdom Temples." In *Current Research in Egyptology 2006*, edited by Maria Cannata, pp. 66–84. Oxford: Oxbow Books.
Forthcoming "Links between the Rekhyt and Doorways in Ancient Egypt." *Proceedings of the Tenth International Congress of Egyptologists, University of the Aegean, Rhodes, 22-29 May 2008*, edited by Panagiotis Kousoulis and Nikolaos Lazaridis. Leuven: Peeters.

Griffith, F. L., editor
1900 *Beni Hasan*, Part IV: *Zoological and Other Details*. Archaeological Survey of Egypt 7. London: Egypt Exploration Society.

Griffiths, John Gwyn
1970 *Plutarch's de Iside et Osiride*. Cardiff: University of Wales Press.

Grossman, Mary Louise, and John N. Hamlet
1964 *Birds of Prey of the World*. New York: C. N. Potter.

Guglielmi, Waltraud
1973 *Reden, Rufe und Leider auf altägyptischen Darstellungen der Landwirtschaft, Viehzucht, des Fisch- und Vogelfangs vom Mittleren Reich bis zur Spätzeit*. Tübinger ägyptologische Beiträge 1. Bonn: Rudolf Habelt.

Gumpenberger, Michaela, and Wolfgang Henninger
2001 "The Use of Computed Tomography in Avian and Reptile Medicine." *Seminars in Avian and Exotic Pet Medicine* 4: 174–80.

Gustave-Lübcke Museum, Hamm
1996 *Ägypten, Schätze aus dem Wüstensand: Kunst und Kultur der Christen am Nil*. Wiesbaden: Ludwig Reichert Verlag.

Hall, Emma Swan
1986 *The Pharaoh Smites His Enemies: A Comparative Study*. Münchner ägyptologische Studien 44. Munich: Deutscher Kunstverlag.

Hamilton-Dyer, Sheila
1997 "The Domestic Fowl and Other Birds from the Roman Site of Mons Claudianus, Egypt." *International Journal of Osteoarchaeology* 7: 326–29.

Harcum, Cornelia G.
1921 "Roman Cooking Utensils in the Royal Ontario Museum of Archaeology." *American Journal of Archaeology* 25/1: 37–54.

Harpur, Yvonne, and Paolo J. Scremin
2006 *The Chapel of Kagemni: Scene Details*. Egypt in Miniature 1. Reading: Oxford Expedition to Egypt.

Harris, J. R.
1961 *Lexicographical Studies in Ancient Egyptian Minerals*. Berlin: Akademie-Verlag.

Hartwig, Melinda K.
2004 *Tomb Painting and Identity in Ancient Thebes, 1419-1372 BCE*. Monumenta Aegyptiaca 10. Brussels: Fondation égyptologique Reine Élisabeth; Turnhout: Brepols.

Hayes, William
1935 *Royal Sarcophagi of the XVIII Dynasty*. Princeton: Princeton University Press.
1959 *The Scepter of Egypt: A Background for the Study of the Egyptian Antiquities in the Metropolitan Museum of Art*, Part 2: *The Hyksos Period and the New Kingdom (1675-1080 BC)*. Cambridge: Harvard University Press.

Helbig, A. J.; I. Seibold; W. Bednarek; P. Gaucher; D. Ristow; W. Scharlau; D. Schmidl; and M. Wink
1994 "Phylogenetic Relationships among Falcon Species (Genus *Falco*) According to DNA Sequence Variation of the Cytochrome b Gene." In *Raptor Conservation Today: Proceedings of the IV World Conference on Birds of Prey and Owls*, edited by R. D. Chancellor and B.-U. Meyburg, pp. 593–99. Berlin, London, Paris: World Working Group on Birds of Prey and Owls.

Helck, Wolfgang, and Eberhard Otto
1972–92 *Lexikon der Ägyptologie*. 6 volumes. Wiesbaden: Harrassowitz.

Hendrickx, Stan
2000 "Autruches et flamants: les oiseaux représentés sur la céramique prédynastique de la catégorie *Decorated*." *Cahiers Caribéens d'Égyptologie* 1: 21–52.
2010 "L'iconographie de la chasse dans le contexte social prédynastique." *Archeo-Nil* 20: 106–33.

Hendrickx, Stan; Heiko Riemer; Frank Förster; and John C. Darnell
2009 "Late Predynastic/Early Dynastic Rock Art Scenes of Barbary Sheep Hunting from Egypt's Western Desert: From Capturing Wild Animals to the Women of the 'Acacia House.'" In *Desert Animals in the Eastern Sahara: Status, Economic Significance and Cultural Reflection in Antiquity* (Proceedings of an interdisciplinary ACACIA workshop held at the University of Cologne, December 14–15, 2007), edited by Heiko Riemer, Frank Förster, Michael Herb, and Nadja Pöllath, pp. 189–244. Cologne: Heinrich-Barth Institut.

Henein, Nessim Henry
2002 "Filets hexagonaux à oiseaux représentés dans la tombe de Méhou à Saqqâra." *Bulletin de l'Institut français d'archéologie orientale* 102: 259–66.
2010 *Pêche et chasse au lac Manzala*. Bibliothèque d'Étude 149. Cairo: Institut français d'archéologie orientale.

Hermann, Alfred
1932 "Das Motiv der Ente mit zurückgewendetem Kopfe im ägyptischen Kunstgewerbe." *Zeitschrift für ägyptische Sprache und Altertumskunde* 68: 86–105.

Hill, Marsha
2009 "Snake Charting: Situating the Sculptors' Models / Votives of the Late and Ptolemaic Periods." In *Sitting Beside Lepsius: Studies in Honour of Jaromir Malek at the Griffith Institute*, edited by Diana Magee, Janine Bourriau, and Stephen Quirke, pp. 237–56. Orientalia Lovaniensia Analecta 185. Leuven: Peeters.

Hoffmann, Friedhelm
1989 "Zu den 'Pirolen' auf dem Relief Kairo, Temporary Number 6/9/32/1." *Göttinger Miszellen* 107: 77–80.

Holm-Rasmussen, Torben
1979 "On the Statue Cult of Nektanebos II." *Acta Orientalia* 40: 21–25.

Hölscher, Uvo
1951 The Excavation of Medinet Habu IV. *The Mortuary Temple of Ramses III*, Part 2. Oriental Institute Publications 55. Chicago: University of Chicago Press.

Hornung, Erik
1996 *Conceptions of God in Ancient Egypt: The One and the Many*. Ithaca: Cornell University Press.

Hornung, Erik, and Betsy M. Bryan, editors
2002 *The Quest for Immortality: Treasures of Ancient Egypt*. New York: National Gallery of Art.

Hornung, Erik; Rolf Krauss; and David A. Warburton
2006 *Ancient Egyptian Chronology*. Handbook of Oriental Studies 83. Leiden: Brill.

Hornung, Erik, and Elisabeth Staehelin
1976 *Skarabäen und andere Siegelamulette aus Basler Sammlungen*. Ägyptische Denkmäler in der Schweiz 1. Mainz: Philipp von Zabern.

Houlihan, Patrick F.
1986 *The Birds of Ancient Egypt*. The Natural History of Egypt 1. Warminster: Aris & Phillips. Reprinted in 1988.
1996 *The Animal World of the Pharaohs*. London: Thames & Hudson.
2001 "Poultry." In *The Oxford Encyclopedia of Ancient Egypt*, edited by Donald B. Redford, vol. 3, pp. 59–61. New York: Oxford University Press.

BIBLIOGRAPHY

Hughes, George R.
1958 "A Demotic Letter to Thoth." *Journal of Near Eastern Studies* 17: 1–12.

Hughes, George R., and Richard Jasnow
1997 *Oriental Institute Hawara Papyri: Demotic and Greek Texts from an Egyptian Family Archive in the Fayum (Fourth to Third Century BC)*, edited by George R. Hughes and Richard Jasnow, pp. 95–103. Oriental Institute Publications 113. Chicago: The Oriental Institute.

Hunt, C. H.; C. P. Wood; F. E. Diehn; L. J. Eckel; K. M. Schwartz; and B. J. Erickson
2012 "Emerging Trends in the Volume and Format of Outside Examinations Submitted for Secondary Interpretation." *American Journal of Roentgenology* 198/4: 764–68.

Husselman, Elinor M.
1953 "The Dovecotes of Karanis." *Transactions of the American Philological Association* 84: 81–91.

Huyge, Dirk
2009 "Late Palaeolithic and Epipalaeolithic Rock Art in Egypt: Qurta and El-Hosh." *Archeo-Nil* 19: 109–20.

Huyge, Dirk, and Salima Ikram
2009 "Animal Representation in the Late Palaeolithic Rock Art of Qurta (Upper Egypt)." In *Desert Animals in the Eastern Sahara: Status, Economic Significance and Cultural Reflection in Antiquity* (Proceedings of an interdisciplinary ACACIA workshop held at the University of Cologne, December 14–15, 2007), edited by Heiko Riemer, Frank Förster, Michael Herb, and Nadja Pöllath, pp. 175–88. Cologne: Heinrich-Barth Institut.

Ikram, Salima
1995 *Choice Cuts: Meat Production in Ancient Egypt*. Orientalia Lovaniensia Analecta 69. Leuven: Peeters.
2004 "Victual, Ritual, or Both? Food Offerings from the Funerary Assemblage of Isitemkheb." *Studi di Egittologia e di Papirologia* 1: 87–92.
2005a *Divine Creatures: Animal Mummies in Ancient Egypt*. Cairo: American University in Cairo Press.
2005b "A Monument in Miniature: The Eternal Resting Place of a Shrew." In *Structure and Significance: Thoughts on Ancient Egyptian Architecture*, edited by Peter Jánosi, pp. 335–40. Untersuchungen der Zweigstelle Kairo 25. Vienna: Verlag der Österreichischen Akademie der Wissenschaften.
2007 "Animals in the Ritual Landscape at Abydos: A Synopsis." In *The Archaeology and Art of Ancient Egypt: Essays in Honor of David B. O'Connor*, edited by Zahi A. Hawass and Janet Richards, vol. 1, pp. 417–32. Supplément aux annales du service des antiquités de l'Égypte 36. Cairo: Conseil Suprême des Antiquités de l'Égypte.
In prep "A Re-analysis of Part of Prince Amenemhat Q's Eternal Menu."

Ikram, Salima, and Aidan Dodson
1998 *The Mummy in Ancient Egypt: Equipping the Dead for Eternity*. London: Thames & Hudson.

Ikram, Salima, and Nasry Iskander
2002 *Catalogue Général of the Egyptian Museum: Non-Human Mummies*. Cairo: Supreme Council of Antiquities Press.

Iversen, Erik
1958 *Papyrus Carlsberg Nr. VII: Fragments of a Hieroglyphic Dictionary*. Det Kongelige Danske Videnskabernes Selskab, Historisk-Filologiske Skrifter 3:2. Copenhagen: Ejnar Munksgaard.

Jackson, J. Bianca; J. Bowen; G. Walker; J. Labaune; Gérard Mourou; Michel Menu; and Kaori Fukunaga
2011 "A Survey of Terahertz Application in Cultural Heritage Conservation Science." *IEEE Transactions on Terahertz Science and Technology* 1: 220–31.

James, T. G. H.
2000 *Tutankhamun*. Vercelli: White Star.

Janák, Jiri
2007 "Migratory Spirits: Remarks on the *akh* Sign." In *Current Research in Egyptology 2006* (proceedings of the seventh annual symposium, University of Oxford, April 2006), edited by Maria Cannata, pp. 116–19. Oxford: Oxbow Books.
2010 "Spotting the *Akh*: The Presence of the Northern Bald Ibis in Ancient Egypt and Its Early Decline." *Journal of the American Research Center in Egypt* 46: 17–31.

Janssen, Jac. J.
1979 "The Role of the Temple in the Egyptian Economy During the New Kingdom." In *State and Temple Economy in the Ancient Near East*, edited by Edward Lipiński, vol. 2, pp. 505–15. Leuven: Department Orientalistiek.

Jasnow, Richard
1997 "The Greek Alexander Romance and Demotic Egyptian Literature." *Journal of Near Eastern Studies* 56/2: 95–103.
Forthcoming "'Caught in the Web of Words.' Remarks on the Imagery of Writing and Hieroglyphs in the Book of Thoth." *Journal of the American Research Center in Egypt*.

Jasnow, Richard, and Karl-Theodor Zauzich
2005 *The Ancient Egyptian Book of Thoth*. 2 volumes. Wiesbaden: Harrassowitz.
Forthcoming *The Book of Thoth: A New Translation*.

Jelinková-Reymond, Eva
1956 *Les inscriptions de la statue guérisseuse de Djed-Her-le-Sauveur*. Bibliothèque d'Étude 23. Cairo: Institut français d'archéologie orientale.

Kahl, Jochem
1991 "Von ḥ bis ḵ. Indizien für eine 'alphabetische' Reihenfolge einkonsonantiger Lautwerte in spätzeitlichen Papyri." *Göttinger Miszellen* 122: 33–47.

Kákosy, László
1981 "Problems of the Thoth-Cult in Roman Egypt." *Selected Papers (1956–73)*, pp. 41–46. Studia Aegyptiaca 7. Budapest: Études publiées par les chaires d'histoire ancienne de l'Université Loránd Eötvös de Budapest.

Kammerzell, Frank
2001 "Die Entstehung der Alphabetreihe: Zum ägyptischen Ursprung der semitischen und westlichen Schriften." In *Hieroglyphen-Alphabete-Schriftreformen: Studien zu Multiliteralismus, Schriftwechsel und Orthographieneuregelungen*, edited by Dörte Borchers, Frank Kammerzell, and Stefan Weninger, pp. 117–58. Lingua Aegyptia-Studia Monographica 3. Göttingen: Seminar für Ägyptologie und Koptologie.

Kanawati, Naguib
2001 *Tombs at Giza*, Volume 1: *Kaiemankh (G4561) and Seshemnefer I (G4940)*. Australian Centre for Egyptology, Reports 16. Warminster: Aris & Phillips.

Kanawati, Naguib, and Mahmoud Abder-Raziq
1998 *The Teti Cemetery at Saqqara*, Volume 3: *The Tombs of Nefereshemre and Seankhuiptah*. Australian Centre for Egyptology, Reports 11. Warminster: Aris & Phillips.
1999 *The Teti Cemetery at Saqqara*, Volume 5: *The Tomb of Hesi*. Australian Centre for Egyptology, Reports 13. Warminster: Aris & Phillips.
2000 *The Teti Cemetery at Saqqara*, Volume 6: *The Tomb of Nikauisesi*. Australian Centre for Egyptology, Reports 14. Warminster: Aris & Phillips.

Kanawati, Naguib, and A. Hassan
1997 *The Teti Cemetery at Saqqara*, Volume 2: *The Tomb of Ankhmahor*. Australian Centre for Egyptology, Reports 9. Warminster: Aris & Phillips.

Kanawati, Naguib, and Alexandra Woods
2010 *Beni Hassan: Art and Daily Life in an Egyptian Province*. Cairo: Supreme Council of Antiquities Press.

Kanawati, Naguib; Alexandra Woods; Sameh Shafik; and Effy Alexakis
2010 *Mereruka and His Family*, Part 3.1: *The Tomb of Mereruka*. Australian Centre for Egyptology, Reports 29. Oxford: Aris & Phillips.

BIBLIOGRAPHY

Kantor, Helene J.
1948 "A Predynastic Ostrich Egg with Incised Decoration." *Journal of Near Eastern Studies* 7/1: 46–51.

Kaplony, Peter
1972 "Die Prinzipien der Hieroglyphenschrift." In *Textes et langages de l'Égypte pharaonique: Cent cinquante années de recherches, 1822–1972; hommage à Jean-François Champollion*, pp. 3–14. Bibliothèque d'Étude 64. Cairo: Institut français d'archéologie orientale.
1976 *Studien zum Grab des Methethi*. Riggisberg: Abegg-Stiftung Bern.

Kees, Hermann
1961 *Ancient Egypt: A Cultural Topography*. Chicago: University of Chicago Press.

Keimer, Louis
1951 "Les hiboux constituant des prototypes de la lettre 'M' de l'alphabet égyptien." *Hawliyat Kulliyat al-Adab* 1: 73–83.

Kemp, Barry J.
2006 *Ancient Egypt: Anatomy of a Civilization*. 2nd edition. London: Routledge.

Kessler, Dieter
1989 *Die heiligen Tiere und der König*, Volume 1: *Beiträge zu Organisation, Kult und Theologie der spätzeitlichen Tierfriedhöfe*. Ägypten und Altes Testament 16. Wiesbaden: Harrassowitz.
2010 "Ibis-Vögel mit Eigennamen: Tiere des Festes und des Orakels." In *Honi soit qui mal y pense: Studien zum pharaonischen, griechisch-römischen und spätantiken Ägypten zu Ehren von Heinz-Josef Thissen*, edited by H. Knuf, C. Leitz, and D. von Recklinghausen, pp. 261–72. Orientalia Lovaniensia Analecta 194. Leuven: Peeters.

Kessler, Dieter, and Abdel el Halim Nur el-Din
2005 "Tuna El-Gebel: Millions of Ibises and Other Animals." In *Divine Creatures: Animal Mummies in Ancient Egypt*, edited by Salima Ikram, pp. 120–63. Cairo: American University in Cairo Press.

Killen, Geoffrey
1980 *Ancient Egyptian Furniture*, Volume 1: *4000–1300 BC*. Warminster: Aris & Phillips.

Kircher, Athanasius
1636 *Prodromus coptus sive aegyptiacus*. Rome: Typio S. Cong.

Kitchen, Kenneth A.
1975 *Ramesside Inscriptions: Historical and Biographical*. Volume 1. Oxford: B. H. Blackwell.
1979 *Ramesside Inscriptions: Historical and Biographical*, Volume 2. Oxford: B. H. Blackwell.
1982 *Ramesside Inscriptions: Historical and Biographical*. Volume 4. Oxford: B. H. Blackwell.
1983 *Ramesside Inscriptions: Historical and Biographical*. Volume 5. Oxford: B. H. Blackwell.

Koefoed-Petersen, Otto
1951 *Catalogue des sarcophages et cercueils égyptiens*. Ny Carlsberg Glyptotek Publications 4. Copenhagen: Fondation Ny Carlsberg.

Kozloff, Arielle P.; Betsy M. Bryan; and Lawrence M. Berman
1992 *Egypt's Dazzling Sun: Amenhotep III and His World*. Cleveland: The Cleveland Museum of Art in cooperation with Indiana University Press.

Kristensen, T. L. T.; Withawat Withayachumnankul; P. U. Jepsen; and D. Abbott
2010 "Modeling Terahertz Heating Effects on Water." *Optics Express* 18: 4727–39.

Kuhlmann, Klaus Peter
2002 "The 'Oasis Bypath' or the Issue of Desert Trade in Pharaonic Times." In *Tides of the Desert - Gezeiten der Wüste: Contribution to the Archaeology and Environmental History of Africa in Honour of Rudolph Kuper*, edited by Tilman Lenssen-Erz, Ursula Tegmeier, and Stefan Kröpelin, pp. 125–70. Africa Praehistorica 14. Cologne: Heinrich-Barth-Institut.

Kurth, Dieter
1998 *Edfou* VIII. Die Inschriften des Tempels von Edfu 1. Wiesbaden: Harrassowitz.

Lacau, Pierre
1914 "Suppressions et modifications de signes dans les textes funéraires." *Zeitschrift für ägyptische Sprache und Altertumskunde* 51: 1–64.

Lacovara, Peter, and Betsy Teasley Trope, editors
2001 *The Realm of Osiris: Mummies, Coffins, and Ancient Egyptian Funerary Art in the Michael C. Carlos Museum*. Atlanta: Emory University.

Ladynin, Ivan
2009 "'Nectanebos-the-Falcons': Sculpture Images of Nectanebo II before the God Horus and Their Concept." *Vestnik drevney istorii* 4: 1–26.

Lambert-Zazulak, Patricia
2000 "The International Ancient Egyptian Mummy Tissue Bank at the Manchester Museum." *Antiquity* 74: 44–48.

Lambert-Zazulak, P.; P. Rutherford; and A. R. David
2003 "The International Ancient Egyptian Mummy Tissue Bank at the Manchester Museum as a Resource for the Palaeoepidemiological Study of Schistosomiasis." *World Archaeology* 35/2: 223–40.

Lansing, A.
1920 "The Egyptian Expedition 1918–1920. Excavations at Thebes 1918–19." *The Metropolitan Museum of Art Bulletin* 15/12: 4–12.

Lapp, Günther
2006 *Totenbuch Spruch 17*. Totenbuchtexte 1. Basel: Orientverlag.

Leclant, Jean
1961 "Sur un contrepoids de Menat au nom de Taharqa: allaitement et 'apparition' royale." In *Mélanges Mariette*, pp. 251–84. Bibliothèque d'Études 32. Cairo: Institut français d'archéologie orientale.

Legrain, Georges
1890 *Livre des transformations (Papyrus Démotique 3.452 du Louvre)*. Paris: Ernest Leroux.

Leitz, Christian, editor
2002 *Lexikon der ägyptischen Götter und Götterbezeichnungen*. 8 volumes. Orientalia Lovaniensia Analecta 110–116, 129. Leuven: Peeters.

Lentacker, An, and Wim van Neer
1996 "Bird Remains from Two Sites on the Red Sea Coast and Some Observations on Medullary Bones." *International Journal of Osteoarchaeology* 6: 488–96.

Lepsius, C. Richard
1842 *Das Todtenbuch der Ägypter nach dem hieroglyphischen Papyrus in Turin*. Leipzig: Georg Wigand.
1849–59 *Denkmäler aus Ägypten und Äthiopien*. 12 volumes. Berlin: Nicolaische Buchhandlung. Reprinted Geneva: Éditions de Belles-lettres, 1972–73. Available online at: http://edoc3.bibliothek.uni-halle.de/lepsius/

Leroy, Jules
1974 *Les manuscrits coptes et coptes-arabes illustrés*. Institut français d'archéologie de Beyrouth. Bibliothèque archéologique et historique 96. Paris: Paul Geuthner.

Lewis, Thomas Hayter
1882 "Tel-El-Yahoudeh (the Mound of the Jew)." *Transactions of the Society of Biblical Archaeology* 7: 177–92.

Lichtheim, Miriam
1957 *Demotic Ostraca from Medinet Habu*. Oriental Institute Publications 80. Chicago: University of Chicago Press.
1980 *Ancient Egyptian Literature*, Volume 2: *The New Kingdom*. Berkeley: University of California Press.

BIBLIOGRAPHY

Lilyquist, Christine
    1998   "The Use of Ivories as Interpreters of Political History." *Bulletin of the American Schools of Oriental Research* 310: 25–33.

Lilyquist, Christine, editor
    2003   *The Tomb of Three Foreign Wives of Tuthmosis III.* New York: The Metropolitan Museum of Art.

Linseele, Veerle; Wim van Neer; and Renée F. Friedman
    2009   "Special Animals from a Special Place? The Fauna from HK29A at Predynastic Hierakonpolis." *Journal of the American Research Center in Egypt* 45: 105–36.

Loat, L. S.
    1914   "The Ibis Cemetery at Abydos." *Journal of Egyptian Archaeology* 1/1: 40.

Loeben, Christian E.
    1987   "A Throwstick of Princess *Nfr-Nfrw-Rꜥ*, with Additional Notes on Throwsticks of Faience." *Annales du Service des Antiquités de l'Égypte* 71: 143–49.

Lortet, Louis C. É., and Claude Gaillard
    1901   *Les oiseaux momifiés de l'ancienne Égypte.* Paris: n.p.
    1903   *La faune momifiée de l'ancienne Égypte.* Archives du Muséum d'histoire naturelle de Lyon 8. Lyon: Librairie de la Faculté de Médecine et de la Faculté de Droit.
    1905–09   *La faune momifiée de l'ancienne Égypte.* 5 volumes. Lyon: Henri Georg.

Lucchesi-Palli, Elisabetta
    1991   "Symbols in Coptic Art: Eagle." In *The Coptic Encyclopedia*, edited by Aziz Suryal Atiya, vol. 7, pp. 2167–70. New York: Macmillan.

Lüscher, Barbara
    1990   *Untersuchungen zu ägyptischen Kanopenkästen: Vom Alten Reich bis zum Ende der Zweiten Zwischenzeit.* Hildesheimer ägyptologische Beiträge. Hildesheim: Gerstenberg Verlag.

MacDonald, Kevin C., and David N. Edwards
    1993   "Chickens in Africa: The Importance of Qasr Ibrim." *Antiquity* 67/256: 584–90.

Maguire, Eunice Dauterman; Henry P. Maguire; and Maggie J. Duncan-Flowers
    1989   *Art and Holy Powers in the Early Christian House.* Illinois Byzantine Studies 2. Urbana: Krannert Art Museum, University of Illinois at Urbana-Champaign.

Mahmoud, Osama
    1991   *Die wirtschaftliche Bedeutung der Vögel im Alten Reich.* Europäische Hochschulschriften 35. Frankfurt am Main: Peter Lang.

Malaise, Michel
    1988   "Les animaux dans l'alimentation des ouvriers égyptiens de Deir el-Medineh au Nouvel Empire." *Anthropozoologica* Numéro spécial 2: 65–72.

Manniche, Lise
    1988   *Lost Tombs: A Study of Certain Eighteenth Dynasty Monuments in the Theban Necropolis.* Studies in Egyptology. London: Kegan Paul International.

Marcus, Gary F.
    2006   "Startling Starlings." *Nature* 440 (April 27): 1117–18.

Marfoe, Leon
    1982   *A Guide to the Oriental Institute Museum.* Chicago: The Oriental Institute.

Markowitz, Yvonne J., and Peter Lacovara
    1999   "Crafts and Industries at Amarna." In *Pharaohs of the Sun: Akhenaten, Nefertiti, Tutankhamun*, edited by Rita E. Freed, Yvonne J. Markowitz and Sue H. D'Auria, pp. 131–43. Boston: Museum of Fine Arts.

Matoïan, Valérie, and Henri Loffet
    1997   *Les antiquités égyptiennes et assyriennes du Musée Auguste Grasset de Varzy.* Études et Documents 1. Nevers: Atelier d'impression du Conseil Général de la Nièvre.

McDowell, A. G.
    1990   *Jurisdiction in the Workmen's Community of Deir el-Medîna.* Egyptologische Uitgaven 5. Leiden: Nederlands Instituut voor het Nabije Oosten.

McKnight, Lidija M.
    2010   *Imaging Applied to Animal Mummification in Ancient Egypt.* British Archaeology Reports, International Series 2175. Cambridge: Archaeopress.

McKnight, Lidija M.; Stephanie D. Atherton; and A. Rosalie David
    2011   "Introducing the Ancient Egyptian Animal Bio Bank at the KNH Centre for Biomedical Egyptology, University of Manchester." *Antiquity* 85/329.

McLeod, W.
    1982   *Self Bows and Other Archery Tackle from the Tomb of Tutankhamun.* Tutankhamun Tomb Series 4. Oxford: Griffith Institute.

McMillan, M. C.
    1994   "Imaging Techniques." In *Avian Medicine: Principles and Applications*, edited by Branson W. Ritchie, Greg J. Harrison, and Linda R. Harrison, pp. 246–326. 2nd edition. Lake Worth: Wingers.

Meinertzhagen, R.
    1930   *Nicoll's Birds of Egypt.* London: Hugh Rees.

Meininger, Peter L., and G. Atta
    1994   *Ornithological Studies in Egyptian Wetlands 1989/90.* Foundation for Ornithological Research in Egypt, Report No. 94-01. Zeist: Netherlands.

Meininger, Peter L., and Wim C. Mullié
    1981   *The Significance of Egyptian Wetlands for Wintering Waterbirds.* New York: Holy Land Conservation Fund.

Mekkawy, Fawzy, and Sabry Khater
    1990   "A Granite Statue of Horus as a Hawk from Buto." *Cahier de Recherches de l'Institut de Papyrologie et d'Égyptologie de Lille* 12: 87–88.

Mellado, Esther Pons
    1995   *Terracotas egipcias de época Greco-Romana del Museo del Oriente Bíblico del Monasterio de Montserrat.* Aula Orientalis Supplementa 9. Barcelona: Editorial AUSA.

Menu, Bernadette M.
    2001   "Economy: Private Sector." In *The Oxford Encyclopedia of Ancient Egypt*, edited by Donald B. Redford, vol. 1, pp. 430–33. New York: Oxford University Press.

Migahid, Abd-el-Gawad
    1986   *Demotische Briefe an Götter von der Spät- bis zur Römerzeit.* PhD dissertation, University of Würzburg.

Milde, H.
    1991   *The Vignettes in the Book of the Dead of Neferrenpet.* Egyptologische Uitgaven 7. Leiden: Nederlands Instituut voor het Nabije Oosten.

Minar, Edwin L. Jr.; F. H. Sandbach; and W. C. Helmbold
    1969   *Plutarch's Moralia*, Volume 9: *697 C–771 E*. Loeb Classical Library 425. Cambridge: Harvard University Press.

Montet, Pierre
    1925   *Scènes de la vie privée dans les tombeaux égyptiens de l'Ancien Empire.* Strasbourg: Librairie Istra.
    1928   *Byblos et l'Égypte: quatre campagnes de fouilles à Gebeil, 1921-1922-1923-1924.* Bibliothèque archéologique et historique 11. 2 volumes. Paris: Paul Geuthner.
    1951   *Les constructions et le tombeau de Psousennès à Tanis.* La nécropole royale de Tanis 2. Paris: Centre national de la recherche scientifique.

Moodie, Roy Lee
    1931   *Roentgenologic Studies of Egyptian and Peruvian Mummies.* Chicago: Field Museum of Natural History.

BIBLIOGRAPHY

Moran, William L., editor
1992 *The Amarna Letters*. Baltimore: Johns Hopkins University Press.

Moret, Alexandre
1931 "La légende d'Osiris à l'époque thébaine d'après l'hymne à Osiris du Louvre." *Bulletin de l'Institut français d'archéologie orientale* 30: 725–50.

Morrow, Maggie; Peter Cherry; and Toby A. H. Wilkinson, editors
2010 *Desert RATS: Rock Art Topographical Survey in Egypt's Eastern Desert*. British Archaeological Reports, International Series 2166. Oxford: Archaeopress.

Moussa, Ahmed M., and Hartwig Altenmüller
1971 *The Tomb of Nefer and Ka-hay*. Mainz am Rhein: Philipp von Zabern.
1977 *Das Grab des Nianchchnum und Chnumhotep*. Mainz am Rhein: Philipp von Zabern.

Muir, Arthur H., and Renée F. Friedman
2011 "Analysis of Predynastic Ostrich Eggshells from Hierakonpolis and Beyond." In *Egypt at Its Origins* 3, edited by Renée F. Friedman and Peter N. Fiske, pp. 571–93. Orientalia Lovaniensia Analecta 205. Leuven: Peeters.

Munro, Peter
1973 *Die spätägyptischen Totenstelen*. 2 volumes. Ägyptologische Forschungen 25. Glückstadt: J. J. Augustin.

Murray, Margaret Alice
1904 *Saqqara Mastabas*. Volume 1. London: British School of Archaeology in Egypt.

Museum of Fine Arts, Boston
1982 *Egypt's Golden Age: The Art of Living in the New Kingdom, 1558–1085 BC*. Boston: Museum of Fine Arts.

Nasr el-Dine, Hassan
2010 "Bronzes d'ibis provenant de Touna el-Gebel." *Bulletin de l'Institut français d'archéologie orientale* 110: 235–49.

Nelson, Harold H.
1949 "Certain Reliefs at Karnak and Medinet Habu and the Ritual of Amenophis I – Concluded." *Journal of Near Eastern Studies* 8/4: 310–45.
1981 *The Great Hypostyle Hall at Karnak*, Volume 1, Part 1: *The Wall Reliefs*. Edited by William J. Murnane. Oriental Institute Publications 106. Chicago: The Oriental Institute.

Newberry, Percy E.
1893 *Beni Hasan*, Part 1. Egypt Exploration Society, Archaeological Survey of Egypt Memoir 1. London: Egypt Exploration Society.
1895 *El Bersheh*, Part 1: *The Tomb of Tehuti-Hetep*. Archaeological Survey of Egypt 3, edited by F. L. Griffith. London: Egypt Exploration Fund.
1900 *Beni Hasan*, Part 4: *Zoological and Other Details*. Egypt Exploration Society, Archaeological Survey of Egypt Memoir 7. London: Egypt Exploration Society.
1937 *Funerary Statuettes and Model Sarcophagi*. 3 volumes. Catalogue général des antiquités égyptiennes du Musée du Caire 86. Cairo: Institut français d'archéologie orientale.
1951 "The Owls in Ancient Egypt." *Journal of Egyptian Archaeology* 37: 72–74.

Nicholson, Paul T.
1995 "The Sacred Animal Necropolis at North Saqqara." *Journal of Egyptian Archaeology* 81: 6–9.
2000 "Egyptian Faience." In *Ancient Egyptian Materials and Technology*, edited by Paul T. Nicholson and Ian Shaw, pp. 177–78. Cambridge: Cambridge University Press.
2005 "The Sacred Animal Necropolis at North Saqqara: The Cults and Their Catacombs." In *Divine Creatures: Animal Mummies in Ancient Egypt*, edited by Salima Ikram, pp. 44–71. Cairo: American University in Cairo Press.

Nicholson, Paul T., and Harry S. Smith
1996 "Fieldwork, 1995–6: The Sacred Animal Necropolis at North Saqqara." *Journal of Egyptian Archaeology* 82: 8–11.

O'Connor, David
2009 *Abydos: Egypt's First Pharaohs and the Cult of Osiris*. London: Thames & Hudson.

Ohrström, L.; A. Bitzer; M. Walther; and F. J. Rühli
2010 "Technical Note: Terahertz Imaging of Ancient Mummies and Bone." *American Journal of Physical Anthropology* 142/3: 497–500.

Oldfather, C. H., translator
1967 *Diodorus of Sicily in Twelve Volumes*. Volume 2:35–4:58. Cambridge: Harvard University Press.

Oliver, Andrew
1977 *Silver for the Gods: 800 Years of Greek and Roman Silver*. Toledo: Toledo Museum of Art.

Osborn, Dale J., and J. Osbornova
1998 *The Mammals of Ancient Egypt*. Warminster: Aris & Phillips.

Owen, Lidija M.
2000 *A Radiographic Study of Thirty-Nine Animal Mummies from Ancient Egypt*. BSc dissertation, University of York.
2001 *A Radiographic Investigation of the Ancient Egyptian Animal Mummies from the Manchester Museum*. MSc dissertation, University of Manchester.

Paget, R. F. E., and A. Pirie
1896 *The Tomb of Ptah-hetep*. London: Histories and Mysteries of Man.

Papazian, Hratch
2009 "Slab Stelae of the Giza Necropolis." *Journal of Near Eastern Studies* 68/1: 59.

Parkinson, Richard B.
1991 *Voices from Ancient Egypt: An Anthology of Middle Kingdom Writings*. London: British Museum Press.
2008 *The Painted Tomb-Chapel of Nebamun: Masterpieces of Ancient Egyptian Art in the British Museum*. London: British Museum Press.

Parlasca, Klaus
1974 "Falkenstelen aus Edfu: Bemerkungen zu einer Gruppe zerstören Reliefs des Berliner Museums." In *Festschrift zum 150 jährigen Bestehen des Berliner Ägyptischen Museums*, pp. 483–88. Mitteilungen aus der ägyptischen Sammlung, Staatliche Museen zu Berlin 8. Berlin: Akademie-Verlag.

Paszthory, Emmerich
1992 *Salben, Schminken und Parfüme im Altertum*. Zaberns Bildbande zur Archäologie 4. Mainz am Rhein: Philipp von Zabern.

Patch, Diana Craig
2011 *Dawn of Egyptian Art*. New York: Metropolitan Museum of Art.

Pearce, Sarah
2007 *The Land of the Body: Studies in Philo's Representation of Egypt*. Tübingen: Mohr Siebeck.

Peet, T. Eric
1914 "The Year's Work at Abydos." *Journal of Egyptian Archaeology* 1/1: 37–39.

Peet, T. Eric, and L. S. Loat
1913 *The Cemeteries of Abydos*, Part 3: *1912–1913*. London: Egypt Exploration Fund.

Perrins, Christopher
1979 *Birds: Their Life, Their Ways, Their World*. Pleasantville: Reader's Digest Association.

Peterson, Bengt
1987 "Egyptian Symbols of Love." *Medelhavsmuseet Bulletin* 22: 23–27.

BIBLIOGRAPHY

Petrie, William M. Flinders
- 1905   *Ehnasya 1904*. Excavation Memoir 26. London: Egypt Exploration Fund.
- 1914   *Amulets*. London: Constable.
- 1927   *Objects of Daily Use*. Publications of the British School of Archaeology in Egypt 42. London: British School of Archaeology in Egypt.
- 1953   *Ceremonial Slate Palettes and Corpus of Proto-Dynastic Pottery*. Publications of the British School of Egyptian Archaeology in Egypt 66. London: British School of Archaeology in Egypt.

Petrie, William M. Flinders, and Ernest Mackay
- 1915   *Heliopolis, Kafr Ammar and Shurafa*. Publications of the British School of Archaeology in Egypt 24. London: British School of Archaeology in Egypt.

Petrie, William M. Flinders, and James Edward Quibell
- 1896   *Naqada and Ballas 1895*. London: Bernard Quaritch.

Phillips, Jacke S.
- 2009   "Ostrich Eggshell." In *UCLA Encyclopedia of Egyptology*, edited by Willeke Wendrich, pp. 1–4. Los Angeles: University of California, Los Angeles. Available online at: http://escholarship.org/uc/item/0tm87064

Picardo, Nicholas S.
- 2004   "Dealing with Decapitation Diachronically." *Nekhen News* 16: 13–14.

Price, F. G. Hilton
- 1908   *A Catalogue of the Egyptian Antiquities in the Possession of F. G. Hilton Price*. London: Bernard Quaritch.

Prisse d'Avennes, Émile
- 1879   *Histoire de l'art égyptien d'après les monuments*. Paris: Arthus Bertrand.

Proctor, Noble S., and Patrick J. Lynch
- 1993   *Manual of Ornithology: Avian Structure and Function*. New Haven: Yale University Press.

Quack, Joachim Friedrich
- 1993   "Ägyptisches und südarabisches Alphabet." *Revue d'Égyptologie* 44: 141–51.
- 1994   "Notwendige Korrekturen." *Revue d'Égyptologie* 45: 197.
- 2003   "Die spätägyptische Alphabetreihenfolge und das 'südsemitische' Alphabet." *Lingua Aegyptia* 11: 163–84.

Quibell, James Edward
- 1898   *The Ramesseum*. Egyptian Research Account 1896. London: Bernard Quaritch.
- 1908   *Tomb of Yuaa and Thuiu (Nos. 51001–51191)*. Catalogue général des antiquités égyptiennes du Musée du Caire 43. Cairo: Institut français d'archéologie orientale.

Quibell, James Edward, and Frederick W. Green
- 1902   *Hierakonpolis 2*. Egypt Research Account 5. London: Bernard Quaritch.

Quirke, Stephen
- 2008   "Creation Stories in Ancient Egypt." In *Imagining Creation*, edited by Markham J. Geller and Mineke Shipper, pp. 61–86. Institute of Jewish Studies, Studies in Judaica 5. Leiden: Brill.

Radwan, Ali
- 1975   "Zur bildlichen Gleichsetzung des ägyptischen Königs mit der Gottheit." *Mitteilungen des Deutschen Archäologischen Instituts, Abteilung Kairo* 31: 99–108.
- 1985   "Einige Aspekte der Vergöttlichung des ägyptischen Königs." In *Ägypten, Dauer und Wandel*, pp. 53–69. Deutsches Archäologisches Institut, Abteilung Kairo 18. Mainz am Rhein: Philipp von Zabern.

Ranke, Hermann
- 1936   *The Art of Ancient Egypt*. Vienna: Phaidon Verlag.

Raven, Maarten, and Wybren K. Taconis
- 2005   *Egyptian Mummies: Radiological Atlas of the Collections in the National Museum of Antiquities in Leiden*. Turnhout: Brepols.

Ray, John D.
- 1976   *The Archive of Ḥor*. London: Egypt Exploration Society.
- 2002   *Reflections of Osiris: Lives from Ancient Egypt*. Oxford: Oxford University Press.
- 2011   *Texts from the Baboon and Falcon Galleries: Demotic, Hieroglyphic and Greek Inscriptions from the Sacred Animal Necropolis, North Saqqara*. Texts from Excavations 15. London: Egypt Exploration Society.

Redford, Donald B.
- 1995   "The Concept of Kingship during the Eighteenth Dynasty." In *Ancient Egyptian Kingship*, edited by David O'Connor and David P. Silverman, pp. 157–84. Probleme der Ägyptologie 9. Leiden: Brill.

Rice, E. E.
- 1983   *The Grand Procession of Ptolemy II Philadelphus*. Oxford: Oxford University Press.

Riefstahl, Elizabeth
- 1949   "A Sacred Ibis." *Brooklyn Museum Bulletin* 11/1: 5–9.

Riemer, Heiko; Nadja Pöllath; Stefanie Nussbaum; Ines Teubner; and Hubert Berke
- 2008   "El Kharafish: A Sheikh Muftah Desert Camp Site between the Oasis and the Nile." In *Egypt at Its Origins 2*, edited by Beatrix Midant-Reynes and Yann Tristant, pp. 585–608. Orientalia Lovaniensia Analecta 172. Leuven: Peeters.

Riggs, Christina
- 2003   "The Egyptian Funerary Tradition at Thebes in the Roman Period." In *The Theban Necropolis: Past, Present and Future*, edited by John H. Taylor and Nigel Strudwick, pp. 189–201. London: British Museum Press.
- 2005   *The Beautiful Burial in Roman Egypt*. Oxford: Oxford University Press.

Ritner, Robert K.
- 1993   *The Mechanics of Ancient Egyptian Magical Practice*. Studies in Ancient Oriental Civilization 54. Chicago: The Oriental Institute. Fourth printing 2008.
- 2002   "Necromancy in Ancient Egypt." In *Magic and Divination in the Ancient World*, edited by Jonathan Lee Seidel and Leda Jean Ciraolo, pp. 89–96. Leiden: Brill.
- 2006   "'And Each Staff Transformed into a Snake': The Serpent Wand in Ancient Egypt." In *Through a Glass Darkly: Magic, Dreams and Prophecy in Ancient Egypt*, edited by Kasia M. Szpakowska, pp. 205–25. Swansea: Classical Press of Wales.
- 2008   "Household Religion in Ancient Egypt." In *Household and Family Religion in Antiquity*, edited by Saul M. Olyan and John Bodel, pp. 171–96. Ancient World, Comparative Histories 6. Oxford: Blackwell Publishing.
- 2011   "Theogonies and Cosmogonies in Egyptian Ritual." Paper read at the conference Imagined Beginnings: The Poetics and Politics of Cosmogony, Theogony and Anthropogony in the Ancient World, Chicago, Illinois, April 9, 2011.

Robins, Gay
- 1990   "Problems in Interpreting Egyptian Art." *Discussions in Egyptology* 17: 45–58.
- 1997   *The Art of Ancient Egypt*. Cambridge: Harvard University Press.

Robinson, David M.
- 1941   *Excavations at Olynthus, Part 10: Metal and Minor Miscellaneous Finds, an Original Contribution to Greek Life*. The Johns Hopkins University Studies in Archaeology 31. Baltimore: The Johns Hopkins University Press.

Roeder, Günther
- 1956   *Ägyptische Bronzefiguren*. Berlin: Staatliche Museen zu Berlin.

Roehrig, Catharine H.
- 1988   "Female Offering Bearer." In *Mummies and Magic: The Funerary Arts of Ancient Egypt*, edited by Sue D'Auria, Peter Lacovara, and Catharine H. Roehrig, pp. 102–03. Boston: Museum of Fine Arts.

BIBLIOGRAPHY

Roehrig, Catharine H., editor
2005 *Hatshepsut: From Queen to Pharaoh*. New York: Metropolitan Museum of Art.

Romano, James F.
2001 "Folding Headrest." In *Eternal Egypt: Masterworks of Ancient Art from the British Museum*, edited by Edna Russman, pp. 162–63. Berkeley: University of California Press.

Rosellini, Ippolito
1834 *I monumenti dell'Egitto e della Nubia*, Volume 2: *Monumenti civili*. Pisa: Presso N. Capurro.

Rößler-Köhler, Ursula
1979 *Kapitel 17 des ägyptischen Totenbuches: Untersuchungen zur Textgeschichte und Funktion eines Textes der altägyptischen Totenliteratur*. Göttinger Orientforschung 4. Wiesbaden: Harrassowitz.

Roth, Ann Macy
1995 *A Cemetery of Palace Attendants, Including G 2084-2099, G 2230+2231, and G 2240*. Giza Mastabas 6. Boston: Museum of Fine Arts.

Russman, Edna, editor
2001 *Eternal Egypt: Masterworks of Ancient Art from the British Museum*. Berkeley and Los Angeles: University of California Press.

Rutschowscaya, Marie-Hélène
1990 *Coptic Fabrics*. Paris: Adam Biro.

Sakkara Expedition
1938 *The Mastaba of Mereruka*. Part 1: *Chambers A 1-10*; and Part 2: *Chambers A 11-13, Doorjambs, and Inscriptions of Chambers A 1-21, Tomb Chamber, and Exterior*. Oriental Institute Publications 31 (part 1) and 39 (part 2). Chicago: University of Chicago Press.

Saleh, Mohamed
1984 *Das Totenbuch in den thebanischen Beamtengräbern des Neuen Reiches*. Archäologische Veröffentlichungen 46. Mainz am Rhein: Philipp von Zabern.

Scalf, Foy
Forthcoming "Resurrecting an Ibis Cult: Demotic Votive Texts from the Oriental Institute Museum of the University of Chicago." To be published in the festschrift for Ola el-Aguizy, forthcoming from the Institut français d'archéologie orientale, Cairo.

Scharff, A.
1927 "Ein Denkstein der römischen Kaiserzeit aus Achmim." *Zeitschrift für ägyptische Sprache und Altertumskunde* 62: 86–107.

Schlichting, Robert
1994 "Vom Entenvogel zum Entenvogelboot: Überlegungen zur Entensymbolik in der ägyptischen Kunst." In *Quaerentes Scientiam: Festgabe für Wolfhart Westendorf zu seinem 70. Geburtstag*, edited by Heike Behlmer, pp. 183–88. Göttingen: Seminar für Ägyptologie und Koptologie.

Schmitz, Bettina, and Dina Faltings
1987 *Vögel im alten Ägypten: Informationen zum Thema und Kurzführer durch die Ausstellung*. Informationen und Einführungen für den Museumsbesucher 3. Hildesheim: Pelizaeus-Museum.

Schmuttenmaer, Charles A.
2004 "Exploring Dynamics in the Far-Infrared with Terahertz Spectroscopy." *Chemistry Review* 104: 1759–79.

Scholfield, A. F.
1958 *Aelian. On the Characteristics of Animals*, Volume 1: *Books I–V*. Loeb Classical Library Volume 446. Cambridge: Harvard University Press.

Schorsch, Deborah
1988 "An Egyptian Ibis Sarcophagus in the Virginia Museum of Fine Arts — A Technical Report." *Arts in Virginia* 28: 48–59.

Schott, S.
1956 "Zur Krönungstitulatur der Pyramidenzeit." *Nachrichten der Akademie der Wissenschaften in Göttingen, Philologisch-Historische Klasse, aus dem Jahre 1956*: 55–79.

Schwartze, Moritz Gotthilf
1843 *Das alte Ägypten, oder Sprache, Geschichte, Religion und Verfassung des alten Ägyptens nach den altägyptischen Original-Schriften und den Mittheilungen der nicht-ägyptischen alten Schriftsteller*. Leipzig: J. A. Barth.

Seeber, Christine
1976 *Untersuchungen zur Darstellung des Totengerichts im alten Ägypten*. Münchner ägyptologische Studien 35. Munich: Deutscher Kunstverlag.

Sethe, Kurt
1906–09 *Urkunden der 18. Dynastie*. Urkunden des ägyptischen Altertums 4. Leipzig: J. C. Hinrichs.

1908 *Die altägyptischen Pyramidentexte nach den Papierabdrücken und Photographien des Berliner Museums*. Leipzig: J. C. Hinrichs.

Shedid, Abdel Ghaffar
1994 *Die Felsgräber von Beni Hassan in Mittelägypten*. Zaberns Bildbände zur Archäologie 16. Mainz: Philipp von Zabern.

Shelley, George Ernest
1872 *A Handbook to the Birds of Egypt*. London: J. Van Voorst.

Silverman, David P., editor
1997 *Searching for Ancient Egypt: Art, Architecture, and Artifacts from the University of Pennsylvania Museum of Archaeology and Anthropology*. Dallas: Dallas Museum of Art.

Simon, Catherine
2001 "Geb." In *The Oxford Encyclopedia of Ancient Egypt*, edited by Donald B. Redford, vol. 2, p. 7. Oxford: Oxford University Press.

Simpson, William Kelly
1978 *The Mastabas of Kawab, Khafkhufu I and II (G7110-20, 7130-40 and 7150 and Subsidiary Mastabas of Street G 7100)*. Boston: Museum of Fine Arts.

Smelik, Klaas A. D., and Emily Ann Hemelrijk
1984 "'Who Knows Not What Monsters Demented Egypt Worships?' Opinions on Egyptian Animal Worship in Antiquity as Part of the Ancient Conception of Egypt." In *Aufstieg und Niedergang der römischen Welt: Geschichte und Kultur Roms im Spiegel der neueren Forschung* II.17.4, edited by Wolfgang Haase, pp. 1852–2000. Berlin: Walter de Gruyter.

Smith, Harry S.
1974 *A Visit to Ancient Egypt: Life at Memphis and Saqqara (c. 500-30 BC)*. Warminster: Aris & Phillips.

1975 "The Saqqara Papyri: V. Demotic Literary Papyri and Letters." In *Proceedings of the XIV International Congress of Papyrologists, Oxford, 24-31 July 1974*, pp. 257–59. Graeco-Roman Memoirs 61. London: Egypt Exploration Society.

Smith, Harry S.; C. A. R. Andrews; and Sue Davies
2011 *The Sacred Animal Necropolis at North Saqqara: The Mother of Apis Inscriptions 1-2*. Texts from Excavations 14. London: Egypt Exploration Society.

Smith, Harry S., and William John Tait
1983 *Saqqâra Demotic Papyri I (P. Dem. Saq. I)*. Texts from Excavations 7. London: Egypt Exploration Society.

Smith, Mark J.
1979 The Demotic Mortuary Papyrus Louvre E. 3452. PhD dissertation, University of Chicago.

2002 "Aspects of the Preservation and Transmission of Indigenous Religious Tradition in Akhmim and Its Environs During the Graeco-Roman Period." In *Perspectives on Panopolis: An Egyptian Town from Alexander the Great to the Arab Conquest*, edited by A. Egberts, Brian P. Muhs, and Joep van der Vliet, pp. 233–47. Papyrologica Lugduno-Batava 31. Boston: Brill.

BIBLIOGRAPHY

    2009   *Traversing Eternity: Texts for the Afterlife from Ptolemaic and Roman Egypt.* Oxford: Oxford University Press.

Smith, William Stevenson
    1978   *A History of Egyptian Sculpture and Painting in the Old Kingdom.* London: Oxford University Press.

Smith, William Stevenson, and William Kelly Simpson
    1998   *Art and Architecture of Ancient Egypt.* 3rd edition. New Haven: Yale University Press.

Spiegelberg, Wilhelm
    1914   *Die sogenannte demotische Chronik des Pap. 215 der Bibliothèque nationale zu Paris nebst den auf der Rückseite des Papyrus stehenden Texten.* Demotische Studien 7. Leipzig: J. C. Hinrichs.
    1918   "Demotische Kleinigkeiten." *Zeitschrift für ägyptische Sprache und Altertumskunde* 54: 111–28.
    1927   "Die Falkenbezeichnung des Verstorbenen in der Spätzeit." *Zeitschrift für ägyptische Sprache und Altertumskunde* 62: 27–34.
    1928   *Neue Urkunden zum ägyptischen Tierkultus.* Sitzungsberichte der Bayerischen Akademie der Wissenschaften. Munich: Bayerische Akademie der Wissenschaften.

Spiegelman, M.; S. Ikram; J. Taylor; L. Berger; H. Donoghue; and D. Lambert
    2008   "Preliminary Genetic and Radiological Studies of Ibis Mummification in Egypt." In *Mummies and Science: World Mummies Research,* edited by P. Pena, C. Rodriquez Martin, and M. Rodriguez, pp. 545–52. Santa Cruz de Tenerife: Academia Canaria de la Historia.

Staley, Preston S.; James L. Phillips; and John Desmond Clark
    1974   "Interpretations of Prehistoric Technology from Ancient Egyptian and Other Sources, Part 1: Ancient Egyptian Bows and Arrows and Their Relevance for African Prehistory." *Paléorient* 2/2: 323–88.

Stauffer, Annemarie; M. Hill; H. C. Evans; and D. Walker
    1995   *Textiles of Late Antiquity.* New York: Metropolitan Museum of Art.

Steindorff, Georg
    1892   "Das altägyptische Alphabet und seine Umschreibung." *Zeitschrift der Deutschen Morgenländischen Gesellschaft* 46: 709–30.

Stevenson, Alice
    2009   "Palettes." In *UCLA Encyclopedia of Egyptology,* edited by Willeke Wendrich, pp. 1–9. Los Angeles: University of California Los Angeles. Available online at: http://escholarship.org/uc/item/7dh0x2n0

Störk, Lothar
    1976   "*Dndn* 'der Schwan'?" *Göttinger Miszellen* 19: 57–58.

Strudwick, Nigel
    2006   *Masterpieces of Ancient Egypt.* London: British Museum Press.

Stupko, Anastazja
    2010   "Cranes in the Chapel of Hatshepsut at Deir El-Bahari: Studies on Representations." *Études et Travaux* 23: 158–78.

Szpakowska, Kasia
    2003   "Playing with Fire: Initial Observations on the Religious Uses of Clay Cobras from Amarna." *Journal of the American Research Center in Egypt* 40: 113–22.

Tarboton, W. R.; Peter Pickford; and Beverly Pickford
    1990   *African Birds of Prey.* Ithaca: Cornell University Press.

Taylor, John H.
    2001   *Death and the Afterlife in Ancient Egypt.* London: Trustees of the British Museum.

Taylor, John H., editor
    2010   *Journey through the Afterlife: Ancient Egyptian Book of the Dead.* Cambridge: Harvard University Press.

Teeter, Emily
    1994   "Egyptian Art." *The Art Institute of Chicago: Museum Studies* 20/1: 14–31.
    2003   *Ancient Egypt: Treasures from the Collection of the Oriental Institute.* Oriental Institute Museum Publications 23. Chicago: The Oriental Institute.
    2010a   *Baked Clay Figurines and Votive Beds from Medinet Habu.* Oriental Institute Publications 133. Chicago: The Oriental Institute.
    2010b   "Feathers." In *UCLA Encyclopedia of Egyptology,* edited by Willeke Wendrich, pp. 1–6. Los Angeles: University of California Los Angeles. Available online at: http://escholarship.org/uc/item/4737m1mb
    2011a   *Religion and Ritual in Ancient Egypt.* Cambridge: Cambridge University Press.

Teeter, Emily, editor
    2011b   *Before the Pyramids: The Origins of Egyptian Civilization.* Oriental Institute Museum Publications 33. Chicago: The Oriental Institute.

Teeter, Emily, and Janet H. Johnson, editors
    2009   *The Life of Meresamun: A Temple Singer in Ancient Egypt.* Oriental Institute Museum Publications 29. Chicago: The Oriental Institute.

Thomas, Thelma
    2000   *Late Antique Egyptian Funerary Sculpture.* Princeton: Princeton University Press.

Thompson, Herbert
    1924   *The Gospel of St. John according to the Earliest Coptic Manuscript.* British School of Archaeology in Egypt and Egyptian Research Account 36. London: British School of Archaeology in Egypt.

Tobin, Vincent Arieh
    2001   "Creation Myths." In *The Oxford Encyclopedia of Ancient Egypt,* edited by Donald B. Redford, vol. 2, pp. 469–72. Oxford: Oxford University Press.
    2003a   "The Tale of the Eloquent Peasant." In *The Literature of Ancient Egypt,* edited by William Kelly Simpson, pp. 25–44. 3rd edition. New Haven: Yale University Press.
    2003b   "Selections from the Pyramid Texts." In *The Literature of Ancient Egypt,* edited by William Kelly Simpson, pp. 247–62. 3rd edition. New Haven: Yale University Press.

Tomoun, Nadja Samir
    2005   *The Sculptors' Models of the Late and Ptolemaic Periods: A Study of the Type and Function of a Group of Ancient Egyptian Artefacts.* Translated by Brenda Siller. Cairo: National Center for Documentation of Cultural and Natural Heritage and the Supreme Council of Antiquities, Egypt.

Tooley, Angela M.
    1995   *Egyptian Models and Scenes.* Shire Egyptology 22. Princes Risborough: Shire Publications.
    2001   "Models." In *The Oxford Encyclopedia of Ancient Egypt,* edited by Donald B. Redford, vol. 2, pp. 424–28. New York: Oxford University Press.

Török, László
    2009   *Between Two Worlds: The Frontier Region between Ancient Nubia and Egypt 3700 BC–AD 500.* Probleme der Ägyptologie 29. Leiden: Brill.

Tropper, Josef
    1996   "Ägyptisches, nordwestsemitisches und altsüdarabisches Alphabet." *Ugarit-Forschungen* 28: 619–32.

Troy, Lana
    1986   *Patterns of Queenship in Ancient Egyptian Myth and History.* Boreas: Uppsala Studies in Ancient Mediterranean and Near Eastern Civilizations 14. Uppsala: Uppsala University.

Valeriano Bolzanio, Giovanni Pierio
    1602   *Hieroglyphica sev De sacris ægyptiorum, aliarumque gentium literis commentarii.* Lyon: Paul Frelon.

van den Broek, R.
    1972   *The Myth of the Phoenix According to Classical and Early Christian Traditions.* Leiden: Brill.

BIBLIOGRAPHY

van de Walle, Baudouin
  1978 *La chapelle funéraire de Neferirtenef*. Brussels: Musées Royaux d'Art et d'Histoire.

van Dijk, Jacobus
  1983 "A Ramesside Naophorus Statue from the Teti Pyramid Cemetery." *Oudheidkundige Mededelingen uit het Rijksmuseum van Oudheden te Leiden* 64: 49–60.

van Neer, Wim; Veerle Linseele; and Renée F. Friedman
  2004 "Animal Burials and Food Offerings at the Elite Cemetery HK6 at Hierakonpolis." In *Egypt at Its Origins: Studies in Memory of Barbara Adams*, edited by Stan Hendrickx, Renée F. Friedman, Krzysztof M. Ciałowicz, and Marek Chłodnicki, pp. 67–130. Orientalia Lovaniensia Analecta 138. Leuven: Peeters.

Van Walsem, René
  2005 *Iconography of Old Kingdom Elite Tombs: Analysis and Interpretation, Theoretical and Methodological Aspects*. Mémoires de la Société d'études orientales "Ex Oriente Lux" 35. Leuven: Peeters.

Vandier, Jacques
  1958 *Manuel d'archéologie égyptienne III: les grandes époques. La statuaire*. Paris: A. & J. Picard.
  1969 *Manuel d'archéologie égyptienne*, Volume 5: *Bas-reliefs et peintures, scènes de la vie quotidienne*. Paris: A. & J. Picard.

te Velde, Hermann
  1982 "Geb." In *Lexikon der Ägyptologie*, edited by Wolfhart Westendorf and Wolfgang Helck, vol. 2, cols. 427–29. Wiesbaden: Harrassowitz.

Verhöven, Ursula
  1984 *Grillen, Kochen, und Backen im Alltag und im Ritual Altägyptens: Ein lexikographischer Beitrag*. Rites Égyptiens 4. Brussels: Fondation égyptologique Reine Élisabeth.

Vernus, Pascal, and Jean Yoyotte
  2005 *Bestiaire des pharaons*. Paris: Perrin.

Vittmann, Günter
  1996 "Zum Gebrauch des k₃-Zeichens im Demotischen." *Studi di egittologia e di antichità puniche* 15: 1–12.
  1998 "Tradition und Neuerung in der demotischen Literatur." *Zeitschrift für ägyptische Sprache und Altertumskunde* 125: 62–77.

von Beckerath, Jürgen
  1982 "Menit." In *Lexikon der Ägyptologie*, edited by Wolfgang Helck and Wolfhart Westendorf, vol. 4, cols. 52–54. Wiesbaden: Harrassowitz.

von Bissing, Friedrich Wilhelm
  1904 *Steingefäße*. Catalogue général des antiquités égyptiennes du Musée du Caire 17. Cairo: Egyptian Museum.

von den Driesch, Angela; Dieter Kessler; Frank Steinmann; Véronique Berteaux; and Joris Peters
  2005 "Mummified, Deified, and Buried at Hermopolis Magna: The Sacred Birds from Tuna el-Gebel, Middle Egypt." *Ägypten und Levante* 15: 203–44.

von Droste zu Hülshoff, Vera; B. Schlick-Nolte; and S. Seidlmayer
  1991 *Ägyptische Bildwerke*, Volume 2: *Statuetten, Gefässe und Geräte*. Melsungen: Gutenberg.

von Lieven, Alexandra
  2007 *The Carlsberg Papyri 8: Grundriss des Laufes der Sterne: Das sogenannte Nutbuch*. Carsten Niebuhr Institute of Near Eastern Studies, Publications 31. Copenhagen: Museum Tusculanum Press.

Vycichl, Werner
  1990 *La vocalisation de la langue égyptienne*, Volume 1: *La phonétique*. Bibliothèque d'Étude 16. Cairo: Institut français d'archéologie orientale.

Wade, Andrew D.; S. Ikram; G. J. Conlogue; R. Beckett; A. J. Nelson; R. Colten; B. Lawson; and D. Tampieri
  2012 "Foodstuff Placement in Ibis Mummies and the Role of Viscera in Embalming." *Journal of Archaeological Science* 39/5: 1642–47.

Walker, G. C.; E. Berry; N. N. Zinov'ev; A. J. Fitzgerald; R. E. Miles; J. M. Chamberlain; and M. A. Smith
  2002 "Terahertz Imaging and International Safety Guidelines." *Proceedings of the Society of Photo-Optical Instrumentation Engineers* 4682: 683–90.

Wanscher, Ole
  1980 *Sella Curulis: The Folding Stool, an Ancient Symbol of Dignity*. Copenhagen: Rosenklide and Bagger.

Weaver, Peter
  1981 *The Birdwatcher's Dictionary*. London: A. & T. D. Poyser.

Wendorf, Fred; Romuald Schild; and Angela E. Close
  1980 *Loaves and Fishes: The Prehistory of Wadi Kubbaniya*. Dallas: Department of Anthropology, Institute for the Study of Earth and Man, Southern Methodist University Press.

Wengrow, David
  2006 *The Archaeology of Early Egypt: Social Transformations in North-East Africa, 10,000 to 2650 BC*. Cambridge: Cambridge University Press.

Wente, Edward F.
  1990 *Letters from Ancient Egypt*. Society of Biblical Literature Writings from the Ancient World 1. Edited by Edmund S. Meltzer. Atlanta: Scholars Press.
  2003 "Selections from the Coffin Texts." In *The Literature of Ancient Egypt*, edited by W. K. Simpson, pp. 263–66. 3rd edition. New Haven: Yale University Press.

Westendorf, Wolfhart
  1975 *Göttinger Totenbuchstudien: Beiträge zum Kapitel 17*. Göttinger Orientforschung 4.3. Wiesbaden: Harrassowitz.

Whittemore, Thomas
  1914 "The Ibis Cemetery at Abydos: 1914." *Journal of Egyptian Archaeology* 1: 248–49.

Whyte, Alison
  2012 "Bird Mummy Conservation: A Delicate Balance." *Oriental Institute News & Notes* 214: 28.

Wiese, André, and Andreas Brodbeck, editors
  2004 *Tutankhamun: The Golden Beyond; Tomb Treasures from the Valley of the Kings*. Bonn: Antikenmuseum Basel und Sammlung Ludwig.

Wild, Henri
  1953 *Le Tombeau de Ti*, Volume 2: *La Chapelle*, Part 1. Cairo: Institut français d'archéologie orientale.

Wilkinson, Toby A. H.
  1999 *Early Dynastic Egypt*. London and New York: Routledge.

Williams, Bruce
  1989 *Excavations between Abu Simbel and the Sudan Frontier, Parts 2, 3, and 4. Neolithic, A-Group, and Post-A-Group Remains from Cemeteries W, V, S, Q, T, and a Cave East of Cemetery K*. Oriental Institute Nubian Expedition 4. Chicago: The Oriental Institute.
  2011 "Relations between Egypt and Nubia in the Naqada Period." In *Before the Pyramids: The Origins of Egyptian Civilization*, edited by Emily Teeter, pp. 83–92. Oriental Institute Museum Publications 33. Chicago: The Oriental Institute.

Williams, J. G., and N. Arlott
  1980 *The Collins Field Guide to the Birds of East Africa*. New York: Stephen Greene.

Williams, Malayna Evans
  2011 *Signs of Creation: Sex, Gender, Categories, Religion and the Body in Ancient Egypt*. PhD dissertation, University of Chicago.

Wilson, Karen, and Joan Barghusen
- 1989 *The Oriental Institute Museum: Highlights from the Collection.* Chicago: The Oriental Institute.

Wilson, Penelope
- 1997 *A Ptolemaic Lexikon: A Lexicographical Study of the Texts in the Temple of Edfu.* Orientalia Lovaniensia Analecta 78. Leuven: Peeters.

Winkler, Hans A.
- 1938 *Rock-drawings of Southern Upper Egypt* I. Edited by the Egypt Exploration Society. Archaeological Survey of Egypt, memoir 26–27. London: Humphrey Milford.

Winlock, H. E.
- 1955 *Models of Daily Life in Ancient Egypt from the Tomb of Meket-Re at Thebes.* Publications of the Metropolitan Museum of Art Egyptian Expedition 18. New York: The Metropolitan Museum of Art.

Woods, Christopher, editor
- 2010 *Visible Language: Inventions of Writing in the Ancient Middle East and Beyond.* Oriental Institute Museum Publications 32. Chicago: The Oriental Institute.

Wyatt, John H., and Jackie Garner
- In prep "Birds in Ancient Egypt: A Guide to Identification."

Young, Eric
- 1964 "Sculptors' Models or Votives? In Defense of a Scholarly Tradition." *Metropolitan Museum of Art Bulletin* 22/7: 247–56.

Yoyotte, Jean
- 1959 "Nectanébo II comme faucon divin?" *Kêmi* 15: 70–74.

Žabkar, Louis V.
- 1968 *A Study of the Ba Concept in Ancient Egyptian Texts.* Studies in Ancient Oriental Civilization 34. Chicago: The Oriental Institute.

Zandee, J.
- 1960 *Death as an Enemy.* Leiden: Brill.

Zauzich, Karl-Theodor
- 2000a "Die Namen der koptischen Zusatzbuchstaben und die erste ägyptische Alphabetübung." *Enchoria* 26: 151–57.
- 2000b "Ein antikes demotisches Namenbuch." In *The Carlsberg Papyri* 3: *A Miscellany of Demotic Texts and Studies*, edited by P. J. Frandsen and K. Ryholt, pp. 27–52. Carsten Niebuhr Institute of Near Eastern Studies, Publications 22. Copenhagen: Museum Tusculanum Press.

Ziegler, Christiane
- 1987 "Les arts du métal à la Troisième Période Intermédiaire." In *Tanis: l'or des pharaons*, pp. 85–101. Paris: Association française d'action artistique.
- 1993 *Le mastaba d'Akhethetep: une chapelle funéraire de l'Ancien Empire.* Paris: Réunion des Musées Nationaux.
- 1997 "Sur quelques vases inscrits de l'Ancien Empire." In *Études sur l'Ancien Empire et la nécropole de Saqqâra dédiées à Jean-Philippe Lauer*, edited by Bernard Mathieu and Catherine Berger, pp. 461–89. Montpellier: Université Paul Valéry (Montpellier III).
- 1999 "Jar Inscribed with the Name of King Unis." In *Egyptian Art in the Age of the Pyramids*, pp. 361–62. New York: Metropolitan Museum of Art.
- 2007 *Le mastaba d'Akhethetep.* Paris: Peeters.

Ziegler, Christiane, and Jean-Luc Bovot
- 2001 *L'Égypte ancienne.* Manuels de l'école du Louvre – art et archéologie. Paris: École du Louvre, Réunion des Musées Nationaux.

Zivie, Alain
- 1980 "Ibis." In *Lexikon der Ägyptologie*, edited by Wolfhart Westendorf and Wolfgang Helck, vol. 3, cols. 115–21. Wiesbaden: Harrassowitz.